Rigby

On Our Way to English™

Language, Literacy, and Content for English Language Learners

Thematic Units

Teacher's Guide

Rigby

Language Advisors

Spanish

Elizabeth de la Ossa, Ph.D.
Spanish Educational Publishing, Ltd.

Aurora Colón García
Northside Independent School District (San Antonio), Literacy Specialist

Cecilia Silva, Ph.D.
Texas Christian University

Vietnamese

Phap Dam, Ph.D.
Texas Woman's University

Hmong

Doua Hollie Vu
Fresno Unified School District, Title III Office

Haitian Creole

Flore Zéphir, Ph.D.
University of Missouri–Columbia

Nancy Graham
Miami-Dade County Public Schools, Bilingual Educational Specialist

Cantonese

Beverly Hong-Fincher
University of Kentucky

Helen Yu
New York City Public Schools, Elementary Teacher

Korean

Soohee Kim, Ph.D.
University of Washington

Khmer

Wayne E. Wright
Arizona State University

Russian

Julia Stakhnevich, Ph.D.
Bridgewater State College

Arabic

Younasse Tarbouni
St. Louis University

Tagalog

Maria Sheila Zamar
University of Hawaii at Manoa

On Our Way to English: Thematic Units Teacher's Guide

Grade 2

1000 Hart Road
Barrington, IL 60010
www.rigby.com

Editor-in-Chief: Judy Nyberg; Executive Editors: Lynelle H. Morgenthaler and Sandy Petroshius; Curriculum Advisor: Clara Amador-Watson; Conceptual Design: Lynelle H. Morgenthaler; Design Director: Jeff Wills; Marketing Product Manager: Marilyn Lindgren; Supervising Editors: Eduardo Aparicio, Anne Kaske, Robert McCreight, Nina Tsang, Arianne Weber; Senior Editors: Karen Clevidence, Cathy Tell, Elizabeth Yoder; Editors: Judi Black, Sophia Caribacas, Lisa Chesters, Meg Garcia, Megan Healy, Jennette McClain, Sue Schumer, Mary Susnis, Loretta West; Design Manager: Jackie Ropski; Supervising Designers: Ann Cain, Julie Spielman, Judy Tresnowski; Senior Designer: Phil Meilinger; Designers: Noel Arreola, Michael Beckett; Image Manager: Cecily Rosenwald; Art and Photo Coordinator: Karen McKinlay; Production Manager: Tom Sjoerdsma; Production Specialist: Gwen Plogman; Graphic Services Administrator: Stuart Cook; Publishing Operations Manager: Alayne Zahara; Senior Project Coordinator: Rachel Bachman; Business Associate: Karen Savord; Manufacturing Manager: Theresa Wiener; Manufacturing Coordinators: Tom Behrendt, Vanessa Kirk

09 08 07
10 9 8 7 6 5 4 3 2

Printed in China

ISBN-10: 0-7578-7895-4
ISBN-13: 978-0-7578-7895-4

Program Authors

David Freeman Yvonne Freeman

Dr. Yvonne S. Freeman and Dr. David E. Freeman are professors in the Department of Curriculum and Instruction in the School of Education at University of Texas–Pan American. Yvonne is a professor of bilingual education, and David is a professor of reading. They are interested in literacy education for English language learners. In addition to doing staff development with school districts across the country, they present regularly at international, national, and state conferences. They have published articles on the topics of second language teaching, biliteracy, bilingual education, and second language acquisition. They have coauthored several books together, including *Closing the Achievement Gap, Teaching Reading in Multilingual Classrooms, Between Worlds, Teaching Reading and Writing in Spanish in the Bilingual Classroom*, and *ESL/EFL Teaching Principles for Success.*

Lydia Stack

Lydia Stack is an administrator at the Bilingual Education and Language Academy of the San Francisco Unified School District. She also teaches courses at San Francisco State University and Stanford University. She has been an elementary bilingual/ESL teacher and a high school ESL Department Head. She received the San Francisco Star Teacher Award in 1989, California Mentor Teacher twice, and the CATESOL Sadie Iwataki Award for outstanding service to the profession. She was the 1991–1992 President of TESOL (Teachers of English to Speakers of Other Languages). She is currently involved in curriculum writing and teacher training and has co-authored three previous educational series: *Voices in Literature, Making Connections*, and *WordWays.*

Aurora Colón García

Aurora Colón García is the literacy specialist for the Northside Independent School District in San Antonio, Texas. She is currently a State Trainer for the Texas First and Second Grade Reading Academies. She has been an instructor at Texas Woman's University, Southwest Texas State University, and the University of Texas at San Antonio. She has been a bilingual teacher, a reading specialist, and an adult ESL instructor. She specializes in early literacy intervention training and is a national literacy consultant. Most recently, she has served as a Program Advisor for Rigby *Colección PM* and has authored several children's books in Spanish and in English.

Mary Lou McCloskey

Mary Lou McCloskey is an international educational consultant and an adjunct professor at Georgia State University. She is the 2002–2003 President of TESOL (Teachers of English to Speakers of Other Languages) and was the 1989–1990 President of Georgia TESOL. She has been an elementary school teacher, an adult reading instructor, and a middle school teacher. She has been awarded the 1999 Moss Chair of Excellence in English at the University of Memphis, TESOL's D. Scott Enright Service Award, and the Georgia TESOL Professional Service Award. Her publications include *Teaching Language, Literature, and Culture, Integrating English, Voices in Literature*, and *Making Connections.*

Cecilia Silva

Cecilia Silva is an associate professor in the School of Education at Texas Christian University in Fort Worth, Texas, and is a member of the Center of Urban Education. Having taught in bilingual/ESL elementary classrooms, she currently specializes in ESL, bilingual, and multicultural education. She is interested in the integration of content area learning and literacy development and is a coauthor of the book *Curricular Conversations: Themes in Multilingual and Monolingual Classrooms.*

Margo Gottlieb

Margo Gottlieb is Director of Assessment and Evaluation for the Illinois Resource Center in Des Plaines, Illinois. Margo has had classroom experience as an elementary ESL and bilingual teacher, has been an administrator of bilingual services, and has served as a consultant for universities, school districts, publishers, and educational organizations. In addition to her involvement in assessment efforts in Illinois, Margo has provided technical assistance to states such as Alaska, Texas, and Pennsylvania. She has also designed state assessments for English language learners in Wisconsin and Delaware.

Contents

What Do English Language Learners Need to Succeed? **T6**

***On Our Way to English* Program Structure** **T7**

Why Use Themes in Teaching English Language Learners? T8

- **Unit Lesson Plans** **T10**
- **Center Activities** **T12**
- **Thematic Units Lessons** **T14**

Assessment in *On Our Way to English* T18

Using *On Our Way to English* in Different Classroom Settings T20

Professional Handbook

Developing Children's Oral Language **T23**

Developing Literacy **T30**

Modeled Reading for English Language Learners T31

Shared Reading for English Language Learners T32

Shared-to-Guided Reading for English Language Learners T33

Guided Reading for English Language Learners T34

Independent Reading for English Language Learners T35

Modeled and Shared Writing T36

Interactive, Guided, and Independent Writing T37

Strategic Reading **T38**

From the Authors

How Do We Teach Reading to English Language Learners? T39
Mary Lou McCloskey

How Do We Teach Writing to English Language Learners? T41
Lydia Stack

How Do We Teach the Content Area Subjects to English Language Learners? T43
David and Yvonne Freeman

How Do We Teach English Language Learners at Various Language Proficiencies? T45
Cecilia Silva

Thematic Units

Unit 1: Proud to Be Me U4

Unit 2: Living in America U28

Unit 3: Circle of Life U52

Unit 4: From Farm to You U76

Unit 5: Water Works U100

Unit 6: Disaster Alert U124

Unit 7: How Things Work U148

Unit 8: Choices We Make U172

Appendix

Appendix A1

What Do English Language Learners Need to Succeed?

As the population of English language learners rises steadily in our schools, teachers and administrators are faced with a complex challenge.

Earlier ideas of language instruction embraced the notion that children needed to speak a language before learning to read it. Now research has shown that literacy and oral language instruction should be integrated from the earliest language learning experiences.

Research has also identified the fact that it takes English language learners an average of five to seven years to catch up to their native-speaking peers in the content areas.

What can we do to help English language learners close the gap between themselves and their native-speaking peers?

How can we teach these children to speak English *while* they are learning to read and *while* they are acquiring content area knowledge?

On Our Way to English was designed specifically to meet these challenges by providing children simultaneous access to English oral language development, comprehensive literacy instruction, and standards-based content area information.

As the triangle to the right shows, content area learning is supported by oral language development and literacy learning. In *On Our Way to English*, whole-class instruction in content area themes bridges from chants, songs, and language-learning games to shared reading texts to hands-on content area activities. Meanwhile children are learning to read through engaging phonics songs and through small-group guided reading experiences that feature texts specifically written for English language learners and that highlight content area topics.

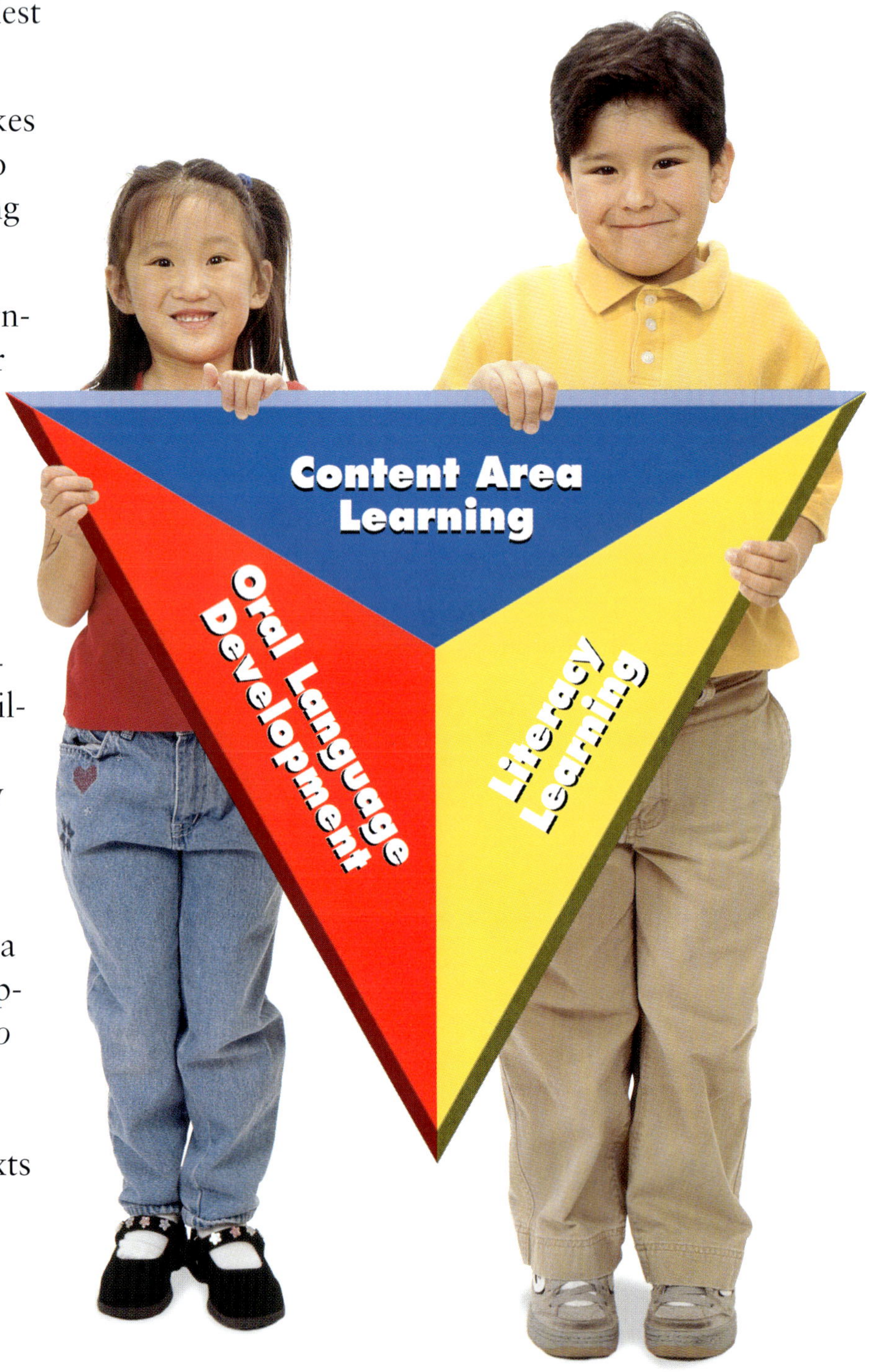

On Our Way to English Program Structure

On Our Way to English Thematic Units, Guided Reading Collection, and Phonics work together to provide the language, literacy, and content instruction necessary to launch English language learners into academic success. The lesson plans in this Teacher's Guide support you in using best practices in language teaching and in literacy instruction. In a step-by-step fashion, the lessons show you how to provide the comprehensible input—instruction that is meaningful to language learners—that these children need in order to succeed. Because the instruction is carefully scaffolded so that each learning experience supports the next, the learning environment in your classroom will become an engaging, motivating arena in which English language learners feel empowered to contribute and achieve.

On Our Way to English—3 key strands

Pacing Chart		
Component	**Daily Pacing**	**Block**
Thematic Units	**30-40 minutes**	**ESL or ELD block**
Phonics	**20 minutes**	**ESL or ELD block**
Guided Reading	**20 minutes per group**	**Reading block**

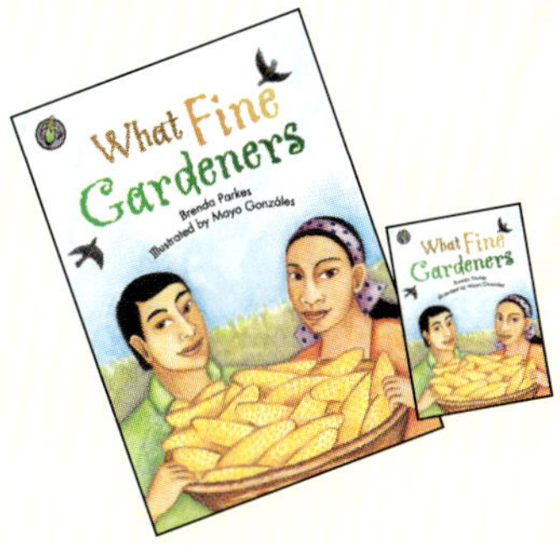

Why Use Themes in Teaching English Language Learners?

What's in Each Unit?

English language learners need simultaneous instruction in language, literacy, and content. Theme teaching provides an ideal backdrop for this three-part learning. It also allows children to reuse and recycle the vocabulary and concepts they are learning—an essential aspect of second language learning as instruction bridges from the spoken to the written word.

The thematic units contain components that are designed to accomplish two primary goals:

1. Oral language development connected to the content area theme
2. Shared reading and writing to develop literacy skills in the context of the theme

Because this is an integrated curriculum, these goals are not mutually exclusive—oral language and literacy skills are integrated into all components of the content area unit.

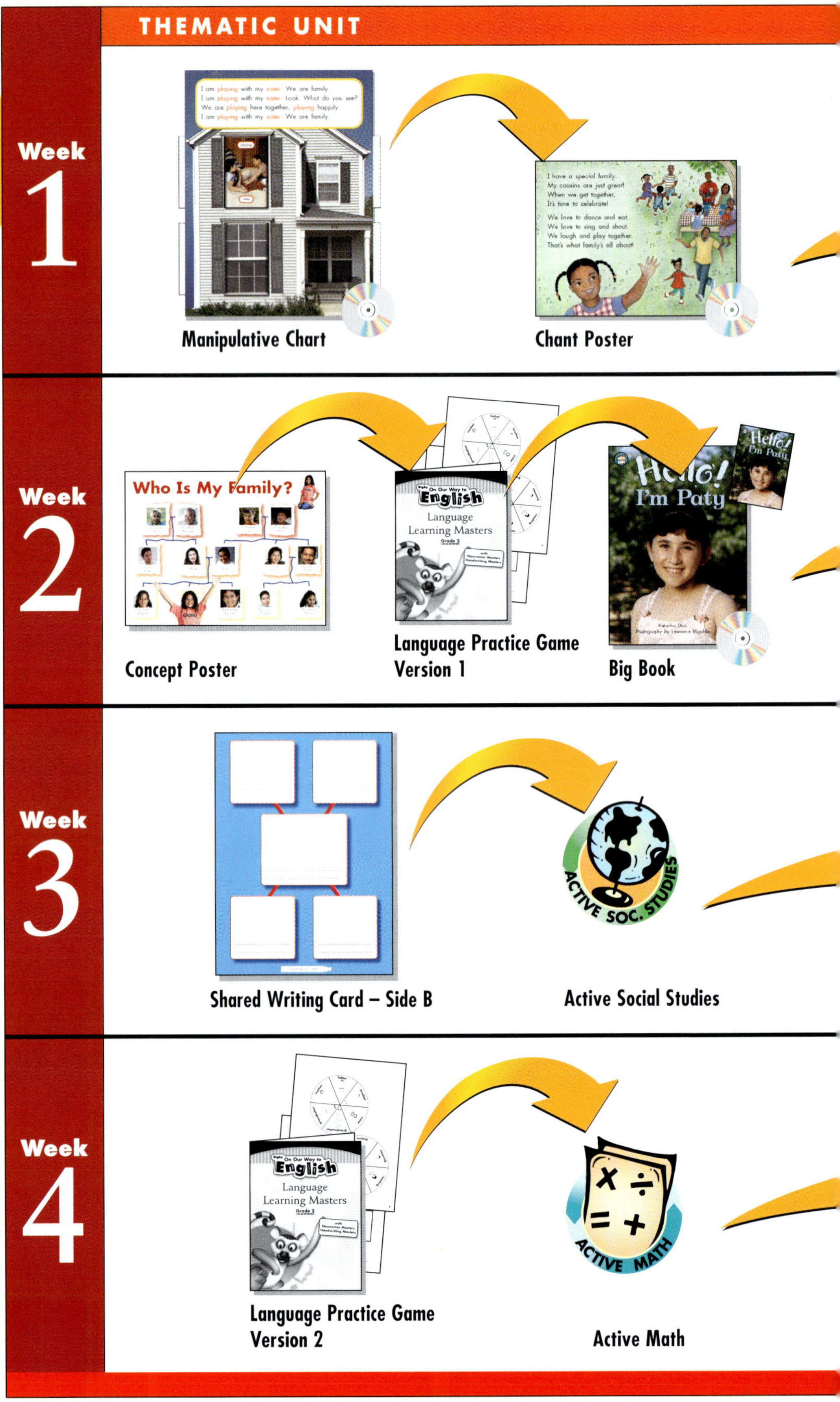

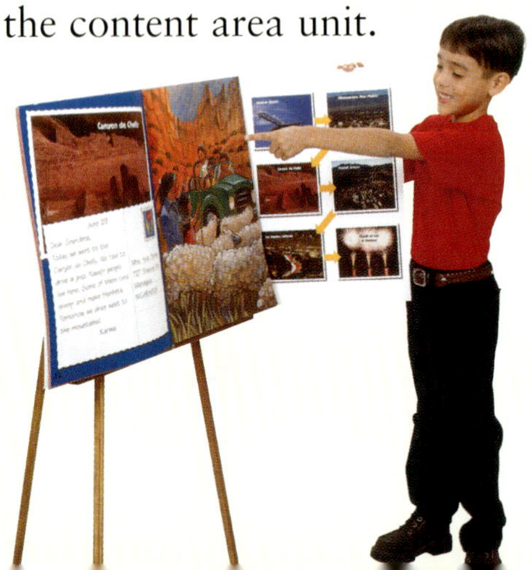

TPR Cards

Newcomer Book

Manipulative Chart provides a first peek at basic unit concepts and vocabulary through song and an interactive format.

Chant Poster follows up with an engaging chant that highlights thematic content.

TPR Cards provide interactive practice with unit vocabulary.

Newcomer Book builds directly on the language practice of the Manipulative Chart and provides an ideal initial literacy experience.

Theme Project

Shared Writing Card – Side A

Concept Poster deepens children's understanding of the unit theme through a highly visual format.

Language Practice Game comes in two versions—it makes language practice fun!

Big Book provides a rich literacy experience within the unit's theme and an opportunity for the teacher to use shared reading techniques to model the behaviors of a good reader. An innovative fold-out back flap provides English language learners with a graphic tool to enhance their reading comprehension.

Theme Project features a hands-on long-term project for collaborative groups that focuses on theme content.

Shared Writing Card springboards from the Big Book's back flap, helping children to connect reading and writing. Side A is an Illustrated graphic organizer on a unit topic for you to label with children and then use as the basis for a class shared writing piece.

Active Science

Writing Planners

Shared Writing Card side B is a blank graphic organizer for repeating the procedure with a class-brainstormed idea.

Active Social Studies features a hands-on social studies activity.

Active Science features a hands-on science activity.

Writing Planners are blackline versions of the shared writing card for use in cooperative-group and independent writing. This step-by-step writing instruction provides the scaffolding children need to move toward independence!

Assessment

Language Practice Game comes in two versions for different degrees of challenge.

Active Math features a hands-on math activity.

Assessment is integrated throughout the unit and provides the tools needed for evaluation purposes.

Unit Lesson Plans

A whole-group lesson plan is provided for each thematic unit that spans four weeks of instruction. Because the instruction is carefully integrated and scaffolded, components are introduced and revisited throughout the four weeks. The opening pages of each unit lesson plan provide a roadmap for coordinating the use of the components to maximize their effectiveness.

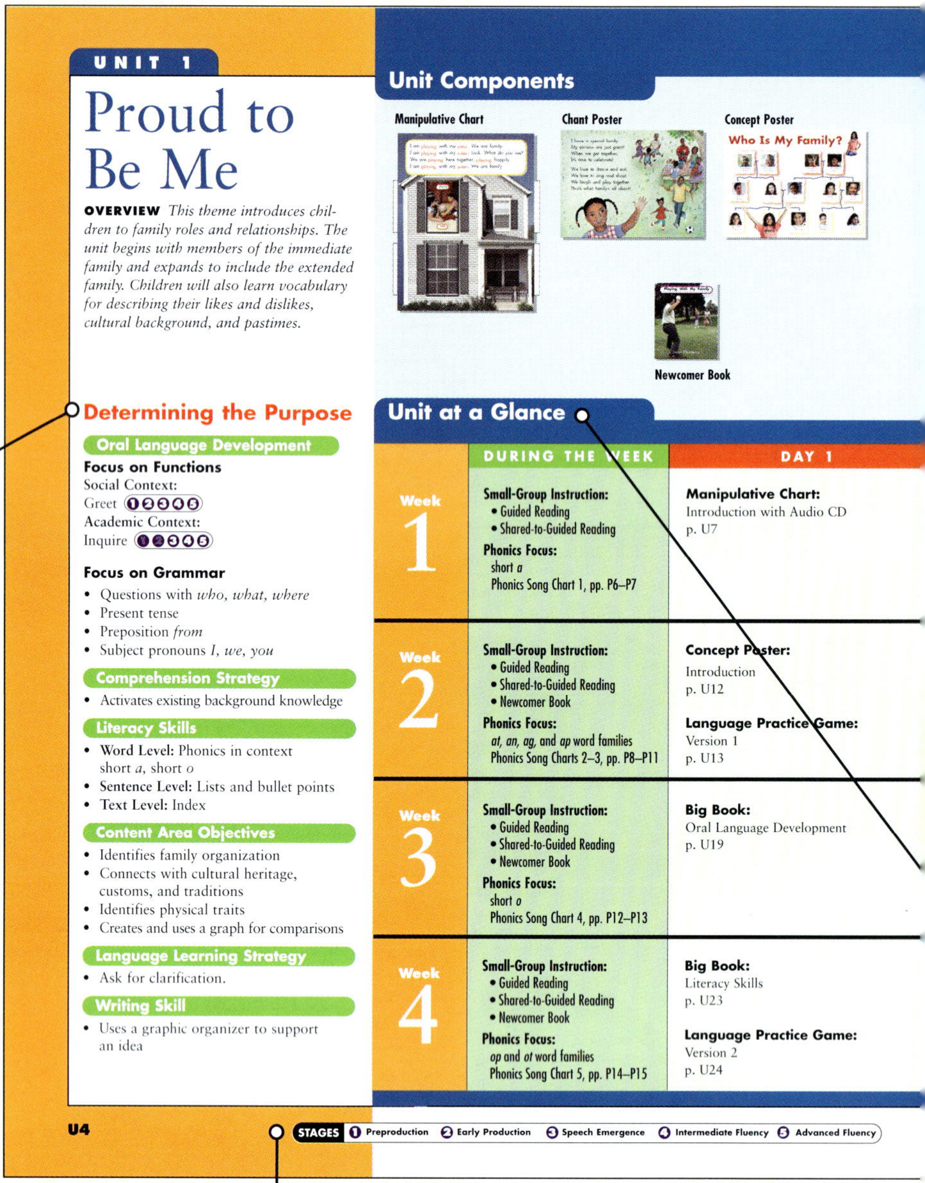
UNIT 1

Proud to Be Me

OVERVIEW *This theme introduces children to family roles and relationships. The unit begins with members of the immediate family and expands to include the extended family. Children will also learn vocabulary for describing their likes and dislikes, cultural background, and pastimes.*

Determining the Purpose

Oral Language Development

Focus on Functions
Social Context:
Greet ❶❷❸❹❺
Academic Context:
Inquire ❶❷❸❹❺

Focus on Grammar
- Questions with *who, what, where*
- Present tense
- Preposition *from*
- Subject pronouns *I, we, you*

Comprehension Strategy
- Activates existing background knowledge

Literacy Skills
- **Word Level:** Phonics in context short *a*, short *o*
- **Sentence Level:** Lists and bullet points
- **Text Level:** Index

Content Area Objectives
- Identifies family organization
- Connects with cultural heritage, customs, and traditions
- Identifies physical traits
- Creates and uses a graph for comparisons

Language Learning Strategy
- Ask for clarification.

Writing Skill
- Uses a graphic organizer to support an idea

Unit Components

Manipulative Chart
Chant Poster
Concept Poster
Who Is My Family?
Newcomer Book

Unit at a Glance

	DURING THE WEEK	DAY 1
Week 1	**Small-Group Instruction:** • Guided Reading • Shared-to-Guided Reading **Phonics Focus:** short *a* Phonics Song Chart 1, pp. P6–P7	**Manipulative Chart:** Introduction with Audio CD p. U7
Week 2	**Small-Group Instruction:** • Guided Reading • Shared-to-Guided Reading • Newcomer Book **Phonics Focus:** *at, an, ag,* and *ap* word families Phonics Song Charts 2–3, pp. P8–P11	**Concept Poster:** Introduction p. U12 **Language Practice Game:** Version 1 p. U13
Week 3	**Small-Group Instruction:** • Guided Reading • Shared-to-Guided Reading • Newcomer Book **Phonics Focus:** short *o* Phonics Song Chart 4, pp. P12–P13	**Big Book:** Oral Language Development p. U19
Week 4	**Small-Group Instruction:** • Guided Reading • Shared-to-Guided Reading • Newcomer Book **Phonics Focus:** *op* and *ot* word families Phonics Song Chart 5, pp. P14–P15	**Big Book:** Literacy Skills p. U23 **Language Practice Game:** Version 2 p. U24

U4

STAGES ❶ Preproduction ❷ Early Production ❸ Speech Emergence ❹ Intermediate Fluency ❺ Advanced Fluency

Determining the Purpose

Determining the Purpose provides a quick overview of the learning goals for each unit.

- **Oral Language Development** objectives highlight two language functions, one social and one academic, along with four or five grammar points.
- **Comprehension Strategy** instruction is clear and direct. You model and children practice a single comprehension strategy while working with the Big Book.
- **Literacy Skills** for the Big Book are highlighted in each unit according to **Word Level, Sentence Level,** and **Text Level** skills Word level skills provide an opportunity for integrating phonics instruction into thematic study. Sentence level skills help children learn to look at sentence structure and use cueing systems to make sense out of sentences. Text level skills teach children to look at the book as a whole, examining literary elements such as text structure, features, and writing style.
- **Content Area Objectives** provide information on the standards-based content goals that each unit fulfills.
- **Language Learning Strategy** mini-lessons facilitate metacognitive thinking about the language learning process.
- **Writing Skills** are taught in the context of the Shared Writing Card and focus on using writing to communicate ideas.

Stage numbers are used to highlight differentiated instruction by language proficiency, as identified in this reference tool.

DAY 2	DAY 3	DAY 4	DAY 5
nipulative Chart: tures and nipulative Fun J8	**Chant Poster:** Introduction p. U9	**TPR Cards:** Introduction p. U10	**Manipulative Chart:** Oral Language Development Student Version p. U11
Book: oduction J15	**Theme Project:** Class Directory p. U16 **Big Book:** Revisiting p. U16	**Big Book:** Comprehension Strategy p. U17 **Chant Poster:** Oral Language Development p. U17	**Shared Writing Card:** Introduction of Side A p. U18 **Concept Poster:** Revisiting p. U18
ared Writing Card: nstorming Side B J20 **ive Social Studies:** ily Trees, J21	**Shared Writing Card:** Writing Together with Side B p. U21 **Manipulative Chart:** Oral Language Development p. U21	**Active Science:** Physical Characteristics p. U22	**Writing Resource Guide:** A Simplified Graphic Organizer Cooperative-Group Writing p. U22
ive Math: Graph J24 **sessment** J24	**Writing Resource Guide:** Individual Writing p. U25 **Assessment** p. U24	**Writing Resource Guide:** Individual Writing p. U25 **Assessment** p. U24	**Theme Project:** Sharing p. U25

Thematic Unit 1 *Proud to Be Me* **U5**

Pictures of unit components provide a ready resource to help you select and organize the pieces you need to teach the unit.

Unit at a Glance clearly outlines the instruction planned for each day. Lesson plans reflecting this day-by-day format provide the support you need to create an optimum learning environment in your classroom. The "During the Week" column in the chart helps you integrate *On Our Way to English* Guided Reading Collection and Phonics with the thematic Unit to provide an integrated, complete English learning curriculum.

Center Activities

On Our Way to English simplifies the management of your classroom by providing suggestions for six easy-to-prepare centers that augment unit activities. Children can work in these centers while you meet with guided reading groups, small groups formed according to Language Acquisition Stages, and individual children for assessment at the end of the unit.

Center Procedures

With each new set of centers, you will need to introduce each activity and its procedures. The procedures to explain to children include:

- expected behavior while working in centers.
- how to clean up the center.
- when and how to change centers.
- where to put completed work.

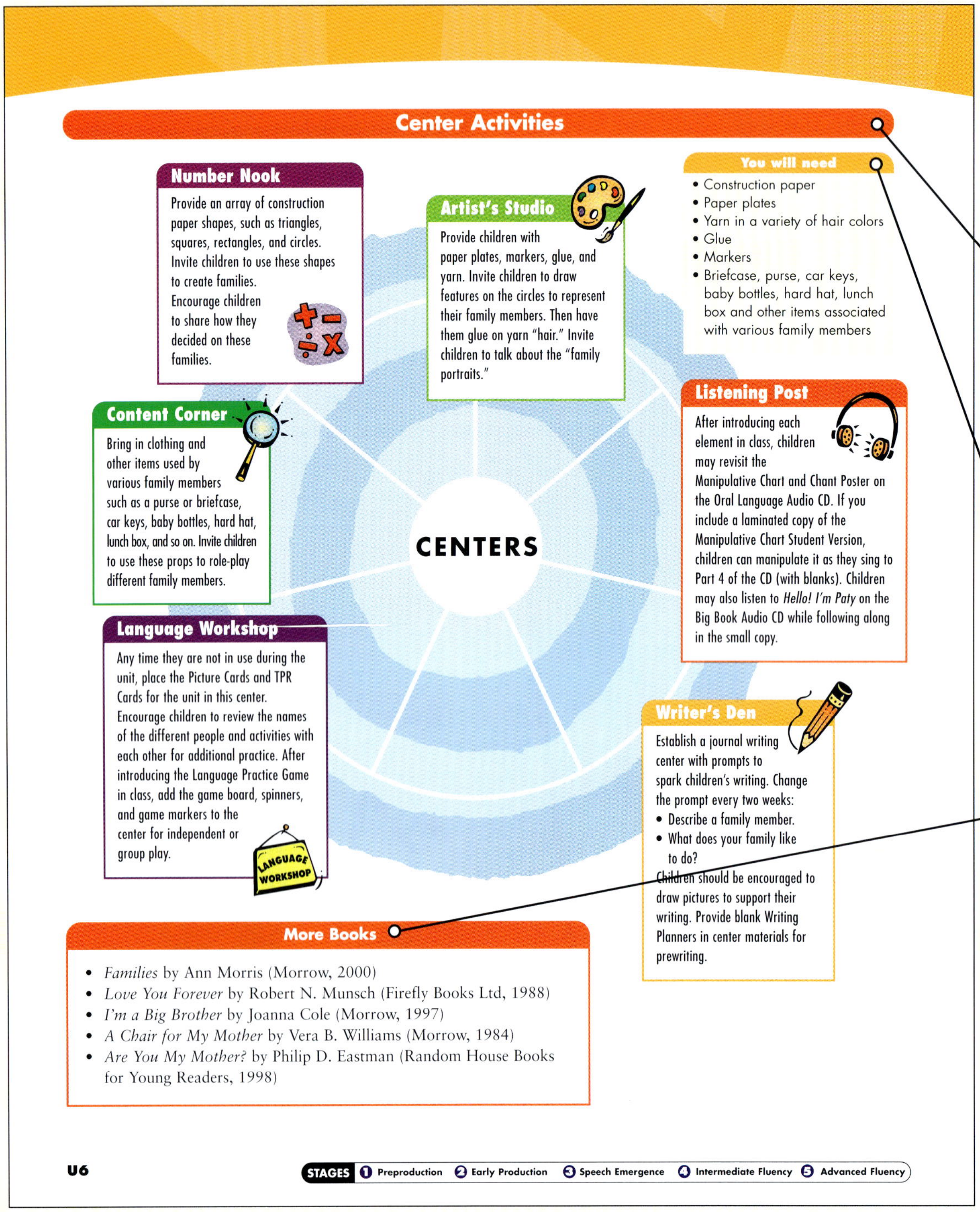

Center Activities

Number Nook

Provide an array of construction paper shapes, such as triangles, squares, rectangles, and circles. Invite children to use these shapes to create families. Encourage children to share how they decided on these families.

Artist's Studio

Provide children with paper plates, markers, glue, and yarn. Invite children to draw features on the circles to represent their family members. Then have them glue on yarn "hair." Invite children to talk about the "family portraits."

You will need

- Construction paper
- Paper plates
- Yarn in a variety of hair colors
- Glue
- Markers
- Briefcase, purse, car keys, baby bottles, hard hat, lunch box and other items associated with various family members

Content Corner

Bring in clothing and other items used by various family members such as a purse or briefcase, car keys, baby bottles, hard hat, lunch box, and so on. Invite children to use these props to role-play different family members.

CENTERS

Listening Post

After introducing each element in class, children may revisit the Manipulative Chart and Chant Poster on the Oral Language Audio CD. If you include a laminated copy of the Manipulative Chart Student Version, children can manipulate it as they sing to Part 4 of the CD (with blanks). Children may also listen to *Hello! I'm Paty* on the Big Book Audio CD while following along in the small copy.

Language Workshop

Any time they are not in use during the unit, place the Picture Cards and TPR Cards for the unit in this center. Encourage children to review the names of the different people and activities with each other for additional practice. After introducing the Language Practice Game in class, add the game board, spinners, and game markers to the center for independent or group play.

LANGUAGE WORKSHOP

Writer's Den

Establish a journal writing center with prompts to spark children's writing. Change the prompt every two weeks:

- Describe a family member.
- What does your family like to do?

Children should be encouraged to draw pictures to support their writing. Provide blank Writing Planners in center materials for prewriting.

More Books

- *Families* by Ann Morris (Morrow, 2000)
- *Love You Forever* by Robert N. Munsch (Firefly Books Ltd, 1988)
- *I'm a Big Brother* by Joanna Cole (Morrow, 1997)
- *A Chair for My Mother* by Vera B. Williams (Morrow, 1984)
- *Are You My Mother?* by Philip D. Eastman (Random House Books for Young Readers, 1998)

STAGES ❶ Preproduction ❷ Early Production ❸ Speech Emergence ❹ Intermediate Fluency ❺ Advanced Fluency

Center Activities complement the theme of each unit. These centers are designed to be introduced at the beginning of the unit and made accessible each day.

You will need provides a list of materials for the centers to facilitate easy center preparation.

More Books lists a selection of trade books, videos, and CD-ROMs that reflect the unit's theme. Use these books to read aloud to children or for children to use in self-selecting independent reading.

Language Workshop

In a classroom that includes English language learners, a center should be devoted specifically to language learning activities. This center will promote independent practice and review with unit elements that promote language learning, such as the Picture Cards, Language Practice Games, and TPR Cards. Children can work independently or with partners to review vocabulary and language patterns from the unit in the context of fun and engaging play.

Supplies for your Language Workshop center:

- envelopes for storing cards and game pieces
- manipulatives that can serve as game markers
- other elements needed for game play

Listening Post

Children develop language skills by listening to recorded stories and songs. By placing the Oral Language Audio CD in the listening center along with a laminated copy of the Manipulative Chart Student Version, children can acquire much-needed oral language practice with the Manipulative Chart and Chant Poster. The Big Book Audio CD and Small Book versions of the Big Book offer a quick and easy way to provide multiple exposures to shared reading texts. As children listen to tapes where expert speakers model spoken English and expert readers model reading with expression and fluency, they too will become better speakers and readers.

Content Corner

The instructional goal of this center will vary with the instructional goals of the unit. Since most themes are based on social studies or science objectives with integrated math content, this center will function as either a social studies or science corner, depending on the unit theme. Children can engage in hands-on exploration of a real-world item connected with the unit or participate in a related activity. Materials needed for the center can be found under "You will need."

Number Nook

This center provides an opportunity for children to explore a math activity in connection with the theme. Children learn math concepts best when engaging in hands-on exploration of shapes, numbers, and patterns. Materials needed for the center can be found under "You will need."

Writer's Den

Writing in response to learning experiences is one of the best ways to reinforce speech-to-print and text-to-writing connections. Since personal writing is often a child's first venture into writing, it is important to promote and encourage journal writing. This center offers children journal prompts, as well as space and materials, that can fuel journal writing, whether it takes the form of simple picture drawing or actual recording of text.

Supplies for the Writer's Den:

- a variety of types of paper
- pencils, crayons, markers, colored pencils
- erasers
- sticky notes
- tape
- stapler
- stickers and stamps
- folders for storing work

Artist's Studio

Art is a powerful form of self-expression and is therefore very appropriate as a response to literature and content learning. Reading, writing, and art all share the purpose of nurturing imagination through the processes of creating, reflecting, and responding. Materials needed for the center can be found under "You will need."

Thematic Units Lessons

Each day's instruction is clearly identified and provided in a step-by-step format.

Setting the Scene offers English language learners the background building instruction they require. *On Our Way to English* understands that these children cannot simply be "talked at" when setting the scene for instruction. Setting the Scene shows you how to provide language support with techniques such as gesturing and Picture Cards. This section also provides sample responses to expect and encourage from English language learners.

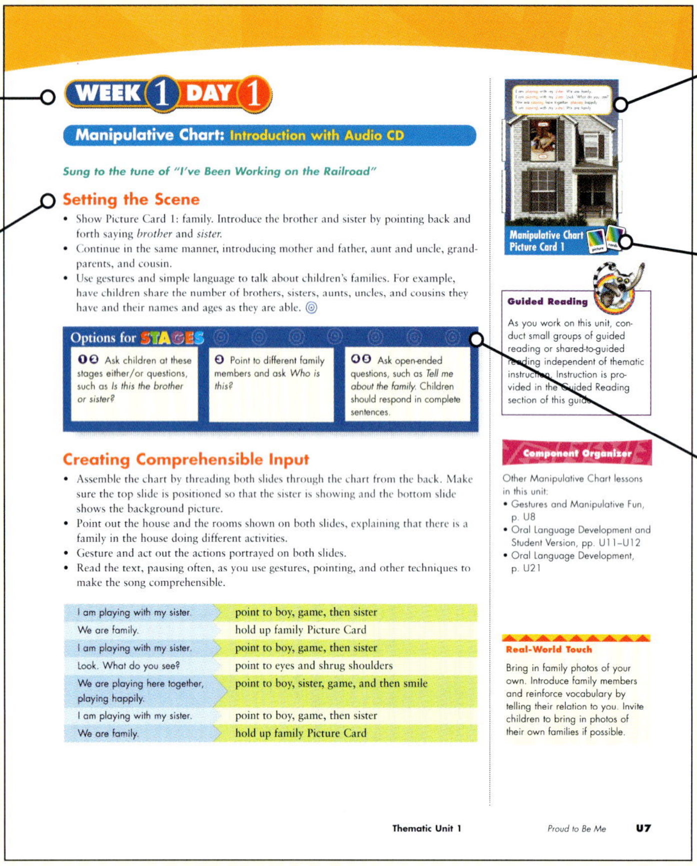

WEEK 1 DAY 1

Manipulative Chart: Introduction with Audio CD

Sung to the tune of "I've Been Working on the Railroad"

Setting the Scene

- Show Picture Card 1: family. Introduce the brother and sister by pointing back and forth saying *brother* and *sister.*
- Continue in the same manner, introducing mother and father, aunt and uncle, grandparents, and cousin.
- Use gestures and simple language to talk about children's families. For example, have children share the number of brothers, sisters, aunts, uncles, and cousins they have and their names and ages as they are able. ◎

Options for STAGES

- ❶❷ Ask children at these stages either/or questions, such as *Is this the brother or sister?*
- ❸ Point to different family members and ask *Who is this?*
- ❹❺ Ask open-ended questions, such as *Tell me about the family.* Children should respond in complete sentences.

Creating Comprehensible Input

- Assemble the chart by threading both slides through the chart from the back. Make sure the top slide is positioned so that the sister is showing and the bottom slide shows the background picture.
- Point out the house and the rooms shown on both slides, explaining that there is a family in the house doing different activities.
- Gesture and act out the actions portrayed on both slides.
- Read the text, pausing often, as you use gestures, pointing, and other techniques to make the song comprehensible.

I am playing with my sister.	point to boy, game, then sister
We are family.	hold up family Picture Card
I am playing with my sister.	point to boy, game, then sister
Look. What do you see?	point to eyes and shrug shoulders
We are playing here together, playing happily.	point to boy, sister, game, and then smile
I am playing with my sister.	point to boy, game, then sister
We are family.	hold up family Picture Card

Manipulative Chart Picture Card 1

Guided Reading

As you work on this unit, conduct small groups of guided reading or shared-to-guided reading independent of thematic instruction. Instruction is provided in the Guided Reading section of this guide.

Component Organizer

Other Manipulative Chart lessons in this unit:
- Gestures and Manipulative Fun, p. U8
- Oral Language Development and Student Version, pp. U11–U12
- Oral Language Development, p. U21

Real-World Touch

Bring in family photos of your own. Introduce family members and reinforce vocabulary by telling their relation to you. Invite children to bring in photos of their own families if possible.

Thematic Unit 1 Proud to Be Me U7

Pictures of components help you to identify quickly what is needed for each lesson.

Picture Cards provide vocabulary development and are integrated into unit instruction.

Options for Stages is a recurring feature that helps you to tailor whole-group activities for children in different Stages of Language Acquisition and to understand what kinds of responses to expect from children in those Stages. ◎This symbol is used to designate a differentiated activity.

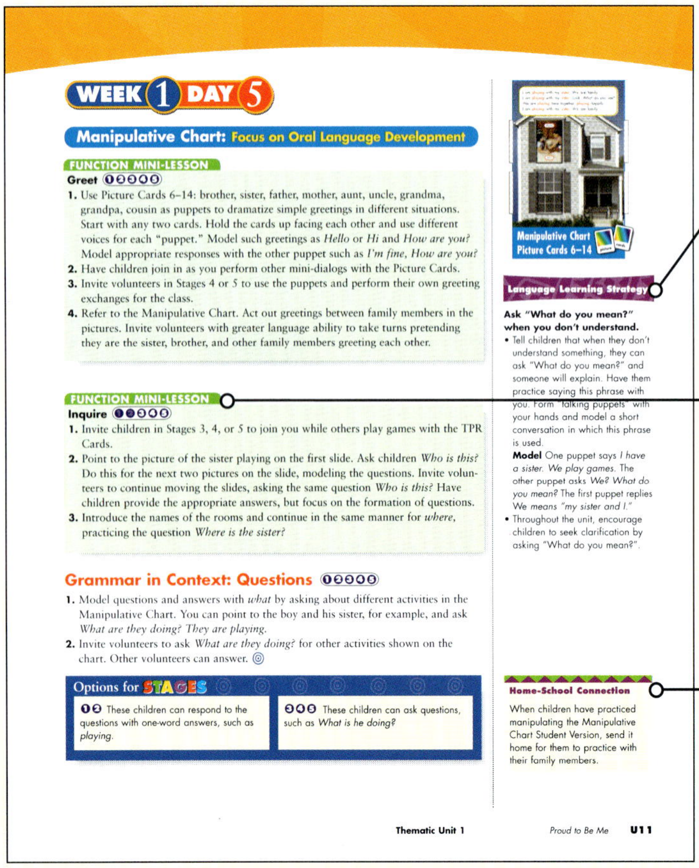

WEEK 1 DAY 5

Manipulative Chart: Focus on Oral Language Development

FUNCTION MINI-LESSON

Greet ❶❷❸❹❺

1. Use Picture Cards 6–14: brother, sister, father, mother, aunt, uncle, grandma, grandpa, cousin as puppets to dramatize simple greetings in different situations. Start with any two cards. Hold the cards up facing each other and use different voices for each "puppet." Model such greetings as *Hello* or *Hi* and *How are you?* Model appropriate responses with the other puppet such as *I'm fine, How are you?*
2. Have children join in as you perform other mini-dialogs with the Picture Cards.
3. Invite volunteers in Stages 4 or 5 to use the puppets and perform their own greeting exchanges for the class.
4. Refer to the Manipulative Chart. Act out greetings between family members in the pictures. Invite volunteers with greater language ability to take turns pretending they are the sister, brother, and other family members greeting each other.

FUNCTION MINI-LESSON

Inquire ❶❷❸❹❺

1. Invite children in Stages 3, 4, or 5 to join you while others play games with the TPR Cards.
2. Point to the picture of the sister playing on the first slide. Ask children *Who is this?* Do this for the next two pictures on the slide, modeling the questions. Invite volunteers to continue moving the slides, asking the same question *Who is this?* Have children provide the appropriate answers, but focus on the formation of questions.
3. Introduce the names of the rooms and continue in the same manner for *where,* practicing the question *Where is the sister?*

Grammar in Context: Questions ❶❷❸❹❺

1. Model questions and answers with *what* by asking about different activities in the Manipulative Chart. You can point to the boy and his sister, for example, and ask *What are they doing? They are playing.*
2. Invite volunteers to ask *What are they doing?* for other activities shown on the chart. Other volunteers can answer. ◎

Options for STAGES

- ❶❷ These children can respond to the questions with one-word answers, such as *playing.*
- ❸❹❺ These children can ask questions, such as *What is he doing?*

Manipulative Chart Picture Cards 6–14

Language Learning Strategy

Ask "What do you mean?" when you don't understand.
- Tell children that when they don't understand something, they can ask "What do you mean?" and someone will explain. Have them practice saying this phrase with you. Form "talking puppets" with your hands and model a short conversation in which this phrase is used.

  Model One puppet says *I have a sister. We play games.* The other puppet asks *We? What do you mean?* The first puppet replies *We means "my sister and I."*
- Throughout the unit, encourage children to seek clarification by asking "What do you mean?".

Home-School Connection

When children have practiced manipulating the Manipulative Chart Student Version, send it home for them to practice with their family members.

Thematic Unit 1 Proud to Be Me U11

Language Learning Strategy supports you in teaching a metacognitive language learning strategy that can accelerate the language learning process.

Function Mini-lessons Language functions focus on the different ways we use language to communicate in various contexts, both social and academic. Each unit in *On Our Way to English* highlights one social and one academic language function. The Stage designations at the top of the lesson help you identify which children should participate in the mini-lesson. Others should engage in center activities.

Home-School Connection Masters bring unit learning into the home by providing parent letters in English and seven other languages, a home activity related to each unit theme, and blackline versions of the Big Book back flaps for retelling.

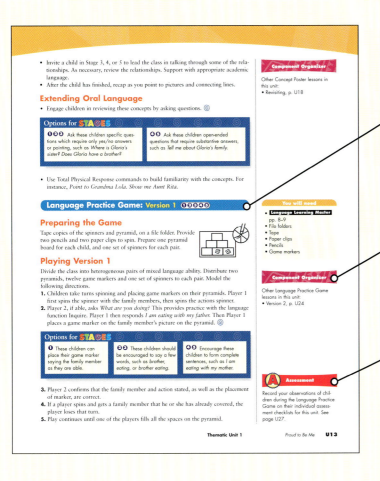

- Invite a child in Stage 3, 4, or 5 to lead the class in talking through some of the relationships. As necessary, review the relationships. Support with appropriate academic language.
- After the child has finished, recap as you point to pictures and connecting lines.

Extending Oral Language

- Engage children in reviewing these concepts by asking questions. ◎

Options for STAGES

❶❷❸ Ask these children specific questions which require only *yes/no* answers or pointing, such as *Where is Gloria's sister? Does Gloria have a brother?*

❹❺ Ask these children open-ended questions that require substantive answers, such as *Tell me about Gloria's family.*

- Use Total Physical Response commands to build familiarity with the concepts. For instance, *Point to Grandma Lola. Show me Aunt Rita.*

Language Practice Game: Version 1 ❶❷❸❹❺

Preparing the Game

Tape copies of the spinners and pyramid, on a file folder. Provide two pencils and two paper clips to spin. Prepare one pyramid board for each child, and one set of spinners for each pair.

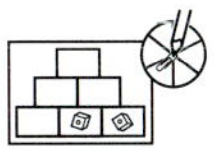

Playing Version 1

Divide the class into heterogeneous pairs of mixed language ability. Distribute two pyramids, twelve game markers and one set of spinners to each pair. Model the following directions.

1. Children take turns spinning and placing game markers on their pyramids. Player 1 first spins the spinner with the family members, then spins the actions spinner.
2. Player 2, if able, asks *What are you doing?* This provides practice with the language function Inquire. Player 1 then responds *I am eating with my father.* Then Player 1 places a game marker on the family member's picture on the pyramid. ◎

Options for STAGES

❶ These children can place their game marker saying the family member as they are able.

❷❸ These children should be encouraged to say a few words, such as *brother, eating,* or *brother eating.*

❹❺ Encourage these children to form complete sentences, such as *I am eating with my mother.*

3. Player 2 confirms that the family member and action stated, as well as the placement of marker, are correct.
4. If a player spins and gets a family member that he or she has already covered, the player loses that turn.
5. Play continues until one of the players fills all the spaces on the pyramid.

Component Organizer

Other Concept Poster lessons in this unit:
- Revisiting, p. U18

You will need
- **Language Learning Master** pp. 8–9
- File folders
- Tape
- Paper clips
- Pencils
- Game markers

Component Organizer

Other Language Practice Game lessons in this unit:
- Version 2, p. U24

Assessment

Record your observations of children during the Language Practice Game on their individual assessment checklists for this unit. See page U27.

Thematic Unit 1 *Proud to Be Me* **U13**

Language Practice Game instruction provides an engaging, enjoyable atmosphere for language practice. A depiction of game assembly and a list of materials are provided.

Component Organizer provides page references for other component lessons within the unit, creating a road map for each component.

Assessment features in the margin signal when to use the unit assessment checklist for observing children during unit instruction.

Comprehensible input chart offers step-by-step guidance in how to make each component understandable to children with limited comprehension of English. Appropriate strategies, such as gesturing, restating, and pointing, are provided to support introduction of vocabulary and concepts.

You will need is a list of materials that lets you know what you will need for each lesson.

Theme Project is an ongoing extended project that engages children in the unit's theme. Projects are designed for collaborative groups.

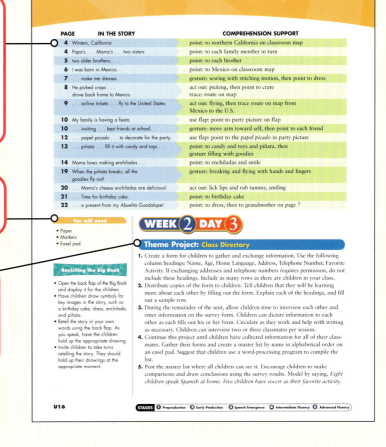

PAGE	IN THE STORY	COMPREHENSION SUPPORT
4	Winters, California	point: to northern California on classroom map
4	Papa's . . . Mama's . . . two sisters	point: to each family member in turn
5	two older brothers, . . .	point: to each brother
6	I was born in Mexico.	point: to Mexico on classroom map
7	. . . make me dresses.	gesture: sewing with stitching motion, then point to dress
8	He picked crops . . . drove back home to Mexico.	act out: picking, then point to crate trace: route on map
9	. . . airline tickets . . . fly to the United States.	act out: flying, then trace route on map from Mexico to the U.S.
10	My family is having a fiesta.	use flap: point to party picture on flap
10	. . . inviting . . . best friends at school.	gesture: move arm toward self, then point to each friend
12	. . . *papel picado* . . . to decorate for the party.	use flap: point to the *papel picado* in party picture
13	. . . piñata . . . fill it with candy and toys . . .	point: to candy and toys and piñata, then gesture filling with goodies
14	Mama loves making enchiladas . . .	point: to enchiladas and smile
19	When the piñata breaks, all the goodies fly out!	gesture: breaking and flying with hands and fingers
20	. . . Mama's cheese enchiladas are delicious!	act out: lick lips and rub tummy, smiling
21	. . . Time for birthday cake.	point: to birthday cake
22	. . . a present from my *Abuelita* Guadalupe!	point: to dress, then to grandmother on page 7

You will need
- Paper
- Markers
- Easel pad

Revisiting the Big Book
- Open the back flap of the Big Book and display it for the children.
- Have children draw symbols for key images in the story, such as a birthday cake, dress, enchilada, and piñata.
- Retell the story in your own words using the back flap. As you speak, have the children hold up the appropriate drawing.
- Invite children to take turns retelling the story. They should hold up their drawings at the appropriate moment.

WEEK 2 DAY 3

Theme Project: Class Directory

1. Create a form for children to gather and exchange information. Use the following column headings: Name, Age, Home Language, Address, Telephone Number, Favorite Activity. If exchanging addresses and telephone numbers requires permission, do not include these headings. Include as many rows as there are children in your class.
2. Distribute copies of the form to children. Tell children that they will be learning more about each other by filling out the form. Explain each of the headings, and fill out a sample row.
3. During the remainder of the unit, allow children time to interview each other and enter information on the survey form. Children can dictate information to each other as each fills out his or her form. Circulate as they work and help with writing as necessary. Children can interview two or three classmates per session.
4. Continue this project until children have collected information for all of their classmates. Gather their forms and create a master list by name in alphabetical order on an easel pad. Suggest that children use a word-processing program to compile the list.
5. Post the master list where all children can see it. Encourage children to make comparisons and draw conclusions using the survey results. Model by saying, *Eight children speak Spanish at home. Five children have soccer as their favorite activity.*

U16 STAGES ❶ Preproduction ❷ Early Production ❸ Speech Emergence ❹ Intermediate Fluency ❺ Advanced Fluency

Language Learning Masters provide practice and extend vocabulary through the Manipulative Chart Student Version, TPR Cards, Language Practice Game, and grammar blackline masters.

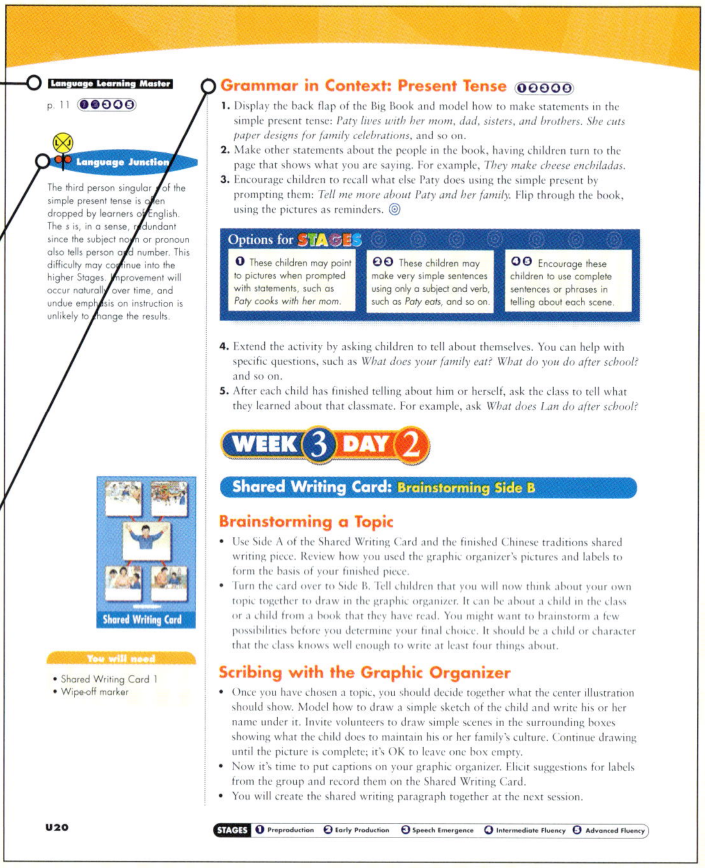

Language Learning Master

p. 11 ❶❷❸❹❺

Language Junction

The third person singular *s* of the simple present tense is often dropped by learners of English. The *s* is, in a sense, redundant since the subject noun or pronoun also tells person and number. This difficulty may continue into the higher Stages. Improvement will occur naturally over time, and undue emphasis on instruction is unlikely to change the results.

Grammar in Context: Present Tense ❶❷❸❹❺

1. Display the back flap of the Big Book and model how to make statements in the simple present tense: *Paty lives with her mom, dad, sisters, and brothers. She cuts paper designs for family celebrations*, and so on.
2. Make other statements about the people in the book, having children turn to the page that shows what you are saying. For example, *They make cheese enchiladas.*
3. Encourage children to recall what else Paty does using the simple present by prompting them: *Tell me more about Paty and her family.* Flip through the book, using the pictures as reminders.

Options for STAGES

❶ These children may point to pictures when prompted with statements, such as *Paty cooks with her mom.*

❷❸ These children may make very simple sentences using only a subject and verb, such as *Paty eats,* and so on.

❹❺ Encourage these children to use complete sentences or phrases in telling about each scene.

4. Extend the activity by asking children to tell about themselves. You can help with specific questions, such as *What does your family eat? What do you do after school?* and so on.
5. After each child has finished telling about him or herself, ask the class to tell what they learned about that classmate. For example, ask *What does Lan do after school?*

WEEK 3 DAY 2

Shared Writing Card: Brainstorming Side B

Shared Writing Card

You will need
- Shared Writing Card 1
- Wipe-off marker

Brainstorming a Topic
- Use Side A of the Shared Writing Card and the finished Chinese traditions shared writing piece. Review how you used the graphic organizer's pictures and labels to form the basis of your finished piece.
- Turn the card over to Side B. Tell children that you will now think about your own topic together to draw in the graphic organizer. It can be about a child in the class or a child from a book that they have read. You might want to brainstorm a few possibilities before you determine your final choice. It should be a child or character that the class knows well enough to write at least four things about.

Scribing with the Graphic Organizer
- Once you have chosen a topic, you should decide together what the center illustration should show. Model how to draw a simple sketch of the child and write his or her name under it. Invite volunteers to draw simple scenes in the surrounding boxes showing what the child does to maintain his or her family's culture. Continue drawing until the picture is complete; it's OK to leave one box empty.
- Now it's time to put captions on your graphic organizer. Elicit suggestions for labels from the group and record them on the Shared Writing Card.
- You will create the shared writing paragraph together at the next session.

U20

STAGES ❶ Preproduction ❷ Early Production ❸ Speech Emergence ❹ Intermediate Fluency ❺ Advanced Fluency

Language Junction provides critical information about how various native languages affect English learning: Spanish, Vietnamese, Hmong, Cantonese, Haitian Creole, Korean, Khmer, Tagalog, Russian, and Arabic. You can use this information to help you refine instruction for these speakers.

Grammar in Context provides contextualized, developmentally appropriate instruction for a specific grammar point. The Stage designations at the top of the lesson help you identify which children should participate in each grammar instruction. Others can engage in center activities.

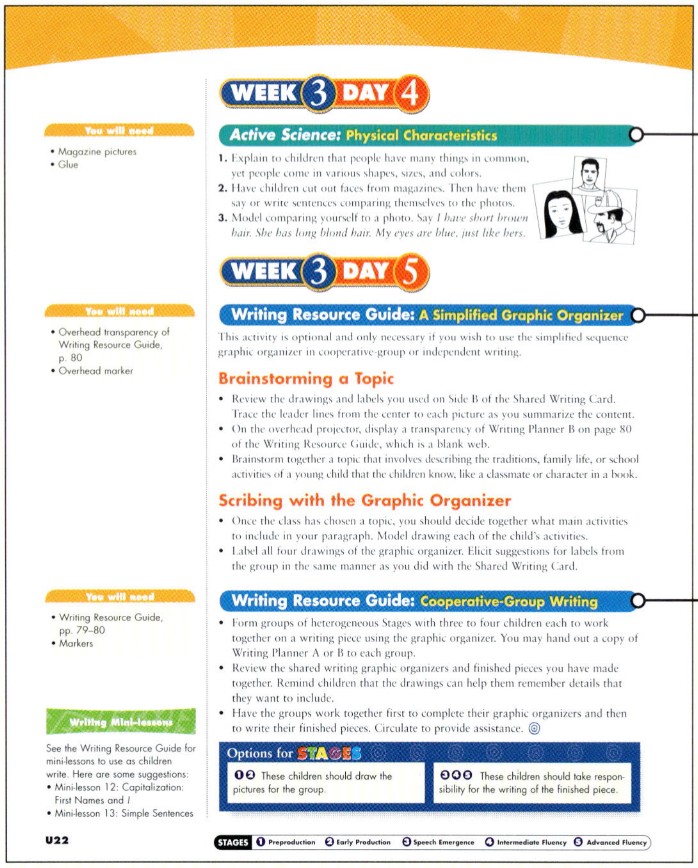

WEEK 3 DAY 4

Active Science: Physical Characteristics

You will need
- Magazine pictures
- Glue

1. Explain to children that people have many things in common, yet people come in various shapes, sizes, and colors.
2. Have children cut out faces from magazines. Then have them say or write sentences comparing themselves to the photos.
3. Model comparing yourself to a photo. Say *I have short brown hair. She has long blond hair. My eyes are blue, just like hers.*

WEEK 3 DAY 5

Writing Resource Guide: A Simplified Graphic Organizer

You will need
- Overhead transparency of Writing Resource Guide, p. 80
- Overhead marker

This activity is optional and only necessary if you wish to use the simplified sequence graphic organizer in cooperative-group or independent writing.

Brainstorming a Topic
- Review the drawings and labels you used on Side B of the Shared Writing Card. Trace the leader lines from the center to each picture as you summarize the content.
- On the overhead projector, display a transparency of Writing Planner B on page 80 of the Writing Resource Guide, which is a blank web.
- Brainstorm together a topic that involves describing the traditions, family life, or school activities of a young child that the children know, like a classmate or character in a book.

Scribing with the Graphic Organizer
- Once the class has chosen a topic, you should decide together what main activities to include in your paragraph. Model drawing each of the child's activities.
- Label all four drawings of the graphic organizer. Elicit suggestions for labels from the group in the same manner as you did with the Shared Writing Card.

Writing Resource Guide: Cooperative-Group Writing

You will need
- Writing Resource Guide, pp. 79–80
- Markers

- Form groups of heterogeneous Stages with three to four children each to work together on a writing piece using the graphic organizer. You may hand out a copy of Writing Planner A or B to each group.
- Review the shared writing graphic organizers and finished pieces you have made together. Remind children that the drawings can help them remember details that they want to include.
- Have the groups work together first to complete their graphic organizers and then to write their finished pieces. Circulate to provide assistance.

Options for STAGES

❶❷ These children should draw the pictures for the group.

❸❹❺ These children should take responsibility for the writing of the finished piece.

Writing Mini-lessons

See the Writing Resource Guide for mini-lessons to use as children write. Here are some suggestions:
- Mini-lesson 12: Capitalization: First Names and *I*
- Mini-lesson 13: Simple Sentences

U22

STAGES ❶ Preproduction ❷ Early Production ❸ Speech Emergence ❹ Intermediate Fluency ❺ Advanced Fluency

Active Social Studies, Active Math, and **Active Science** lessons provide hands-on experiences in the content areas. Each unit offers one lesson in all three content areas.

Writing Resource Guide features blank graphic organizers that match the **Shared Writing Card**. Children use them first in groups and then independently. Mini-lessons provide on-the-spot assistance for use in the "teachable moment" as children write.

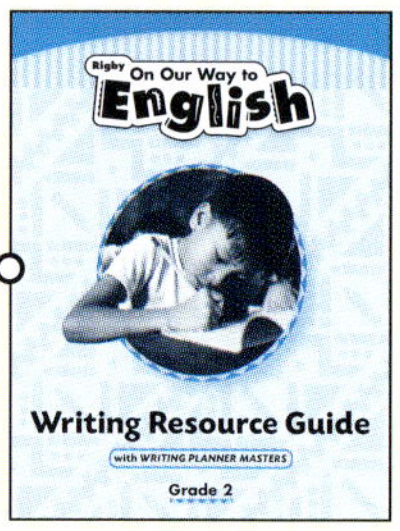

Open-Ended Oral Language Assessment appears at the end of each unit. By using the illustration and prompts to stimulate children's language production, you can assess and reassess children's Stages of Language Acquisition throughout the year.

Open-Ended Oral Language Assessment Reassess children's Language Acquisition Stages. Begin with an open-ended prompt like the first one below. If children are unable to respond, intervene with increasingly directed prompts, such as the second and third ones below.

What can you tell me about the picture? *What are the people in the picture doing?* *I see a sister. Do you see a brother?*

Assessment Directions: Copy this form for each child and place the completed form in the child's portfolio. Locate the child's Language Acquisition Stage for each of the first four activities and assess his or her performance during the unit according to expectations for that Stage. For the Big Book Retelling, pull children to retell the Big Book during end-of-unit assessment time. Use the Open-Ended Oral Language Assessment to reassess children's Language Acquisition Stages with one-fourth of your students for each unit, using the back side of the sheet to take notes. *For more guidance on assessment, see pages T40 and T41.*

Unit 1 Assessment **Name** ______________ **Date** ______________

On Our Way to English Grade 2	STAGE EXPECTATIONS ❶	❷	❸	❹	❺
Fluency Manipulative Chart: Student Version, page U12 *How does the child respond when manipulating the mini-chart along with the Oral Language Audio CD?*	Shows the correct answers. ☐ Yes ☐ Not yet	Shows the correct answers, naming the family member or activity. ☐ Yes ☐ Not yet	Shows the correct answers, approximating sentences and substitutions. ☐ Yes ☐ Not yet	Shows the correct answers, singing the verse with few, if any, errors. ☐ Yes ☐ Not yet	
Content Area Knowledge Language Practice Game: Version 1, page U13 *How does the child demonstrate an understanding of family names and everyday activities?*	Lays the cards down on the appropriate squares in the pyramid. ☐ Yes ☐ Not yet	Lays the cards down in the appropriate squares and uses some appropriate vocabulary, such as *brother eating.* ☐ Yes ☐ Not yet		Lays the cards down on the appropriate squares in the pyramid and says a complete sentence with appropriate vocabulary, such as *I am eating with my mother.* ☐ Yes ☐ Not yet	
Social Language Function Greet, page U17 *How does the child respond during the Function Mini-lesson??*	Responds non-verbally or with a basic word such as *Hello.* ☐ Yes ☐ Not yet		Responds using a short phrases, such as *Hello. How you? I'm fine.* ☐ Yes ☐ Not yet		
Academic Language Function Inquire, page U17 *How does the child respond during the Function Mini-lesson?*			Is able to form very simple questions with key words, such as *Where sister?* ☐ Yes ☐ Not yet	Uses complete, well-formed questions, such as *Where is sister?* ☐ Yes ☐ Not yet	
Big Book Retelling page U16 *Have each child use the back flap and symbols on the board to retell* Hello! I'm Paty. *How does the child retell the book?*	Simply points from Paty to each picture. ☐ Yes ☐ Not yet	Retells using a few words. ☐ Yes ☐ Not yet	Retells using longer phrases or simple sentences. ☐ Yes ☐ Not yet	Retells using complete sentences in connected discourse with few errors. ☐ Yes ☐ Not yet	Retells using story language similar to native-speaking peers. ☐ Yes ☐ Not yet
Open-Ended Oral Language Assessment, page U26 *Use the child's responses to the illustration to reassess the child's Stage of Language Acquisition.*	☐ **STAGE ❶** Uses few or no words; gestures or points.	☐ **STAGE ❷** Uses words or short phrases.	☐ **STAGE ❸** Uses phrases and simple sentences.	☐ **STAGE ❹** Uses sentences in connected discourse.	☐ **STAGE ❺** Uses language comparable to native-speaking peers.

Thematic Unit 1 Proud to Be Me U27

Assessment for each unit can be completed with a checklist to assess each child's performance in Fluency, Content Area Knowledge, Language Functions, and Big Book Retelling. There is also a place to record the child's performance on the Open-Ended Oral Language Assessment.

Standardized Test Practice Masters prepare English language learners for taking state and national tests.

Assessment in On Our Way to English

Program Assessment

- Similar to the retelling tasks found in commercial language tests, the *On Our Way to English* Retelling Pre- and Post-Test (pages A3–A4) provides critical information about a child's Stage of Language Acquisition. Using this information, you can decide how to place the child in appropriate groups for instruction. By administering this test at the start and end of the year, you can gauge a child's progress. We recommend that you audiotape the child's retelling at both points of administration for comparison purposes.
- The *On Our Way to English* Oral Language Rubric (page A5) provides descriptions of each Stage of Language Acquisition. Each description details four areas: Comprehension, Message, Fluency and Sentence Structure, and Word Choice and Academic Language. Although most school systems have their own criteria for transitioning students into the mainstream, children are generally considered ready to exit specialized ESL/ELD services when they have achieved Stage 5 in Language Acquisition and are performing at grade-level standards in literacy and the content areas.
- The *On Our Way to English* Writing Rubric (pages A6–A9) provides a basis for evaluating children's writing. Specifically developed with English language learners in mind, this writing rubric mirrors the four areas of the Oral Language Rubric: Message and Content, Conventions of English, Word Choice and Academic Language, and Fluency and Sentence Structure. To make the rubric accessible to busy teachers and to help guide them in scoring student writing, samples of each of the six Writing Levels are provided.

Thematic Units

- For each thematic unit, *On Our Way to English* offers an Open-Ended Oral Language Assessment based on a rich illustration depicting the content area topic. Children are asked to respond orally to the illustration, demonstrating their speaking ability as well as the content knowledge they have acquired through the unit. We recommend using this unique assessment tool with about one-fourth of your class for each unit so that you will have used this assessment for two units with each child by the end of the year. We also recommend audiotaping one of each child's mid-year performances for the Open-Ended Oral Language Assessment. Together with the Retelling Pre- and Post-Test audiotapings, this audiotape will complete the picture of the child's development in oral language throughout the year.

- Each unit comes with an easy-to-use Assessment Checklist that you can complete for each child. The checklist allows you to effectively observe and analyze children's performance during unit instruction in three areas: Fluency, Content Area Knowledge, and Language Functions. For each of these categories, the checklist provides guidelines for performance expectations that are appropriate to each Language Acquisition Stage. With these guidelines, you know, for example, what to look for in determining whether a Stage 1 child exhibits appropriate growth in Content Area Knowledge versus a Stage 4 child. You also have the opportunity to observe children's ability to retell the Big Book after multiple rereadings and to assess the retelling according to their Stages of Language Acquisition. Finally the checklist provides a space for recording the results of the Open-Ended Oral Language Assessment. The Thematic Unit Assessment Summary Sheet (page A10) provides a handy tool for summarizing each child's unit-by-unit progress throughout the year.

- Selected grammar blackline masters from the Language Learning Masters in each unit are recommended for inclusion in children's portfolios. These provide a record of each child's mastery of key grammar points from the unit and can be analyzed across the school year.

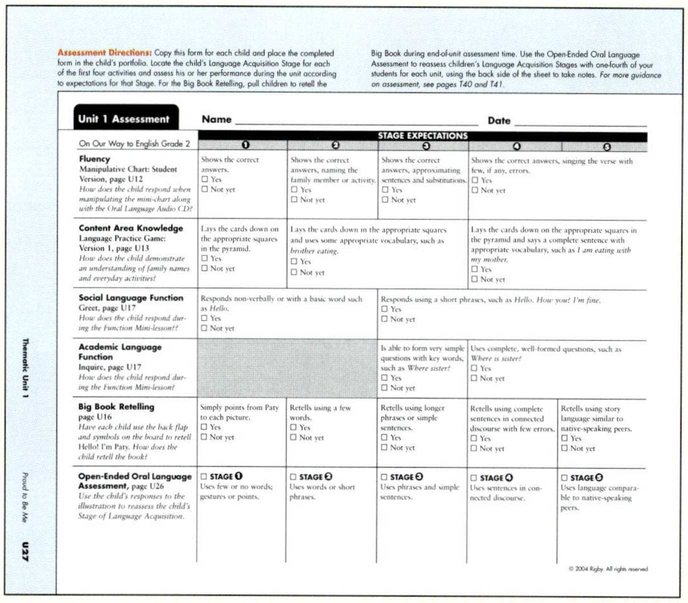

Assessment Directions: Copy this form for each child and place the completed form in the child's portfolio. Locate the child's Language Acquisition Stage for each of the first four activities and assess his or her performance during the unit according to expectations for that Stage. For the Big Book Retelling, pull children to retell the Big Book during end-of-unit assessment time. Use the Open-Ended Oral Language Assessment to reassess children's Language Acquisition Stages with one-fourth of your students for each unit, using the back side of the sheet to take notes. *For more guidance on assessment, see pages T40 and T41.*

Unit 1 Assessment Name ________ Date ________

On Our Way to English Grade 2	STAGE EXPECTATIONS ❶	❷	❸	❹	❺
Fluency Manipulative Chart: Student Version, page U12 *How does the child respond when manipulating the mini-chart along with the Oral Language Audio CD?*	Shows the correct answers. ☐ Yes ☐ Not yet	Shows the correct answers, naming the family member or activity. ☐ Yes ☐ Not yet	Shows the correct answers, approximating sentences and substitutions. ☐ Yes ☐ Not yet	Shows the correct answers, singing the verse with few, if any, errors. ☐ Yes ☐ Not yet	
Content Area Knowledge Language Practice Game: Version 1, page U13 *How does the child demonstrate an understanding of family names and everyday activities?*	Lays the cards down on the appropriate squares in the pyramid. ☐ Yes ☐ Not yet	Lays the cards down in the appropriate squares and uses some appropriate vocabulary, such as *brother eating.* ☐ Yes ☐ Not yet		Lays the cards down on the appropriate squares in the pyramid and says a complete sentence with appropriate vocabulary, such as *I am eating with my mother.* ☐ Yes ☐ Not yet	
Social Language Function Greet, page U17 *How does the child respond during the Function Mini-lesson??*	Responds non-verbally or with a basic word such as *Hello.* ☐ Yes ☐ Not yet		Responds using a short phrases, such as *Hello. How you? I'm fine.* ☐ Yes ☐ Not yet		
Academic Language Function Inquire, page U17 *How does the child respond during the Function Mini-lesson?*			Is able to form very simple questions with key words, such as *Where sister?* ☐ Yes ☐ Not yet	Uses complete, well-formed questions, such as *Where is sister?* ☐ Yes ☐ Not yet	
Big Book Retelling page U16 *Have each child use the back flap and symbols on the board to retell* Hello! I'm Paty. *How does the child retell the book?*	Simply points from Paty to each picture. ☐ Yes ☐ Not yet	Retells using a few words. ☐ Yes ☐ Not yet	Retells using longer phrases or simple sentences. ☐ Yes ☐ Not yet	Retells using complete sentences in connected discourse with few errors. ☐ Yes ☐ Not yet	Retells using story language similar to native-speaking peers. ☐ Yes ☐ Not yet
Open-Ended Oral Language Assessment, page U26 *Use the child's responses to the illustration to reassess the child's Stage of Language Acquisition.*	☐ STAGE ❶ Uses few or no words; gestures or points.	☐ STAGE ❷ Uses words or short phrases.	☐ STAGE ❸ Uses phrases and simple sentences.	☐ STAGE ❹ Uses sentences in connected discourse.	☐ STAGE ❺ Uses language comparable to native-speaking peers.

© 2004 Rigby. All rights reserved.

Thematic Unit 1 Proud to Be Me U27

Using *On Our Way to English* in Different Classroom Settings

The Bilingual and Dual-Language Classrooms

In bilingual and dual-language classrooms, children receive some of their daily instruction in their primary language and some in English. Throughout the country, an increasing emphasis on an organized approach to English language instruction is leading bilingual teachers to establish a clear ESL/ELD curriculum. At the same time, interest in dual-language classrooms—in which native English speakers and, for example, native Spanish speakers are brought together in a single classroom to achieve fluency in two languages—is increasing. Children in both these classrooms are usually at several different Stages of English Language Acquisition. Bilingual and dual-language teachers can use *On Our Way to English* in the following ways.

- Begin English-learning instruction with the thematic Units of *On Our Way to English*, tailoring instruction according to the Stages of Language Acquisition present in your classroom.
- Since current research now emphasizes learning to read in both languages simultaneously, you can use the titles in the Guided Reading Collection (available as separate purchase) simultaneous to native-language literacy instruction with all children. The appropriate Literacy Level for a child might be limited by his or her English-speaking ability—do not expect children to be reading at the same Literacy Level in their first and second languages.
- Phonics instruction in English will depend on the Literacy Level of each child in his or her primary language and on the similarity of the writing system of that primary language to English. Children in bilingual programs usually receive phonics instruction in their first language. Use *On Our Way to English* Phonics (available as separate purchase) by focusing first on phonics elements similar to the native language, then moving on to phonics elements that are new, and concluding with phonics elements that pose transfer difficulties. For more information about these elements, refer to the alternate scopes and sequences by language found on pages P2–P5 in the Phonics Teacher's Guide. There is also helpful information about how children's various native languages influence their acquisition of English in the "Language Junction" notes within the lesson plans.

The Mainstream Classroom

Mainstream classrooms include English language learners at various Stages of Language Acquisition as well as native English speakers. Mainstream classroom teachers can use *On Our Way to English* in the following ways.

- Organize all classroom instruction around the thematic Units in *On Our Way to English*, creating a sense of community and equity for all learners. Use the wide variety of whole-group, small-group, partner, and individual activities provided in the program. This content-based literacy instruction is good instruction for all learners. Tailor activities to the Stages of Language Acquisition present in your classroom.
- Alternatively, you can meet with English language learners for ESL or ELD instruction using the thematic Units while other children participate in independent, collaborative, or center-based activities.
- In your ESL/ELD time, provide *On Our Way to English* Phonics instruction to the whole group of English language learners. However, base your performance expectations on children's Stages of Language Acquisition, as outlined in "Assessment for Stages" within the lesson plans.
- Meet with small groups of English language learners organized into Rigby ELL Levels for Guided Reading, just as you meet with native speakers for guided reading instruction. All *On Our Way to English* titles can be used with native speakers for mixed-grouping purposes.

The ESL Specialist

In schools with lower populations of English language learners, an ESL specialist may work with children either within the classroom or on a pull-out basis. Communication about instructional objectives and ongoing progress of children with the classroom teacher is essential for achieving academic success for English language learners. Sometimes ESL specialists may choose to combine children from several mainstream classrooms who are at similar Stages of Language Acquisition. Others may choose to group children from one mainstream classroom who are at different Stages. ESL specialists using these different instructional groupings will use the components of *On Our Way to English* differently. ESL specialists can use *On Our Way to English* in the following ways.

- *On Our Way to English* Thematic Units can be tailored to suit the group's appropriate Stages of Language Acquisition by following the "Options for Stages" and "Assessment for Stages" features within the lesson plans. Teachers working with one or two Stages at a time will hone instruction to only those activities most appropriate for these Stages.
- Work collaboratively with the classroom teacher to ensure that the specially designed Guided Reading Collection titles are used during small-group time within the mainstream classroom within the Reading/Language Arts block.

The Self-Contained Classroom

Self-contained classrooms are made up entirely of English language learners who are at similar Stages of Language Acquisition, usually Stages 1–3. This homogeneity allows you to create an enriched environment appropriate for the acquisition of language, literacy, and academic content. Keep in mind that, although students may be at the same Stage of Language Acquisition, their Levels of Literacy Development may vary greatly. The self-contained classroom teacher can use *On Our Way to English* in the following ways.

- Use thematic Units for whole-group instruction, following the suggestions in "Options for Stages" within the lesson plans that apply to the Stages of Language Acquisition present in your classroom.
- Group by Rigby ELL Levels for guided reading using the Guided Reading Collection titles designed for English language learners.
- Provide Phonics instruction based on performance expectations for children's Stages of Language Acquisition as outlined in "Assessment for Stages" within the lesson plans.

Developing Children's Oral Language

We need to provide instruction that addresses all of the learners' needs simultaneously.

What Does It Mean to Know a Language?

Learning a new language is a complex undertaking. Children must learn English grammar, sounds, word forms, and word meanings (syntax, phonology, morphology, and semantics). They must be able to use the language to communicate in social situations and also to perform demanding academic functions in all content areas as well. They need to understand the kind of language appropriate to a variety of settings and the conventions which regulate communicating effectively within these settings. For academic success, children must be proficient in all four language processes—reading, writing, speaking, and listening *(Peregoy and Boyle 2001; Freeman and Freeman 2001)*.

It is important to distinguish between two fundamentally different types of language proficiency. Conversational language, sometimes referred to as Basics Interpersonal Communication Skills (BICS), is social language—often called playground language. It is the language used in making friends, meeting basic needs, and comprehending everyday conversation. BICS is developed relatively rapidly and naturally, much as a child acquires his or her first language, through interaction with native speakers and input that is understandable to the child because of physical and visual context. So conversational language is well supported by context and is not cognitively demanding. BICS takes about two years to develop *(Cummins 2000)*.

Academic language, or Cognitive Academic Language Proficiency (CALP), is the type of language necessary for success in school; it is the language of books, math, science, and social studies. It is more complex and abstract, with fewer concrete or visual clues to support

Research has shown that language learners go through a series of predictable stages as they acquire English.

meaning. So academic language typically is not well supported by context and is cognitively demanding. CALP is associated with higher-order thinking skills and is only achieved over time through meaningful language, literacy, and content instruction at children's appropriate Stages of Language Acquisition *(Cummins 2000)*. Academic language proficiency takes between five and seven years to develop.

English language learners do not need to develop CALP before content area learning is introduced. Rather, it is integrated language and content instruction that facilitates the simultaneous acquisition of academic language and academic content (Samway and McKeon 1999). English language learners cannot afford to delay important learning in literacy, math, social studies, and science while they wait to acquire BICS first. We need to provide instruction that addresses all of language learners' needs simultaneously so that they can close the achievement gap between themselves and their native-speaking peers.

How Is Language Acquired?

Research has shown that language learners go through a series of predictable stages as they acquire English.

Preproduction These students are fairly new to English and are not yet comfortable producing English speech. The teacher's goal, therefore, is to build English listening comprehension and vocabulary. Children can indicate understanding through gestures, pointing, and nodding and can answer simple *yes/no* questions. Teaching strategies appropriate for this Stage include slowing down and simplifying speech, enunciating clearly, using gestures and body language, repeating and paraphrasing often, avoiding words with multiple meanings, supporting speech with visuals and manipulatives, using captions to label pictures, and Total Physical Response (see page T26). Group activities are especially successful at this Stage. Literacy instruction should focus on reading aloud, shared reading, and shared-to-guided reading.

Early Production These students are just beginning to understand spoken English and are feeling confident enough to produce one- or two-word answers. They can produce set phrases such as greetings. At this Stage, you will want to continue building their receptive vocabulary and motivating them to produce the vocabulary they understand. Techniques appropriate for this Stage are similar to those above. Literacy instruction should focus on reading aloud, shared reading, and shared-to-guided reading.

Speech Emergent These students produce phrases and short sentences. They understand much of the spoken English in the world around them. Despite the errors in their speech, they are able to communicate socially. Academic language is still limited. Strategies appropriate for this level include clarifying the usage of words with multiple meanings, using graphic organizers, and supporting speech with visual aids. Encourage children to retell and respond to reading, supporting their efforts with visuals and props. Literacy instruction should focus on reading aloud, shared reading, and guided reading.

Intermediate Fluency These students understand most of the spoken English they encounter. Although their speech is not perfect, communication rarely breaks down. However, they are still struggling to master academic language and to expand their abilities in the various content areas. Effective instruction includes the use of strategies such as supporting academic language with graphic organizers or other visual aids. At this Stage, children should be able to understand and communicate with less reliance on manipulatives and real-world objects. Provide opportunities for students to read aloud to others and engage students in meaningful discussions about reading. Literacy instruction should focus on reading aloud, shared reading, and guided reading.

Advanced Fluency These students speak and comprehend spoken English with native-like fluency, although they may still make a few errors with prepositions and idioms. In most educational settings, children at this Stage are transitioned into the mainstream program. However, they may still lag behind their native-speaking peers in academic language and content area knowledge. At this Stage, continue building academic vocabulary and developing higher-order thinking skills and language use in the content areas. Strategies that work well include visual support for academic concepts, opportunities for students to read aloud to others, engaging students in meaningful discussions about reading, and encouraging them to make connections between characters, settings, and ideas across texts. Literacy instruction should focus on reading aloud, shared reading, and guided reading.

While English language learners need to have input that they can understand, they also need to be exposed to language more advanced than they are able to produce in order for their development to progress. Children need ongoing opportunities to learn to express ideas in new ways. Teachers must make efforts to model new language use in increasingly complex contexts.

Children need ongoing opportunities to learn to express ideas in new ways.

Meeting the Needs of English Language Learners

English language learners need to be able to use English to communicate in social settings and to achieve academically in all content areas. In order for this to happen, teachers must provide comprehensible input—language that is understandable to language learners because it is contextualized and meaningful—in both oral and written English. Instruction in the language-learning classroom should be contextualized and supported by strategies such as gesturing, restating, and acting out—strategies that enhance and support meaning. In this way, instruction becomes meaningful (in other words, the input becomes comprehensible) to children whose command of English is limited.

Teachers can make instruction comprehensible to students by using the following techniques:

- Using visuals, real-world objects, models, and audiovisual aids as examples of concepts and vocabulary
- Employing gestures, movements, and other body language to emphasize meaning
- Paraphrasing, or saying the same thing in different ways
- Writing key words and ideas on the board or easel pad so that language input is slowed down and children can remember it

Our first job as teachers of English language learners is to provide comprehensible input.

- Using graphic organizers, semantic webs, and charts to show the relationships between ideas
- Checking frequently for understanding and encouraging children to show they understand with gestures, movements, or short answers
- Asking students to explain concepts and vocabulary to one another in small groups or pairs
- Using frequent repetition and restatement
- Keeping oral explanations short and simple
- Connecting to children's prior knowledge and educational experiences
- Using Total Physical Response, a technique in which children respond physically to commands given orally by the teacher or another student
- Using Language Experience Approach (LEA), a technique in which children dictate words, phrases, or sentences about a shared experience to the teacher
- Previewing and reviewing lessons in students' primary language, whenever possible
- Using children as linguistic and cultural resources

(Freeman and Freeman 1998).

Our first job as teachers of English language learners is to provide comprehensible input. Children often go through a silent period (Preproduction). Once they do start to talk, however, we need to respond to their message rather than correcting what they say. At the same time, we can model correct language as we interact with English learners. If we constantly correct students, they may become afraid to use their developing English. When asked *Go bathroom?*, the teacher can model the correct language in his or her response without interrupting the purpose of the conversation: *You need to go to the bathroom? Sure, you may do that.*

Similarly, the classroom atmosphere should be one that is inviting and comfortable for language learners. If children are nervous or bored, it is as if a filter goes up and blocks them from learning language. On the other hand, if children are motivated and interested, the filter goes down, allowing language acquisition to take place. This is known as lowering the affective filter. We as teachers need to create a low-anxiety environment in which students feel comfortable taking language-learning risks. Rather than calling on children individually and using traditional tests that may raise the affective filter, we need to engage them in collaborative activities, encourage volunteering, validate attempts to produce language, and use a variety of ways to assess performance.

Children need a comfortable, supportive environment for learning in which they feel confident in taking risks with the new language, are given adequate time for developing higher-order thinking skills and academic language, and receive instruction that fulfills their needs in language, literacy, and content learning. Activities should be appropriate for children at a variety of Stages of Language Acquisition, with the teacher skillfully modifying whole-class instruction for groups of children with varying English proficiencies. Children need to be invited to use all of their senses in hands-on, meaningful activities instead of hearing an endless, incomprehensible stream of speech.

Characteristics of Classrooms that Support Language Learning

- **Low affective filter** The classroom atmosphere is encouraging and makes children feel comfortable and willing to participate and take risks.
- **Comprehensible input** Supportive strategies make concepts and vocabulary understandable to children at the various Stages of Language Acquisition.
- **Focus on communication** Language is real and is used for authentic, meaningful purposes rather than merely for its own sake.
- **Contextualized language** Context, visuals, examples, and illustrations provide support for integrated oral language, literacy, and content area instruction.
- **Error acceptance** The message, rather than linguistic correctness, is the focus. Errors are corrected through teacher modeling of correct forms rather than drills and exercises.
- **Increased wait time** Adequate time for formulating responses aids in second language production.
- **Respect for Stages of Language Acquisition** Activities chosen are developmentally appropriate for a variety of Stages of Language Acquisition. Language instruction allows learners to stretch their skills and progress to higher Stages.
- **Student-centered activities** Small group and partner activities provide authentic contexts for communication and language use. Student participation and interaction is encouraged. Teacher-talk is kept to a minimum.
- **Use of first language and home culture** When children are allowed to process information with each other in their first language, they maintain self-esteem, build a sense of community, and are able to transfer learning from one language to another. When home culture is used as an asset to classroom instruction, avenues to student participation are opened.
- **Authentic assessment based on multiple measures** Multiple measures, including oral reading records, anecdotal observations, observational checklists, oral language and writing rubrics, and student work samples—when embedded in instruction—provide the teacher with appropriate information for use in planning further instruction.

The Role of Family Members

It is clear from research that the academic and linguistic growth of students is enhanced when collaborative relationships are established between families and school *(Cummins 2000)*. Children who read to family members make significantly greater progress in literacy and English language development even when their parents are neither fluent speakers of English nor literate. Children whose families are involved in their learning show greater interest in learning and behave better in school than those whose families are not involved.

Family involvement in their children's formal education has often been limited to attendance at open houses and report card conferences. Particularly in low-income schools, parents may come from backgrounds of little or no formal education themselves. School may be intimidating for these individuals and conjure up negative emotions and experiences. They may feel inadequate in dealing with school personnel. Also, the relationship between teachers and parents in their home culture might discourage direct parental involvement *(Valdes 1996; Wong-Fillmore 1990)*. Sometimes this gives the mistaken impression that these parents do not care about their children or are not interested in their academic progress. Schools need to explore ways to encourage these parents to become involved in all aspects of their children's education.

Family involvement is more likely when families see the school and classroom as a welcoming environment. The presence of school staff or volunteers who speak their home language will facilitate family involvement. If asked, parents will often bring a trusted friend or family member who can serve as translator to conferences or meetings at school. This puts parents at ease and solves a problem for the staff members who do not speak the parents' language.

Families of English language learners should be regarded as a valuable resource for their own children and for others in school. They need to be empowered to share in policy- and decision-making about their children and the educational community in general. When schools and families work together, students succeed and communities are strengthened.

> *A child's culture operates as a lens through which he or she views the world.*

The Role of Culture

Acquiring a language involves more than simply speaking, reading, and writing the language. It involves thought patterns, perceptions, cultural values, communication styles, and social organizations.

A child's culture operates as a lens through which he or she views the world. Often the culture and language use in the classroom may conflict with what the child has learned in the home culture and language. Sometimes these differences may interfere with student learning or participation in activities. Test performance, group interactions, responses to questioning, homework practices, and learning styles may all be ways in which the culture of the home conflicts with the culture of the classroom. Awareness of these differences will help you deal with them effectively. As students learn English, their success depends on their ability to adapt to the culture of the community. Teachers can facilitate this acculturation process by bridging the culture and language gap for their students. A variety of routines and approaches can help to increase student comfort and success in your classroom. These include valuing the contributions of home languages and cultures, allowing the use of the home language in the classroom when appropriate, encouraging students to make connections to their past experiences and contribute their viewpoints, fostering family involvement in the classroom and in school, and pursuing specific information about the cultures of the students and their families.

Some Myths and Misconceptions About Language Acquisition

There are a number of myths and misconceptions commonly held in today's society regarding second language acquisition. We hope the research-based facts presented here will help you dispel these myths.

Myth: English language learners simply need to be placed in an English learning environment, and they'll pick up English naturally in one year.

Fact: While this approach works well for the acquisition of social English, the acquisition of academic English requires skillful instruction that reaches the child with a limited command of English. Children who receive little or no instruction tailored to the needs of language learners can take as many as ten years to achieve grade level performance in the content areas (Collier 1995).

Myth: If children can already speak English, they don't need any further specialized instruction.

Fact: Even though English language learners may give the impression of being able to speak English well on the playground or with their peers, we know that it typically takes five to seven years for them to acquire grade-level competence in academic subject areas. Integrated instruction in language, literacy, and content can help children acquire academic skills as they learn language. Effective instruction can help reduce this academic gap (Collier 1995).

Introducing literacy at the outset of English acquisition moves children most rapidly toward academic success.

Myth: Transfer occurs automatically from the primary language to English.

Fact: *Although it is known that some transfer between languages does occur naturally, we can organize our instruction to maximize the transfer of learning. Similarities between the two languages should be explicitly pointed out in instruction so that children develop metalinguistic awareness and the ability to analyze language patterns. With this in mind, we should also recognize that the higher the level of development of the child's primary language, the better his or her chances at success in the second language will be. Therefore, we should encourage parents to maintain the home language and continue to foster its development in their children (Cummins 2000).*

Myth: English language learners should not be exposed to English print until they are orally proficient in English.

Fact: *Although this belief was held widely in the past, we now know that second language acquisition is aided by exposure to literacy. We can and should begin literacy instruction right from the start. Although written language seems to rely upon oral language, there are strategies for developing language and literacy simultaneously. Exposure to print helps children build visual literacy and remember what they have learned. Introducing literacy at the outset of English acquisition allows children to progress most rapidly toward academic success (Freeman and Freeman 2000).*

Myth: Children need to become proficient readers in their native language before learning to read in their second language.

Fact: *While research supports the importance of primary language reading in overall literacy development, current research shows that literacy can proceed simultaneously in two languages, and that there is no reason to delay second language literacy. Reading skills acquired in one language can transfer to the other and vice versa (Cummins 2000).*

Developing Literacy

The balanced literacy instructional approaches—modeled, shared, shared-to-guided, guided, and independent—involve different degrees of teacher and learner responsibility.

These approaches are blended throughout *On Our Way to English* lesson plans to move learners through modeled, shared, shared-to-guided, guided, and independent work. The ultimate goal of balanced literacy instruction is independent readers and writers.

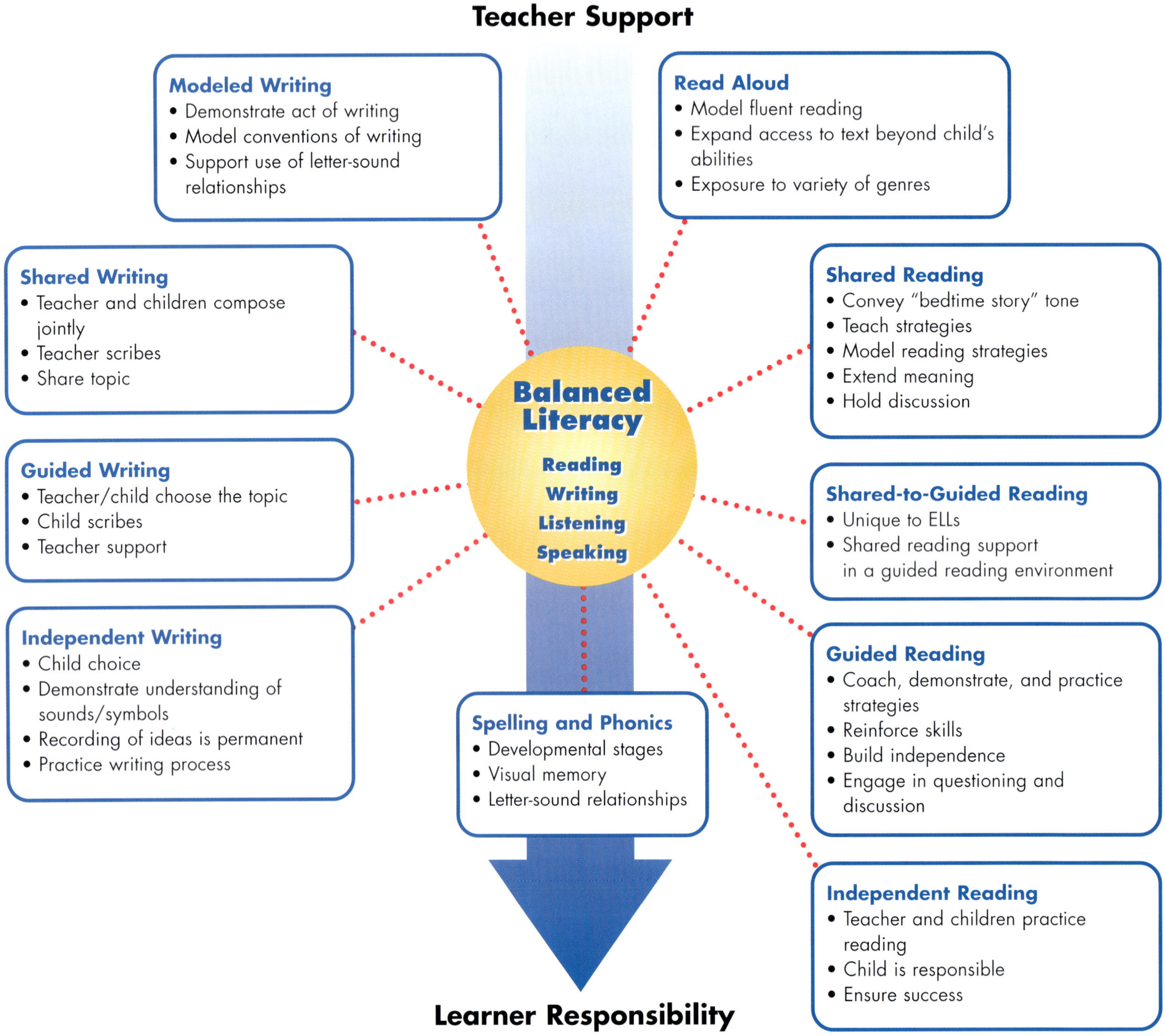

Modeled Reading for English Language Learners

Students at all levels of language proficiency benefit from and enjoy listening to stories, rhymes, poems, chants, and nonfiction. Reading aloud demonstrates the connections between oral and written language and provides a model of both fluent reading and oral production of English. The books chosen for read-alouds expose children to a variety of language patterns and interesting vocabulary as well as popular authors and writing styles. As children respond to the books, they share their common and diverse experiences and build their background knowledge for independent reading of the books. The responsibility lies with the teacher to select the book for a purpose, to read with expression, and to encourage children to interact with the text through words or gestures and pointing as they predict and respond.

Prior to reading the text aloud to children, the teacher might do a picture walk, eliciting predictions about events, topics, or vocabulary that may be encountered in the reading. With English language learners, the teacher needs to creatively encourage a variety of responses for children at different Stages of Language Acquisition, from pointing at pictures to complete oral sentences. Recording these predictions on chart paper or the chalkboard will enhance students' engagement with the reading as they seek to confirm their predictions and will allow them to better remember any new language being introduced. Setting a purpose for reading will increase attentiveness and motivation to listen. Teachers should be aware of the varying levels of prior knowledge of students and build background appropriately, using gestures, real-world items, and pictures to support their spoken language.

Teaching Tips for Reading Aloud to English Language Learners

- Select the book for a purpose.
- Read the book yourself before reading it to children.
- Determine natural breaks for stopping.
- Read with expression and enthusiasm at a natural pace.
- Build comprehensible input through gesturing, pointing, props, and restating.
- Make connections with children's prior experiences.
- Remember that children do not need to understand every single word to enjoy the passage.
- Encourage responses, in gestures or words, or have children repeat phrases.
- Model how a proficient reader makes sense out of reading through think-alouds.
- After reading, have children use props or illustrations to retell their favorite parts.
- Reread the story to develop listening fluency.
- Extend the book's message to other cultures and perspectives.

More Books

- *Families* by Ann Morris (Morrow, 2000)
- *Love You Forever* by Robert N. Munsch (Firefly Books Ltd, 1988)
- *I'm a Big Brother* by Joanna Cole (Morrow, 1997)
- *A Chair for My Mother* by Vera B. Williams (Morrow, 1984)
- *Are You My Mother?* by Philip D. Eastman (Random House Books for Young Readers, 1998)

Suggested trade titles for read-alouds or independent reading are listed in the thematic units lesson plans. Each recommended book relates to the content area theme being explored. You may want to choose some of the recommended books to read aloud and put others in your classroom library.

Shared Reading for English Language Learners

The shared reading approach involves reading in a whole-group setting with enlarged print materials such as Big Books and poetry charts. The teacher begins by reading aloud while children follow along. As they become more familiar with the book, children join in and share in the reading. This enables each child to participate at his or her appropriate Literacy Level and, in the case of the English language learner, at the appropriate Stage of Language Acquisition.

Appropriate texts for shared reading with English language learners are those of a variety of genres in which the reading is slightly more difficult than the instructional level of the children. They should contain rhythm, rhyme, and repetition of concepts and language patterns as well as vocabulary that is useful to English language learners. They should provide frequent opportunities for participation by students using Total Physical Response techniques. Pictures should give maximum support for understanding the text.

Prior to reading the selection, you should relate the Big Book to the theme and children's interests and prior knowledge. Then examine front and back cover illustrations for clues to text content. As you read the text with children, point clearly to each word with a finger or a pointer.

The first reading should be at a natural pace with few stops so that children may enjoy and comprehend the flow of the story. In subsequent readings, build comprehensible input through gesturing, pointing, props, restating, and use of the backflap on the Big Books. Ask questions of students which will elicit responses at their appropriate Stages of Language Acquisition. Encourage children to brainstorm and create movements, actions, or sounds to accompany certain parts of the story. This is particularly helpful to English language learners because it helps them internalize the meanings of words and engages multiple senses in the reading experience. The lesson plans for shared reading in *On Our Way to English* are organized in an instructional sequence for effectiveness with English language learners.

Shared-to-Guided Reading for English Language Learners

Shared-to-guided reading is an instructional technique developed specifically for English language learners to facilitate the transition from shared reading to guided reading. Shared-to-Guided reading is an ideal way to involve children in Stages 1 and 2 in small-group reading sessions. The high level of support provided by the teacher allows children to read their own copies of a book successfully.

Books selected for shared-to-guided reading are those with real-world topics supported by realistic pictures, simple sentence patterns, and text that reflects oral language. Text difficulty should reflect Rigby ELL Levels A through C.

Prior to reading, help children connect speech to print by conducting a picture walk and pointing to the pictures as children describe what they see and make predictions about what they will read. As you read the selection aloud, model such concepts of print as how to hold the book, turn the pages, and track the print from left to right with your finger. Read the entire text through, pointing to pictures to create comprehensible input.

Invite children to assume more and more responsibility for subsequent readings by using techniques such as echo reading or choral reading. In echo reading, you read aloud one phrase, line, or sentence of text and children echo by reading and repeating the line. In choral reading, children read along with you as a group. Then encourage students to read the text with partners or on their own. Provide ongoing access to the books so that students may revisit them during center time or independent reading time.

Guided Reading for English Language Learners

In guided reading, teachers work with two to six children who have been placed in a flexible group according to developmental needs, strategy proficiency, and literacy skill level. With English language learners, these groups should also reflect Language Acquisition Stages: for instance, Stages 1 and 2 reading at Level B will be a in a shared-to-guided reading group and Stages 3 through 5 reading at Level B, in a guided reading group. Each group is matched with a guided reading little book that offers features that ensure some success with known strategies and skills, yet also provides appropriate challenges for children learning to read. A book is at a child's instructional level if the child can read 90% to 94% of the text accurately. Students are considered to be reading accurately even if they use native language pronunciation for English words (e.g., Spanish speakers pronounce *bit* as *beet* or if they drop word endings, e.g., *want* for *wanted*.)

Before reading, set the scene for the guided reading book by building children's background for the text. Because you are working with English language learners, background building takes on additional importance as you work together to explore new ideas and concepts. Now you are ready to do a book talk, in which you use the pictures to build familiarity with book content and provide essential vocabulary for language learners. Using the *On Our Way to English* Reading Strategy Cards (sold separately), you introduce reading strategies appropriate to the Rigby ELL Level of the text by using a demonstration think-aloud, simplifying language, and then making a direct strategy statement.

Each child holds and reads his or her own copy of the book during guided reading. As children read, you act as a coach, reminding children of the reading strategy you are currently working on and of earlier reading strategies they have already mastered. Because children are meant to read the text independently from one another, you should discourage choral reading. Tune into children one by one, observing reading behaviors and supporting problem-solving and meaning-making.

About Flexible Groupings

Flexible groupings are different than traditional groupings because flexible groupings:

- are temporary and change according to children's interests, needs, social interactions, and development.
- allow children to move freely among groups (even skipping a Literacy Level) to address the special needs of a group of children at a specific point in time.
- have names that reference the title, activity, or members' names (*I'd like to meet with the group that read* Omar's Surprise *yesterday*) rather than static labels like "Bluebirds."

Independent Reading for English Language Learners

Children learn to read by reading and need time every day to spend with books they enjoy. Reading independently gives them time to improve their fluency and to independently practice their reading strategies. During a quiet designated time for silent reading, you and the children should read the books you or they have selected. Young children have a "not so silent" reading time because they need to chat or share as they experience the joy of reading. The reading experiences within *On Our Way to English* lead children to discover the kinds of books and authors they enjoy reading independently. Children in Stages 1 and 2 should be encouraged to return to the texts they have encountered already in shared-to-guided reading groups. Children in Stages 3 and above can read books they have self-selected, such as the trade titles listed in "More Books" at the beginning of each thematic unit or books you have identified as appropriate for them. An appropriate book for independent reading poses few challenges for the reader.

English language learners are sometimes faced with unique challenges in independent reading because they are still learning English as they strive toward independence in reading. Remind children that they don't have to be able to say unfamiliar words perfectly or to know the meaning of every word to understand what the book is about. As they read, provide each child in Stages 3–5 with a block of sticky notes that he or she can use while reading. Encourage them to focus on the overall meaning of the text and to take notes that will help them go back to learn unfamiliar vocabulary and sentence structures later. They can also note passages that they like, dislike, and don't understand. Some shorthand for children to use appears above on the right.

When your independent readers in Stages 3–5 have finished reading, gather them into a group. Invite them to share their sticky notes in a group discussion. They may be able to help each other unravel tricky sentences and define unknown words. Invite them to comment on each other's responses to the texts.

sentence	I can't understand this sentence, even when I reread it.
word	I need to figure out what this word means by asking someone or by looking it up in a dictionary. It seems important.
!	That's interesting!
?	I don't get it.
X	I disagree.
♥	I love this part!

Modeled Writing

In modeled writing, you demonstrate the writing process by thinking aloud while composing a text on the board or an easel pad. This technique provides an opportunity to show students how the thinking and writing processes differ according to the type of passage or the purpose for writing. You should discuss how you make decisions about content, vocabulary, grammar, style, and conventions as you write. For English language learners, explain terms or idioms that may be unfamiliar. You might even draw explanatory pictures next to words that are difficult. Keep the modeled writing passages brief, closely related to the theme, and focused on key skills currently being addressed in *On Our Way to English*.

Shared Writing

During shared writing, students work together with the teacher to compose a text. The primary responsibility for composing the text rests with the students while the teacher acts as scribe and shares ideas and strategies. When working with English language learners, the teacher may also need to supply appropriate vocabulary and model correct English usage as she scribes for the class. This technique enables students to engage in writing beyond their independent writing level. Encourage children to share their thinking as they participate, and draw explanatory pictures to support comprehension of difficult words.

Using a graphic organizer to begin shared writing is a vital step for English language learners, who need to collect vocabulary and ideas, as well as visualize the relationships among their ideas, before writing. The Shared Writing Cards in *On Our Way to English* provide English language learners with an effective way to gather ideas and organize information in a graphic organizer during the prewriting phase of the writing process. To help children make the reading-writing connection, each graphic organizer reflects the back flap of the shared reading selection in that unit. When the text is finished, it should be reread many times and displayed in the classroom where children can revisit it independently. A variety of types of writing and purposes for writing are explored in shared writing.

Interactive Writing

Interactive writing is similar to shared writing except that children are invited to share the responsibility for writing. For interactive writing time, you hand out colored markers to children, designating the same color to the same child every day. Then you can use the color of the marker to analyze student input. As you compose a text together, prompt students to say a word of text, stretching the sounds so students are able to hear them. If a child knows which sounds to write, he or she goes to the chart paper or overhead to write the sound or word. If a child does not know a sound, or if it is irregular, the teacher supplies the letter(s). After a new word has been added, the group rereads what has been written. This process is repeated until the whole text is written. Then the whole group rereads the text many times.

Guided Writing

Guided writing is writing done by students with guidance or coaching from the teacher. In *On Our Way to English*, guided writing is done within the Thematic Unit using a blackline of the Shared Writing Card's graphic organizer. When working with English language learners, you must tailor writing expectations to children's Literacy Level and Stage of Language Acquisition. Children unable to produce much oral English will probably also be unable to produce much written English. In this child-centered workshop, children work as a community of learners who support one another through sharing and responding. As children are writing, meet with children individually or in flexible groups to discuss their writing or to conduct mini-lessons specific to their needs in writing process, strategies, or mechanics. The *Writing Resource Guide* is an excellent resource for mini-lessons that you can use in the teachable moment. Encourage children to support each other by modeling their thinking strategies, sharing their writing, and responding to the writing of others as they progress toward independence in writing.

Independent Writing

The writing instruction and activities in *On Our Way to English* will prepare children and motivate them to write independently with enthusiasm and confidence. They will write about what they have learned through oral language development activities and what they have read in shared and guided reading lessons. As children begin to internalize concepts, vocabulary, grammar, and other skills and strategies, they will put these into practice in their independent writing. Provide your students with frequent opportunities, ideas, and materials for independent writing. Thematically connected writing prompts for independent writing are provided in the Writer's Den for each Thematic Unit.

Strategic Reading

Within the rich literacy experiences of a balanced literacy classroom, children develop skills and strategies to help them make meaning of text. By observing how readers use the language cueing systems to gather information and by knowing what strategies expert readers use to make meaning, you can more easily assess how children are progressing as readers. You will gain insight into how children think about what they are reading, including:

- what they know
- what they think they know
- how they think they know it
- what they want to know

For English language learners, using the cueing systems poses some particular difficulties since these children don't have the same linguistics resources to draw on as native-speaking children. The chart below identifies some key differences.

Native English Speakers	English Language Learners
• Can sample print and select key words.	• May not know which words carry the most information. • May not know all the sound-symbol relationships and use them to sample.
• Can predict what is about to be read using the meaning and structure of English.	• May not have sufficient background knowledge, cultural knowledge, or knowledge of English grammatical structures to predict. • May often rely heavily on phonics cues instead.
• Can check predictions and confirm or reject them later.	• May not be able to tell whether a prediction "sounds right" or makes sense as a native English speaker would.
• Can self-correct using multiple sources of information.	• May not recognize a miscue. • May not have the vocabulary to correct a miscue with a more appropriate word.

From the Authors

How Do We Teach Reading to English Language Learners?

Mary Lou McCloskey

Mary Lou McCloskey

My favorite teaching moments are those miraculous times watching children's faces light up with the wonder of learning to read. As educators, we have the privilege of sharing the joy but also the responsibility to look beyond the wonder to understand the process of developing literacy. Literacy involves all aspects of language—listening, speaking, reading, and writing. When children develop literacy, they learn to construct and convey meaning from written texts. They begin to have effective ways to learn about the world, to interact with people in the world, and to influence what happens in the world through the written word. Our goals for young English learners are to help them develop beyond merely being able to do these things—we want our students to become learners who *choose* to read and write, who *delight* in reading and writing.

Oral Language Development and Literacy Development

For English language learners, we can employ literacy development strategies that parallel those of effective oral language development. These include providing comprehensible input and social interaction that lead students toward mature reading and writing. They also include a model of phonics that helps children learn phonetic systems in a manner that is compatible with their cognitive and language development. There are a number of ways in which literacy development is unlike oral language development, however. Most children require explicit instruction for successful literacy development. Effective balanced literacy instruction requires a print-rich environment in which teachers continue the development of oral language, teach text processing and production strategies, ensure cultural background knowledge, and develop decoding and encoding skills *(Cloud et al. 2000)*. The classroom setting provides input—both oral and written—that is understandable to them and at the right instructional level. It provides social interaction with and about texts and explicit instruction in strategies and processes used to make meaning from text.

What Is Unique About English Language Learners Who Are Developing Literacy?

Most linguists and child development specialists agree that it is easier for children to learn to read and write a language that they already speak *(Snow et al. 1998)*. When possible, it is preferable for children to develop literacy first (or simultaneously) in their mother tongue. However, because of the needs of multilingual classrooms and the chosen instructional methods of many districts or states, many English language learners are learning to read in English. This presents unique challenges for young English learners. Though the development of English language learners who are acquiring literacy in a new language has many parallels to first language literacy development, there are a number of important distinctions for teachers to keep in mind.

1. What Our Students Bring

Our English language learners bring a great deal with them to the literacy table. They already know at least one language and use it in sophisticated and age-appropriate ways. They have the same cognitive maturity as their native-speaking peers. They may have some exposure to literacy in their mother tongue and may have acquired many literacy skills and strategies as applied in another language system. They bring rich experiences in one or more cultures. Each day they move between home culture and school culture—and the two cultures may have wide differences in values and expectations. As teachers, we must respect, use, and celebrate what English language learners already know and the unique contributions they bring to our classrooms. Culturally sensitive and responsive programs, such as *On Our Way to English*, are important supports for teachers who want to use the strengths their young language learners bring with them.

2. What Our Students Need

Language development takes time. Researchers estimate the average time that young learners take to acquire native-like academic language as about 5 to 7 years *(Cummins, 1994, Collier, 1995)*. But we can't wait for full acquisition of oral language before we begin literacy instruction as we do with native speakers. In fact, we need to provide instruction in which oral language development, literacy development, and content learning all support one another. As we provide instruction for children's literacy development, we provide many opportunities for oral language development through rich conversations about the materials they read and the content they read about. And we remain conscious of the various aspects of language that learners are acquiring—including words and word meanings, sounds and sound systems, language patterns and grammar, and cultural and social contexts.

Words and meanings

Native speakers generally learn to read words they already use in speech. Learners of English also have to learn what the words mean and how to say them as they learn to read, often using sounds they've never encountered before. While we don't need to delay reading instruction until oral language is well developed, we must be careful to integrate oral language development with literacy instruction. We need to carefully assess our students' oral and reading comprehension and employ direct teaching of vocabulary when needed. We introduce new words in contexts which make them more easily understood, recycling and reusing new words through thematic instruction in order to provide the many encounters students will need to learn these terms thoroughly.

Sound patterns and spelling

As they learn to read and write, native speakers learn to connect sound patterns of words they already know with spelling patterns. Learners of English have to do more. They don't just learn how to make connections between letters or spelling patterns and sounds they already use. Rather, they first have to learn to hear the sounds, then to know what the words mean, and then to read and write those sounds and patterns. Therefore, it is very important to introduce these new sounds in meaningful contexts using words students know. If the words are new to learners, they must be introduced with pictures and other contextual cues that provide support and in the context of meaningful, purposeful language use *(Enright & McCloskey, 1988)*.

Language patterns and grammar

Learners of English don't just connect print to language patterns they recognize but rather must learn new patterns for constructing grammatical language. For these children, it is even more important than for native English speakers to use meaningful print that is both linguistically and culturally accessible. Texts should have characteristics that make it easier to remember and learn: rhyme, rhythm, and repetition. Language patterns should be those frequently encountered in their school and community experiences.

Cultural and social contexts

Native speakers are often familiar with different ways language is used with different conversation partners in different settings. New learners of English who come from other countries and cultures don't just learn to read the words and language forms that are befitting in various sociolinguistic contexts; they must also learn what language is appropriate when and where. They must learn these language and nonverbal behaviors for a very new cultural setting.

By integrating oral language development in the context of thematic instruction, phonological awareness and phonics instruction, and contextualized grammatical instruction with best practices in literacy instruction, we can help children discover the joy and power of reading. *On Our Way to English* provides the tools teachers need to lead English language learners to literacy-learning and language-learning success.

How Do We Teach Writing to English Language Learners?

Lydia Stack

What Are the Similarities in Writing Development for Native Speakers and English Language Learners?

Lydia Stack

In many ways, English writing development is similar for both English language learners and native English speakers *(Peregoy and Boyle, 1997)*. Both use their developing English language knowledge, their background knowledge, and their understanding of the conventions of print to write. Both know how to use the English they have to create texts for different audiences and different purposes *(Edelskey, 1981a, 1981b)*. In the beginning, all students support their writing by drawing pictures *(Hudelson, 1996; Peregoy & Boyle, 1990a)*. It is in the process of writing and talking about their writing that students come to understand and discover what they want to write about. This process expands their thinking and understanding of the world around them.

What Are the Differences Between Writing Development for Native Speakers and English Language Learners?

The difference between native speakers and English language learners is that the development of English writing for the language learner depends upon his or her Stage of Language Acquisition and the ability to read and write in the native language. Even though beginning English learners may have very limited oral skills in English, research has shown that they can benefit from English literacy instruction while they are developing oral English fluency *(Hudelson, 1984, 1986)*. Both oral proficiency and writing skills can develop at the same time. In contrast, native English speakers develop oral skills from birth and formal writing instruction begins at age four or five. A significant support for English language learners can be primary language writing ability since they can usually transfer some of what they know about writing to the task of writing in English *(Cummins, 1981)*.

While all children learn to use the writing process—prewriting, drafting, revising, and publishing—to produce pieces of writing, the initial phase of the writing process, prewriting, takes on additional importance for English language learners. These children need to use graphic organizers, picture drawing, and lists as a way to stimulate vocabulary and concepts before drafting can begin. Since using the English language poses a difficulty for them, they need to concentrate on using tools that help them access their language skills in a productive way and visualize relationships between ideas. *On Our Way to English* offers a step-by-step process for introducing children to using graphic organizers for prewriting by first modeling their use for children, then using them in collaborative groups, and then introducing them for individual use.

What Does a Teacher Need to Know to Teach Writing to English Language Learners?

Although research indicates that it is preferable for young children to develop literacy skills in their first language, this is not always possible. Gibbons (1993) points out a number of important issues that teachers of English language learners need to understand to teach writing to these students.

Orthography and Sound-Symbol Relationships

Many students speak a language with a written script (orthography) that is different than English, such as Chinese, Arabic, Korean, and so on. These students need to be taught the Roman alphabet and English sound-symbol relationships. Others students speak a language that uses the same alphabet but assigns different sounds to different letters. For instance, the letter e in Spanish is pronounced like a long *a* in English. Sometimes children's inability to perceive English sounds correctly creates spelling difficulties in English. Finally an understanding of punctuation is based on the intonation patterns of the spoken language. Students need to control the speech patterns of English before they can punctuate correctly.

Reference Words

When we speak, we use reference words such as *this, that, there, here, it*, and so on. We point to the object or person but do not always name the object or person. In writing, reference words can only be used for something that has already been mentioned in the text. Children learning to write in English need to understand how to use reference words when they write.

Text Types or Forms of Writing

English language learners need to learn that each text type, or form, of writing has its own particular language features.

- the overall structure or organization of the text
- the order of the parts
- the key words that add cohesion to the text
- the specific grammatical features of the text

When evaluating writing, teachers of language learners are often tempted to laboriously correct errors, thereby focusing on the mechanics of writing rather than the child's message. As with oral language instruction, good writing instruction focuses on helping children develop the ability to communicate a message first and then to refine the form of that message. An environment in which English language learners feel safe taking risks is crucial to the development of writing skills. As children use the writing process, they need to be encouraged to get their message across in early drafts and to use the revision process to refine their language use.

What Practices Build Good Writers of English?

Modeled Writing

English learners need high quality models to follow. Teachers should read to students daily, exposing them to a variety of genres and writing styles. Modeling writing is an activity where the teacher acts as a guide in composing and writing a story while modeling good reading and writing strategies. This technique is described in detail on page T54.

Shared and Interactive Writing

Shared and interactive writing are collaborative literacy events in which English language learners and their teacher compose short but accurate texts together. In shared writing, the teacher scribes for the group. The Shared Writing Card in *On Our Way to English* provides a unique vehicle for supporting shared writing. In interactive writing, the teacher hands out colored markers to children and children share in the responsibility for writing. This technique is featured in *On Our Way to English* Phonics. A full description of shared and interactive writing appears on pages T54–T55.

Writer's Workshop

Writer's Workshop is a classroom structure that allows teachers to meet the individual writing needs of English learners. Second language learners are given class time to write. Teachers present mini-lessons on the writing process, different genres of writing, and mechanics. They hold writing and editing conferences as they guide children. The mini-lessons in the *On Our Way to English* Writing Resource Guide support teachers in providing effective writing guidance.

Good writing instruction for English language learners mirrors good instruction for all learners. However, knowledge of the specific needs of language learners leads us to emphasize some techniques and modify others in a way that most benefits these children. *On Our Way to English* offers a variety of tools that support teachers in providing good writing instruction which is specifically tailored to the needs of English language learners.

How Do We Teach the Content Area Subjects to English Language Learners?

David and Yvonne Freeman

David and Yvonne Freeman

English language learners face a number of challenges in school. They are expected to learn English, and they are expected to keep up with native English-speaking classmates in the different content areas including language arts, social studies, science, and math. They vary considerably in their ability to speak English and in their knowledge of content area subject matter. As a result, teachers also face a challenge as they work with the English language learners in their classes.

Teaching English Through Content

In some schools, English language learners are placed in bilingual classes. In these classes, students can study academic subjects in their native language while they are learning English. However, most second language students are placed directly in mainstream or English as a Second Language classes, and their teachers must teach them both English and academic content. The best way to do this is to teach English *through* the different content areas. There are three reasons to take this approach:

1. Students get both language and content.

Research in second language acquisition shows that students develop proficiency in a second language when they receive comprehensible input—messages they understand. If the input is a science or a social studies lesson, then the students get both English and the academic concept at the same time.

2. Language is kept in its natural context.

Traditional approaches to teaching English focused on vocabulary and grammar presented in lists or short exercises. These lessons provided little context for the English language. In contrast, when language is taught through content, the language is kept in its natural context. For example, students learn science terms in English as they study lessons about weather patterns and temperatures. Some English language learners can understand the teacher and carry on conversations with their classmates. They have what Cummins (1996) calls conversational proficiency. What they lack is the academic language of books. One benefit of teaching language through content is that the language students develop is the academic language they need for school success. Conversational language develops naturally in an English-speaking environment as students interact with their friends in and out of school. Academic language develops only as students read, talk, and write about the different content areas.

3. Students have reasons to use language for real purposes.

Many traditional approaches to teaching English give students words and phrases, but the students have no immediate need to use this language. However, when teachers teach language through content, students use the new English words and structures as they write, read, and talk with classmates in the course of investigating interesting content area topics.

Using Themes to Organize Instruction

Many teachers who teach language through content organize their curriculum around meaningful themes. Similarly, *On Our Way to English* has been organized around themes. Organizing curriculum around meaningful themes *(Freeman and Freeman 1998)* provides several benefits for English language learners:

1. Students see the big picture so they can make sense of English language instruction.

Themes provide a unifying framework for different activities. When teachers organize around themes, they make it easier for English language learners to follow the lessons. The students know the general topic, so they can better connect the particular activities to the main idea. For example, if the theme is "How can we conserve water?" an English language learner can make more sense of a science lesson based on the water cycle.

Knowing the theme makes it easier for students to understand the details of each lesson.

2. Content areas (math, science, social studies, literature) are interrelated.

Thematic organization helps teachers connect the different content areas during the day. The math lesson, for example, can reinforce and expand the concepts and language introduced in the science lesson, and the story a teacher reads during language arts time can further unify and develop the academic content and vocabulary.

3. Vocabulary is repeated naturally as it appears in different content area studies.

Students acquire English as the result of hearing and seeing the same words in different contexts. They need multiple exposures to academic vocabulary, and this is what they get when teachers organize around themes. The same terms come up in the discussion of a story, in a social studies lesson, and in a science chapter when the entire curriculum is based on a theme.

4. Through themes based on big questions, teachers can connect curriculum to students' lives. This makes curriculum more interesting.

Many school materials are based on the experiences of mainstream Americans. English language learners bring different experiences to the classroom. They may not see themselves in the stories or content area texts they read. However, themes based on big questions are universal. Teachers can draw on the life experiences of all their students as they discuss topics such as natural disasters. In fact, English language learners with their varied cultural backgrounds serve as a rich resource for the class. When curriculum touches students' lives, they become more involved, and they learn more.

5. Because the curriculum makes sense, English language learners are more fully engaged and experience more success.

Even students with little English-speaking ability can make sense of a curriculum organized around meaningful themes. Because the instruction makes sense, students invest more energy in trying to follow the lessons. As they more fully engage with lessons, they acquire more English and develop higher levels of content area knowledge and skills.

6. Since themes deal with universal human topics, all students can be involved, and lessons and activities can be adjusted to different Stages of English Language Acquisition.

In most classes, some English language learners are beginners, others are intermediates, and a few may be advanced. Keeping all these students involved is often difficult. By teaching language through content organized around themes, teachers can involve students at different Stages of Language Acquisition, adapting the instruction to their needs. The beginners may listen to a taped story while the teacher carries out a math activity with the intermediates. Beginners may respond by labeling pictures while the more advanced students may write a paragraph or short essay about the topic being studied. All the students are studying the same theme, but the kinds of activities they do and their responses differ depending on their Stage of Language Acquisition.

English language learners face a difficult challenge. They need to develop English, literacy, and academic subject content. Teachers can help their students meet this challenge by organizing their curriculum around meaningful themes and helping students develop the academic language and concepts they need as they teach language through content. *On Our Way to English* provides the tools teachers need to implement thematic instruction effectively in their classrooms.

How Do We Teach English Language Learners at Various Language Proficiencies?

Cecilia Silva

Cecilia Silva

One of the most significant changes in ESL practices has been the shift from program models that focus solely on language development to those in which students are expected to acquire English as well as develop academic content. This shift, in turn, has created new challenges for second language teachers. Often we struggle with the question of how to provide curriculum access to English language learners who differ in language and in literacy proficiencies. When considering this question, we need to examine how teachers differentiate instruction in order to make content language comprehensible for English language learners at various levels of proficiency.

Teaching Beginning Language Learners

In the beginning Stages of Language Acquisition (Preproduction and Early Production), teachers make language comprehensible by modifying their speech and making use of extralinguistic cues to convey meaning. Engaged in what is generally described as foreigner talk or caregiver speech, teachers consciously modify their input by slowing down their speech rate, simplifying grammatical structures, and restricting the length of their communication. Another way language is made more comprehensible is by the use of repetition. Key words or phrases are also emphasized through variation in intonation. Teachers take most of the responsibility for beginning conversational topics and topics are grounded in the here and now. At these Stages of Language Acquisition, teachers rely on extralinguistic cues—gestures, actions, pictures—to clarify meanings that otherwise might not be apparent to their students. The Comprehensible Input charts found in the *On Our Way to English* Teacher's Guide lessons support teachers in making academic content accessible to all learners. Extralinguistic cues can also be made available through the utilization of technology such as computer software, videos, CD-ROMs, or laser-disks.

Another way of differentiating instruction while maximizing extralinguistic cues is by integrating the use of various communication systems in the classroom. Often schools rely on language as the only communication system to access the curriculum. For English language learners, alternate forms of communication provide alternate ways of accessing the curriculum. In addition to the use of language, English language learners can make use of art, music, movement, and mathematics for amplifying, exploring, and expressing meaning. As students read and discuss a story, for example, they may be asked to explore the feelings of the main character through art or music. Similarly, English language learners can use movement to demonstrate their understanding of abstract science or social studies concepts, such as evaporation or immigration.

For students in the beginning Stages of Language Acquisition, reading activities provide opportunities for further language input. Predictable books are particularly useful because of their highly repetitive language and simplified text. Chants and songs also offer students the opportunity to gain familiarity with content vocabulary and language patterns. Teachers can scaffold the language of the text through engagements such as read-alouds and shared reading. The Concept Posters, Chant Posters, Newcomer Books, and the books in Enhanced Reading Levels A–C available in *On Our Way to English* are examples of the type of materials that provide students in the beginning Stages of Language Acquisition with comprehensible input while encountering key academic concepts.

Teaching Intermediate and Advanced Language Learners

As students become more proficient in English, teachers continue to scaffold language use and to use extralinguistic cues to support language. With students at the Intermediate levels of proficiency (Speech Emergence and Intermediate Fluency), teachers increase language speed and complexity. At this point, however, one of the ways teachers scaffold language use is by consciously reducing their own input and offering students the opportunity to take responsibility for more of the language input. Providing opportunities for language learners to use their developing language skills is even more important for Advanced language learners (Advanced Fluency).

As oral language and literacy develop, so do the reading and writing demands of the academic curriculum. One of the ways teachers differentiate instruction is through lessons that scaffold academic language. Strategy lessons to make English language learners aware of text structure and text organization are important in making content language comprehensible. Teachers continue to rely on extralinguistic cues to embed language in meaningful contexts. Graphic organizers, in particular, support second language readers and writers by visually highlighting aspects of text.

For these students, the visual structure of graphic organizers limits the linguistic demands of the text while highlighting important information or relationships. The Big Book and Class Collections backflaps and the Shared Writing Cards are useful when scaffolding common text structures and organization within various content areas. In addition, these materials also present a number of helpful graphic organizers to support English language learners in coping with the linguistic demands of more challenging texts.

By providing language learners multiple points of entry into the curriculum, *On Our Way to English* supports teachers in providing a full range of English language learners access to the core curriculum that all students need to succeed. While not all students will achieve the same level of language, literacy, and content area development, all will be simultaneously moving toward the same goal along different paths. As teachers use the differentiated instruction built into the Teacher's Guide lessons, they provide opportunities for all language learners to succeed.

Teacher Notes

Rigby

On Our Way to English

Thematic Units

Thematic Units

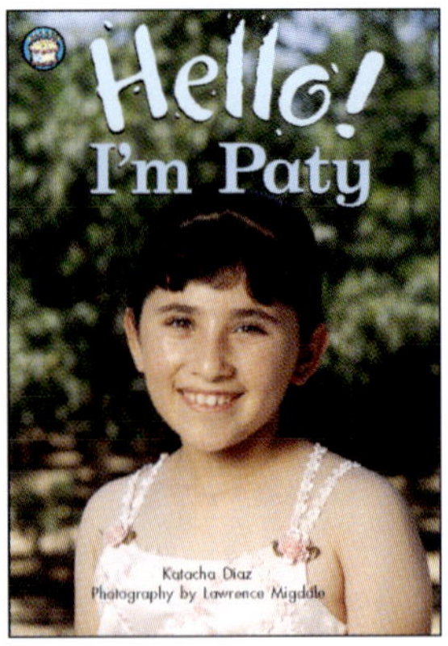

Unit 1 Proud to Be Me U4
Big Book: *Hello, I'm Paty*
by Katacha Díaz

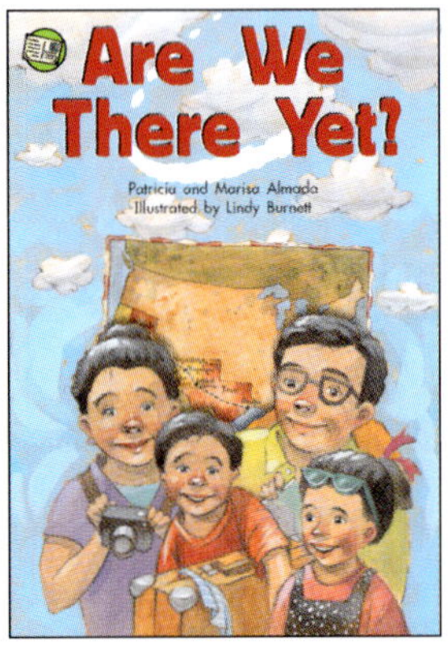

Unit 2 Living in America U28
Big Book: *Are We There Yet?*
by Patricia and Marisa Almada

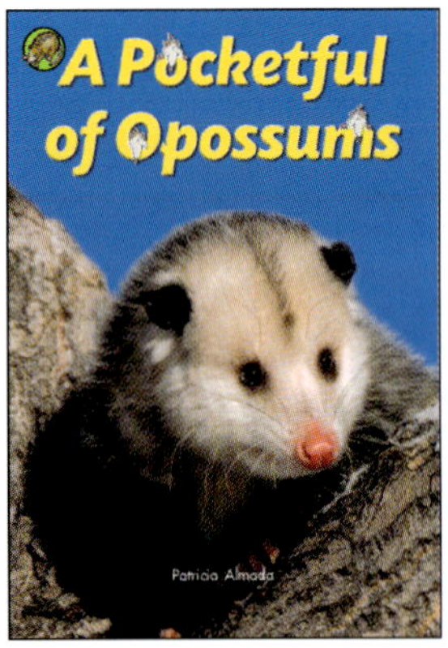

Unit 3 Circle of Life U52
Big Book: *A Pocketful of Opossums*
by Patricia Almada

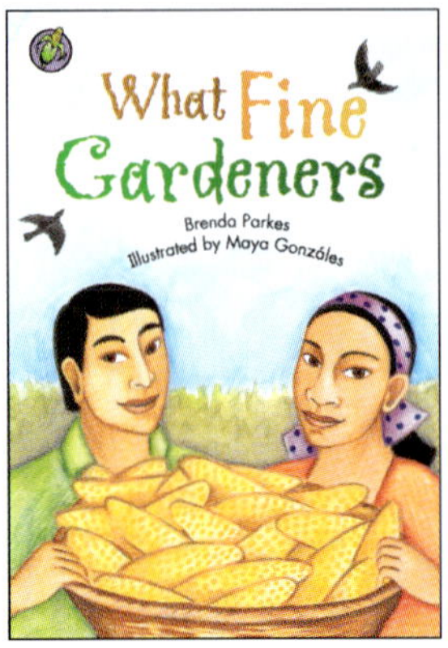

Unit 4 From Farm to You U76
Big Book: *What Fine Gardeners*
by Brenda Parkes

Unit 5 Water Works U100
Big Book: *Water Detective*
by Carol Alexander

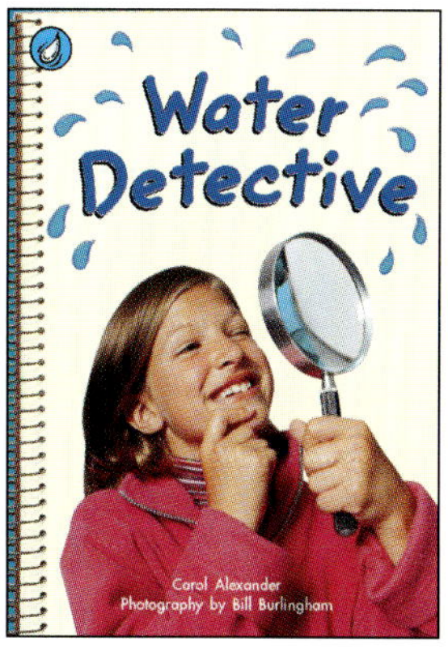

Unit 6 Disaster Alert U124
Big Book: *Barge Cat*
by Martin Waddell

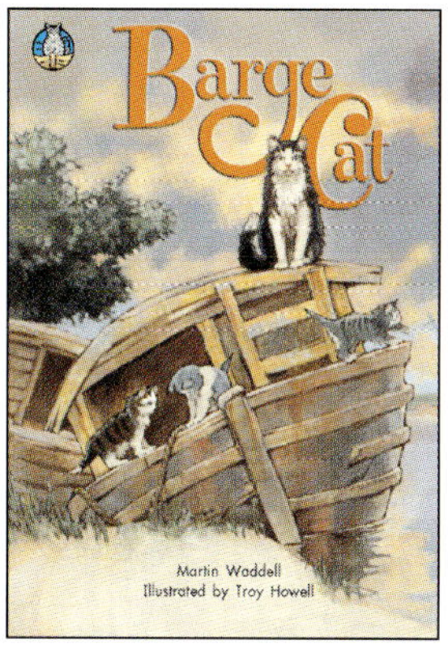

Unit 7 How Things Work U148
Big Book: *How Bicycles Work*
by Lloyd Kajikawa

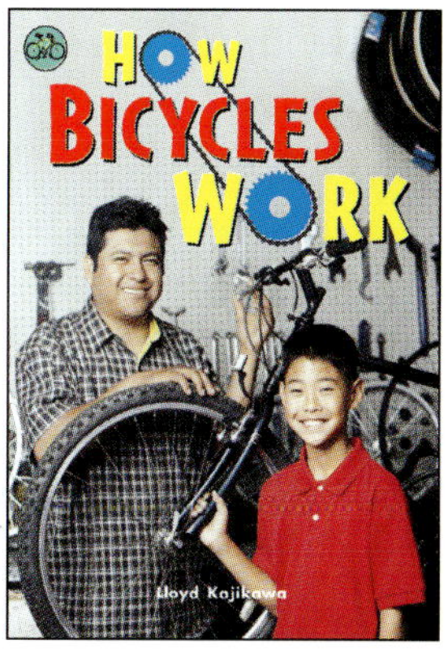

Unit 8 Choices We Make U172
Big Book: *Ibis and Jaguar's Dinner*
by Isabel Campoy

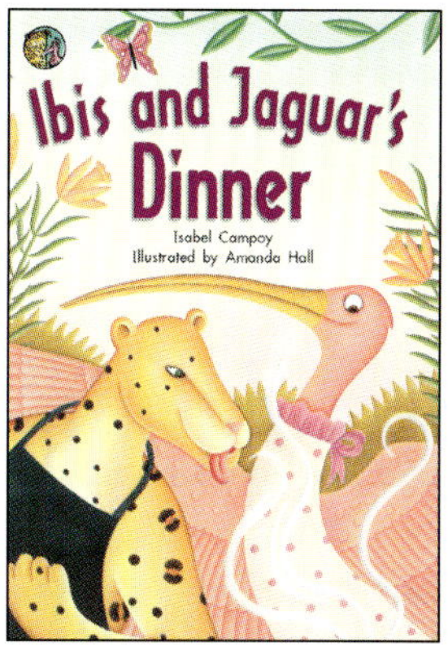

UNIT 1

Proud to Be Me

OVERVIEW *This theme introduces children to family roles and relationships. The unit begins with members of the immediate family and expands to include the extended family. Children will also learn vocabulary for describing their likes and dislikes, cultural background, and pastimes.*

Unit Components

Manipulative Chart

Chant Poster

Concept Poster

Newcomer Book

Determining the Purpose

Oral Language Development

Focus on Functions

Social Context:
Greet 1 2 3 4 5
Academic Context:
Inquire 1 2 3 4 5

Focus on Grammar

- Questions with *who, what, where*
- Present tense
- Preposition *from*
- Subject pronouns *I, we, you*

Comprehension Strategy

- Activates existing background knowledge

Literacy Skills

- **Word Level:** Phonics in context short *a*, short *o*
- **Sentence Level:** Lists and bullet points
- **Text Level:** Index

Content Area Objectives

- Identifies family organization
- Connects with cultural heritage, customs, and traditions
- Identifies physical traits
- Creates and uses a graph for comparisons

Language Learning Strategy

- Ask for clarification.

Writing Skill

- Uses a graphic organizer to support an idea

Unit at a Glance

	DURING THE WEEK	DAY 1
Week 1	**Small-Group Instruction:** • Guided Reading • Shared-to-Guided Reading **Phonics Focus:** short *a* Phonics Song Chart 1, pp. P6–P7	**Manipulative Chart:** Introduction with Audio CD p. U7
Week 2	**Small-Group Instruction:** • Guided Reading • Shared-to-Guided Reading • Newcomer Book **Phonics Focus:** *at, an, ag,* and *ap* word families Phonics Song Charts 2–3, pp. P8–P11	**Concept Poster:** Introduction p. U12 **Language Practice Game:** Version 1 p. U13
Week 3	**Small-Group Instruction:** • Guided Reading • Shared-to-Guided Reading • Newcomer Book **Phonics Focus:** short *o* Phonics Song Chart 4, pp. P12–P13	**Big Book:** Oral Language Development p. U19
Week 4	**Small-Group Instruction:** • Guided Reading • Shared-to-Guided Reading • Newcomer Book **Phonics Focus:** *op* and *ot* word families Phonics Song Chart 5, pp. P14–P15	**Big Book:** Literacy Skills p. U23 **Language Practice Game:** Version 2 p. U24

STAGES 1 Preproduction 2 Early Production 3 Speech Emergence 4 Intermediate Fluency 5 Advanced Fluency

Oral Language Audio CD

Big Book with Audio CD and Small Book

Home-School Connection Masters

Picture Cards

Shared Writing Card

Writing Resource Guide

Language Learning Masters

DAY 2	DAY 3	DAY 4	DAY 5
Manipulative Chart: Gestures and Manipulative Fun p. U8	**Chant Poster:** Introduction p. U9	**TPR Cards:** Introduction p. U10	**Manipulative Chart:** Oral Language Development Student Version p. U11
Big Book: Introduction p. U15	**Theme Project:** Class Directory p. U16 **Big Book:** Revisiting p. U16	**Big Book:** Comprehension Strategy p. U17 **Chant Poster:** Oral Language Development p. U17	**Shared Writing Card:** Introduction of Side A p. U18 **Concept Poster:** Revisiting p. U18
Shared Writing Card: Brainstorming Side B p. U20 **Active Social Studies:** Family Trees, p. U21	**Shared Writing Card:** Writing Together with Side B p. U21 **Manipulative Chart:** Oral Language Development p. U21	**Active Science:** Physical Characteristics p. U22	**Writing Resource Guide:** A Simplified Graphic Organizer Cooperative-Group Writing p. U22
Active Math: Age Graph p. U24 **Assessment** p. U24	**Writing Resource Guide:** Individual Writing p. U25 **Assessment** p. U24	**Writing Resource Guide:** Individual Writing p. U25 **Assessment** p. U24	**Theme Project:** Sharing p. U25

Center Activities

You will need

- Construction paper
- Paper plates
- Yarn in a variety of hair colors
- Glue
- Markers
- Briefcase, purse, car keys, baby bottles, hard hat, lunch box and other items associated with various family members

CENTERS

Number Nook

Provide an array of construction paper shapes, such as triangles, squares, rectangles, and circles. Invite children to use these shapes to create families. Encourage children to share how they decided on these families.

Artist's Studio

Provide children with paper plates, markers, glue, and yarn. Invite children to draw features on the circles to represent their family members. Then have them glue on yarn "hair." Invite children to talk about the "family portraits."

Content Corner

Bring in clothing and other items used by various family members such as a purse or briefcase, car keys, baby bottles, hard hat, lunch box, and so on. Invite children to use these props to role-play different family members.

Listening Post

After introducing each element in class, children may revisit the Manipulative Chart and Chant Poster on the Oral Language Audio CD. If you include a laminated copy of the Manipulative Chart Student Version, children can manipulate it as they sing to Part 4 of the CD (with blanks). Children may also listen to *Hello! I'm Paty* on the Big Book Audio CD while following along in the small copy.

Language Workshop

Any time they are not in use during the unit, place the Picture Cards and TPR Cards for the unit in this center. Encourage children to review the names of the different people and activities with each other for additional practice. After introducing the Language Practice Game in class, add the game board, spinners, and game markers to the center for independent or group play.

Writer's Den

Establish a journal writing center with prompts to spark children's writing. Change the prompt every two weeks:

- Describe a family member.
- What does your family like to do?

Children should be encouraged to draw pictures to support their writing. Provide blank Writing Planners in center materials for prewriting.

More Books

- *Families* by Ann Morris (Morrow, 2000)
- *Love You Forever* by Robert N. Munsch (Firefly Books Ltd, 1988)
- *I'm a Big Brother* by Joanna Cole (Morrow, 1997)
- *A Chair for My Mother* by Vera B. Williams (Morrow, 1984)
- *Are You My Mother?* by Philip D. Eastman (Random House Books for Young Readers, 1998)

WEEK 1 DAY 1

Manipulative Chart: Introduction with Audio CD

Sung to the tune of "I've Been Working on the Railroad"

Setting the Scene

- Show Picture Card 1: family. Introduce the brother and sister by pointing back and forth saying *brother* and *sister.*
- Continue in the same manner, introducing mother and father, aunt and uncle, grandparents, and cousin.
- Use gestures and simple language to talk about children's families. For example, have children share the number of brothers, sisters, aunts, uncles, and cousins they have and their names and ages as they are able. ◎

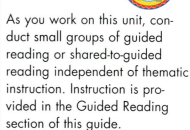

Options for STAGES

❶❷ Ask children at these stages either/or questions, such as *Is this the brother or sister?*

❸ Point to different family members and ask *Who is this?*

❹❺ Ask open-ended questions, such as *Tell me about the family.* Children should respond in complete sentences.

Creating Comprehensible Input

- Assemble the chart by threading both slides through the chart from the back. Make sure the top slide is positioned so that the sister is showing and the bottom slide shows the background picture.
- Point out the house and the rooms shown on both slides, explaining that there is a family in the house doing different activities.
- Gesture and act out the actions portrayed on both slides.
- Read the text, pausing often, as you use gestures, pointing, and other techniques to make the song comprehensible.

I am playing with my sister.	point to boy, game, then sister
We are family.	hold up family Picture Card
I am playing with my sister.	point to boy, game, then sister
Look. What do you see?	point to eyes and shrug shoulders
We are playing here together, playing happily.	point to boy, sister, game, and then smile
I am playing with my sister.	point to boy, game, then sister
We are family.	hold up family Picture Card

Guided Reading

As you work on this unit, conduct small groups of guided reading or shared-to-guided reading independent of thematic instruction. Instruction is provided in the Guided Reading section of this guide.

Component Organizer

Other Manipulative Chart lessons in this unit:

- Gestures and Manipulative Fun, p. U8
- Oral Language Development and Student Version, pp. U11–U12
- Oral Language Development, p. U21

Real-World Touch

Bring in family photos of your own. Introduce family members and reinforce vocabulary by telling their relation to you. Invite children to bring in photos of their own families if possible.

Home-School Connection

Choose one of the versions of the parent letter to send home with each child, according to the child's home language (pages 8–15 in the Home-School Connection Masters). Also send home the activity on page 16.

Manipulative Chart

Journal Writing Reminder

Children should be writing in their journals during the course of the unit. Journal writing provides an opportunity for personal writing, an important aspect of children's early writing. See Writer's Den for suggested journal prompts.

Introducing the Audio CD

- Play Part 1 of the Oral Language Audio CD, the spoken song, as you say the song and track the print on the Manipulative Chart with your finger or a pointer. Replay Part 1 several times, encouraging children to chime in whenever they can.
- Introduce the song by playing the song at natural speed, Part 2 of the Audio CD, to help children get a feel for the song. Allow the Audio CD to continue playing through Part 3, the song at instructional pace. Track the print as the Audio CD plays. Repeat Part 3 again, this time singing along, making clear lip movements without exaggerating. Revisit Part 3 several times to help children learn the song.

WEEK 1 DAY 2

Manipulative Chart: Gestures and Manipulative Fun

Gesturing the Song

Introduce these simple gestures to accompany the song:

I am playing with my sister.	point to self, then sister and skip
We are family.	hold arms in front of you in a circle
I am playing with my sister.	point to self, then sister and skip
Look. What do you see?	point to eyes and hold up arms to indicate a question
We are playing here together, playing happily.	interlace fingers of both hands to indicate "together" and smile
I am playing with my sister.	point to self, then sister and skip
We are family.	hold arms in front of you in a circle

Manipulating the Chart

- Show children how to move the slide in the Manipulative Chart so that different pictures show in the openings. Have them return the top slide to the background before manipulating the bottom slide and vice versa. The items on the slide can be substituted for the words in red. Turn to *singing/brother,* sing the verse, and emphasize using *singing* and *brother* instead of *playing* and *sister* each time they appear in the song.
- Play Part 4 of the Oral Language Audio CD while you say *brother* in the blank space.
- Continue introducing and naming the family members and activities on each slide in this manner.
- Invite volunteers to manipulate the Manipulative Chart for the class as you sing the verse together or give Total Physical Response commands, such as *Show me the grandpa talking.*
- Invite children to help you create new gestures for the activities shown on the slides.
- You can revisit this activity many times during the unit.

WEEK 1 DAY 3

Chant Poster: Introduction

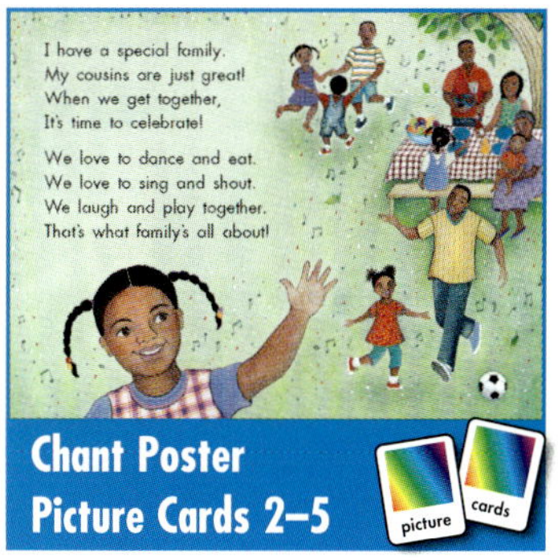

Setting the Scene

- Use Picture Cards 2–4: play, sing, eat, to review these verbs.
- Show Picture Card 5: dance. Introduce the card by saying *The girl loves to dance.*
- Introduce the verbs *shout* and *laugh* by acting out each one. To teach *shout*, cup your hands around your mouth while saying in a raised voice *I am shouting.* Then act out laughing heartily saying *I am laughing.*
- Give Total Physical Response commands, such as *laugh and eat.* Ask children what they are doing.

Options for STAGES

❶❷ These children may respond to the Total Physical Response command or say one-word responses, such as *laugh* or *eat.*	❸❹❺ Encourage these children to approximate a sentence, such as *I am laughing.*

Creating Comprehensible Input

- Displaying the Chant Poster, tell children that it shows a family at a picnic.
- Read the text with frequent pauses as you use gestures, pointing, and other techniques to make the chant comprehensible.

I have a special family.	point to self, then hold arms up and out
My cousins are just great!	point to children on poster, then smile
When we get together,	bring hands together in encompassing gesture
It's time to celebrate!	smile, clap hands, and tap feet
We love to dance and eat.	act out dancing and eating
We love to sing and shout.	sing this line, raising voice on shout
We laugh and play together.	act out laughing and playing
That's what family's all about!	nod head emphatically

Chanting the Poster

- Say *A chant is a kind of poem. Some poems have rhymes. Rhyming words are words that have the same ending sounds. For example, these words rhyme:* great *and* celebrate. *As we are chanting the poem, raise your hand when you hear a word that thymes with* shout.
- Encourage children to chime in as you chant the rhyme several times. You can chant the first stanza as a class, and then have two groups alternate lines in the second verse.
- Introduce the chant on Oral Language Audio CD as you and the children move to the rhythm of the chant. Tell them they can listen on their own later at the Listening Post.
- Practice saying the chant in different ways, such as while clapping and stomping to help create a sense of rhythm and celebration.
- Revisit the chant often with children. Invite them to perform the various actions.

Component Organizer

Other Chant Poster lessons in this unit:

- Oral Language Development, pp. U17–U18

WEEK 1 DAY 4

You will need

- **Language Learning Master** p. 7
- Scissors
- Crayons

TPR Cards: Introduction

Introducing the Cards with Total Physical Response

- Provide one copy of page 7 of the Language Learning Masters to each child. Have children color and cut out the cards.
- Introduce a few cards at a time by holding them up one by one and saying the words clearly. Select first the words which have already been introduced in previous activities.
- Ask children to pick up the correct cards as you call out a word. Model the desired outcome. Add one new card at a time and keep reviewing in a game-like atmosphere. Children may want to say the word as they pick up the card.
- Now invite children to respond to your full-sentence commands, such as *Show me the grandmother. Hold up the brother.*
- Assign partners so you can add commands like *Give the sister to Mai.*
- As children increase their familiarity with the TPR Cards and the game, add funny commands, such as *Put the brother on your nose.*
- Invite volunteers in Stages 3, 4, or 5 to give commands to their classmates.
- Extend language to discuss the gender of the family members. ◎

Options for STAGES

❶❷ Have these children group family members by gender. Encourage them to say *male* or *female*.

❸❹❺ Children in these stages should state the gender of family members with phrases or complete sentences.

- Repeat this activity several times throughout the unit.

Language Learning Master p. 10 ❶❷❸❹❺

Grammar in Context: Questions ❶❷❸❹❺

1. You will be introducing questions with *who* and *where* to the children.
2. Model questions and answers by holding up the grandmother TPR Card and saying *Who is this? This is the grandmother.* Repeat with several other family cards. Invite children to repeat the question and answer for each of the cards.
3. Invite volunteers in Stages 4 or 5 to pose *who* questions to the class about the TPR Cards.
4. Place the cards in various locations to create a context for forming *where* questions. Say *Where is the brother? The brother is on the desk.* Continue with other cards and invite volunteers in Stages 4 or 5 to then pose their own *where* questions. ◎

Options for STAGES

❶❷ These children can respond in one word answers, such as *grandma*, as they are able.

❸ These children can answer with short phrases, such as *She is sister.*

❹❺ These children can ask *who* and *where* questions.

WEEK 1 DAY 5

Manipulative Chart: Focus on Oral Language Development

FUNCTION MINI-LESSON

Greet

1. Use Picture Cards 6–14: brother, sister, father, mother, aunt, uncle, grandma, grandpa, cousin as puppets to dramatize simple greetings in different situations. Start with any two cards. Hold the cards up facing each other and use different voices for each "puppet." Model such greetings as *Hello* or *Hi* and *How are you?* Model appropriate responses with the other puppet such as *I'm fine, How are you?*
2. Have children join in as you perform other mini-dialogs with the Picture Cards.
3. Invite volunteers in Stages 4 or 5 to use the puppets and perform their own greeting exchanges for the class.
4. Refer to the Manipulative Chart. Act out greetings between family members in the pictures. Invite volunteers with greater language ability to take turns pretending they are the sister, brother, and other family members greeting each other.

FUNCTION MINI-LESSON

Inquire

1. Invite children in Stages 3, 4, or 5 to join you while others play games with the TPR Cards.
2. Point to the picture of the sister playing on the first slide. Ask children *Who is this?* Do this for the next two pictures on the slide, modeling the questions. Invite volunteers to continue moving the slides, asking the same question *Who is this?* Have children provide the appropriate answers, but focus on the formation of questions.
3. Introduce the names of the rooms and continue in the same manner for *where*, practicing the question *Where is the sister?*

Grammar in Context: Questions

1. Model questions and answers with *what* by asking about different activities in the Manipulative Chart. You can point to the boy and his sister, for example, and ask *What are they doing? They are playing.*
2. Invite volunteers to ask *What are they doing?* for other activities shown on the chart. Other volunteers can answer.

Options for STAGES

1 2 These children can respond to the questions with one-word answers, such as *playing.*

3 4 5 These children can ask questions, such as *What is he doing?*

Manipulative Chart
Picture Cards 6–14

Language Learning Strategy

Ask "What do you mean?" when you don't understand.

- Tell children that when they don't understand something, they can ask "What do you mean?" and someone will explain. Have them practice saying this phrase with you. Form "talking puppets" with your hands and model a short conversation in which this phrase is used.
  Model One puppet says *I have a sister. We play games.* The other puppet asks *We? What do you mean?* The first puppet replies *We means "my sister and I."*
- Throughout the unit, encourage children to seek clarification by asking "What do you mean?"

Home-School Connection

When children have practiced manipulating the Manipulative Chart Student Version, send it home for them to practice with their family members.

You will need

- **Language Learning Master** pp. 5–6
- Scissors

Assessment

Record your observations of children on their individual assessment checklists for this unit. See page U27.

Manipulative Chart: Student Version

- Model assembling the pages according to the directions.
- Circulate to provide assistance as children assemble their pull-through charts.
- Encourage children to color and decorate their charts.
- Invite children to carefully pull through the slides on their charts as you manipulate the pull-through slide on the Manipulative Chart. Then encourage them to match the picture to what you do as you say different words in the song.
- Have children respond to your Total Physical Response commands: *Show me the boy and the grandma reading.*
- Play Part 4 of the Oral Language Audio CD and model how children can manipulate their Student Versions as they sing along. Tell children that they will later be able to listen to the Audio CD and manipulate this mini-chart in the Listening Post.

WEEK 2 DAY 1

Concept Poster
Picture Cards 1, 10–14

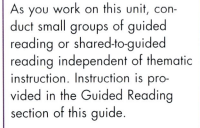

Concept Poster: Introduction

Setting the Scene

- Show children Picture Card 1: family and review the names of the different family members. Children may chime in naturally.
- Share information about your own family, saying, for example *I have two sisters. One sister's name is Chantal. The other sister's name is Gabrielle.*
- Invite volunteers to share information about their own families. Be aware of different family situations, and do not presume that all children have both parents at home. Ask *Who lives in your house?*

Creating Comprehensible Input

- Display Picture Card 1: family. Reinforce that these are all people in a family. Then show the Concept Poster and read the title "Who Is My Family?" Introduce the child (Gloria) shown at the bottom. Explain that the poster shows other members of her family. Talk through these relationships with a think-aloud, tracing the lines to show how each person is related to Gloria.
  Model *This is Gloria. This is her family. This line shows the relationships. This is Dolores, Gloria's sister. This is Pancho, Gloria's brother. Mom and Dad are her parents.*
- Recap this in simple language as you point to the pictures and connecting lines: *Gloria; Gloria's brother and sister; Gloria's mom and dad. They are a family.*
- Display Picture Card 10, 11, 14: aunt, uncle, cousin. Remind children what each family member is called.
- Talk through the relationships between Gloria and her aunt, uncles, and cousins as you did for Gloria's immediate family, recapping the relationships in simple language.
- Display Picture Card 12: grandma and Picture Card 13: grandpa. Talk through their relationships to Gloria in a similar manner as above.
- Summarize the chart by saying *This poster shows Gloria's family. It is a family tree. It shows all of Gloria's relatives and it gives their names. The people at the top are Gloria's grandparents. The people in the second row are her parents, uncles, and aunt. At the bottom are Gloria, her brother and sister, and her cousins.*

Guided Reading

As you work on this unit, conduct small groups of guided reading or shared-to-guided reading independent of thematic instruction. Instruction is provided in the Guided Reading section of this guide.

- Invite a child in Stage 3, 4, or 5 to lead the class in talking through some of the relationships. As necessary, review the relationships. Support with appropriate academic language.
- After the child has finished, recap as you point to pictures and connecting lines.

Extending Oral Language

- Engage children in reviewing these concepts by asking questions. ◎

Options for STAGES

❶❷❸ Ask these children specific questions which require only *yes/no* answers or pointing, such as *Where is Gloria's sister? Does Gloria have a brother?*	❹❺ Ask these children open-ended questions that require substantive answers, such as *Tell me about Gloria's family.*

- Use Total Physical Response commands to build familiarity with the concepts. For instance, *Point to Grandma Lola. Show me Aunt Rita.*

Component Organizer

Other Concept Poster lessons in this unit:

- Revisiting, p. U18

Language Practice Game: Version 1 ❶❷❸❹❺

Preparing the Game

Tape copies of the spinners and pyramid, on a file folder. Provide two pencils and two paper clips to spin. Prepare one pyramid board for each child, and one set of spinners for each pair.

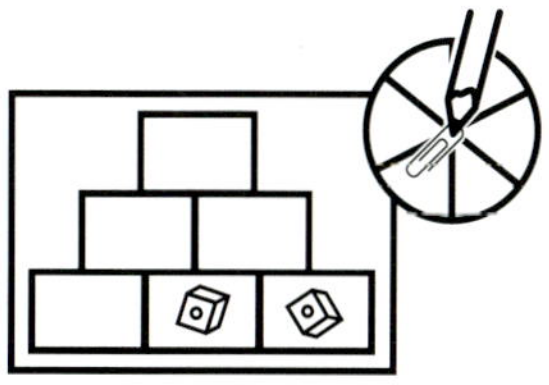

Playing Version 1

Divide the class into heterogeneous pairs of mixed language ability. Distribute two pyramids, twelve game markers and one set of spinners to each pair. Model the following directions.

1. Children take turns spinning and placing game markers on their pyramids. Player 1 first spins the spinner with the family members, then spins the actions spinner.
2. Player 2, if able, asks *What are you doing?* This provides practice with the language function Inquire. Player 1 then responds *I am eating with my father.* Then Player 1 places a game marker on the family member's picture on the pyramid. ◎

Options for STAGES

❶ These children can place their game marker saying the family member as they are able.	❷❸ These children should be encouraged to say a few words, such as *brother, eating,* or *brother eating.*	❹❺ Encourage these children to form complete sentences, such as *I am eating with my mother.*

3. Player 2 confirms that the family member and action stated, as well as the placement of marker, are correct.
4. If a player spins and gets a family member that he or she has already covered, the player loses that turn.
5. Play continues until one of the players fills all the spaces on the pyramid.

You will need

- **Language Learning Master** pp. 8–9
- File folders
- Tape
- Paper clips
- Pencils
- Game markers

Component Organizer

Other Language Practice Game lessons in this unit:

- Version 2, p. U24

Assessment

Record your observations of children during the Language Practice Game on their individual assessment checklists for this unit. See page U27.

Newcomer Book: Small-Group Instruction

Playing with My Family

Written by Karen Clevidence

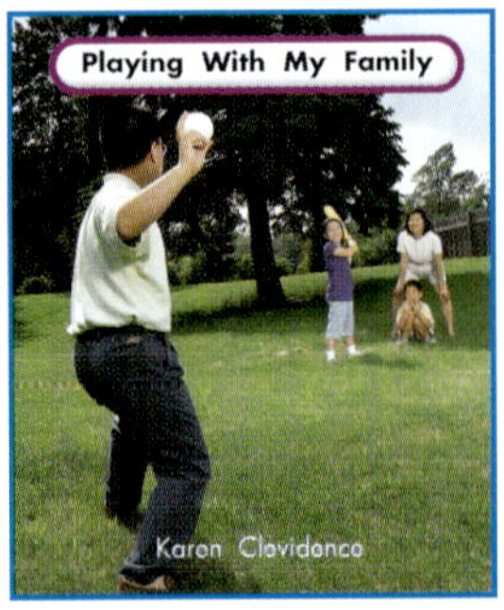

OVERVIEW *Family members like to have fun together.*

The Newcomer Book is supported by the language of the Manipulative Chart and should be integrated into small-group instruction this week when children have had enough practice with vocabulary and concepts in this unit.

Language Pattern

I am playing with my ___________.

Text Vocabulary

family members

Vocabulary Extenders

colors

Reading the Text

Book Talk

- Work with a small group of four children at one time who exhibit similar literacy-learning behaviors.
- Engage children in a book talk as you flip through the pages of your copy of the book. ◎

Options for STAGES

❶❷ Encourage these children to name family members, as they are able.	❸❹❺ Ask children to identify each family member with sentences such as *That's the brother,* as you encounter them.

INSTRUCTIONAL PATHS

❶❷❸❹❺ **All Readers:** Shared-to-Guided Reading	❶❷❸❹❺ **Emergent Readers:** Guided Reading	❶❷❸❹❺ **Early Readers:** Independent Reading no lesson provided

INDIVIDUAL READING

Shared-to-Guided Reading — **3–4 sessions**
❶❷❸❹❺ **All Readers**

1. Read the book to children.
   - Invite children to sit near you as you read a copy of the book. Begin with the cover and title page.
   - Turn to page 2 and begin reading the words as you point to them. Draw children's attention to the pictures.
2. Read the book with children.
   - Encourage children to follow along in their own copies of the book, turning the pages as you read together and using their own fingers to point to the words from left to right.
   - Invite children to chime in when they are comfortable.
   - Reread the book in this manner over several sessions.
3. Have children buddy read the book.
4. Invite children to read the book independently.

Assess

- Did children hold the book appropriately?
- Did children look from left to right as you read together?

Guided Reading — **2 sessions**
❶❷❸❹❺ **Emergent Readers**

1. Provide copies of the book to children. Use one child's book and turn to page 2. Introduce the book's pattern to children by reading the sentence and pointing to each word as you read *I am playing with my uncle.*
2. Have each child read at his or her own pace while remaining in the group. Discourage choral reading. Observe as they read.

Assess

- Did children use the pictures to help them read the words?
- Did children use the first letter of words to figure them out?

REVISITING THE NEWCOMER BOOK

If children seem ready, you may also use the book to extend their knowledge of colors by naming the color of the girl's shirt on each page.

WEEK 2 DAY 2

Big Book: Introduction

Hello! I'm Paty

Written by Katacha Díaz *Photographed by Lawrence Migdale*

OVERVIEW *Paty is getting ready for her birthday party. All her friends and family will come on Saturday.*

Warming Up

Begin the lesson by revisiting the Manipulative Chart, Chant Poster, or a familiar Big Book. You may ask a volunteer to choose one.

Setting the Scene

- Review the names of different family members using Picture Cards 1 and 6–14. Also review the verbs *play, sing,* and *dance* using Picture Cards 2, 3, and 5.
- If you have photos of you and your family celebrating a special occasion or traditional holiday, share them with the class. With or without photos, tell the class about your family members and celebrations.
- Ask children to tell about traditional holidays that their families celebrate. Ask *What do you eat? What do you wear? Do you sing special songs? Do you dance? What else do you do?* Encourage them to respond with words or gestures, as they are able.
- Display the cover. Say *This is Paty. In this book, we will read about her and what she and her family do to celebrate special occasions.*
- Make predictions about the book. *What do you think the book will tell us about how Paty and her family celebrate?* Help children determine a purpose for listening. Say *As we turn the pages, see if you can find information about ways of celebrating.*

Reading the Text

- Read the title page. Have children make an additional prediction about the book. *Who else might be in this book about Paty?*
- As you read through the book, use a pointer or your finger to draw children's attention to the text. Focus on the enjoyment of the book, while pointing out items in the photographs to support your reading. You will return later to build children's understanding of the text. In future rereadings, children should be encouraged to chime in.
- If you have children in Stages 3, 4, or 5, pause after reading page 17 for a prediction of what will happen next. *What do you think Paty, her family, and her friends will do at the party?*

Creating Comprehensible Input

- Open the back flap of the book, which shows key scenes from the book. Leave it open as you read to help build comprehension of Paty's family's traditions when preparing for and celebrating a birthday party.
- Use the comprehension supports in the following chart to help you build comprehensible input with children at all Stages of Language Acquisition.

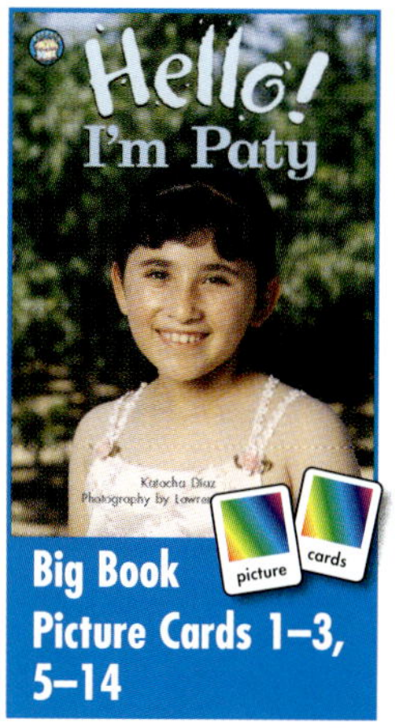

Component Organizer

Other Big Book lessons in this unit:

- Revisiting, p. U16
- Comprehension Strategy, p. U17
- Oral Language Development, pp. U19–U20
- Literacy Skills, p. U23

Idiom Note

The phrase, *all the goodies* may be an unfamiliar. Explain that goodies may be delicious things to eat, toys, or other treats. Point to the candy in the Big Book, smiling to demonstrate meaning.

PAGE	IN THE STORY	COMPREHENSION SUPPORT
4	Winters, California	point: to northern California on classroom map
4	Papa's . . . Mama's . . . two sisters	point: to each family member in turn
5	two older brothers, . . .	point: to each brother
6	I was born in Mexico.	point: to Mexico on classroom map
7	. . . make me dresses.	gesture: sewing with stitching motion, then point to dress
8	He picked crops . . . drove back home to Mexico.	act out: picking, then point to crate trace: route on map
9	. . . airline tickets . . . fly to the United States.	act out: flying, then trace route on map from Mexico to the U.S.
10	My family is having a fiesta.	use flap: point to party picture on flap
10	. . . inviting . . . best friends at school.	gesture: move arm toward self, then point to each friend
12	. . . *papel picado* . . . to decorate for the party.	use flap: point to the *papel picado* in party picture
13	. . . piñata . . . fill it with candy and toys . . .	point: to candy and toys and piñata, then gesture filling with goodies
14	Mama loves making enchiladas . . .	point: to enchiladas and smile
19	When the piñata breaks, all the goodies fly out!	gesture: breaking and flying with hands and fingers
20	. . . Mama's cheese enchiladas are delicious!	act out: lick lips and rub tummy, smiling
21	. . . Time for birthday cake.	point: to birthday cake
22	. . . a present from my *Abuelita* Guadalupe!	point: to dress, then to grandmother on page 7

You will need

- Paper
- Markers
- Easel pad

Revisiting the Big Book

- Open the back flap of the Big Book and display it for the children.
- Have children draw symbols for key images in the story, such as a birthday cake, dress, enchilada, and piñata.
- Retell the story in your own words using the back flap. As you speak, have the children hold up the appropriate drawing.
- Invite children to take turns retelling the story. They should hold up their drawings at the appropriate moment.

WEEK 2 DAY 3

Theme Project: Class Directory

1. Create a form for children to gather and exchange information. Use the following column headings: Name, Age, Home Language, Address, Telephone Number, Favorite Activity. If exchanging addresses and telephone numbers requires permission, do not include these headings. Include as many rows as there are children in your class.
2. Distribute copies of the form to children. Tell children that they will be learning more about each other by filling out the form. Explain each of the headings, and fill out a sample row.
3. During the remainder of the unit, allow children time to interview each other and enter information on the survey form. Children can dictate information to each other as each fills out his or her form. Circulate as they work and help with writing as necessary. Children can interview two or three classmates per session.
4. Continue this project until children have collected information for all of their classmates. Gather their forms and create a master list by name in alphabetical order on an easel pad. Suggest that children use a word-processing program to compile the list.
5. Post the master list where all children can see it. Encourage children to make comparisons and draw conclusions using the survey results. Model by saying, *Eight children speak Spanish at home. Five children have soccer as their favorite activity.*

WEEK 2 DAY 4

Big Book: Focus on Comprehension Strategy

Activates Existing Background Knowledge

1. Read pages 6 and 7 in *Hello! I'm Paty.* Demonstrate activating existing background knowledge with a think-aloud.
   Model *When I read* I miss my friends and relatives there, especially my grandmother, *I realize that I really understand what Paty's saying because I moved away from my family, too. It helps me understand this page better when I stop and think about how I felt when I moved.*
2. Invite children to share their own background knowledge as it relates to other pages in the book. ◎

Options for STAGES

❶ Allow these children to point to and name familiar items, like *mother.*	❷❸ Ask these children to relate the book to their own life: *How many brothers and sisters do you have?*	❹❺ Ask these children to tell what is familiar to them: *Have you ever done something like this?*

Chant Poster: Focus on Oral Language Development

FUNCTION MINI-LESSON

Greet ❶❷❸❹❺

1. Revisit the chant together, saying it several times.
2. Review informal greetings, which were introduced on Week 1 Day 5.
3. Have children pretend to be different family members shown on the chart, and role play greetings for the class. Model vocabulary and intonation. ◎

Options for STAGES

❶❷ These children can greet each other with *hi, hello,* and so on.	❸❹❺ Have these children use a variety of greetings in short dialogs, such as *Hi! How are you? Fine, thanks.*

FUNCTION MINI-LESSON

Inquire ❶❷❸❹❺

1. Reread the chant together, stopping to ask such questions as *Who is just great?* and *What do they love to do?*
2. Continue in the same manner, modeling and then asking other "What" questions, such as *What are they doing?*
3. Finish by asking the children where they think the family is.

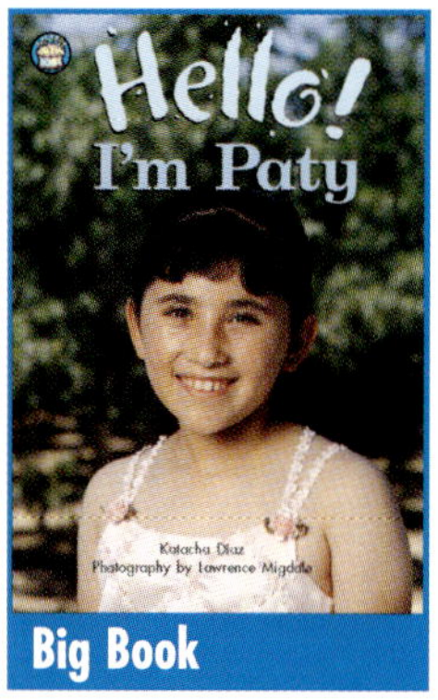

Assessment

Use a retelling of the Big Book to assess comprehension. Have children use the back flap for support. See page U27.

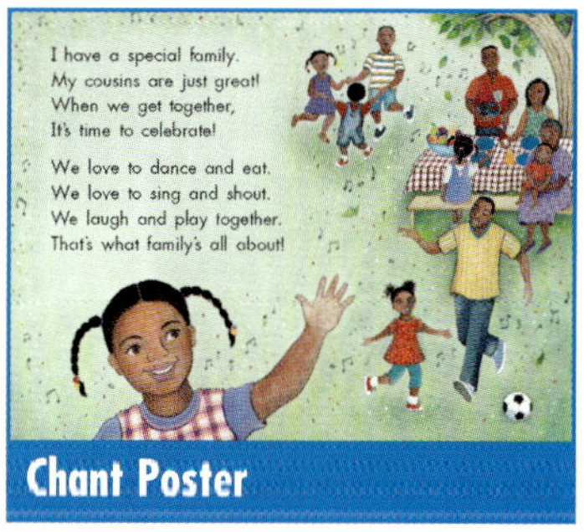

Home Culture Sharing

- Point out to children that Paty calls her parents "Mama" and "Papa." Tell children about familiar terms you use for your family members. Then invite children to share terms they use for different members of their families and if there is a special reason for the names.

Assessment

Record your observations of children during these mini-lessons on their individual assessment checklists for this unit. See page U27.

Grammar in Context: Present Tense ❶❷❸❹❺

1. Reread the chant. Then pose questions about the poster. Ask *What does this family do when they get together?* Model responses, such as *They play; They dance; They eat,* while pointing to each activity. Have children repeat your responses and then provide their own.
2. Extend the activity by asking *What do you do with your family?*

WEEK 2 DAY 5

Shared Writing Card: Introduction of Side A

You will need

- Shared Writing Card 1
- Wipe-off marker
- Regular marker
- Easel pad

Setting the Scene

- Use the back flap of the Big Book to review the key scenes of *Hello! I'm Paty.* Talk about Paty's family and the different things they do to maintain their Mexican traditions. Use words like *and, also,* and *another.*
- Tell the class that they will now be working together to complete a writing organizer about a boy.

Creating Comprehensible Input

- Display Shared Writing Card 1 Side A. It shows a web with four scenes of a boy and what he does to maintain his Chinese heritage. Begin by pointing to and naming individual items.

  Model *This boy is Chinese. His family is from China. These are chopsticks for eating. Here's some rice in bowls. Here's a Chinese parade. These are special Chinese pastries called mooncakes. This is Chinese writing.*
- Go back to the center illustration and use think-alouds to talk through the illustrations. Point to each illustration as you discuss it, tracing the lines with your finger.

  Center: *Here is a picture of a boy. He is Chinese.*

  Illustration 1: *In this picture, he is eating with his father and mother. They are using chopsticks to eat Chinese food.*

  Illustration 2: *Here he is watching a parade. It is a Chinese New Year parade. It's a Chinese celebration.*

  Illustration 3: *In this picture, the boy is eating Chinese mooncakes with his family for a special holiday.*

  Illustration 4: *In this picture, he is learning how to write in Chinese.*
- Explain that the boxes and lines on the Shared Writing Card help us understand more about what's in the center. Point to each outer illustration, saying *This is what the boy and his family do to keep their Chinese traditions.* Elicit from children that this will be the main idea of your paragraph.
- Invite a volunteer from Stages 3, 4, or 5 to retell the illustrations in his or her own words. Repeat with other volunteers.

Scribing with the Graphic Organizer

- After children become comfortable with the content of the illustrations, use the wipe-off marker provided to scribe while you brainstorm labels. Since you are creating a graphic organizer, not a finished product, well-crafted sentences are not necessary.

Revisiting the Concept Poster

- Revisit the Concept Poster, inviting volunteers to name as many family members as they can.
- Use self-stick notes to cover only the titles of each person on the family tree. Invite children to recall as many family titles as they can.

- Think aloud as you write so that children have insight into the writing process.
- Here is an example of simple shared writing for the illustrations:
  Illustration 1: eating food with chopsticks
  Illustration 2: watching Chinese New Year's parade
  Illustration 3: eating mooncakes
  Illustration 4: practicing how to write in Chinese

Writing Together from the Graphic Organizer

- You will again be holding the pen while you work with children to create a shared writing piece together. This time, you will model how to use the labels from the Chinese boy graphic organizer to create a finished paragraph on your easel pad.
- Begin with a think-aloud.
  Model *We started with* Chinese boy. *That isn't a complete sentence. Let's see. How about* This boy is Chinese? *Now I need to say what my writing is going to be about. Let me look at all the pictures and labels. How does* He and his family practice some special Chinese traditions *sound?*
- Write down the first one or two sentences you agree upon with children, being sure to include the main idea.
- As you move to the next illustration, read the label and then invite children to help you create the sentence based on the picture and the label. When children offer sentences with errors in them, correct them without being overt. Encourage children to use classroom resources, such as the Word Wall.
- When you have finished your shared writing piece, read it together several times. Then hang it up on the wall where it can be displayed during the rest of the unit and reread many times. For now, do not erase your labels on Side A.

Phonics in Context

Shared writing provides an ideal opportunity for reviewing the phonics skills children are learning. Highlight the sounds in words like ***o***n and ***an***d as you reread the writing.

Sample Shared Writing

The boy is Chinese. He and his family practice some special Chinese traditions. They eat with chopsticks. They also watch the Chinese New Year's parade. On special days, they eat mooncakes. The boy also practices how to write in Chinese.

WEEK 3 DAY 1

Big Book: Focus on Oral Language Development

Reread the Big Book and return to the text to focus on oral language development.

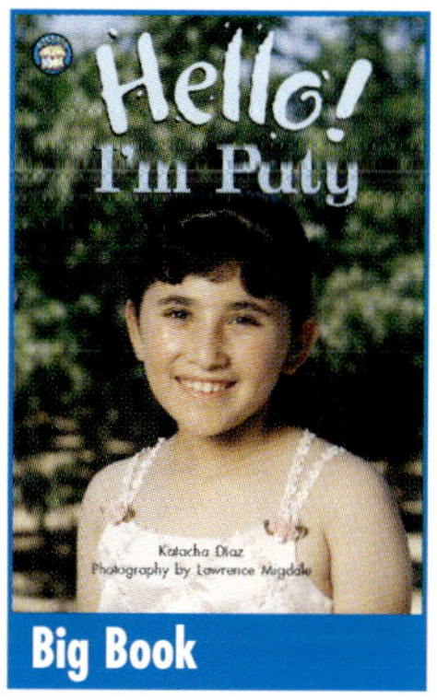

Grammar in Context: Preposition 1 2 3 4 5

1. Open the Big Book to page 6 and read the text. Restate by saying *Paty was born in Mexico. I can say that a different way. I can say: Paty is from Mexico.* Emphasize *from* as you repeat the sentence.
2. Tell where your family is from, and then go around the room asking children where their families are from. If most children are from the same country, they can say what region, state, or city they are from.
3. Use a classroom map for support and help children with the names of their countries.
4. Put a self-stick note with each child's name on it on their family's country or region of origin.

Guided Reading

As you work on this unit, conduct small groups of guided reading or shared-to-guided reading independent of thematic instruction. Instruction is provided in the Guided Reading section of this guide.

Language Learning Master

p. 11 (1 2 3 4 5)

Language Junction

The third person singular *s* of the simple present tense is often dropped by learners of English. The *s* is, in a sense, redundant since the subject noun or pronoun also tells person and number. This difficulty may continue into the higher Stages. Improvement will occur naturally over time, and undue emphasis on instruction is unlikely to change the results.

Grammar in Context: Present Tense (1 2 3 4 5)

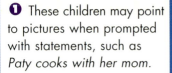

1. Display the back flap of the Big Book and model how to make statements in the simple present tense: *Paty lives with her mom, dad, sisters, and brothers. She cuts paper designs for family celebrations*, and so on.
2. Make other statements about the people in the book, having children turn to the page that shows what you are saying. For example, *They make cheese enchiladas.*
3. Encourage children to recall what else Paty does using the simple present by prompting them: *Tell me more about Paty and her family.* Flip through the book, using the pictures as reminders.

Options for STAGES

1 These children may point to pictures when prompted with statements, such as *Paty cooks with her mom.*	2 3 These children may make very simple sentences using only a subject and verb, such as *Paty eats*, and so on.	4 5 Encourage these children to use complete sentences or phrases in telling about each scene.

4. Extend the activity by asking children to tell about themselves. You can help with specific questions, such as *What does your family eat? What do you do after school?* and so on.
5. After each child has finished telling about him or herself, ask the class to tell what they learned about that classmate. For example, ask *What does Lan do after school?*

WEEK 3 DAY 2

Shared Writing Card: Brainstorming Side B

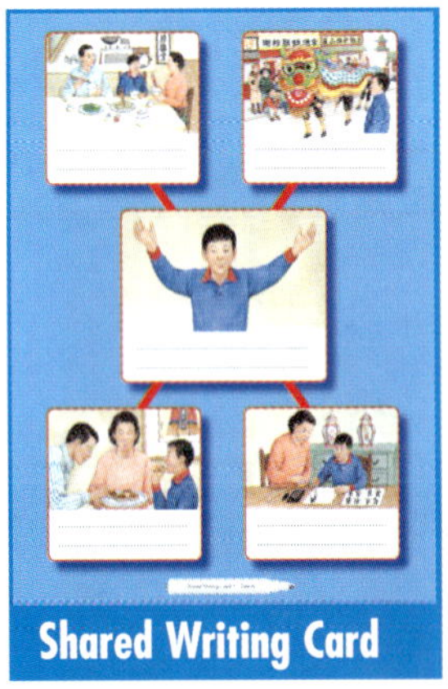

You will need

- Shared Writing Card 1
- Wipe-off marker

Brainstorming a Topic

- Use Side A of the Shared Writing Card and the finished Chinese traditions shared writing piece. Review how you used the graphic organizer's pictures and labels to form the basis of your finished piece.
- Turn the card over to Side B. Tell children that you will now think about your own topic together to draw in the graphic organizer. It can be about a child in the class or a child from a book that they have read. You might want to brainstorm a few possibilities before you determine your final choice. It should be a child or character that the class knows well enough to write at least four things about.

Scribing with the Graphic Organizer

- Once you have chosen a topic, you should decide together what the center illustration should show. Model how to draw a simple sketch of the child and write his or her name under it. Invite volunteers to draw simple scenes in the surrounding boxes showing what the child does to maintain his or her family's culture. Continue drawing until the picture is complete; it's OK to leave one box empty.
- Now it's time to put captions on your graphic organizer. Elicit suggestions for labels from the group and record them on the Shared Writing Card.
- You will create the shared writing paragraph together at the next session.

Active Social Studies: Family Trees

1. Ask children to bring in photos of family members. Photocopy the pictures and have children take home the originals.
2. If children are unable to bring in photos, they can draw family member portraits on white paper squares.
3. Have children glue the family portraits on large pictures of paper, using the Concept Poster of Gloria's family as a model. However, they do not have to arrange them in traditional order as in the Concept Poster. This will ensure that children from alternative family structures can participate fully.
4. Invite volunteers to share their family trees, using gestures and words to tell about each member.

You will need

- Family photos
- Drawing paper
- Construction paper
- Crayons and markers
- Scissors
- Glue

WEEK 3 DAY 3

Shared Writing Card: Writing Together with Side B

- As with Side A, you will work together with children to create a finished writing piece from the graphic organizer on Side B of Shared Writing Card 1.
- Model writing from the center illustration, using think-alouds as you go. Show children how to use resources like the Word Wall. Work together on difficult spellings or tricky passages.
- When you have finished your shared writing piece, read it together several times. Then hang it up on the wall where it can be displayed during the rest of the unit. At the end of the unit, you should erase both sides of the Shared Writing Card.

Shared Writing Card

Manipulative Chart: Focus on Oral Language Development

Grammar in Context: Subject Pronouns ❶❷❸❹❺

1. Point to yourself as you make two statements about yourself to model the use of the pronoun *I;* for example, *My name is Ms. Hinojosa. I am the teacher.* Emphasize the word *I* as you point to yourself. Have Stage 4 or 5 children introduce themselves.
2. Demonstrate the use of the pronoun *we* by making statements about yourself and the children. You might gather several children around you as you gesture and say *Sophia, Kim, and I are in front of the class. We are standing together.* Emphasize *we* as you make an inclusive gesture. Continue in the same manner for the pronoun *you.*
3. Explain that *I, we,* and *you* can take the place of people's names. Reinforce by repeating the names (such as *Sophia, Kim, I*) and then saying *we.* Ask volunteers to make their own sentence pairs, one with proper names and the other using a pronoun.
4. Draw children's attention to the Manipulative Chart. Read the words to the song, asking children to listen for the words *I, we,* and *you.*
5. Sing the song with children, having them clap each time they hear these pronouns.
6. In heterogeneous pairs, have children write sentences using people's names as subjects of the sentences. Then have children rewrite each sentence, replacing the subject noun with a pronoun as they are able.

Language Learning Master

p. 12 ❶❷❸❹❺

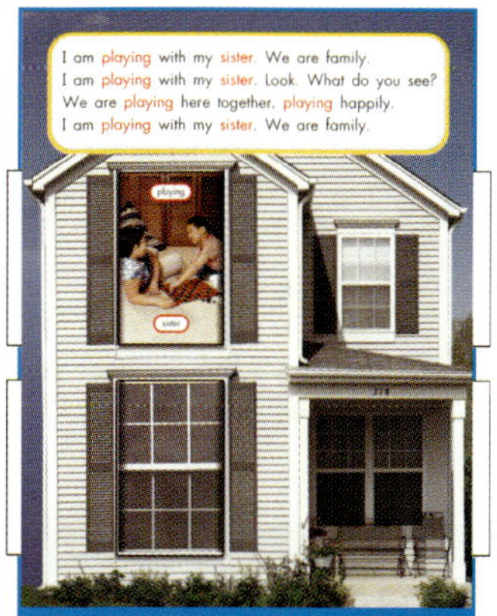

Manipulative Chart

WEEK 3 DAY 4

You will need

- Magazine pictures
- Glue

Active Science: Physical Characteristics

1. Explain to children that people have many things in common, yet people come in various shapes, sizes, and colors.
2. Have children cut out faces from magazines. Then have them say or write sentences comparing themselves to the photos.
3. Model comparing yourself to a photo. Say *I have short brown hair. She has long blond hair. My eyes are blue, just like hers.*

WEEK 3 DAY 5

You will need

- Overhead transparency of Writing Resource Guide, p. 80
- Overhead marker

Writing Resource Guide: A Simplified Graphic Organizer

This activity is optional and only necessary if you wish to use the simplified sequence graphic organizer in cooperative-group or independent writing.

Brainstorming a Topic

- Review the drawings and labels you used on Side B of the Shared Writing Card. Trace the leader lines from the center to each picture as you summarize the content.
- On the overhead projector, display a transparency of Writing Planner B on page 80 of the Writing Resource Guide, which is a blank web.
- Brainstorm together a topic that involves describing the traditions, family life, or school activities of a young child that the children know, like a classmate or character in a book.

Scribing with the Graphic Organizer

- Once the class has chosen a topic, you should decide together what main activities to include in your paragraph. Model drawing each of the child's activities.
- Label all four drawings of the graphic organizer. Elicit suggestions for labels from the group in the same manner as you did with the Shared Writing Card.

You will need

- Writing Resource Guide, pp. 79–80
- Markers

Writing Resource Guide: Cooperative-Group Writing

- Form groups of heterogeneous Stages with three to four children each to work together on a writing piece using the graphic organizer. You may hand out a copy of Writing Planner A or B to each group.
- Review the shared writing graphic organizers and finished pieces you have made together. Remind children that the drawings can help them remember details that they want to include.
- Have the groups work together first to complete their graphic organizers and then to write their finished pieces. Circulate to provide assistance. ◎

Options for STAGES

❶❷ These children should draw the pictures for the group.	❸❹❺ These children should take responsibility for the writing of the finished piece.

Writing Mini-lessons

See the Writing Resource Guide for mini-lessons to use as children write. Here are some suggestions:

- Mini-lesson 12: Capitalization: First Names and *I*
- Mini-lesson 13: Simple Sentences

WEEK 4 DAY 1

Big Book: Focus on Literacy Skills

Word Level: Phonics in Context

1. You will need the Word Wall Starters with the birthday cake symbol on them: *clap*, *hot*. These are pictured in the back of the Big Book.
2. Tell children that you want to choose some special words from the story for them to look at more closely.
3. Introduce the word *clap* by saying it clearly, emphasizing the *ap* sound, and drawing attention to the highlighting behind the *ap*. Then say */ap/-/ap/-/ap/. The letters* a *and* p *together make the* ap *sound. Let's say the word* clap *together: clap. Can you hear how* clap *ends with* ap? *Now let's sing a song.* Review Phonics Song Chart 3.
4. Say *I'm going to put the word* clap *below the* short a *label.* Walk to your Word Wall and place *clap* under the *short a* label. Remind children that they can use the birthday cake symbol to help them remember where they "met" that word before.
5. Repeat a similar procedure for the other words and phonics skills.

Sentence Level: Lists and Bullet Points

1. Read the text on pages 14 and 15, pointing out the list of ingredients for cheese enchiladas. As you read the items in the list, point to each one to emphasize the list format.
2. Point out that each thing in a list is on a separate line and that sometimes there's a number next to each item in a list, and sometimes there are bullets or pictures.
   Model *When I see the list of ingredients, I know exactly what I need to make cheese enchiladas. Each ingredient is on a separate line. This helps me remember.*
3. Ask children to help you find other lists in the classroom, noting the style used. Discuss how it's helpful to have that information in list form.
4. Ask volunteers to dictate or write simple lists of their own, such as foods needed to make something or people to invite to a special celebration. Remind them to put a bullet, number, or picture in front of each item.

Text Level: Index

1. Open the Big Book to the Index on page 24. Introduce children to this part of a book using simple language and gestures. Say *This is an index. It is a list of different words and ideas in the book, and the page where you can find that word or idea.*
2. Demonstrate how to use an index by reading the entries, noting their alphabetical order. Have children tell which part they'd like to read again and why.

Options for STAGES

1 2 These children can find the page to turn to, stating what they are looking for as they are able.	3 4 5 These children can say what they want to read more about and why.

3. Explain to children that an index tells us what page to turn to when we want to read about one particular thing.
4. Extend the activity by having children work with indices in other classroom books.

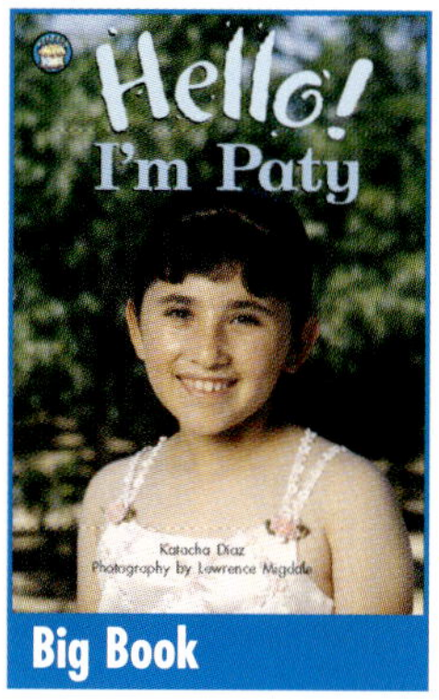

Guided Reading

As you work on this unit, conduct small groups of guided reading or shared-to-guided reading independent of thematic instruction. Instruction is provided in the Guided Reading section of this guide.

Home-School Connection

Send home page 17 of the Home-School Connection Masters for children to use in retelling *Hello! I'm Paty* to their families. They should retell the story in English and then talk about it in either English or their home language.

You will need

- TPR Cards
- Previously prepared game boards

Language Practice Game: Version 2

Divide children in Stages 3, 4, or 5 into pairs. Provide each pair with a pyramid game board and give each child an identical set of the six action TPR cards. Model the following directions for this information gap game.

1. Have partners sit back to back.
2. Player 1 places one set of the TPR Cards on various family members on the pyramid.
3. When both partners are ready, Player 2 asks "who" or "what" questions about the family members, such as *Who is playing?* or *What is Grandfather doing?*
4. Player 1 responds with sentences, such as *Brother is playing* or *Grandfather is eating.*
5. Player 2 arranges his or her cards according to Player 1's response.
6. When Player 2 is finished, both players check their boards to make sure they match.
7. Partners switch roles and play again.

WEEK 4 DAY 2

You will need

- Index cards
- Pencils
- Chalk
- Tape

Active Math: Age Graph

1. Distribute index cards to children and have them write their names on the cards. Write the numerals 6, 7, and 8 on the board and identify the numbers. Make sure that all ages represented by children are included.
2. Beginning with the first age, ask *How many children are six years old?* Collect these cards and tape them in a column under the appropriate age on the board.
3. Have children help you tally the cards in each column. Ask them to make global statements about the graph: *How many children are in our class? Who is eight? How old is Ali? Are there more six-year-olds or more seven-year-olds?*

6	7	8
Ali	Bao	Kim
San	Sue	Luc
Ana	Jin	
Luz	Lee	
Kia	Eva	
	Gil	
	Mai	
	Van	

You will need

A copy of page U27 at the end of this unit for each child

A End-of-Unit Assessment

- While children are engaged in activities this week, pull them individually for the Big Book retelling, using page U27 at the end of this unit.
- Select a number of children with whom you would like to use the Open-Ended Oral Language Assessment on pages U26–U27 of this unit and pull them individually during activities this week. We recommend assessing about one-fourth of your class each unit.
- You should also have gathered the following for their assessment portfolio:
  - page 10 of the Language Learning Masters
  - page 11 of the Language Learning Masters
  - finished writing piece assessed according to the Writing Rubric on page A6.

WEEK 4 DAY 3–4

Writing Resource Guide: Individual Writing

- Children have engaged in a step-by-step writing process moving toward independence. They began with teacher-led shared writing, moved to cooperative groups, and are now ready to work individually.
- Provide a copy of Writing Planner A or B to each child. They may need individual conferencing on choosing a topic. ◎

Options for STAGES

❶❷ and Emergent Level
These children can draw different aspects of the child's life on the web. They can either label the drawings on their own or dictate labels to you.

❸❹❺ Early Level and Above
These children should also use drawings and labels on the graphic organizer to record their topic. They should then use the graphic organizer to create a finished piece.

- When children have completed their finished product, whether graphic organizer or paragraph, you should assess it using the Writing Rubric on page A6 of this Teacher's Guide.

You will need

- Writing Resource Guide, pp. 79–80
- Markers

Assessment

Continue pulling some children for the Big Book Retelling and Open-Ended Oral Language Assessment as others write.

WEEK 4 DAY 5

Theme Project: Sharing

- Conclude the unit by reviewing the class directory. Invite children to take turns coming to the front of the class and giving information about themselves and one or two other classmates.
- Ask questions as necessary to help children with their presentations. For example: *How old is Indira? Where does Marcos live?* and so on.
- Post the directory on the bulletin board so that children can review it as they wish.

Open-Ended Oral Language Assessment Reassess children's Language Acquisition Stages. Begin with an open-ended prompt like the first one below. If children are unable to respond, intervene with increasingly directed prompts, such as the second and third ones below.

What can you tell me about the picture?

What are the people in the picture doing?

I see a sister. Do you see a brother?

Assessment Directions: Copy this form for each child and place the completed form in the child's portfolio. Locate the child's Language Acquisition Stage for each of the first four activities and assess his or her performance during the unit according to expectations for that Stage. For the Big Book Retelling, pull children to retell the Big Book during end-of-unit assessment time. Use the Open-Ended Oral Language Assessment to reassess children's Language Acquisition Stages with one-fourth of your students for each unit, using the back side of the sheet to take notes. *For more guidance on assessment, see pages T33 and T34.*

Unit 1 Assessment

Name ____________________ **Date** __________

On Our Way to English Grade 2	STAGE EXPECTATIONS ❶	❷	❸	❹	❺
Fluency Manipulative Chart: Student Version, page U12 *How does the child respond when manipulating the mini-chart along with the Oral Language Audio CD?*	Shows the correct answers. ☐ Yes ☐ Not yet	Shows the correct answers, naming the family member or activity. ☐ Yes ☐ Not yet	Shows the correct answers, approximating sentences and substitutions. ☐ Yes ☐ Not yet	Shows the correct answers, singing the verse with few, if any, errors. ☐ Yes ☐ Not yet	
Content Area Knowledge Language Practice Game: Version 1, page U13 *How does the child demonstrate an understanding of family names and everyday activities?*	Lays the cards down on the appropriate squares in the pyramid. ☐ Yes ☐ Not yet	Lays the cards down in the appropriate squares and uses some appropriate vocabulary, such as *brother eating.* ☐ Yes ☐ Not yet		Lays the cards down on the appropriate squares in the pyramid and says a complete sentence with appropriate vocabulary, such as *I am eating with my mother.* ☐ Yes ☐ Not yet	
Social Language Function Greet, page U17 *How does the child respond during the Function Mini-lesson??*	Responds non-verbally or with a basic word such as *Hello.* ☐ Yes ☐ Not yet		Responds using a short phrases, such as *Hello. How you? I'm fine.* ☐ Yes ☐ Not yet		
Academic Language Function Inquire, page U17 *How does the child respond during the Function Mini-lesson?*			Is able to form very simple questions with key words, such as *Where sister?* ☐ Yes ☐ Not yet	Uses complete, well-formed questions, such as *Where is sister?* ☐ Yes ☐ Not yet	
Big Book Retelling page U16 *Have each child use the back flap and symbols on the board to retell* Hello! I'm Paty. *How does the child retell the book?*	Simply points from Paty to each picture. ☐ Yes ☐ Not yet	Retells using a few words. ☐ Yes ☐ Not yet	Retells using longer phrases or simple sentences. ☐ Yes ☐ Not yet	Retells using complete sentences in connected discourse with few errors. ☐ Yes ☐ Not yet	Retells using story language similar to native-speaking peers. ☐ Yes ☐ Not yet
Open-Ended Oral Language Assessment, page U26 *Use the child's responses to the illustration to reassess the child's Stage of Language Acquisition.*	☐ **STAGE ❶** Uses few or no words; gestures or points.	☐ **STAGE ❷** Uses words or short phrases.	☐ **STAGE ❸** Uses phrases and simple sentences.	☐ **STAGE ❹** Uses sentences in connected discourse.	☐ **STAGE ❺** Uses language comparable to native-speaking peers.

UNIT 2

Living in America

OVERVIEW *This theme focuses on learning about North America, its countries, its people, and their communities. The unit begins with maps of North America and the United States. It then continues with urban, suburban, and rural settings, as well as several states in the southwest United States.*

Determining the Purpose

Oral Language Development

Focus on Functions

Social Context:

Express likes and dislikes ❶❷❸❹❺

Academic Context:

Evaluate ❶❷❸❹❺

Focus on Grammar

- Conjunction *and*
- Subject pronouns *it* and *they*
- Adverbs—time
- Regular and irregular past tense

Comprehension Strategy

- Considers author's viewpoint, purpose, and style

Literacy Skills

- **Word Level:** Phonics in context short *i*, short *u*
- **Sentence Level:** Distinguishing fact from opinion
- **Text Level:** Comparing and contrasting plot, settings, and characters

Content Area Objectives

- Identifies features of U.S. geography
- Distinguishes cardinal directions (north, south, east, west)
- Recognizes urban, suburban, and rural settings
- Understands that many U.S. residents come from other parts of the world
- Recognizes Canada, United States, and Mexico on a map of North America

Language Learning Strategy

- Use your home language to help you understand a word.

Writing Skill

- Uses a graphic organizer to sequence events

Unit Components

Manipulative Chart

Chant Poster

Concept Poster

Newcomer Book

Unit at a Glance

Week	DURING THE WEEK	DAY 1
Week 1	**Small-Group Instruction:** • Guided Reading • Shared-to-Guided Reading **Phonics Focus:** short *i* Phonics Song Chart 6, pp. P16–P17	**Manipulative Chart:** Introduction with Audio CD p. U31
Week 2	**Small-Group Instruction:** • Guided Reading • Shared-to-Guided Reading • Newcomer Book **Phonics Focus:** *ip* and *in* word families Phonics Song Chart 7, pp. P18–P19	**Concept Poster:** Introduction p. U36 **Language Practice Game:** Version 1 p. U37
Week 3	**Small-Group Instruction:** • Guided Reading • Shared-to-Guided Reading • Newcomer Book **Phonics Focus:** short *u* Phonics Song Chart 8, pp. P20–P21	**Big Book:** Oral Language Development p. U43
Week 4	**Small-Group Instruction:** • Guided Reading • Shared-to-Guided Reading • Newcomer Book **Phonics Focus:** *un* and *ug* word families Phonics Song Chart 9, pp. P22–P23	**Big Book:** Literacy Skills p. U47 **Language Practice Game:** Version 2 p. U48

STAGES ❶ Preproduction ❷ Early Production ❸ Speech Emergence ❹ Intermediate Fluency ❺ Advanced Fluency

Oral Language Audio CD

Big Book with Audio CD and Small Book

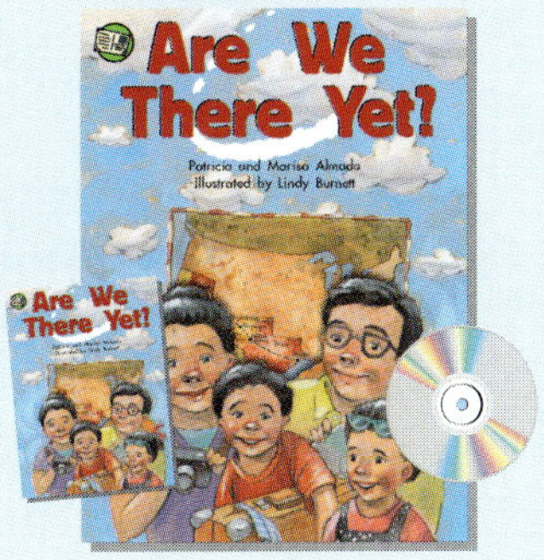

Home-School Connection Masters

Picture Cards

Shared Writing Card

Writing Resource Guide

Language Learning Masters

DAY 2	DAY 3	DAY 4	DAY 5
Manipulative Chart: Gestures and Manipulative Fun p. U32	**Chant Poster:** Introduction p. U33	**TPR Cards:** Introduction p. U34	**Manipulative Chart:** Oral Language Development Student Version p. U35
Big Book: Introduction p. U39	**Theme Project:** Newcomers Gallery p. U40 **Big Book:** Revisiting p. U40	**Big Book:** Comprehension Strategy p. U41 **Chant Poster:** Oral Language Development p. U41	**Shared Writing Card:** Introduction of Side A p. U42 **Concept Poster:** Revisiting p. U42
Shared Writing Card: Brainstorming Side B p. U44 **Active Social Studies:** Where Will We Go? p. U44	**Shared Writing Card:** Writing Together with Side B p. U45 **Manipulative Chart:** Oral Language Development p. U45	**Active Science:** Crystal Garden p. U45	**Writing Resource Guide:** A Simplified Graphic Organizer Cooperative-Group Writing p. U46
Active Math: Road Mileage p. U48 **Assessment** p. U49	**Writing Resource Guide:** Individual Writing p. U49 **Assessment** p. U49	**Writing Resource Guide:** Individual Writing p. U49 **Assessment** p. U49	**Theme Project:** Sharing p. U49

Center Activities

You will need

- U.S. map
- Scissors
- Markers
- Index cards
- Markers and crayons
- Brochures and postcards from U.S., Canada, Mexico

Number Nook

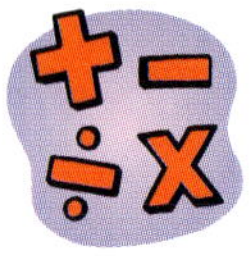

Create puzzles of the United States by copying and laminating maps and cutting along state lines. Invite children to assemble the puzzles and then to practice counting the states.

Artist's Studio

Provide index cards, markers, and crayons. Invite children to create their own picture postcards for places that they have been to or would like to visit.

Content Corner

Bring in brochures and postcards from different regions of the United States, Canada, and Mexico. Invite children to explore these items together.

CENTERS

Listening Post

After introducing each element in class, children may revisit the Manipulative Chart and Chant Poster on the Oral Language Audio CD. If you include a laminated copy of the Manipulative Chart Student Version, children can manipulate it as they sing to Part 4 of the CD (with blanks). Children may also listen to *Are We There Yet?* on the Big Book Audio CD while following along in the small copy.

Language Workshop

Any time they are not in use during the unit, place the Picture Cards for the unit in this center. Encourage children to review the names with each other for additional practice. After introducing the Language Practice Game in class, add the game board, TPR Cards, and foil ball to the center for independent group play.

Writer's Den

Establish a journal writing center with prompts to spark children's writing. Change the prompt every two weeks:

- Is there a place you want to visit in North America?
- Which do you think is the best place to live: the city, the suburbs, or the country?

Children should be encouraged to draw pictures to support their writing. Provide blank Writing Planners in center materials for prewriting.

More Books

- *Dreaming of America: An Ellis Island Story* by Eve Bunting (HarperTrophy, 1997)
- *On the Go* by Ann Morris (Lothrop, Lee & Shepard, 1990)
- *Stringbean's Trip to the Shining Sea* by Vera B. Williams (Mulberry, 1999)
- *Going Home* by Eve Bunting (HarperTrophy, 1998)
- *Greetings from America: Postcards From Donovan & Daisy* by Ray Nelson Jr. and Douglas Kelly (Flying Rhinocerous, 1995)

WEEK 1 DAY 1

Manipulative Chart: Introduction with Audio CD

Sung to the tune of "Dem Bones"

Setting the Scene

- Show Picture Card 1: plane. Ask *Who has seen a plane? Who has been on a plane?* Have children share their experiences as they are able.
- Show Picture Card 2: directions. Point to the location and the names of the four directions. Say *north, south, east, and west.*
- Introduce Picture Cards 3–5: United States, Mexico, Canada. Children may join in as you pronounce these names.
- Hold Picture Card 1 and have it "land" on different places in the classroom, including Picture Cards 3–5. Each time, ask *Where did the plane land?* ◎

Options for STAGES

❶❷ Have these children, if they are able, say the name of the place where the plane has landed.

❸❹❺ Encourage children at these Stages to make sentences with the pattern *It landed on the desk.*

Creating Comprehensible Input

- The Manipulative Chart shows a map of North America. There are Velcro™ pads in the three countries. The plane piece has a Velcro™ pad so that it can "land" in various locations.
- Tell children that this is a map. Point out the names and location of the countries and the four cardinal directions shown on the map.
- Read the text, pausing often, as you use gestures, pointing, and other techniques to make the song comprehensible.

That plane, that plane,	hold up plane
It flew around.	move the plane in a figure-eight
That plane, that plane,	hold up plane
It touched down.	attach plane to Velcro™ pad in center of the United States
That plane, that plane,	point to plane
It's on the ground.	tap site with finger
Where did it land?	shrug shoulders

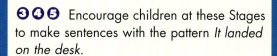

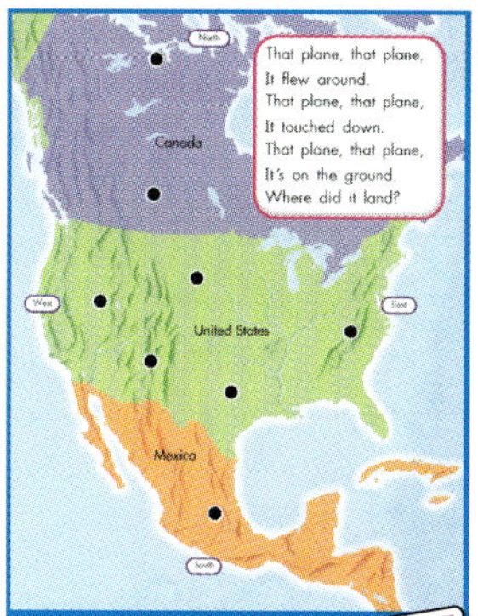

Manipulative Chart
Picture Cards 1–5

Guided Reading

As you work on this unit, conduct small groups of guided reading or shared-to-guided reading independent of thematic instruction. Instruction is provided in the Guided Reading section of this guide.

Component Organizer

Other Manipulative Chart lessons in this unit:

- Gestures and Manipulative Fun, p. U32
- Oral Language Development and Student Version, pp. U35–U36
- Oral Language Development, p. U45

Real-World Touch

Bring in postcards from North America. Point out the front photo, the caption on the back, and the spaces for the message and address, and any postmark or stamp.

Home-School Connection

Choose one of the versions of the parent letter to send home with each child, according to the child's home language (pages 18–25 in the Home-School Connection Masters). Also send home the activity on page 26.

Manipulative Chart

Journal Writing Reminder

Children should be writing in their journals during the course of the unit. Journal writing can help children to activate their prior knowledge, which prepares them to participate in classroom activities. See Writer's Den for suggested journal prompts.

Introducing the Audio CD

- Play Part 1 of the Oral Language Audio CD, the spoken song, as you say the song and track the print on the Manipulative Chart with your finger or a pointer. Replay Part 1 several times, encouraging children to chime in whenever they can.
- Introduce the song by playing the song at natural speed, Part 2 of the Audio CD, to help children get a feel for the song. Allow the Audio CD to continue playing through Part 3, the song at instructional pace. Track the print as the Audio CD plays. Repeat Part 3 again, this time singing along, making clear lip movements without exaggerating. Revisit Part 3 several times to help children learn the song.

WEEK 1 DAY 2

Manipulative Chart: Gestures and Manipulative Fun

Gesturing the Song

Introduce these simple gestures to accompany the song:

That plane, that plane,	extend arms as "wings"
It flew around.	move arms through the air in flying motion
That plane, that plane,	extend arms as "wings"
It touched down.	bring arms down and stop movement
That plane, that plane,	extend arms as "wings"
It's on the ground.	point to the ground
Where did it land?	shrug shoulders

Manipulating the Chart

- Show children how to attach the plane piece to different parts of the Manipulative Chart. The cardinal directions and/or country names can be shouted out, depending on where the plane "lands," in response to the question at the end of the song. Position the plane in the United States, sing the song, and then have children shout out "In the United States!" along with you.
- Play Part 4 of the Oral Language Audio CD. Shout "In the United States!" at the end of the song.
- Continue introducing and naming the other directions and country names on the chart in this manner.
- Invite volunteers to manipulate the plane for the class as you sing the verse together or give Total Physical Response commands, such as *Fly to Canada.*
- You can revisit this activity many times during the unit.

WEEK 1 DAY 3

Chant Poster: Introduction

Setting the Scene

- Display a world map. Identify some countries, such as Haiti, Mexico, China, Vietnam, Pakistan, and Russia. Ask *What other countries do you know?*
- Trace lines of immigration with your finger as you say *People come to the United States from many different places. Some people come from Mexico. Some people come from China,* and so on. Make sure all children's national backgrounds are mentioned. Have children join in as you say the names of these countries. Ask *Where is your family from?* ◎

Options for STAGES

❶❷ Invite these children to point to their country of origin or just to say the country name as they are able.

❸❹❺ Have these children trace lines of immigration from their countries of origin to the U.S. and tell where their families are from in complete sentences.

- Invite volunteers to tell about their countries of origin.

Creating Comprehensible Input

- Displaying the Chant Poster, identify the planes, the bus, and the United States.
- Read the text with frequent pauses as you use gestures, pointing, and other techniques to make the chant comprehensible.

So many people	point to children in poster
So many faces.	trace a circle around the faces of the children
People in the United States	trace border of U.S.
Come from so many places!	point to several routes of entry shown by planes and bus
Maybe they were born here,	pretend to cradle a baby
Or came by plane or bus.	point to planes and bus
Everyone knows that U.S.	trace outline of U.S. on poster
Spells one big US.	round arms in encompassing gesture

Chanting the Poster

- Encourage children to join in as you chant the rhyme together several times. Invite eight children to stand in front of the class, one to chant each stanza.
- Introduce the chant on the Oral Language Audio CD as you and the children move to the rhythm. Tell them that they can listen on their own later at the Listening Post.
- Practice saying the chant very softly, loudly, quickly, and slowly.
- Revisit the chant often, inviting children to create new gestures.

Chant Poster

Component Organizer

Other Chant Poster lessons in this unit:

- Oral Language Development, pp. U41–U42

WEEK 1 DAY 4

You will need

- **Language Learning Master** p. 15
- Scissors
- Crayons

TPR Cards: Introduction

Introducing the Cards with Total Physical Response

- Provide one copy of page 15 of the Language Learning Masters to each child. Have children color and cut out the cards.
- Introduce a few cards at a time by holding them up one by one and saying the words clearly. Select first the words that have already been introduced in previous activities.
- Ask children to pick up the correct cards as you call out a word. Model the desired outcome. Add one new card at a time and keep reviewing in a game-like atmosphere. Children may want to say the word as they pick up the card.
- Now invite children to respond to your full-sentence commands, such as *Point to Mexico. Pick up the mountain.*
- Assign partners so you can add commands like *Give the bus to Alicia.*
- As children increase their familiarity with the TPR Cards and the game, add silly commands, such as *Put the river in the plane.*
- Invite volunteers in Stages 3, 4, or 5 to give commands to their classmates.
- Extend language to discuss where the children live. ◎

Options for STAGES

❶❷ Have these children point to and name, as they are able, cards that show where they live. They can point to more than one card.	❸❹❺ Have these children point to cards and say complete sentences, as they are able, about where they live.

- Repeat this activity several times throughout the unit.

Grammar in Context: Conjunction *and* ❶❷❸❹❺

1. Display a world map and ask two children whose families are from the same country where they are from. Have the children point to this place on the map. Summarize the information, saying, for example, *Van is from Vietnam. Tran is from Vietnam.* Then model how to combine them into one sentence with *and*, as in *Van is from Vietnam, and Tran is from Vietnam, too.* Continue with other children whose families are from the same country.
2. Position the plane and the bus TPR Cards at different starting points on the map. Ask two volunteers to move the plane and the bus over the map to the same destination. Model how to form a sentence with the conjunction *and*, as in *The plane flew to Mexico, and the bus drove to Mexico, too.*
3. Ask two other volunteers to come forward and repeat this procedure using other "destinations" on the map. For variation, you can tape the mountain, river, and ocean cards to the board with correction tape and manipulate the plane and bus cards as you make sentences such as *The plane flew to the mountains, and the bus drove to the mountains, too.*
4. Invite volunteers to come forward and manipulate the plane card and bus card as they make sentences with the conjunction *and* as they are able.

WEEK 1 DAY 5

Manipulative Chart: Focus on Oral Language Development

FUNCTION MINI-LESSON

Express Likes and Dislikes ❶❷❸❹❺

1. Using facial expressions and gestures to support comprehension, tell children what you like/don't like about travel. For example, *I like flying in planes. I don't like long car trips.*
2. Ask the children to share what they like/don't like about travel. ◎

Options for STAGES

❶❷ Ask these children yes/no questions, such as *Do you like to fly?*

❸❹❺ These children can use phrases and complete sentences, such as *like train* or *I like the train.*

FUNCTION MINI-LESSON

Evaluate ❶❷❸❹❺

1. Invite children in Stages 3, 4, and 5 to join you while others play games with the TPR Cards.
2. Hold the mountain, river, and ocean TPR Cards next to these same features on the Manipulative Chart, explaining that this is how these features are often represented on a map.
3. Using gestures to support comprehension, evaluate the benefits/challenges of living next to each of these, such as *It's good to live next to the ocean because you can swim and catch fish, but there might be bad weather and big waves sometimes.*

Grammar in Context: Subject Pronoun *it* ❶❷❸❹❺

1. Sing the song on the Manipulative Chart with children. Tell them to clap when they hear the word *it*.
2. Reread the first sentence. With your finger draw a circle around the word *plane* and then trace a line to the word *it*. Say *We use* it *to talk about one thing. What is* it *here? That's right,* it *is the plane.*
3. Hold up a common object, such as a pencil. Say *This is a pencil. It is yellow.*
4. Ask children to take turns holding up an object within their reach and to make two simple statements about it, the second one with the subject pronoun *it*. ◎

Options for STAGES

❶❷ These children can say the name of the object then say *it* as they are able.

❸❹❺ Encourage these children to say phrases or sentences with the name of the object and then *it*, such as *This is my book. It is red.*

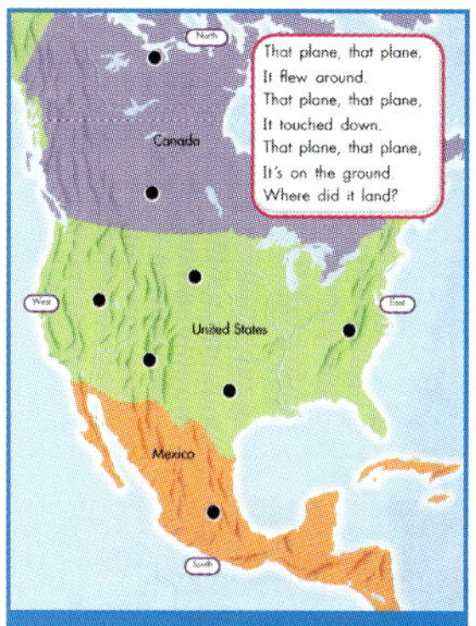

Manipulative Chart

Language Learning Strategy

Use your home language to help you understand a word.
Use this strategy for children in Stages 2–5.

- Tell children that sometimes words in other languages sound like the same word in English. Knowing this may help them understand new words in English.
  Model The word *tren* is a Spanish word. What word does it sound like in English? That's right, it sounds like *train*. In Spanish, *tren* means *train*. So, a word in your home language that sounds the same as a new word in English may mean the same thing.
- Throughout the unit, encourage children to identify cognates in English with equivalents in their home languages.

Home-School Connection

When children have practiced manipulating the Student Version of the Manipulative Chart, send it home for them to practice with their family members.

You will need

- **Language Learning Master** pp. 13–14
- Crayons
- Scissors

Assessment

Record your observations of children on their individual assessment checklists for this unit. See page U51.

Concept Poster
Picture Cards 6–9, 11

Guided Reading

As you work on this unit, conduct small groups of guided reading or shared-to-guided reading independent of thematic instruction. Instruction is provided in the Guided Reading section of this guide.

Manipulative Chart: Student Version

- Have children color each of the seven airplane cards a different color and cut them out.
- Circulate to provide assistance as necessary. Encourage children to color and decorate their charts.
- Invite children to move their planes over their charts as you manipulate the plane with the Manipulative Chart. Have them "land" their labeled planes on the corresponding labeled areas of their charts. Lead them in calling out the name of that place in response to the question at the end of the chant.
- Have children respond to your Total Physical Response commands: *Fly your red plane to the United States.*
- Play Part 4 of the Oral Language Audio CD and model how children can manipulate their Student Versions as they sing along. Tell children that they will later be able to listen to the Audio CD and manipulate this mini-chart in the Listening Post.

WEEK 2 DAY 1

Concept Poster: Introduction

Setting the Scene

- Show Picture Card 6: apartment building. Say *Sometimes there are many homes in one apartment building.*
- Display Picture Card 8: house and Picture Card 11: farm. Explain what these cards show. Point to the house on Picture Card 11 and introduce *farmhouse.*
- Ask questions about Picture Cards 6, 8, and 11 to check comprehension, such as *What building is this? Is this a farmhouse or an apartment?*
- Encourage children to share what type of home they live in.

Creating Comprehensible Input

- Introduce Picture Card 6: apartment building and Picture Card 7: city. Direct children's attention toward the first line of photographs on the Concept Poster. Demonstrate how to talk through the relationship between the pictures with a think-aloud.
  Model *The first picture is an apartment building. Many different people live in this building. Let's follow the arrow to the next picture. It shows the neighborhood around the apartment building. The neighborhood has many buildings and cars close together. In the last picture, we get an even bigger view. This is the city where the neighborhood with all the buildings and cars are.*
- Recap this in simple language as you point at the pictures and connecting arrows: *The apartment building; The apartment building is in this neighborhood with many buildings and cars; This neighborhood is in the city.*
- Display Picture Card 9: suburb. Explain that a suburb is near a city. Invite a child in Stages 3, 4, or 5 to lead the class in talking through the pictures in the second row. Review key vocabulary, using the Picture Cards as necessary, to facilitate the discussion. Support with appropriate academic language.
- After the child has finished, recap in simple language, pointing to pictures and connecting arrows.

- Repeat the procedure for the third row. You might want to point out that neighborhoods can be very different from place to place. Some neighborhoods are all apartments, some are all houses, and some have different kinds of buildings.

Extending Oral Language

- Engage children in reviewing these concepts by asking questions. ◎

Options for STAGES

❶❷ Ask these children either/or questions that can be answered with one-word answers or by pointing, such as *Is the farm in the country or the city?*	❸❹❺ Ask these children open-ended questions that require substantive answers, such as *What is in the city? Where are the suburbs?*

- Use Total Physical Response commands to build familiarity with the concepts. For instance, *Point to the apartment building. Show me the city.*

Language Practice Game: Version 1 ❶❷❸❹❺

Preparing the Game

Tape copies of pages 18 and 19 of the Language Learning Masters to two facing sides of a file folder to give each game board some durability. Assemble one file folder game board for each group. Crumple a piece of aluminum foil into a small ball for each group. Position books around playing area.

Playing Version 1

Divide the class into heterogeneous groups of mixed language abilities with four children each. Provide each group with a game board. Give each player a set of TPR Cards for north, south, east, west, Canada, Mexico, and United States. Model the following directions.

1. Players place their TPR Cards faceup in front of them.
2. Players take turns rolling a foil ball onto the game board, trying to land in or near one of the labeled areas. ◎

Options for STAGES

❶❷ These children should be encouraged to say the name of the corresponding TPR Card, as they are able, when they turn it over.	❸❹❺ Encourage these children to make phrases or approximate sentences as they turn the card over: *in Canada* or *It landed in Canada.*

3. Players can only turn over one card at a time, even if the ball lands near two different labels, or a location qualifies as two places, such as the United States and the West. If a player lands where he or she has already landed, no card is turned over and it is then the next player's turn.
4. The first player to turn over all of his or her cards is the winner.

Component Organizer

Other Concept Poster lessons in this unit:
- Revisiting, p. U42

You will need

- **Language Learning Master** pp. 18–19
- File Folder
- Tape
- Foil ball
- TPR Cards

Component Organizer

Other Language Practice Game lessons in this unit:
- Version 2, p. U48

Assessment

Record your observations of children during the Language Practice Game on their individual assessment checklists for this unit. See page U51.

Newcomer Book: Small-Group Instruction

We Come from Everywhere

Written by Karen Clevidence

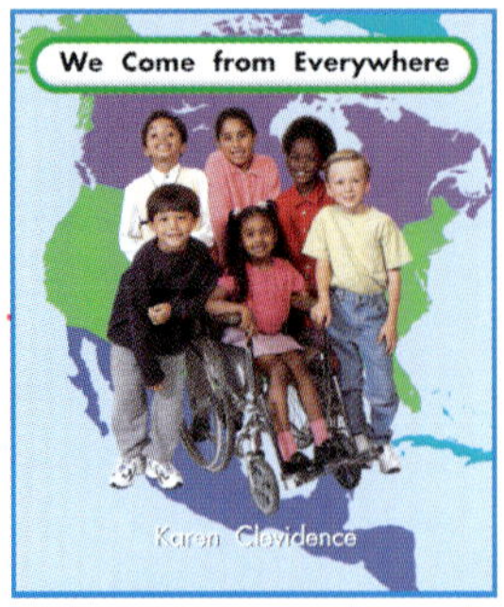

OVERVIEW *People come to the United States from the north, south, east, and west—from everywhere!*

The Newcomer Book is supported by the language of the Chant Poster and should be integrated into small-group instruction this week when children have had enough practice with vocabulary and concepts in this unit.

Language Pattern

I come from ________.

Text Vocabulary

cardinal directions, country names

Vocabulary Extenders

clothing

Reading the Text

Book Talk

- Work with a small group of four children at one time who exhibit similar literacy-learning behaviors.
- Engage children in a book talk as you flip through the pages of your copy of the book. ◎

Options for STAGES

1 2 Identify the names of the four directions and country names for these children. Encourage them to say the names after you as they are able.

3 4 5 Ask children to identify each direction and country as you encounter them in the text.

INSTRUCTIONAL PATHS

1 2 3 4 5 **All Readers:** Shared-to-Guided Reading	1 2 3 4 5 **Emergent Readers:** Guided Reading	1 2 3 4 5 **Early Readers:** Independent Reading no lesson provided

INDIVIDUAL READING

Shared-to-Guided Reading **3–4 sessions**

1 2 3 4 5 **All Readers**

1. Read the book to children.
   - Invite children to sit near you as you read a copy of the book. Begin with the cover and title page.
   - Turn to page 2 and begin reading the words as you point to them. Draw children's attention to the pictures.
2. Read the book with children.
   - Encourage children to follow along in their own copies of the book, turning the pages as you read together and using their own fingers to point to the words from left to right.
   - Invite children to chime in when they are comfortable.
   - Reread the book in this manner over several sessions.
3. Have children buddy read the book.
4. Invite children to read the book independently.

A Assess

- Did the children look at the pictures?
- Did the children point to each word with a finger as you read together?

Guided Reading **2 sessions**

1 2 3 4 5 **Emergent Readers**

1. Provide copies of the book to children. Use one child's book and turn to page 2. Introduce the book's pattern to children by reading the sentence and pointing to each word as you read *I come from the north.*
2. Have each child read at his or her own pace while remaining in the group. Discourage choral reading. Observe as they read.

A Assess

- Did the children look at the words from left to right?
- Did the children check the picture clue against the first letter to read a word?

REVISITING THE NEWCOMER BOOK

If children seem ready, you may also use the book to extend their knowledge of clothing by identifying these items in the photos.

WEEK 2 DAY 2

Big Book: Introduction

Are We There Yet?

Written by Patricia and Marisa Almada *Illustrated by Lindy Burnett*

OVERVIEW *Karina and Javier send postcards to their relatives in Nicaragua as their family makes their way from Texas to California by car. What will they see on their trip?*

Warming Up

Begin the lesson by revisiting the Manipulative Chart, Chant Poster, or a familiar Big Book. You may ask a volunteer to choose one.

Setting the Scene

- Display a world map. Hold Picture Card 1: plane over Nicaragua and identify *Managua, Nicaragua.* Slowly move the plane over the map from Managua to Houston, Texas, as you explain *This book is about a family that travels from Managua, Nicaragua, to Houston, Texas, in the United States.*
- Trace a route from Houston to Ventura, California. Say *From Houston, the family drives to Ventura, a city in California. They pass through other states on their trip.*
- Tap into children's prior knowledge. Ask *Have you ever been to any of these places? What did you see there? What do you know about these places?* Invite volunteers to share what they know about Texas, New Mexico, Arizona, or California.
- Look at the cover together and retrace the route the family takes from Houston to Ventura. Say *In this story, we will learn about places in the states between Texas and California. As we turn the pages, let's see what we learn about these places.*
- Make predictions about the book. *What do you think the family will see on their trip? What do you think the weather will be like?*

Reading the Text

- Read the title page. Tell children that this title is another way of saying *Is the trip finished?* Have children make an additional prediction. *Do you think the trip will seem long to Karina and Javier? Why?*
- As you read through the book, use a pointer or your finger to draw children's attention to the text. Point out items in the pictures to support your reading. You will return later to build children's understanding of the text. In future rereadings, children should be encouraged to chime in.
- If you have children in Stages 3, 4, or 5, pause after page 12 for a prediction of what they will see and do in the mountains.

Creating Comprehensible Input

- Open up the back flap of the book, which shows six postcards from the story in sequential order. Leave it open as you read to help build comprehension of the sequence of the text.
- Use the comprehension supports in the following chart to help you build comprehensible input with children at all Stages of Language Acquisition.

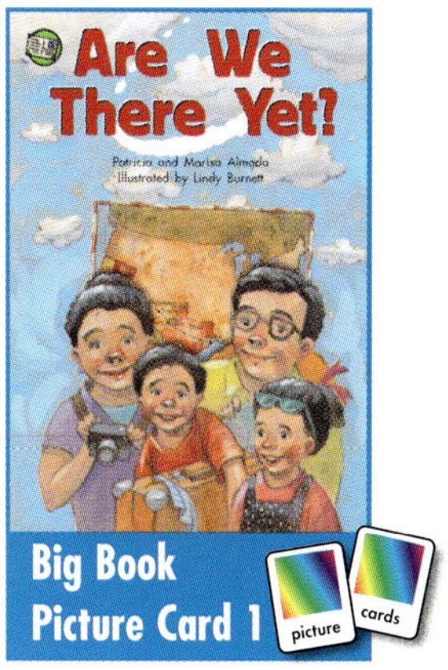

Component Organizer

Other Big Book lessons in this unit:

- Revisiting, p. U40
- Comprehension Strategy, p. U41
- Oral Language Development, pp. U43–U44
- Literacy Skills, p. U47

PAGE	IN THE STORY	COMPREHENSION SUPPORT
2	. . . plane landed . . .	gesture: plane landing with arms extended
2	. . . lots of skyscrapers . . .	point: to skyscrapers on page 4
2	. . . airport is busy . . . People are rushing . . .	explain: *airport* is where planes land; act out: rushing
4	. . . long drive to California.	trace route on cover, emphasizing long duration
6	. . . herding cows.	act out: herding cows together
6	. . . open space here in the country.	gesture: wide open space with sweeping motion
10	. . . outside of Albuquerque.	point: to outside of Albuquerque on map
10	It's a desert.	explain: desert is where it's dry and hot
12	. . . make blankets.	point: to blanket and gesture weaving
12	. . . west to the mountains!	trace: from Canyon de Chelly to Flagstaff on map
16	. . . from the country to the city.	explain: We grow things in the country to bring to the city
16	. . . working in fields and orchards.	explain: Fields are where we grow plants, and orchards are where we grow trees
18	. . . crowded highways.	explain: *Crowded highways* means big streets with lots of cars close together
22	. . . neighborhood . . .	explain: *neighborhood* is all the houses and stores near someone's home

WEEK 2 DAY 3

Theme Project: Newcomers Gallery

1. Divide the class into heterogeneous groups of mixed language abilities with four to five children each.
2. Tell children that they will make a "Newcomers Gallery." Each group will interview a newcomer to the United States and then display their work.
3. Choose subjects to interview. They may be people who have recently immigrated or have lived here for a long period of time. Interviewees may be found among the school staff, in children's families, or in your community.
4. Brainstorm a list of questions to ask. For example, *When did you come to the United States? Where did you come from? How did you get here? Have you always lived in your neighborhood? Where else have you lived? Which place do you like best? Why?* You can help a scribe write these questions. For each group, assign the roles of interviewer, scribe, photographers, and illustrators. Then assign the roles of researcher to children who will find information in an encyclopedia about where the newcomers are from.
5. Have available disposable cameras, tape recorders, drawing paper, and writing paper. At the interview, the interviewer asks questions while the scribe takes notes, and so on for other roles.
6. After the interviews, help children write about the interviewee using a word-processing program if available. They can glue their reports to one side of folded tagboard cards. On the other side, they can attach photos and drawings.
7. Guide children in arranging their displays.

You will need

- Disposable camera
- Tape recorder and cassette
- Paper
- Pens and crayons
- Tagboard
- Glue

Revisiting the Big Book

- Display the back flap of the book, which shows six postcards from the family's trip. Ask children to tell you about each card.
- Distribute six index cards to each child and have children make their own postcards of each place.
- Have partners practice retelling the story with their postcards. Invite volunteers in Stages 4 or 5 to retell the story for the class with their postcards.

WEEK 2 DAY 4

Big Book: Focus on Comprehension Strategy

Considers Author's Viewpoint, Purpose, and Style

1. Look at the cover of the Big Book and ask children if they remember who is telling the story. Flip through the book, noting who signs each postcard: Karina or Javier.
2. Confirm that the story is told by Karina and her brother Javier. Ask *How do they tell the story?* Point out the postcards and help children see that this story is told through the use of postcards.
3. Have children extend the story by writing one last postcard from either Karina or Javier. ◎

Options for STAGES

1 2 These children can simply draw a picture and perhaps label it. They can also sign the back of the card with *Karina* or *Javier*.	**3** Have these children write or dictate simple words and phrases for the message on the back of their cards. Allow for developmental spelling.	**4 5** Encourage these children to write complete sentences in their postcard messages.

Chant Poster: Focus on Oral Language Development

FUNCTION MINI-LESSON

Express Likes and Dislikes 1 2 3 4 5

1. Review how to make statements about likes and dislikes, which was introduced on Week 1 Day 5.
2. Point out your location in the United States on the Chant Poster. Say *This is where we live. There are some things I like here, but some things I don't like. I like all the trees, but I don't like the heat.*
3. Start a chart on the board with the headings "Like" and "Don't Like." Draw a smiling face next to "Like" and a frowning face next to "Don't Like." Ask children to tell you about things they like and don't like about where you live. Write their ideas on the chart, noting children's names next to each entry.
4. Make statements and ask questions using information from the chart, such as *Marlon likes his house, but he misses his grandmother. What does Olga like?*

FUNCTION MINI-LESSON

Evaluate 1 2 3 4 5

1. Engage children in a discussion about the reasons that people move to a new place. Have them evaluate reasons for moving, such as a house is too small, a parent gets a new job, or other reasons they suggest.
2. Record children's ideas in a list. Then have children evaluate reasons why they might like or not like to move. For example, a child might like to move to a new place if the child will have a bigger yard to play in.

Big Book

Assessment

Use a retelling of the Big Book to assess comprehension. Have children use the back flap for support. See page U51.

Chant Poster

Home Culture Sharing

Remember that some children may have moved to the United States as refugees. These children may or may not choose to share their reasons for moving.

Assessment

Record your observations of children during these mini-lessons on their individual assessment checklists for this unit. See page U51.

Language Learning Master

p.18 ❶❷❸❹❺

Shared Writing Card
Picture Cards 7, 9

You will need

- Shared Writing Card 2
- Wipe-off marker
- Regular marker
- Easel pad

Revisiting the Concept Poster

- Revisit the Concept Poster, inviting volunteers to talk you through the pictures as much as possible.
- Extend the activity by inviting children to tell about where they live (the city, suburbs, or country).

Grammar in Context: Subject Pronoun *they* ❶❷❸❹❺

1. Read the chant and have children clap when they hear *they*.
2. Reread the last sentence of the first stanza and the first sentence in the second stanza. With your finger, draw a circle around *People* and trace a line to *they*. Say *"They" here means* people.
3. Say *People come from so many places*. Then model the substitution *They come from so many places*.
4. Repeat with other sentences, such as *Karina and Javier live in Ventura*.

WEEK 2 DAY 5

Shared Writing Card: Introduction of Side A

Setting the Scene

- Use the back flap of the Big Book to review the sequence of events in *Are We There Yet?* Talk about what happened first, next, and last.
- Display Picture Card 9: suburb and Picture Card 7: city. Ask children what kinds of things a family from the suburbs might see on a trip to the city. Record their ideas on the board.

Creating Comprehensible Input

- Display Shared Writing Card 2 Side A, with illustrations of a suburban family's visit to the city inside a sequential graphic organizer. Begin by pointing to and describing individual activities.
  Model *Look, a family outside their house. This is a suburb. Oh look, a bus. Look at all the buildings. This is a big city. Here's a hot dog stand . . . and a fountain. Here's the bus back in the suburbs again.*
- Go back to the first illustration and use think-alouds to talk through the illustrations. Point to the illustrations one by one and trace the arrows with your finger.
  Illustration 1: *Here is a mother, a father, and their child. They live in the suburbs.*
  Illustration 2: *Now they are getting on a bus to go somewhere.*
  Illustration 3: *Here they are looking up at skyscrapers in the city.*
  Illustration 4: *They are buying hot dogs to eat.*
  Illustration 5: *Now they are taking a walk in the park. They see lots of different people and a fountain there.*
  Illustration 6: *They are getting off the bus now. They saw many things in the city.*
- Explain that the arrows on the Shared Writing Card help us to understand the order of events. Review sequence words as you point to the illustrations.

Scribing with the Graphic Organizer

- After children have become comfortable with the content of the illustrations, you can use the wipe-off marker provided to scribe while you brainstorm together labels for the graphic organizer. Since you are creating a graphic organizer, not a finished product, well-crafted sentences are not necessary.
- Think aloud as you write so that children have insight into the writing process.

- Here is an example of simple shared writing labeling for the illustrations.
  Illustration 1: *leave suburbs*
  Illustration 2: *take a bus to the city*
  Illustration 3: *look at skyscrapers*
  Illustration 4: *buy lunch at hot dog stand*
  Illustration 5: *look at fountain in the park*
  Illustration 6: *go back home*

Writing Together from the Graphic Organizer

- You will again be holding the pen while you work with children to create a shared writing piece together. This time, you will model how to use the labels from the graphic organizer to create a finished paragraph on your easel pad.
- Begin with a think-aloud.
  Model *We used* leave suburbs *for the first picture. That isn't a complete sentence. How can we make it a complete sentence? How about* The family leaves the suburbs. *We need to tell why they are leaving, too. How about this:* The family leaves the suburbs for a trip to the city.
- Write down the sentence you agree upon with children. Say the sentence aloud, pausing often as you write it, to reinforce natural phrases.
- As you move to the second illustration, read the label and the invite children to help you create the sentence based on the picture and label. Write down what children say. When children offer sentences with errors in them, correct them without being overt. Encourage children to use classroom resources, such as the Word Wall.
- When you have finished your shared writing piece, read it together several times. Then hang it up on the wall where it can be displayed during the rest of the unit and reread many times. For now, do not erase your labels on Side A.

Phonics in Context

Shared writing provides an ideal opportunity for reviewing the phonics skills children are learning. Highlight the sounds in words like *tr**ip*** and ***f**un* as you reread the writing.

Sample Shared Writing

The family leaves the suburbs for a trip to the city. They take a bus. First they look at tall skyscrapers. Then they buy lunch at a hot dog stand. After lunch they go for a walk in the park. They look at a fountain. At the end of the day, they take the bus back home. Their trip to the city was fun!

WEEK 3 DAY 1

Big Book: Focus on Oral Language Development

Reread the Big Book and return to the text to focus on oral language development.

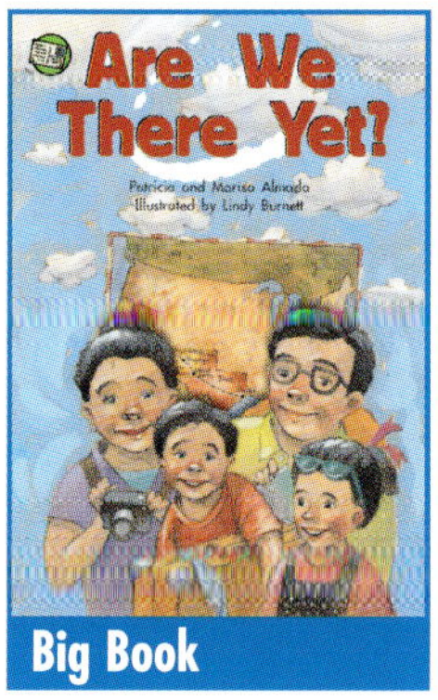

Grammar in Context: Adverbs—Time ❶❷❸❹❺

1. Point to a calendar and say, for example, *Today is Tuesday. Yesterday was Monday. Tomorrow will be Wednesday.* Point out that the words *yesterday, today,* and *tomorrow* tell what day things happen.
2. Model sentences about classroom activities, such as *Yesterday we read a story. Today we are having a spelling test. Tomorrow we will go on a trip.* Encourage children to provide their own phrases or sentences with time adverbs. ◎

Language Learning Master

p. 19 ❶❷❸❹❺

Options for STAGES

❶ These children may simply point to the appropriate day on the calendar in response to your sentences.	❷❸ These children may make statements about the past, present, and future, such as *Yesterday soccer, Today paint, Tomorrow home.*	❹❺ Encourage these children to use complete sentences in making statements about the past, present, and future.

3. Reread Big Book pages 6, 8, and 12, and ask questions, such as *When did the family see real cowboys?* to elicit answers using time adverbs.

Guided Reading

As you work on this unit, conduct small groups of guided reading or shared-to-guided reading independent of thematic instruction. Instruction is provided in the Guided Reading section of this guide.

Language Junction

Speakers of many languages tend to omit the *-ed* ending in the past tense. In addition, the pronunciation of *-ed* can be a problem because of its three possible forms: /d/, /t/, and /id/ and because of the resulting final consonant clusters (for example, /kt/ in *looked*). Some languages, like Arabic, do not have such clusters.

You will need

- Shared Writing Card 2
- Wipe-off marker

You will need

- U.S. map
- Marker
- Picture postcards, encyclopedias, travel brochures

Grammar in Context: Past Tense (1)(2)(3)(4)(5)

1. On the first page of the Big Book, point out the verb *landed.* Then, using Picture Card 1: plane, "land" the plane on the desk. After it lands, say *The plane landed.*
2. Point out the *-ed* at the end of *landed.* Explain that when an action is finished, we usually put *ed* at the end of the word.
3. Have children look through the Big Book for other regular past tense verbs with *ed.* Ask the children if they know other *ed* verbs.
4. Now go to page 2 and read the sentence with saw. Using gestures, explain that this is the verb *see* in the past tense. The action is finished. Tell children that some verbs don't have *ed* at the end for the past tense. Start a list of irregular verbs.
5. Go through the Big Book, adding all irregular verbs to the list: *went, rode, had,* and *met.*

WEEK 3 DAY 2

Shared Writing Card: Brainstorming Side B

Brainstorming a Topic

- Use Side A of the Shared Writing Card and your finished writing piece about the family's trip to the city. Review how you used the graphic organizer's pictures and labels to form the basis of your finished piece.
- Turn the card over to Side B. Tell children that you will now think of your own topic together to draw in the graphic organizer. Brainstorm a topic that involves going on a trip or outing. You can suggest a picnic, field trip, or even a trip to or from school.

Scribing with the Graphic Organizer

- Once the class has chosen a topic, you should decide together what the first drawing should show. Model how to draw the first picture. It should show the main character or characters getting ready to leave for their trip. Invite volunteers to draw subsequent scenes as the class decides on them. Continue drawing until the process is complete.
- Now elicit suggestions for labels and record them on the Shared Writing Card.
- You will create the shared writing paragraph together in the next session.

Active Social Studies: Where Will We Go?

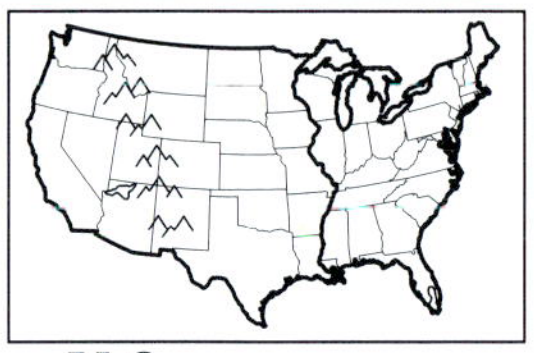

1. Display a U.S. map and mark the name of your city and state. Point out the locations of sites, such as the Grand Canyon, the Everglades, and Niagara Falls. Show pictures of these places in encyclopedias, postcards, and travel brochures.
2. Form four groups of children. Have each group plan a trip using a U.S. map.
3. Invite groups to tell about their trips—direction of travel, and states and sights.

Options for STAGES

(1) These children can draw the route on the group's map.	(2)(3) These children can give directions, such as *Go south to Everglades.*	(4)(5) These children can lead the group discussion and summarize for the class.

WEEK 3 DAY 3

Shared Writing Card: Writing Together with Side B

- As with Side A, you will scribe as you work together with children to create a finished writing piece from the graphic organizer on Side B of Shared Writing Card 2.
- Model writing from the first drawing, using think-alouds as you go. Show children how to use resources like the Word Wall. Work together to puzzle out difficult spellings or tricky passages.
- When you have finished your shared writing piece, read it together several times. Then hang it up on the wall where it can be displayed during the rest of the unit. At the end of the unit, you should erase both sides of the Shared Writing Card.

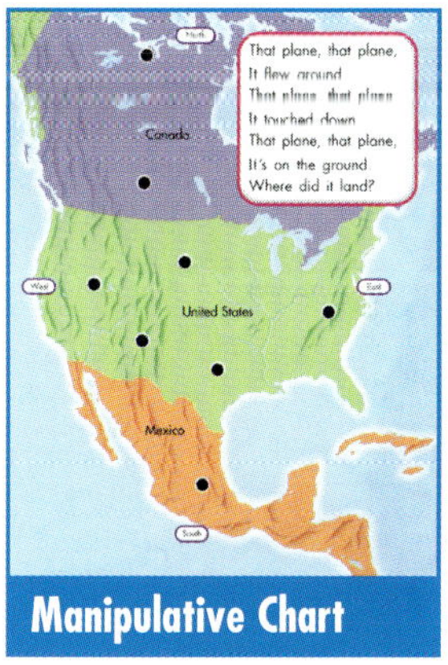

Manipulative Chart: Focus on Oral Language Development

Grammar in Context: Past Tense ❶❷❸❹❺

1. Move the plane piece over the map on the Manipulative Chart toward the west coast as you say *The plane is flying to the west.*
2. Attach the plane to a Velcro™ pad in the west and look at the class to emphasize that the action has been completed. Say *The plane flew to the west.* Children may want to chime in with you.
3. Repeat, as above, this time modeling the past tense of the verbal phrase *touch down,* inviting children to chime in with you.
4. Have children take turns flying the plane and saying an appropriate sentence with "fly" or "touch down" in the past tense after the action has been completed. ◎

Language Learning Master

p. 20 ❶❷❸❹❺

Options for STAGES

❶❷ These children can say *flew* or *touched down* as they are able.	❸ These children should be encouraged to say a few words, such as *plane land west.*	❹❺ Encourage these children to say complete sentences, such as *The plane landed in the west.*

WEEK 3 DAY 4

Active Science: Crystal Garden

You will need

- Water
- Pencil
- Salt
- Thread or string
- Glass jar
- Magnifying glass

1. Tell children that the "strange rocks" in the Big Book on pages 8 and 9 are a kind of crystal. Display a piece of rock candy (if available) to illustrate the shapes of crystals. Then create a crystal garden.
2. Fill a jar half full with warm water.
3. Stir salt into water until no more salt will dissolve.
4. Attach a thread or string to a pencil and hang it in the solution. Do not let the thread touch the bottom of the jar.
5. Leave at room temperature for at least a day.

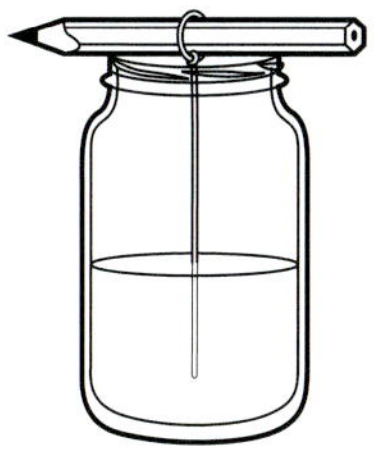

6. Observe your salt crystals each day. As the water evaporates, cubic salt crystals will form on the thread. Use a magnifying glass to examine the salt crystals.
7. Note the experiment steps and children's observations on chart paper. Then have children create their own drawings of the crystals.

WEEK 3 DAY 5

You will need

- Overhead transparency of Writing Resource Guide, p. 82
- Overhead marker

Writing Resource Guide: A Simplified Graphic Organizer

This activity is optional and only necessary if you wish to use the simplified sequence graphic organizer in cooperative-group or independent writing.

Brainstorming a Topic

- Review the drawings and labels you used on Side B of the Shared Writing Card. Trace the sequence of the pictures with your finger.
- On the overhead projector, display a transparency of Writing Planner B on page 82 of the Writing Resource Guide, which is a sequence graphic organizer with four boxes.
- Brainstorm together a simple topic that involves an outing or trip of some sort. The trip should have a clear beginning, middle, and end.

Scribing with the Graphic Organizer

- Once the class has chosen a topic, you should decide together what the different scenes might be. Model drawing the scenes in a logical order.
- Label all four drawings in your graphic organizer. Elicit suggestions for labels from the group in the same manner as you did with the Shared Writing Card.

You will need

- Writing Resource Guide, pp. 81–82
- Markers

Writing Resource Guide: Cooperative-Group Writing

- Form cooperative groups of heterogeneous Stages with three to four children each to work together on a writing piece using the graphic organizer. You may hand out a copy of Writing Planner A or B.
- Review the shared writing graphic organizers and finished pieces you have made together. Remind children that the drawings can help them remember the order—what happened first, next, and last.
- Have the groups work together first to complete their graphic organizers and then to construct finished pieces. Circulate to provide assistance. ◎

Options for STAGES

❶❷ These children should draw the pictures for the group.	❸❹❺ These children should take responsibility for the writing of the finished piece.

Writing Mini-lessons

See the Writing Resource Guide for mini-lessons to use as children write. Here are some suggestions:
- Mini-lesson 18: Naming Words
- Mini-lesson 19: Action Words

WEEK 4 DAY 1

Big Book: Focus on Literacy Skills

Word Level: Phonics in Context

1. You will need the Word Wall Starters with the postcard symbol on them: *ch__in__*, *f__un__*. These are pictured in the back of the Big Book.
2. Tell children that you want to choose some special words from the story for them to take a closer look at.
3. Introduce the word *chin* by saying it clearly, emphasizing the *in* sound, and drawing attention to the highlighting behind the *in*. Then say /in/-/in/-/in/. Say *The letters* i *and* n *together make the* in *sound. Let's say the word* chin *together:* chin. *Hear how* chin *ends with* in? *Let's sing a song together!* Review Phonics Song Chart 7 together.
4. Say *I'm going to put the word* chin *below the* short i *label.* Walk to your Word Wall and place the card *chin* under the *short i* label, taking care to group word families together. Remind children that they can use the postcard symbol to help them remember where they "met" that word before.
5. Repeat a similar procedure for the other word and phonics skill.

Guided Reading

As you work on this unit, conduct small groups of guided reading or shared-to-guided reading independent of thematic instruction. Instruction is provided in the Guided Reading section of this guide.

Sentence Level: Distinguishing Fact from Opinion

1. Reread page 2 of the Big Book. Tell children *Some of these sentences tell about things that are true and can be proved. They are facts. Some sentences tell what Karina thinks, feels, or believes. They are Karina's opinions.*
2. Reread the sentence *It's a big city.* Say *This sentence is true. It's a fact.* Then read the sentence *The United States is an exciting place!* Say *This is an opinion. Karina __thinks__ it is true, but someone else might not think the same way.*
3. As you continue to read the Big Book, provide a few more examples of facts and opinions. Then ask children to determine whether other sentences are facts or opinions.
4. Encourage children in Stages 4 or 5 to create their own sentences and ask partners to tell if the sentence is a fact or an opinion.

Text Level: Comparing and Contrasting Plot, Settings, and Characters

1. Review the main events of the Big Book by displaying the back flap and asking children to tell what they remember about each of the scenes shown. Tell children that the things that happen in a story are the plot, or story problem.
2. Ask children where this story takes place (Texas, Arizona, New Mexico, and California). Tell children that these places are the setting of the story.
3. Ask children about the people in the story. *Who wrote the postcards? Who else is in the story?* Tell children that these are the characters.

Home-School Connection

Send home page 27 of the Home-School Connection Masters for children to use in retelling *Are We There Yet?* to their families. They should retell the story in English and then talk about it in either English or their home language.

4. Have children help you create a story chart. Write column headings *Plot, Setting,* and *Characters* and add children's responses. ◎

Options for STAGES

❶❷ These children can point to scenes in the Big Book and give one-word responses to help you fill out the chart.

❸❹❺ Encourage children at these Stages to use complete sentences, such as *Karina and Javier are characters in the story.*

5. Ask students to think about another familiar story. Then have them complete a story chart for this story. Discuss the similarities and differences in plots, settings, and characters of the two stories.

You will need

- TPR Cards

Language Practice Game: Version 2

Divide children in Stages 3, 4, and 5 into groups and give each group three sets of TPR Cards. The first pile should have 6 buses and 6 planes in random order. The second pile should have four cards each of the mountain, river, and ocean cards, in random order. The third pile has two each of the United States, Mexico, north, south, east, and west cards, also in random order. Then model these directions.

1. Each player draws one card from each pile and says a sentence with the pattern *I went to a mountain in Mexico by plane*. The player then goes on to say *I like/don't like mountains/planes*. This provides practice with the language function *Express Likes and Dislikes*.
2. Other team players check and confirm that the first sentence corresponds with the cards. If the other players agree that it corresponds with the cards, the player keeps the cards. If they do not agree, the player loses those cards.
3. Play continues until the cards are all used up. The player with the most cards wins.

WEEK 4 DAY 2

You will need

- U.S. maps and mileage charts
- Paper
- Pens and highlighters

Active Math: Road Mileage

1. Provide U.S. maps and mileage charts to heterogeneous groups of mixed language ability. First find your location on the map, then choose a destination. Ask children how many miles they think it is to the destination.
2. Demonstrate how to use the chart by tracing the row and column that the two cities are in until they meet at the trip mileage. Compare the actual mileage to children's predictions.
3. Have each group choose a city on the chart that they would like to visit. Tell them to locate it on the map and then use a highlighter to connect your town with that city. Then have them find the trip mileage. Provide assistance as needed.
4. Write the mileage for each trip on the board. Work together to determine which trip is the shortest and which is the longest. Challenge children to find a mileage sign in their community and share the information.

Mileage Chart	Atlanta	Boston	Chicago
Atlanta		1079	714
Boston	1079		983
Chicago	714	983	

End-of-Unit Assessment

- While children are engaged in activities this week, pull them individually for the Big Book retelling, using page U51 at the end of this unit.
- Select a number of children with whom you would like to use the Open-Ended Oral Language Assessment on pages U50–U51 of this unit and pull them individually during activities this week. We recommend assessing about one-fourth of your class each unit.
- You should also have gathered the following for their assessment portfolio:
  - page 21 of the Language Learning Masters
  - page 22 of the Language Learning Masters
  - finished writing piece assessed according to the Writing Rubric on page A6.

You will need

A copy of page U51 at the end of this unit for each child

WEEK 4 DAY 3–4

Writing Resource Guide: Individual Writing

- Children have engaged in a step-by-step writing process moving toward independence. They began with teacher-led writing, moved to cooperative groups, and are now ready to work individually.
- Provide a copy of writing planner A or B to each child. They may need individual conferencing on choosing a topic.

You will need

- Writing Resource Guide, pp. 81–82
- Markers

Options for STAGES

1 2 and Emergent Level
These children should draw the sequential scenes in their graphic organizer. They should label pictures on their own or dictate labels to you.

3 4 5 Early Level and Above
These children should also use drawings and labels on the graphic organizer to record their topic. They should then use the graphic organizer to create a finished piece.

- When children have arrived at the finished product, whether graphic organizer or paragraph, you should assess it using the Writing Rubric on page A6 of this Teacher's Guide.

Assessment

Continue pulling some children for the Big Book Retelling and Open-Ended Oral Language Assessment as others write.

WEEK 4 DAY 5

Theme Project: Sharing

- Have children arrange their newcomer reports and portraits in various locations around the classroom. Ask for volunteers to be "docents." Have them practice giving guided tours around the "Newcomers Gallery." Invite children from other classes to visit the gallery for guided tours. If possible, you may want to invite the interviewees to share details about the items on exhibit.
- After the presentations, allow time for questions and feedback from the class. Model appropriate feedback for the presenters by making the first comment yourself—for example, *Galia, your drawings told me so much about the person you interviewed. Next you might want to try to write some words about each picture.*

Open-Ended Oral Language Assessment Reassess children's Language Acquisition Stages. Begin with an open-ended prompt like the first one below. If children are unable to respond, intervene with increasingly directed prompts, such as the second and third ones below.

What can you tell me about the picture?

What places do you see on the map?

I see Mexico. Show me the United States.

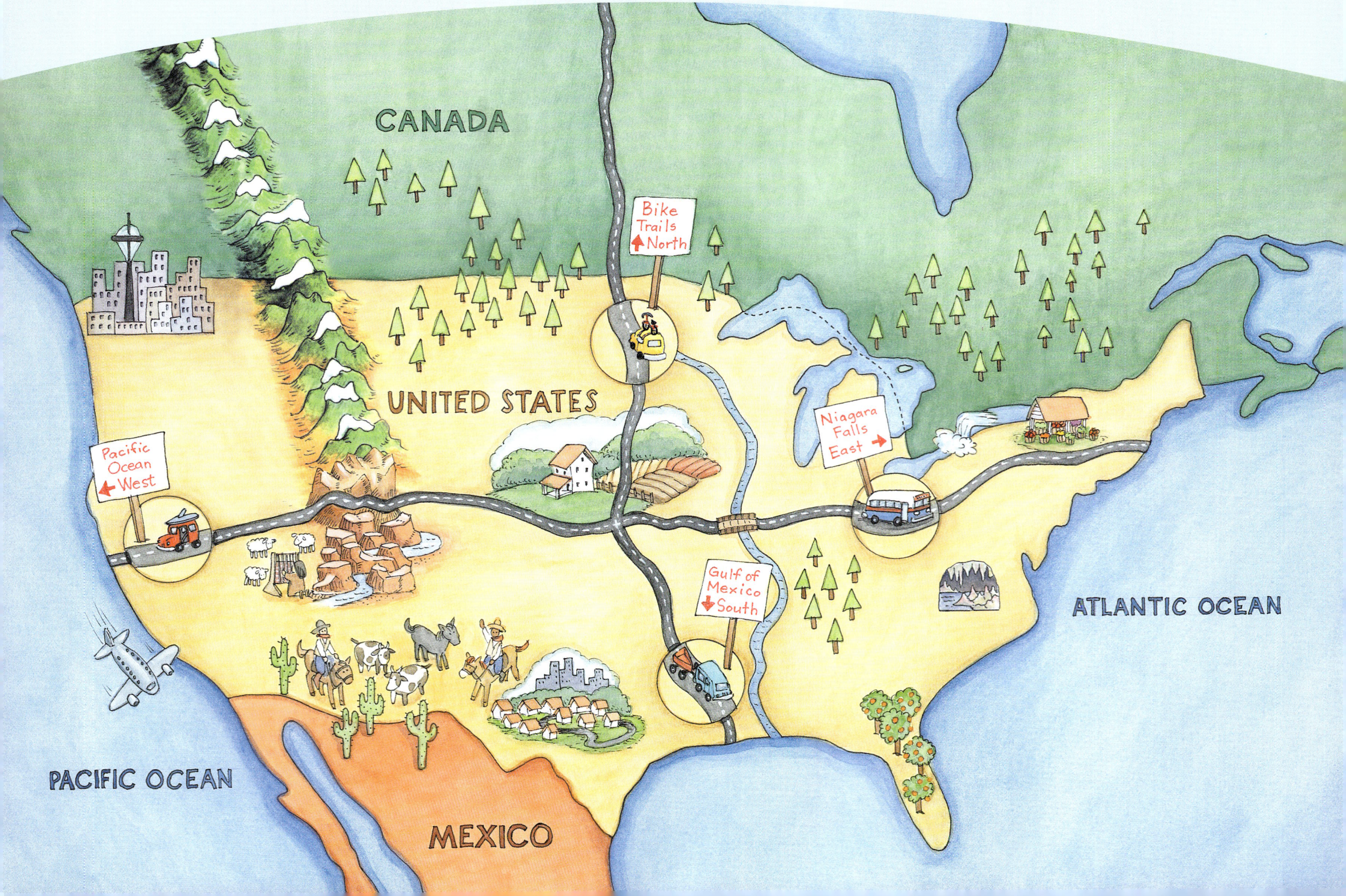

Assessment Directions: Copy this form for each child and place the completed form in the child's portfolio. Locate the child's Language Acquisition Stage for each of the first four activities and assess his or her performance during the unit according to expectations for that Stage. For the Big Book Retelling, pull children to retell the Big Book during end-of-unit assessment time. Use the Open-Ended Oral Language Assessment to reassess children's Language Acquisition Stages with one-fourth of your students for each unit, using the back side of the sheet to take notes. *For more guidance on assessment, see pages T33 and T34.*

Unit 2 Assessment

Name ____________________ **Date** ____________

On Our Way to English Grade 2	STAGE EXPECTATIONS ❶	❷	❸	❹	❺
Fluency Manipulative Chart: Student Version, page U36 *How does the child respond when manipulating the mini-chart along with the Oral Language Audio CD?*	Shows the correct answers. ☐ Yes ☐ Not yet	Shows the correct answers, naming the direction or country name. ☐ Yes ☐ Not yet	Shows the correct answers, approximating sentences and substitutions. ☐ Yes ☐ Not yet	Shows the correct answers, singing the verse with few, if any, errors. ☐ Yes ☐ Not yet	
Content Area Knowledge Language Practice Game: Version 1, page U37 *How does the child demonstrate an understanding of places and directions?*	Turns over the appropriate card, naming the item as he or she is able. ☐ Yes ☐ Not yet		Turns over the appropriate card and uses phrases or complete sentences, such as *In Canada* or *It landed in the north.* ☐ Yes ☐ Not yet		
Social Language Function Express Likes and Dislikes, page U41 *How does the child respond during the Function Mini-Lesson?*	Answers yes/no questions, such as *Do you like the weather here?* ☐ Yes ☐ Not yet		Approximates a sentence, such as *like school.* ☐ Yes ☐ Not yet	Responds with a phrase or complete sentence, such as *I like my house in the United States.* ☐ Yes ☐ Not yet	
Academic Language Function Evaluate, page U41 *How does the child respond during the Mini-Lesson?*			Participates in the discussion using simple words and phrases, such as *more for job.* ☐ Yes ☐ Not yet	Participates in the discussion using complete sentences to express thoughts and ideas. ☐ Yes ☐ Not yet	
Big Book Retelling page U41 *Have children use index cards to make their own postcards of the places shown on the back flap (page 40). How does the child retell the story?*	Puts each card in sequential order, naming the places as he or she is able. ☐ Yes ☐ Not yet		Puts each card in sequential order, using key words and phrases to tell about each place. ☐ Yes ☐ Not yet	Retells using complete sentences in connected discourse with few errors. ☐ Yes ☐ Not yet	Retells using story language similar to native-speaking peers. ☐ Yes ☐ Not yet
Open-Ended Oral Language Assessment, page U50 *Use the child's responses to the illustration to reassess the child's Stage of Language Acquisition.*	☐ **STAGE ❶** Uses few or no words; gestures or points.	☐ **STAGE ❷** Uses words or short phrases.	☐ **STAGE ❸** Uses phrases and simple sentences.	☐ **STAGE ❹** Uses sentences in connected discourse.	☐ **STAGE ❺** Uses language comparable to native-speaking peers.

UNIT 3

Circle of Life

OVERVIEW *This theme focuses on building an understanding of the growth cycle. The unit begins with the human growth cycle and then bridges to animals.*

Unit Components

Manipulative Chart

Chant Poster

Concept Poster

Newcomer Book

Determining the Purpose

Oral Language Development

Focus on Functions

Social Context:
Wish and hope ❶❷❸❹❺
Academic Context:
Compare ❶❷❸❹❺

Focus on Grammar

- Comparative and Superlative
- Infinitives
- Adjectives
- Possessives with *'s*

Comprehension Strategy

- Asks questions to clarify meaning

Literacy Skills

- **Word Level:** Phonics in context: short *e*, short vowels with *ck*, short vowels with *ll*
- **Sentence Level:** Labels
- **Text Level:** Time lines

Content Area Objectives

- Identifies physical characteristics of humans and animals
- Understands the life cycle
- Relates how healthful foods help us grow

Language Learning Strategy

- Listen for parts you know.

Writing Skill

- Uses a graphic organizer to show a cycle

Unit at a Glance

	DURING THE WEEK	DAY 1
Week 1	**Small-Group Instruction:** • Guided Reading • Shared-to-Guided Reading **Phonics Focus:** short *e* Phonics Song Chart 10, pp. P24–P25	**Manipulative Chart:** Introduction with Audio CD p. U55
Week 2	**Small-Group Instruction:** • Guided Reading • Shared-to-Guided Reading • Newcomer Book **Phonics Focus:** *et* and *ed* word families Phonics Song Chart 11, pp. P26–P27	**Concept Poster:** Introduction p. U60 **Language Practice Game:** Version 1 p. U61
Week 3	**Small-Group Instruction:** • Guided Reading • Shared-to-Guided Reading • Newcomer Book **Phonics Focus:** *ick* and *ack* word families Phonics Song Chart 12, pp. P28–P29	**Big Book:** Oral Language Development p. U67
Week 4	**Small-Group Instruction:** • Guided Reading • Shared-to-Guided Reading • Newcomer Book **Phonics Focus:** *ill* and *ell* word families Phonics Song Chart 13, pp. P30–P31	**Big Book:** Literacy Skills p. U71 **Language Practice Game:** Version 2 p. U72

STAGES ❶ Preproduction ❷ Early Production ❸ Speech Emergence ❹ Intermediate Fluency ❺ Advanced Fluency

Oral Language Audio CD

Picture Cards

Shared Writing Card

Big Book with Audio CD and Small Book

Home-School Connection Masters

Writing Resource Guide

Language Learning Masters

DAY 2	DAY 3	DAY 4	DAY 5
Manipulative Chart: Gestures and Manipulative Fun p. U56	**Chant Poster:** Introduction p. U57	**TPR Cards:** Introduction p. U58	**Manipulative Chart:** Oral Language Development Student Version p. U59
Big Book: Introduction p. U63	**Theme Project:** From Young to Old and Old to Young, p. U64 **Big Book:** Revisiting p. U64	**Big Book:** Comprehension Strategy p. U65 **Chant Poster:** Oral Language Development p. U65	**Shared Writing Card:** Introduction of Side A p. U66 **Concept Poster:** Revisiting p. U66
Shared Writing Card: Brainstorming Side B p. U68 **Active Science:** Butterfly Beginnings p. U69	**Shared Writing Card:** Writing Together with Side B p. U69 **Manipulative Chart:** Oral Language Development p. U69	**Active Social Studies:** Life Stages p. U70	**Writing Resource Guide:** A Simplified Graphic Organizer Cooperative-Group Writing p. U70
Active Math: Measure Up! p. U72 **Assessment** p. U73	**Writing Resource Guide:** Individual Writing p. U73 **Assessment** p. U73	**Writing Resource Guide:** Individual Writing p. U73 **Assessment** p. U73	**Theme Project:** Sharing p. U73

Center Activities

You will need

- Balance scale
- Food items
- Pictures of animal life cycles
- Paper plates
- Personal photo albums

CENTERS

Number Nook

Provide a variety of healthful foods, such as nuts, an orange, a box of pasta, and a can of tuna. Also provide a balance scale. Invite children to use the balance scale to compare the weights of food items.

Artist's Studio

Provide pictures of animal life cycles, such as butterfly and frog. Also provide paper plates. Have children choose an animal and draw each stage of its life cycle around the edge of the plate.

Content Corner

Bring in a family photo album. Point out photos of yourself and your family members as babies, teenagers, adults, and grandparents. Invite children to bring in their own family pictures and add them to the center.

Listening Post

After introducing each element in class, children may revisit the Manipulative Chart and Chant Poster on the Oral Language Audio CD. If you include a laminated copy of the Manipulative Chart Student Version, children can manipulate it as they sing to Part 4 of the CD (with blanks). Children may also listen to *A Pocketful of Opossums* on the Big Book Audio CD while following along in the small copy.

Language Workshop

Any time they are not in use, place the Picture Cards for the unit in this center. Encourage children to review the names of the animals and the people with each other for additional practice. After introducing the Language Practice Game in class, add the game board and TPR Cards to the center for independent group play.

Writer's Den

Establish a journal writing center with prompts to spark children's writing. Change the prompt every two weeks:

- Plan a meal for your family. Make a list of foods.
- How have you changed since you were five years old?

Children should be encouraged to draw pictures to support their writing. Provide blank Writing Planners in center materials for prewriting.

More Books

- *Biggest, Strongest, Fastest* by Steve Jenkins (Houghton Mifflin Co., 1997)
- *Changes* by Marjorie N. Allen and Shelley Rotner (Simon & Schuster Children's Books, 1991)
- *Waiting for Wings* by Lois Ehlert (Harcourt, 2001)
- *Oliver's Vegetables* by Vivian French (Orchard Books, 1995)

WEEK 1 DAY 1

Manipulative Chart: Introduction with Audio CD

Sung to the tune of "Farmer in the Dell"

Setting the Scene

- Use simple language to talk about growing up and changing. Show Picture Card 1: baby. Use gestures such as cradling and rocking arms to ask each child if there is a baby at home. Children may indicate by nodding or shaking their heads.
- Continue talking and gesturing with Picture Cards 2–5: child, teenager, adult, grandparent. For example, point to a child for Picture Card 2: child, or point to yourself for Picture Card 4: adult.
- Display Picture Cards 1–5: baby, child, teenager, adult, grandparent. Discuss each life stage with children. ◎

Options for STAGES

❶ These children can answer either/or questions, such as *Is this the baby or the adult?*	❷❸ Shuffle Picture Cards 1–5. Model arranging the cards in order from youngest to oldest. Then have these children arrange and name the cards in order.	❹❺ Have these children say what each person becomes next, such as *A baby becomes a child.*

Creating Comprehensible Input

- Point to each photo in the background. Tell children who it is.
- Read the text, pausing often, as you use gestures, pointing, and other techniques to make the chant comprehensible.

Look at the baby	point to the baby
Use her arms to crawl.	point to arms; make crawling gestures
She is growing older	stretch arms up
Each and every day.	point to school calendar, touching each day
The baby becomes a child,	trace finger from crawling baby to girl in the family photo
Then a teenager as she grows tall.	trace finger from girl to teenager
She becomes an adult soon,	trace finger from teenager to adult
Then a grandparent last of all.	trace finger from adult to grandparent

Guided Reading

As you work on this unit, conduct small groups of guided reading or shared-to-guided reading independent of thematic instruction. Instruction is provided in the Guided Reading section of this guide.

Component Organizer

Other Manipulative Chart lessons in this unit:

- Gestures and Manipulative Fun, p. U56
- Oral Language Development and Student Version, pp. U59–U60
- Oral Language Development, p. U69

Real-World Touch

Invite children to try on clothing and use props, such as dolls, to role-play growing up and changing. Place these in the Content Corner for creative play.

Home-School Connection

Choose one of the versions of the parent letter to send home with each child, according to the child's home language (pages 28–35 in the Home-School Connection Masters). Also send home the activity on page 36.

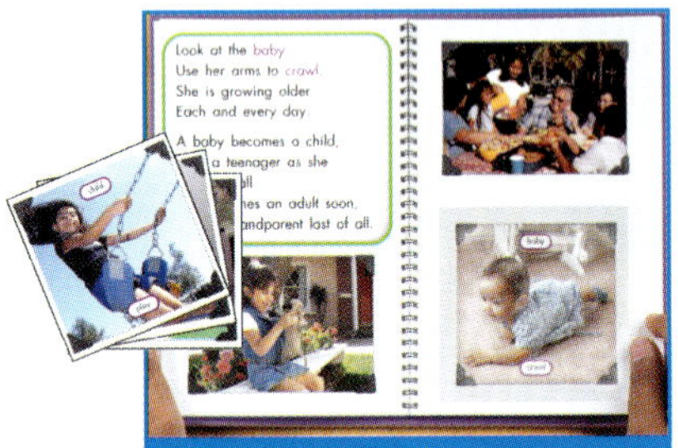

Manipulative Chart

Journal Writing Reminder

Children should be writing in their journals during the course of the unit. This allows children to reflect on their own observations in a non-threatening way. See Writer's Den for suggested journal prompts.

Introducing the Audio CD

- Play Part 1 of the Oral Language Audio CD, the spoken song, as you say the song and track the print on the Manipulative Chart with your finger or a pointer. Replay Part 1 several times, encouraging children to chime in whenever they can.
- Introduce the song by playing the song at natural speed, Part 2 of the Audio CD, to help children get a feel for the song. Allow the Audio CD to continue playing through Part 3, the song at instructional pace. Track the print as the Audio CD plays. Repeat Part 3 again, this time singing along, making clear lip movements without exaggerating. Revisit Part 3 several times to help children learn the song.

WEEK 1 DAY 2

Manipulative Chart: Gestures and Manipulative Fun

Gesturing the Song

Introduce these simple gestures to accompany the song:

Look at the baby	act out cradling and rocking
Use her arms to crawl.	bend down; gesture crawling
She is growing older	hold hand one ft., then two ft. from ground
Each and every day.	count with fingers on left hand
The baby becomes a child,	act out cradling; point to children
Then a teenager as she grows tall.	hold hand over a child's head
She becomes an adult soon,	point to yourself
Then a grandparent last of all.	give self hug

Manipulating the Chart

- Show children how to add pictures to the pocket. The items on the pocket pictures can be substituted for the words in purple. Slide the *child/play* picture into the pocket and sing the verse, emphasizing using *child* and *play* instead of *baby* and *crawl* each time they appear in the song.
- Play Part 4 of the Oral Language Audio CD while you say *child* in the blank spaces.
- Continue introducing and identifying the people in each picture as children place different cards in the pocket.
- Invite volunteers to place different cards in the pocket for the class as you sing the verse together or practice Total Physical Response commands, such as *Find the card that shows a teenager. Put it in the pocket.*
- Invite children to help you create new gestures for the people and actions on the cards.
- You can revisit this activity many times during the unit.

WEEK 1 DAY 3

Chant Poster: Introduction

Setting the Scene

- Display Picture Card 6: food. Say the word and allow children to repeat it. Then display a variety of plastic foods and packaged foods. Invite volunteers to call out names of foods they see. Ask children to point to or name those foods they eat for breakfast, lunch, or dinner.
- Help children understand that they need to eat healthful foods to grow big and strong. Say *We are going to learn about how foods help us grow big and strong. What foods do you like to eat?* Encourage children to point to displayed foods or Picture Card 6, or to name their favorite foods and tell why they like them. ◎

Options for STAGES

❶❷ Invite these children to name other foods from their home cultures.

❸❹❺ These children can tell, as they are able, what their favorite foods are.

Creating Comprehensible Input

- Displaying the Chant Poster, point to and name the different foods, making comparisons to Picture Cards, as appropriate.
- Read the text, pausing often, as you use gestures, pointing, and other techniques to make the chant comprehensible.

I want to be healthy.	point to self, then stand tall and smile
I want to be strong.	point to self, then make muscles with both arms
I eat the right foods	chew and rub stomach
To help me live long.	march in place
I like to eat well	point to self, then chew and rub stomach
Every day, every night,	lift arm up to show sun; hands together at head to show sleep
So my eyes and my ears	point to eyes, then point to ears
And my body work right!	gesture to whole body

Chanting the Poster

- Encourage children to join in as you chant the rhyme together several times. You may wish to divide the groups into boys and girls and alternate lines.
- Introduce the chant on the Oral Language Audio CD as you and children move to the rhythm of the chant. Tell them they can listen to it on their own later at the Listening Post.

Chant Poster
Picture Card 6

Component Organizer

Other Chant Poster lessons in this unit:
- Oral Language Development, pp. U65–U66

- Practice saying the chant, encouraging the children to join in with the rhythm by clapping or tapping out the beat.
- Revisit the chant often. You can increase the volume and the speed of the chant.

WEEK 1 DAY 4

You will need

- **Language Learning Master** p. 23
- Scissors

TPR Cards: Introduction

Introducing the Cards with Total Physical Response

- Provide one copy of page 23 of the Language Learning Masters to each child. Have children color and cut out the cards.
- Introduce a few cards at a time by holding them up one by one and saying the words clearly. Select first the words which have already been introduced in previous activities.
- Ask children to pick up the correct card as you call out the word. Model the desired outcome. Add one card at a time and review in a game-like atmosphere. Children may want to say the word as they pick up the card.
- Now invite children to respond to your full-sentence commands, such as *Point to the baby. Pick up the adult.*
- Assign partners so you can add commands like *Give the adult to Kim.*
- As children increase their familiarity with the TPR Cards and the game, add funny commands, such as *Put the cub on your nose.*
- Invite volunteers in Stages 3, 4, or 5 to give commands to their classmates.
- Extend language to discuss life cycles.

Options for STAGES

❶❷ Invite these children to group same species cards together, naming each card as they are able.

❸❹❺ Have these children make a sentence based the TPR Cards, such as *A chick becomes a chicken.*

- Repeat this activity several times throughout the unit.

Grammar in Context: Comparative and Superlative ❶❷❸❹❺

1. Display three familiar small objects of varying sizes, such as an eraser, small scissors, and a pencil. Ask children to look carefully at the objects and think about their sizes. Using gestures, ask *Are these things big or small?* Model, then tell children *Put the objects in order of small, smaller, smallest.*
2. Repeat the words *small, smaller, smallest* and add *big, bigger, biggest*, using gestures to show differences.
3. Continue with other sets of classroom objects. Have volunteers arrange them and compare their size, length, and height.
4. Use a similar procedure with the TPR Cards. Have children arrange sets of cards in order of *small, smaller, smallest* and *big, bigger, biggest,* such as *cub, chick, tadpole.*

WEEK 1 DAY 5

Manipulative Chart: Focus on Oral Language Development

FUNCTION MINI-LESSON

Wish and Hope ❶❷❸❹❺

Props: Newspaper or magazine pictures of people in careers.

1. Invite Stage 3, 4, or 5 children to join you while others play games with the TPR Cards.
2. As you think aloud, model a statement that expresses a wish. *Hmm . . . I wish that I could go swimming today.* Explain that *wish* means almost the same as *want.*
3. Ask *What do you wish?* Have volunteers answer in a similar fashion.
4. Refer to the Manipulative Chart. Point to the child. Explain that sometimes children hope to have a special job when they grow up. Ask *What to do you hope to be when you grow up?*
5. Have children select pictures of what they want to be, make statements about the pictures, and place them in the pocket of the Manipulative Chart.

FUNCTION MINI-LESSON

Compare ❶❷❸❹❺

1. Draw a T-chart on the board. Label one side "Same" and the other side "Different."
2. Select two children. Model as you gesture and point to different physical features. *Monica's eyes are blue. She has long hair. Carmen has blue eyes, too. Her hair is short.* Write what is the same or different about each child in the appropriate column.
3. Choose two different pictures from the Manipulative Chart. Invite children to identify the people. Ask *Does she have blue eyes? Who is older?* Stage 1 or 2 children can point to the correct picture. Help children identify and describe the pictures.
4. Continue with other comparisons as appropriate (*smaller, shorter, younger*).

Grammar in Context: Comparative ❶❷❸❹❺

1. Remind children how they compared Monica to Carmen. Invite children to name the features that were compared (eyes, hair).
2. Then ask a volunteer to stand next to you and tell or show his or her age. Say *Van is 7. He is a child. He is young.* Indicate yourself and say *I am an adult. I am older than Van.*
3. Point to and identify the child on the Manipulative Chart. Then point to an older person on the chart and ask, for example, *Who is older: the child or the teenager?* Model the response *The teenager is older.*
4. Continue pointing to other people on the chart. Ask other comparison questions. ◎

Manipulative Chart

Language Learning Strategy

Listen for parts you know.
Use this strategy for children in Stages 2–5.

- Explain to children that they can learn the meaning of a sentence by listening to parts of the sentence that are familiar. This is called listening for parts you know.

  Model *Let's do some writing. Take out a piece of paper and a pencil. Hmm . . . What if you aren't sure what I said? Think about words you know. Maybe you know* paper *and* pencil*. That would help you know what I was talking about.*
- As you continue the unit, encourage children to listen for parts of a sentence they already know. That will help when they need to learn the meaning of something that is being said.

You will need

- **Language Learning Master** p. 26 ❶❷❸❹❺

Home-School Connection

When children have practiced manipulating the Manipulative Chart Student Version, send it home for them to practice with their family members.

Options for STAGES

❶❷ These children may respond to the comparison questions by pointing or with one-word responses, such as *teenager.*

❸❹❺ Encourage these children to respond to the comparison questions with phrases or complete sentences, such as *teenager older* or *The teenager is older.*

5. Have children raise their hands every time they hear the word *older* as you sing the song together.

You will need

- **Language Learning Master** pp. 21–22
- Scissors

Manipulative Chart: Student Version

- Have children color the pages. Then model cutting the pages according to the directions, as you provide assistance.
- Have children keep their small pictures in an envelope.
- Invite children to lay their pictures one on top of the other to match the picture you slide into the pocket as you say different words in the song.
- Have children respond to your Total Physical Response commands: *Show me the baby.*
- Play Part 4 of the Oral Language Audio CD and model how children can manipulate their Student Versions as they sing along. Tell children that they will later be able to listen to the Audio CD and manipulate this mini-chart in the Listening Post.

A Assessment

Record your observations of children on their individual assessment checklists for this unit. See page U75.

WEEK 2 DAY 1

Concept Poster: Introduction

Concept Poster
Picture Cards 1–4, 7–11

Setting the Scene

- Display Picture Cards 1–4: baby, child, teenager, adult. Ask children to identify what they see. Discuss that babies grow and become children, then teenagers, and later adults.
- Shuffle the four Picture Cards and invite volunteers to arrange them in order.
- Say *Other living things can have babies that grow, too.*

Creating Comprehensible Input

- Revisit Picture Cards 1–4: baby, child, teenager, adult. Direct children's attention to the first row of photographs on the Concept Poster. Trace with your finger as you tell how living things change over time.

  Model *This is a baby lion—a cub. This arrow tells me that this picture goes with the next one on the right. Now the cub is bigger. I follow the arrow to the right and see a young lion. The cub has grown into a lion. When I follow the arrow again, I see the young lion has grown up to become a full-grown lion.*
- Recap this in simple language as you trace the connecting arrows: *a cub; The cub is growing; a young lion; The lion is now full-grown.*
- Display Picture Card 7: chicken eggs. Ask children if they remember what these are called. Continue with Picture Card 8: chicken. Reinforce the concept of change by moving from left to right as you point to the two Picture Cards.

Guided Reading

As you work on this unit, conduct small groups of guided reading or shared-to-guided reading independent of thematic instruction. Instruction is provided in the Guided Reading section of this guide.

- Invite a child in Stage 3, 4, or 5 to lead the class in talking through the pictures in the second row. As necessary, review the concept of growth and change (child to adult) from the Manipulative Chart. Support with appropriate academic language.
- After the child has finished, recap in simple language, pointing to the pictures and the connecting arrows.
- Repeat the procedure for the third and fourth rows, providing support with Picture Cards 9–11: tadpole, frog, and frog eggs for the third row.

Extending Oral Language

- Engage children in reviewing these concepts by asking questions. ◎

Options for STAGES

❶❷ Ask these children specific questions that require only naming or pointing, such as *What does a chick grow up to be?*	❸❹❺ Ask these children open-ended questions that require substantive answers, such as *Tell me about the chick.*

- Use Total Physical Response commands to build familiarity with the concepts. For instance, *Show me the eggs. Point to the chicken.*

Language Practice Game: Version 1 ❶❷❸❹❺

Preparing the Game

Tape the copies of pages 24–25 of the Language Learning Masters to two facing sides of a file folder to give each game board some durability. Assemble one file folder game for each group.

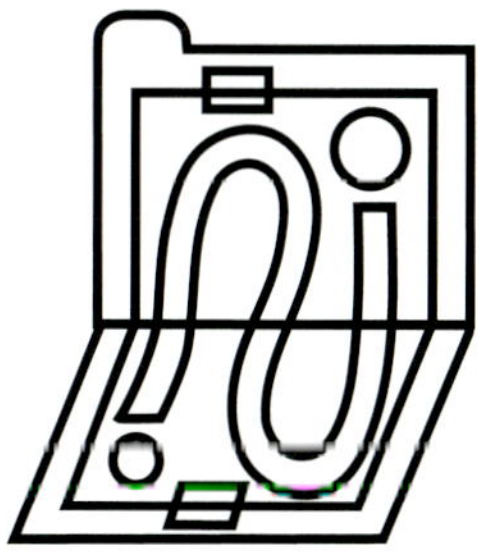

Playing Version 1

Divide the class into heterogeneous groups of mixed language abilities with four children each. Provide a game board and die to each group.

1. Children take turns rolling a die and then moving the number of spaces shown. To move they must complete this pattern: *A ____ becomes a ____*. For example, they say *A tadpole becomes a frog* if they land on either a frog or a tadpole. ◎

Options for STAGES

❶ These children can simply point to the space they're on and then to the next corresponding space, naming one or both as they are able.	❷❸ These children should be encouraged to say a few words, such as *tadpole frog.*	❹❺ Encourage these children to make a complete sentence, such as *A cub becomes a lion.*

2. The other players must decide whether the player's choice is correct. If they agree, the child moves ahead to the corresponding space. If there is no corresponding space ahead, they lose a turn.
3. The winner is the first player to reach the end of the path in this way.

Component Organizer

Other Concept Poster lessons in this unit:

• Revisiting, p. U66

You will need

- **Language Learning Master** pp. 24–25
- File folders
- Tape
- Die

Component Organizer

Other Language Practice Game lessons in this unit:

• Version 2, p. U72

Assessment

Record your observations of children during the Language Practice Game on their individual assessment checklists for this unit. See page U75.

Look at Us

Written by Karen Clevidence

OVERVIEW *Let's see who is eating dinner!*

The Newcomer Book is supported by the language of the Manipulative Chart and should be integrated into small-group instruction this week when children have had enough practice with vocabulary and concepts in this unit.

Language Pattern

Look at the ______.

Text Vocabulary

people

Vocabulary Extenders

food

Reading the Text

Book Talk

- Work with a small group of four children at one time who exhibit similar literacy-learning behaviors.
- Engage children in a book talk as you flip through the pages of your copy of the book. ◎

Options for STAGES

❶❷ Identify each person in the picture. Encourage these children to repeat the names with you.

❸❹❺ Ask these children to identify each person as you turn to each page.

INSTRUCTIONAL PATHS

❶❷❸❹❺ **All Readers:** Shared-to-Guided Reading	❶❷❸❹❺ **Emergent Readers:** Guided Reading	❶❷❸❹❺ **Early Readers:** Independent Reading no lesson provided

INDIVIDUAL READING

Shared-to-Guided Reading **3–4 sessions**
❶❷❸❹❺ **All Readers**

1. Read the book to children.
   - Invite children to sit near you as you read a copy of the book. Begin with the cover and title page.
   - Turn to page 2 and begin reading the words as you point to them. Draw children's attention to the pictures.
2. Read the book with children.
   - Encourage children to follow along in their own copies of the book, turning the pages as you read together and using their own fingers to point to the words.
   - Invite children to chime in when they are comfortable.
   - Reread the book in this manner over several sessions.
3. Have children buddy-read the book.
4. Invite children to read the book independently.

Ⓐ Assess

- Did children chime in on rereadings?
- Did children know when to turn the page?

Guided Reading **2 sessions**
❶❷❸❹❺ **Emergent Readers**

1. Provide copies of the book to children. Use one child's book and turn to page 2. Introduce the book's pattern to children by reading the sentence and pointing to each word as you read *Look at the baby.*
2. Have each child read at his or her own pace while remaining in the group. Discourage choral reading. Observe as they read.

Ⓐ Assess

- Did children point to the words as they read?
- Did children identify and point to a high-frequency word?

REVISITING THE NEWCOMER BOOK

For those children who are ready, you may use the photos to extend children's food vocabulary by naming the items on each page.

WEEK 2 DAY 2

Big Book: Introduction

A Pocketful of Opossums

Written by Patricia Almada

OVERVIEW *Have you ever seen an opossum? Maybe not. Let's meet some!*

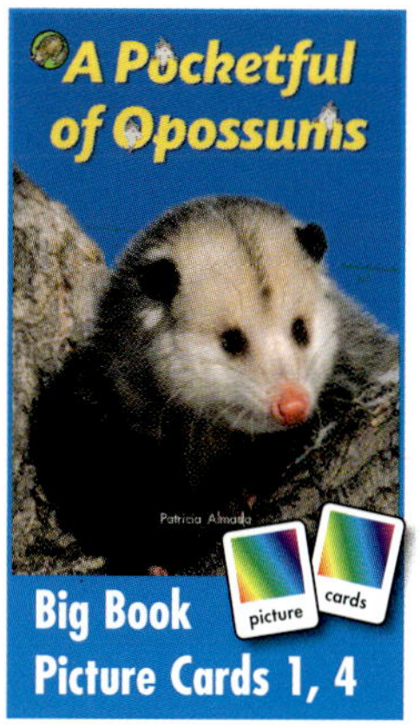

Warming Up

Begin the lesson by revisiting the Manipulative Chart, Chant Poster, or a familiar Big Book. You may ask a volunteer to choose one.

Setting the Scene

- Display Picture Card 1: baby and 4: adult. Using gestures as you point to the title page, explain that opossums, like humans, start as babies and grow up to become adults.
- Tap into children's prior knowledge. *Have you ever seen an opossum? Where have you seen it?* Invite children to nod, shake their heads, or respond in words.
- Refer to the picture of the opossum on the cover. *This is an opossum.*
- Introduce the book and provide children with an overview of the story.
- Make predictions about the book. *How big is an opossum? How long does it take before an opossum becomes an adult? Where do the little babies live? How do they change as they grow?*
- This book gives us information about these questions and more. As we turn the pages, see if you can find places where we can find answers to our questions.

Reading the Text

- Read the title page. Have children make an additional prediction based on this picture. *Why do you think these babies are in a pocket?*
- As you read through the book, use a pointer or your finger to draw children's attention to the text. In future rereadings, children should be encouraged to chime in. Point out items in the pictures to support your reading. You will return later to build children's understanding of the text.
- If you have children in Stages 3, 4, or 5, pause after reading page 13 for a prediction of what will happen next. *What do you think a baby opossum does when it leaves its mom?*

Creating Comprehensible Input

- Open up the back flap of the book, which shows an opossum at different stages in its life. Leave the flap open as you read to help build comprehension of the life cycle.
- Use the comprehension supports in the following chart to help you build comprehensible input with children at all Stages of Language Acquisition.

Component Organizer

Other Big Book lessons in this unit:

- Revisiting, p. U64
- Comprehension Strategy, p. U65
- Oral Language Development, pp. U67–U68
- Literacy Skills, pp. U71–U72

Idiom Note

The phrase *getting around* on page 13 may not be familiar to most children. You can demonstrate the meaning by walking around the classroom and say *I'm getting around the classroom. I'm moving from one place to another.* It is not, however, essential that children understand this idiom for comprehension of the text.

PAGE	IN THE STORY	COMPREHENSION SUPPORT
4	These tiny opossums . . .	use flap: point to pictures for Day 1 gesture: use thumb and index finger to make *tiny*
5	The babies cannot see or hear.	act out: cover eyes, cover ears, shake head
6	The babies use their front feet to climb . . .	act out: climbing with claws
10	They are now about 5 inches long.	use ruler: indicate 5 inches use flap: point to picture for Day 56
12	They ride on their mom's back by hanging on tightly . . .	point: to babies on mother's back
13	The extra weight on her back makes it hard for the mother to get around. . . .	act out: walking with difficulty while carrying doll or stuffed animal around shoulders
15	They are now able to . . . climb, and find food on their own.	act out: climbing, pawing for food, finding food, and eating
16	The opossums have learned to hide during the day and to look for food at night.	act out: hiding, pawing for and finding food point: to picture showing night
18	They are shy . . .	act out: cover face and turn away as if shy
19	Opossums can live from 5 to 7 years . . .	restate: *They live to be about as old as you are now.* use flap: point to picture of adult

You will need

- Writing and drawing paper
- Markers and crayons
- Scissors
- Camera or video camera
- Easel pad and chart paper

Revisiting the Big Book

- Give seven Stage 1, 2, or 3 children each a prop corresponding to those that appear in the headings: a candle and/or balloon, a yardstick, a ruler, a watch, binoculars, a flashlight, and a doll.
- Plan stopping points in the book that correspond to the headings: Day 1, Day 35, Day 56, Day 70, Day 90, Day 100, and Adult. At each stopping point, invite the child with the corresponding prop to come forward to form a time line.
- Once children have formed the time line, invite Stage 4 or 5 children to summarize the key points of the book as each child in the time line holds up or manipulates his or her prop in turn.

WEEK 2 DAY 3

Theme Project: From Young to Old and Old to Young

1. Work with children to plan a Grandparents' Day. Children can invite grandparents, senior neighbors, or friends. (You may wish to contact retired teachers, who might like to visit.)
2. Before the visit, have children make invitations. Display samples. In a shared writing experience, model writing an invitation. Encourage children to participate, either by nodding to tell if information is correct or by contributing information.
3. Brainstorm questions that children will discuss with the visitors. Say *Let's ask our visitors how they got to school every day. We can ask what kinds of games they played when they were children.* Prompt children to ask about what it was like growing up years ago and how it is different today. Guide children as you write the questions on chart paper.
4. Prepare for the visit by practicing introductions. Stages 1 or 2 children may be able to provide single-word greetings, such as *hello* or *welcome*. Decorate the classroom with work from this and previous units.
5. On the day of the visit, team up visiting seniors with small groups of children of mixed language abilities (including cross-age tutors who may work as scribes). Have groups interview their guest and later draw pictures and write captions or stories about each senior friend. Encourage children to use a word-processing program if available.
6. Take photographs or videotape the event, if equipment is available.
7. Provide books about topics, places or events that were discussed at the visit. Encourage children to choose information to display.
8. Create a bulletin board displaying pictures, stories, books, and drawings. Children can later use the bulletin board as a prompt to discuss the visit.

WEEK 2 DAY 4

Big Book: Focus on Comprehension Strategy

Asks Questions to Clarify Meaning

1. As you read through the book, stop when you have questions. Model, for example, *I wonder what* transparent *means. How can I find out?* or *I wonder why the opossum in the Day 90 heading has sticks in its tail. I'm going to read this page to find out.*
2. As you read through the book thinking aloud, encourage children to stop you when they have a question as well.
3. Help children understand that we ask ourselves questions to help make sense of the book. ◎

Options for STAGES

❶ These children can signal the teacher when to stop for clarification.	❷❸ These children can use one-word questions, such as *Who? What?*, or phrases, such as *Who carry?*	❹❺ Encourage these children to ask complete questions, such as *What do the babies do when they leave the pouch?*

Chant Poster: Focus on Oral Language Development

FUNCTION MINI-LESSON

Wish and Hope ❶❷❸❹❺

1. Revisit the chant together, saying it several times.
2. Review wishing and hoping with a statement, which was introduced on Week 1, Day 5.
3. Point to the boy on the Chant Poster and ask *What does he wish?* Remind children that *wish* is like *want.*

FUNCTION MINI-LESSON

Compare ❶❷❸❹❺

1. Read the chant as you substitute a different food in the line *I eat* ______.
2. Invite children to fill in the word from the Chant Poster.
3. Ask children to draw pictures of what they like to eat to make themselves healthy and strong.
4. Help children compare what they like to eat to what their classmates and the boy on the Chant Poster eat with statements like *I eat fish, and the boy eats fish, too.*

Big Book

Assessment

Use a retelling of the Big Book to assess comprehension. See page U75.

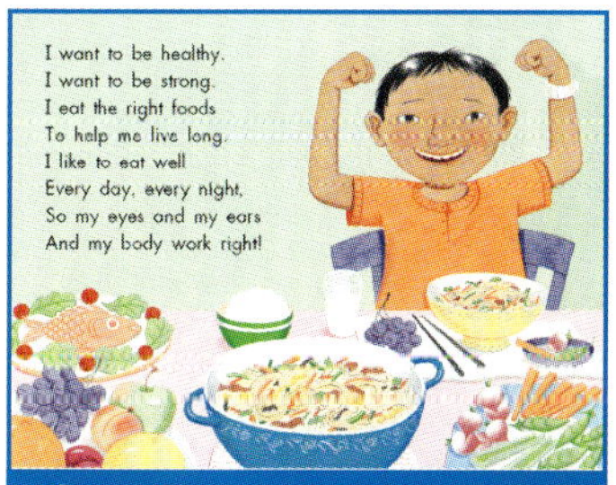

Chant Poster

Home-Culture Sharing

- As you review the pictures of what the boy is eating and what the children eat, invite children to use their home languages to name foods they eat at home.

Assessment

Record your observations of children during these mini-lessons on their individual assessment checklists for this unit. See page U75.

Grammar in Context: Infinitives ①②③④⑤

1. Revisit the chant, inviting children to chime in and move along.
2. Say *We do things to keep ourselves healthy.* Act out exercising. Say *I am exercising.* Ask *Will exercise help me to be healthy?* Say *I drink juice to help me live long,* and act out the sentence. Ask *What do you do to stay healthy, to be strong and to help you live long?* emphasizing the infinitive phrase.
3. Have children supply answers. Help them write sentences so they include the infinitive phrases *to help me live long, to be healthy,* and *to be strong.* Have students work in heterogeneous pairs to edit their sentences as they are able.

WEEK 2 DAY 5

Shared Writing Card: Introduction of Side A

Shared Writing Card
Picture Cards 1–5, 12

You will need

- Shared Writing Card 3
- Wipe-off marker
- Regular marker
- Easel pad

Setting the Scene

- Use the back flap of the Big Book to review the growth and change in the life of an opossum. Follow the circle with your finger and explain how the babies grow older and change every day.
- Tape Picture Cards 1–5: baby, child, teenager, adult, grandparent in a circle on the board. Repeat the procedure as with the Big Book back flap.
- Show Picture Card 12: butterfly. Ask *Who has seen a butterfly? Does it change from baby to adult?* Let children know that butterflies begin as tiny eggs. Then they grow and change just like other living things.

Creating Comprehensible Input

- Display Shared Writing Card 3 Side A with the growth stages of a butterfly in a sequential graphic organizer. Begin by pointing to and naming each item.
  Model *This is a butterfly egg. Here I see a caterpillar on the leaf. I think the caterpillar is inside this chrysalis. Look! This is the full-grown butterfly!*
- Go back to the first illustration and use think-alouds to talk through the illustrations. Point to the illustrations one by one and trace the arrows with your finger.
  Illustration 1: *This butterfly egg looks very tiny on this big leaf.*
  Illustration 2: *The egg grows and changes. It becomes a caterpillar.*
  Illustration 3: *The chrysalis protects the caterpillar so it can grow and change.*
  Illustration 4: *Wow! The caterpillar changes into a beautiful butterfly.*
- Explain that the order of the boxes and the arrows show the change from an egg to a butterfly. Point to the illustrations again, noting the changes as you trace the circle and emphasize the order of growth.
- Invite a volunteer from Stages 3, 4, or 5 to retell the illustrations in his or her own words. Repeat with other volunteers.

Scribing with the Graphic Organizer

- After children have become comfortable with the content of the illustrations, use the wipe-off marker provided to scribe while you brainstorm together labels for the graphic organizer. Since you are creating a graphic organizer, not a finished product, well-crafted sentences are not necessary.

Revisiting the Concept Poster

- Revisit the Concept Poster and invite volunteers to talk about a row of pictures.
- Assign groups to different rows of pictures. Have them role-play the four stages in the life cycle of their chosen living thing.

- Think aloud as you write so children gain insight into the writing process.
- Here is an example of simple shared writing labeling for the illustrations.
  Illustration 1: *egg sticks to leaf*
  Illustration 2: *caterpillar eats leaf*
  Illustration 3: *caterpillar in chrysalis*
  Illustration 4: *butterfly comes out*

Writing Together from the Graphic Organizer

- You will again be holding the pen as you work together with children to create a shared writing piece. In this instance, you will model how to use the words and phrases from the butterfly organizer to create a finished paragraph on your easel pad.
- Begin with a think-aloud.
  Model *Under the first picture we wrote* egg sticks to leaf. *This doesn't sound like a complete sentence. We also want to say that this is how a butterfly starts its life. Let's see . . . What about a sentence like this:* A butterfly starts as a little egg that sticks to a leaf. *That tells what this is about.*
- Write down the sentence that you and the children agree upon. You might point out that the word *little* helps tell what the egg looks like.
- As you move around to the second illustration, read the label and then invite children to help create a sentence based on the picture and label. Write down what children say as you work to make sentences with them. When children offer sentences with errors in them, correct them discreetly. Encourage children to use classroom resources, such as the Word Wall.
- When you have finished your shared writing piece, read it together several times. Then hang it up on the wall where it can be displayed during the rest of the unit and reread many times. For now, do not erase your labels on Side A.

WEEK 3 DAY 1

Big Book: Focus on Oral Language Development

Reread the Big Book and return to the text to focus on oral language development.

Grammar in Context: Adjectives ❶❷❸❹❺

1. Using the photo of an opossum on pages 2–3, point out the labels *long whiskers* and *long scaly tail*. . . . Trace along the whiskers and tail emphasizing their length.
2. Turn to other photos to describe the opossum's tail, whiskers, snout, and anything else that is long.
3. Repeat the same procedure as above for *tiny* in the text on pages 4 and 10 and for *thin* on page 4. *Heavy* can be drawn from page 13.
4. Allow children to use other objects, personal belongings, or items in the classroom to hold up and describe.

Options for STAGES

❶❷ Encourage these children to say just the adjective or to answer *yes* or *no*.

❸❹❺ Encourage these children to make phrases or simple sentences using adjectives, such as *The snout is long.*

Phonics in Context

Shared writing provides an ideal opportunity for reviewing the phonics skills children are learning. Highlight the sounds in words like *st**ick**s*, *b**ed***, and *w**ill*** as you reread the writing.

Sample Shared Writing

A butterfly starts as a little egg that sticks to a leaf. A caterpillar hatches. It eats the leaf to grow strong. Then the caterpillar makes a chrysalis. This is like a bed where the caterpillar rests and grows. Soon a beautiful butterfly will come out and fly away.

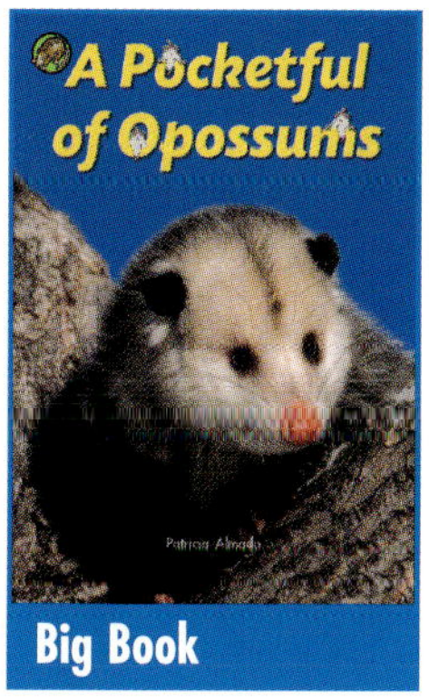

Language Junction

Speakers of Spanish may have several areas of difficulty with adjectives. Since adjectives come after nouns in Spanish, learners at first may carry over that order into English: *I like house big.* For comparatives and superlatives, they may tend to use *more* and *most* (*I am more old than my brother*) instead of the suffixes *-er* and *-est*.

Language Learning Master
p. 27 ❶❷❸❹❺

Guided Reading

As you work on this unit, conduct small groups of guided reading or shared-to-guided reading independent of thematic instruction. Instruction is provided in the Guided Reading section of this guide.

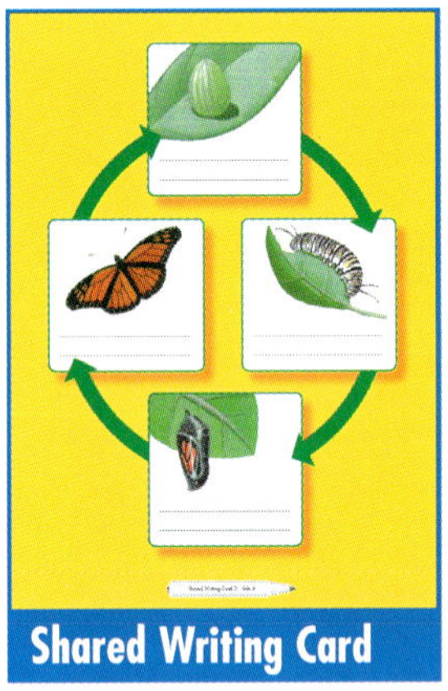

You will need

- Shared Writing Card 3
- Wipe-off marker

Grammar in Context: Possessives with *'s* ❶❷❸❹❺

1. Ask children to display one item on their desks. Point to the first child's item and say *Igor's keychain.* Point to another child's object and say *Viola's backpack.* Continue around the room and encourage children to join in when they understand the pattern.
2. Write *Viola's backpack* on the board and underline the *'s* with a colored marker. Emphasize the *s/z/* as you say it. Invite children to say it along with you. Help them understand that this means that the backpack belongs to Viola.
3. Refer to the Big Book. Turn to the back flap. The pictures labeled Day 56 and Day 70 both have the word *mother's.* Read the captions first, then with the children. Ask *Where are the babies? In the pouch? On the back?* Pointing to each picture ask *Whose pouch? Whose back? Mother's?* Elicit the responses *the mother's pouch, the mother's back.*
4. Have the children go on a scavenger hunt in the Big Book, putting sticky notes under possessives with *'s* as in *mother's.* Revisit those pages and ask questions as above to elicit the possessive words.

WEEK 3 DAY 2

Shared Writing Card: Brainstorming Side B

Brainstorming a Topic

- Use Side A of the Shared Writing Card and your finished butterfly shared writing piece. Review how you used the graphic organizer's pictures and labels to form the basis of your finished piece.
- Turn the card over to Side B. Tell the children that you will now think of your own topic together to draw in the graphic organizer. Brainstorm together a topic that involves a growth sequence. You can steer them either toward a specific classroom plant or pet, or toward a generally familiar growth process, such as that of a person. (Your process should have four or fewer stages.)

Scribing with the Graphic Organizer

- Once the class has agreed on a topic, you should decide together what the first stage would be. Show them how to draw the first picture, such as a baby. Invite volunteers to step up to the card and draw subsequent stages as the class decides on them. Continue drawing stages until the growth process is complete; it's OK to leave a box empty.
- Now it's time to put labels on your graphic organizer. Elicit suggestions for labels from the group in the same manner as you did for Side A and record them on the Shared Writing Card.
- You will create the shared writing paragraph in the next session.

Active Science: Butterfly Beginnings

1. Set up an observation journal labeled "From Caterpillar to Butterfly." Label the top of the first page with the date that the observations begin.
2. If season and weather permit, invite children on a caterpillar hunt. Look for caterpillars on leaves and stems of plants. Remove the caterpillar and place it in a wide-mouth container with a supply of leaves. Include fresh twigs. (As an alternative, you may use Butterfly in a Box™ or a similar product, available at education supply stores.)

3. Use the Concept Poster and Shared Writing Card to review the process of growth and change.
4. Assign children to one of five groups and show the groups how to make observation entries in the journal by modeling the first entry.
5. Assign each group a day of the week to record observations until the butterfly or moth emerges. Then release it and watch it fly away.
6. Collect the data and write them in the form of the Concept Poster. Encourage children to contribute information as they are able.

You will need

- Caterpillars (from nature or science kit)
- Leaves and stems of plants, fresh twigs
- Wide-mouth container

WEEK 3 DAY 3

Shared Writing Card: Writing Together with Side B

- As with Side A, you will scribe as you work together with the children to create a finished writing piece from the graphic organizer on Side B of Shared Writing Card 3.
- Model writing from the first drawing, using think-alouds as you go. Show children how to use resources like the Word Wall. Work together on difficult spellings and passages.
- When you have finished with your shared writing piece, read it together several times. Then hang it up on the wall where it can be displayed during the rest of the unit. At the end of the unit, you should erase both sides of the Shared Writing Card.

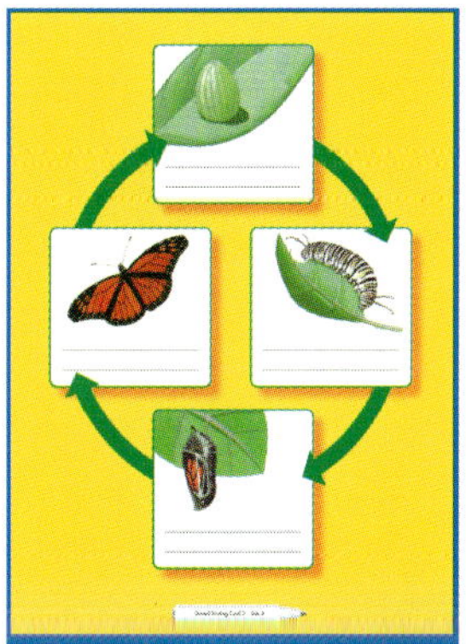

Shared Writing Card

Manipulative Chart: Focus on Oral Language Development

Grammar in Context: Infinitives

1. Sing the song together, allowing volunteers to move the cards in the chart and determine the next verse.
2. Point out the picture of the baby crawling. Read the line *Use her arms to crawl,* and make arm movements to indicate crawling. Have children say the line while making the same arm gestures.
3. Point out the picture of the child playing. Read the line *Use her arms to play,* and make arm movements to indicate playing. Have the children say the line while making the same arm gestures. Repeat the same instruction as above, using the infinitives *to help, to work,* and *to hug* with their corresponding pictures. Invite children to use their arms to show these ways people use their arms.

Manipulative Chart

Language Learning Master

p. 28

WEEK 3 DAY 4

You will need

- Magazines
- Paper
- Glue

Active Social Studies: Life Stages

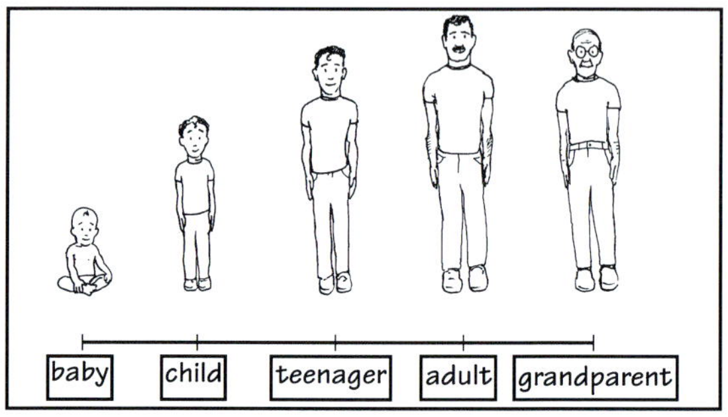

1. Draw a life stage line on the board. Label each stage in order from youngest to oldest.
2. Have children cut out pictures of people from magazines.
3. Then they can glue their pictures onto their own life stage line and label it as they are able.
4. Children can summarize the life stages using their pictures for support. They can also make comparisons between stages, such as *A child is bigger than a baby.*

WEEK 3 DAY 5

You will need

- Overhead transparency of Writing Resource Guide, p. 84
- Overhead marker

Writing Resource Guide: A Simplified Graphic Organizer

This activity is optional and necessary only if you wish to use the simplified sequence graphic organizer in cooperative-group or independent writing.

Brainstorming a Topic

- Review the drawings and labels you used on Side B of the Shared Writing Card. Trace the sequence of the pictures with your fingers.
- On the overhead projector, display a transparency of page 84 of the Writing Resource Guide, which is a cycle graphic organizer with only three boxes.
- Brainstorm together a topic that involves a simple growth process, such as a robin. Your process should have only three steps.

Scribing with the Graphic Organizer

- Once the class has chosen a topic, you should decide together what the stages might be. Model drawing each of the three stages.
- Label each of the three drawings on your graphic organizer. Elicit suggestions for labels from the group in the same manner as you did with the Shared Writing Card.

You will need

- Writing Resource Guide, pp. 83–84
- Markers

Writing Resource Guide: Cooperative-Group Writing

- Form cooperative groups of heterogeneous Stages with three to four children each to work together on a writing piece using the graphic organizer. You may hand out a copy of Writing Planner A or B to each group.
- Review the shared writing graphic organizers and finished pieces you have completed together. Remind children that the drawings help them remember the order.

- Have the groups work together first to complete their graphic organizers and then to write their finished pieces. Circulate to provide assistance. ◎

Options for STAGES

❶❷ These children should draw the pictures for the group.	❸❹❺ These children should take responsibility for the writing of the finished piece.

WEEK 4 DAY 1

Big Book: Focus on Literacy Skills

Word Level: Phonics in Context

1. You will need the Word Wall Starters with the opossum symbol on them: *g__et__*, *b__ack__*, *w__ill__*. These are pictured in the back of the Big Book.
2. Tell children that you want to choose some special words from the book for them to look at more closely.
3. Introduce the word *get* by saying it clearly, emphasizing the *et* sound and drawing attention to the highlighting behind the *et*. Then say /et/-/et/-/et/. *The letters* e *and* t *together make the* et *sound.* Say *Let's say the word* get *together:* get. *Can you hear how* get *ends with* et? *Let's sing a song!* Review Phonics Song Chart 11 together.
4. Say *I'm going to put the word* get *underneath the* short e *label.* Walk over to the Word Wall and place the card *get* under the *short e* label, taking care to group word families together. Remind children to use the opossum symbol to help them remember where they "met" that word before.
5. Repeat a similar procedure for the other words and phonics skills.

Sentence Level: Labels

1. Reread pages 2 and 3 from the Big Book. Point out the labels in the picture of the opossum. Think aloud to explain how labels help you know the parts of a picture.
   Model *The opossum has so many different parts. I know some of the parts, but these labels help me know other parts. When I see the label* pouch, *I know what an opossum's pocket is called.*
   Point to the label *pouch* and follow the line to that part. Continue modeling with one or two more labels. ◎

Options for STAGES

❶❷ These children may answer *yes* or *no* when asked whether a part and a name match.	❸❹❺ Encourage these children to reply with phrases and sentences when asked *What part of the opossum is this?*

2. Read page 9, discussing how the labels show us where the eyes and ears are.

Writing Mini-lessons

See the Writing Resource Guide for mini-lessons to use as children write. Here are some suggestions:

- Mini-lesson 25: Organizing Your Writing
- Mini-lesson 45: Editing for Subject-Verb Agreement

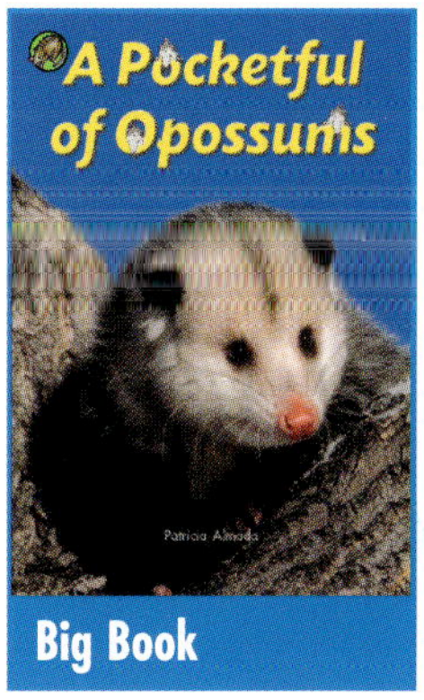

Guided Reading

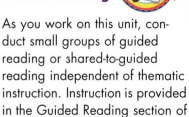

As you work on this unit, conduct small groups of guided reading or shared-to-guided reading independent of thematic instruction. Instruction is provided in the Guided Reading section of this guide.

Home-School Connection

Send home page 37 of the Home-School Connection Masters for children to use in retelling *A Pocketful of Opossums* to their parents. They should first retell in English and then in the home language.

Text Level: Time Lines

1. Reread pages 22–23 of the Big Book. Think aloud how time lines help us understand what we read.
   Model *When I see a time line, I know that it will show me important events and when they happened all on the same page. This helps me remember what I read on all the other pages, and it helps me remember when things happen.*
2. Point to Day 1. Tell children that this is the start of the time line. Continue with the other boxes as you go along, tracing the line with your finger. Stop at each labeled day, pointing to the corresponding pictured stage of development.
3. Ask questions that help children see how the time line helps us know when things happen: *Can the opossums ride on their mothers on Day 35 or Day 70? When can the opossums get their own food?* and so forth.
4. Invite children to say their ages. Write each child's year (and month) of birth on the board. Use chart paper to plot children's years of birth on a simple time line.

You will need

- TPR Cards

Language Practice Game: Version 2 ❶❷❸❹❺

Group children into heterogeneous groups of mixed language abilities with four children each. Provide 5–6 pairs of TPR Cards for each group.

1. Have the children mix the cards well and line them up in rows face down.
2. The children may then play Concentration with the TPR Cards. They can make matches, such as *baby* with *baby.*
3. When a match is made, the child should say *They are the same.* This provides practice with the language function *Compare.*
4. When no more matches can be made, the child with the most matches wins.

Options for STAGES

❶❷ These children may simply make the match or say the words for the cards.

❸❹❺ Encourage these children to produce sentences or sentence approximations.

WEEK 4 DAY 2

You will need

- String
- Tape
- Self-stick notes
- Scissors
- Retractable tape measure
- Markers
- Chart paper

Active Math: Measure Up!

1. Have volunteers stand against the wall. Tape string to the bottom of the wall and stretch it to the top of the child's head, then cut the string and tape it at the top. Measure and label each string with the child's name and height in inches on self-stick notes. Continue until at least six children have been measured.
2. Point to the notes. Ask *Who is tallest? shortest?*
3. Start a chart. Continue until all children have been measured and entered on the chart.

Inches	Student
50	
49	Jae Young
48	Christophe, Irina
47	Sharif, Pang
46	Dora
45	

End-of-Unit Assessment

- While children are engaged in activities this week, pull them individually for the Big Book retelling, using page U75 at the end of this unit.
- Select children with whom you would like to use the Open-Ended Oral Language Assessment on pages U74–U75 of this unit and pull them individually during activities this week. We recommend assessing about one-fourth of your class each unit.
- You should also have gathered the following for their assessment portfolio:
  - page 27 of the Language Learning Masters
  - page 28 of the Language Learning Masters
  - finished writing piece assessed according to the Writing Rubric on page A6.

You will need

A copy of page U75 at the end of this unit for each child

WEEK 4 DAY 3–4

Writing Resource Guide: Individual Writing

- Children have engaged in a step-by-step writing process moving toward independence. They began with teacher-led shared writing, moved to cooperative groups, and are now ready to work individually.
- Provide a copy of Writing Planner A or B to each child. They may need individual conferencing on choosing a topic.

Options for STAGES

❶❷ and Emergent Level
These children should draw the steps of their process on their graphic organizers. They should label writing on their own or dictate labels to you.

❸❹❺ Early Level and Above
These children should also use drawings and labels on the graphic organizers to record their topics. They should then use the graphic organizers to create a finished piece.

- When children have completed the finished product, whether a graphic organizer or a paragraph, you should assess it using the Writing Rubric on page A6 of this Teacher's Guide.

You will need

- Writing Resource Guide, pp. 83–84
- Markers

Assessment

Continue pulling some children for the Big Book Retelling and Open-Ended Oral Language Assessment as others write.

WEEK 4 DAY 5

Theme Project: Sharing

- Invite groups to present their group reports and bulletin board display to each other. Assign children to be presenters.
- After the presentations are over, model appropriate feedback for the class by making the first comment yourself; for example, say *Yasmin, it was very interesting. Would you recommend this project to another class?*

Open-Ended Oral Language Assessment Reassess children's Language Acquisition Stages. Begin with an open-ended prompt like the first one below. If children are unable to respond, intervene with increasingly directed prompts, such as the second and third ones below.

What can you tell me about the picture?

Tell me about animals growing.

I see an egg. What comes next?

Assessment Directions: Copy this form for each child and place the completed form in the child's portfolio. Locate the child's Language Acquisition Stage for each of the first four activities and assess his or her performance during the unit according to expectations for that Stage. For the Big Book Retelling, pull children to retell the Big Book during end-of-unit assessment time. Use the Open-Ended Oral Language Assessment to reassess children's Language Acquisition Stages with one-fourth of your students for each unit, using the back side of the sheet to take notes. *For more guidance on assessment, see pages T33 and T34.*

Unit 3 Assessment

Name ______________________ **Date** ____________

On Our Way to English Grade 2	STAGE EXPECTATIONS ❶	❷	❸	❹	❺
Fluency Manipulative Chart Student Version, page U60 *How does the child respond when manipulating the mini-chart along with the Oral Language Audio CD?*	Shows the correct answers. ☐ Yes ☐ Not yet	Shows the correct answers, naming the people in the pictures. ☐ Yes ☐ Not yet	Shows the correct answers, approximating sentences and substitutions. ☐ Yes ☐ Not yet	Shows the correct answers, singing the verse with few, if any, errors. ☐ Yes ☐ Not yet	
Content Area Knowledge Language Practice Game: Version 1, page U61 *How does the child demonstrate an understanding of the growth stages while playing the game?*	Moves correctly, naming the animals as they are able. ☐ Yes ☐ Not yet	Uses some appropriate vocabulary, such as *cub lion*. ☐ Yes ☐ Not yet		Says a complete sentence, such as *A cub becomes a lion.* ☐ Yes ☐ Not yet	
Social Language Function Wish and hope, page U65 *How does the child respond during the Function Mini-lesson?*	Responds nonverbally or with a basic word or phrase, such as *strong*. ☐ Yes ☐ Not yet		Approximates a sentence, such as *He wish strong.* ☐ Yes ☐ Not yet	Responds with a complete and appropriate sentence. ☐ Yes ☐ Not yet	
Academic Language Function Compare, page U65 *How does the child respond during the Function Mini-lesson?*	Responds nonverbally or with a basic word or phrase. ☐ Yes ☐ Not yet		Responds using short phrases or basic words. ☐ Yes ☐ Not yet	Responds with a complete, correct sentence. ☐ Yes ☐ Not yet	
Big Book Retelling page U65 *Have each child use the time line to retell* A Pocketful of Opossums. *How does the child retell the book?*	Retells by pointing and using gestures nonverbally. ☐ Yes ☐ Not yet	Retells using a few words. ☐ Yes ☐ Not yet	Retells using longer phrases or simple sentences. ☐ Yes ☐ Not yet	Retells using complete sentences in connected discourse with few errors. ☐ Yes ☐ Not yet	Retells using book language similar to native-speaking peers. ☐ Yes ☐ Not yet
Open-Ended Oral Language Assessment, page U74 *Use the child's responses to the illustration to reassess the child's Stage of Language Acquisition.*	☐ **STAGE ❶** Uses few or no words; gestures or points.	☐ **STAGE ❷** Uses words or short phrases.	☐ **STAGE ❸** Uses phrases and simple sentences.	☐ **STAGE ❹** Uses sentences in connected discourse.	☐ **STAGE ❺** Uses language comparable to native-speaking peers.

From Farm to You

OVERVIEW *This unit focuses on the stages of plant growth and what plants need to grow. It then discusses how food gets from the farm to our table.*

Unit Components

Manipulative Chart

Chant Poster

Brown seeds, black seeds,
Green seeds, more!
Speckled seeds, striped seeds,
Wrinkled seeds, more!
Flying seeds, floating seeds,
Sticking seeds, more!

Concept Poster

Where Does Peanut Butter Come From?

What Makes Plants Grow?

Newcomer Book

Determining the Purpose

Oral Language Development

Focus on Functions

Social Context:
Use social etiquette ① ② ③ ④ ⑤

Academic Context:
Sequence ① ② ③ ④ ⑤

Focus on Grammar

- Object pronouns
- Sequence words
- Adjectives with *–ing*
- Infinitives
- Present continuous tense

Comprehension Strategy

- Sequences ideas and story events

Literacy Skills

- **Word Level:** Phonics in context: long *a*, long *o*
- **Sentence Level:** Rhythm, rhyme, and alliteration
- **Text Level:** Identifying characters and setting

Content Area Objectives

- Identifies the parts of a plant
- Understands how plants grow and change
- Identifies steps in food production
- Counts, reads, and writes numbers

Language Learning Strategy

- Work with a friend to help you understand.

Writing Skill

- Uses a graphic organizer to sequence

Unit at a Glance

	DURING THE WEEK	DAY 1
Week 1	**Small-Group Instruction:** • Guided Reading • Shared-to-Guided Reading **Phonics Focus:** *ake* and *ale* word families Phonics Song Chart 14, pp. P32–P33	**Manipulative Chart:** Introduction with Audio CD p. U79
Week 2	**Small-Group Instruction:** • Guided Reading • Shared-to-Guided Reading • Newcomer Book **Phonics Focus:** *ail* and *ain* word families Phonics Song Chart 15, pp. P34–P35	**Concept Poster:** Introduction p. U84 **Language Practice Game:** Version 1 p. U85
Week 3	**Small-Group Instruction:** • Guided Reading • Shared-to-Guided Reading • Newcomer Book **Phonics Focus:** *oke* and *ope* word families Phonics Song Chart 16, pp. P36–P37	**Big Book:** Oral Language Development p. U91
Week 4	**Small-Group Instruction:** • Guided Reading • Shared-to-Guided Reading • Newcomer Book **Phonics Focus:** *oad* and *old* word families Phonics Song Chart 17, pp. P38–P39	**Big Book:** Literacy Skills p. U95 **Language Practice Game:** Version 2 p. U96

STAGES ① Preproduction ② Early Production ③ Speech Emergence ④ Intermediate Fluency ⑤ Advanced Fluency

Oral Language Audio CD

Big Book with Audio CD and Small Book

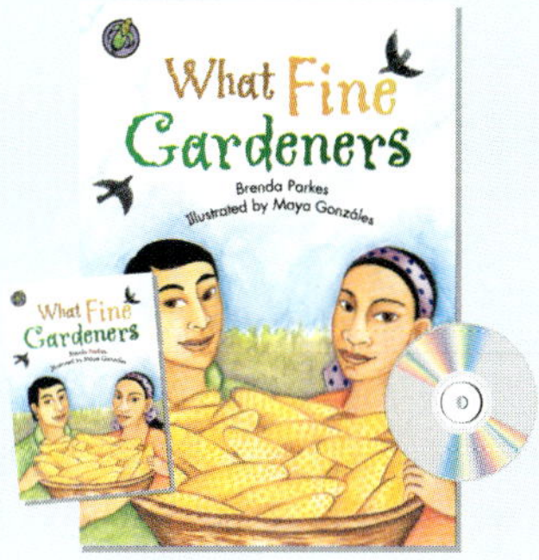

Home-School Connection Masters

Picture Cards

Shared Writing Card

Writing Resource Guide

Language Learning Masters

DAY 2	DAY 3	DAY 4	DAY 5
Manipulative Chart: Gestures and Manipulative Fun p. U80	**Chant Poster:** Introduction p. U81	**TPR Cards:** Introduction p. U82	**Manipulative Chart:** Oral Language Development Student Version p. U83
Big Book: Introduction p. U87	**Theme Project:** Plant Parts on Our Table p. U88 **Big Book:** Revisiting p. U88	**Big Book:** Comprehension Strategy p. U89 **Chant Poster:** Oral Language Development p. U89	**Shared Writing Card:** Introduction of Side A p. U90 **Concept Poster:** Revisiting p. U90
Shared Writing Card: Brainstorming Side B p. U92 **Active Social Studies:** Working Together p. U93	**Shared Writing Card:** Writing Together with Side B p. U93 **Manipulative Chart:** Oral Language Development p. U93	**Active Science:** Soil, Sun, and Water p. U94	**Writing Resource Guide:** A Simplified Graphic Organizer Cooperative-Group Writing p. U94
Active Math: Bean Counters p. U96 **Assessment** p. U97	**Writing Resource Guide:** Individual Writing p. U97 **Assessment** p. U97	**Writing Resource Guide:** Individual Writing p. U97 **Assessment** p. U97	**Theme Project:** Sharing p. U97

Center Activities

Number Nook

Provide several containers of beans. Have children estimate and record how many beans are in each container. Later, children can verify their estimations by counting the beans. Change the amount of beans each week.

Artist's Studio

Provide colored scrap paper, tissue paper, paper cups, pipe cleaners, modeling clay, twigs, and leaves. Invite children to make their own three-dimensional plants, flowers, and gardens.

You will need

- Beans
- Plastic containers
- Scrap paper
- Tissue paper
- Paper cups
- Pipe cleaners
- Modeling clay
- Twigs and leaves
- Seed packets, beans, nuts
- Packaged and play foods

CENTERS

Content Corner

Bring in seed packets, beans, and nuts, as well as nonperishable packaged or play foods that come from those sources, such as peanut butter and chips. Invite children to match the foods to their sources.

Listening Post

After introducing each element in class, children may revisit the Manipulative Chart and Chant Poster on the Oral Language Audio CD. If you include a laminated copy of the Manipulative Chart Student Version, children can manipulate it as they sing to Part 4 of the CD (with blanks). Children may also listen to *What Fine Gardeners* on the Big Book Audio CD while following along in the small copy.

Language Workshop

Any time they are not in use during the unit, place the Picture Cards and TPR Cards for the unit in this center. Encourage children to sequence the ways in which a plant grows from seed to flower. After introducing the Language Practice Game in class, add the game board, spinners and game markers to the center for independent group play.

Writer's Den

Establish a journal writing center with prompts to spark children's writing. Change the prompt every two weeks:

- What do you want to plant in a garden?
- Draw and write about a plant.

Children should be encouraged to draw pictures to support their writing. Provide blank Writing Planners in center materials for prewriting.

More Books

- *The Milk Makers* by Gail Gibbons (Simon & Schuster Children's Books, 1996)
- *From Seed to Plant* by Gail Gibbons (Holiday House, 1993)
- *The Surprise Garden* by Zoe Hall (Blue Sky Press, Scholastic, 1998)
- *The Tiny Seed* by Eric Carle (Little Simon, 1998)
- *The Town Mouse and the Country Mouse, an Aesop Fable* adapted by Janet Stevens (Holiday House, 1989)

WEEK 1 DAY 1

Manipulative Chart: Introduction with Audio CD

Sung to the tune of "Did You Ever See a Lassie?"

Setting the Scene

- Show children Picture Card 1: flower. Using gestures, explain why you like it. Ask children to describe or draw flowers they know or like on the chalkboard.
- Display Picture Cards 1–8: flower, seeds, soil, sun, water, leaf, stem, root. Show Picture Card 2: seeds. Use gestures, such as placing a seed in the ground. Continue pointing and gesturing to Picture Cards to emphasize the process of planting and the stages of plant growth.

Options for STAGES

❶❷ These children can answer yes/no or either/or questions, such as *Is this a flower?* or *Is this a root or a leaf?*

❸ Shuffle the Picture Cards. Model, then encourage these children to name plant parts.

❹❺ Encourage these children to tell about the stages of plant growth using phrases or complete sentences.

- Use Picture Cards 3–5: soil, sun, water. Say the words and allow children to repeat them. Use gestures and acting out to show that these things help plants grow.

Creating Comprehensible Input

- Point out parts of the picture, such as the boy, water, sun, soil, and seed.
- Read the text, pausing often, as you use gestures, pointing, and other techniques to make the song comprehensible.

Do you know	point to children, point to head
What makes a seed grow	point to seed, shrug shoulders
A seed grow	point to seed, move up with finger
A seed grow?	repeat
Do you know	point to children, shrug shoulders
What makes a seed grow?	point to seed, shrug shoulders
It's soil, sun, and water.	point to soil, point to sun, point to water drops

Guided Reading

As you work on this unit, conduct small groups of guided reading or shared-to-guided reading independent of thematic instruction. Instruction is provided in the Guided Reading section of this guide.

Component Organizer

Other Manipulative Chart lessons in this unit:

- Gestures and Manipulative Fun, p. U80
- Oral Language Development and Student Version, pp. U83–U84
- Oral Language Development, p. U93

Real-World Touch

Invite children to bring in fruits such as apples, oranges, peaches, and plums. Help children remove the seeds or pits to examine and compare them. Keep the seeds and pits for counting and sorting.

Home-School Connection

Choose one of the versions of the parent letter to send home with each child, according to the child's home language (pages 38–45 in the Home-School Connection Masters). Also send home the activity on page 46.

Manipulative Chart

Journal Writing Reminder

Children should be writing in their journals during the course of the unit. Journal writing gives children the opportunity to practice newly learned language. See Writer's Den for suggested journal prompts.

Introducing the Audio CD

- Play Part 1 of the Oral Language Audio CD, the spoken song, as you say the song and track the print on the Manipulative Chart with your finger or a pointer. Replay Part 1 several times, encouraging children to chime in whenever they can.
- Introduce the song by playing the song at natural speed, Part 2 of the Audio CD, to help children get a feel for the song. Allow the Audio CD to continue playing through Part 3, the song at instructional pace. Track the print as the Audio CD plays. Repeat Part 3 again, this time singing along, making clear lip movements without exaggerating. Revisit Part 3 several times to help children learn the song.

WEEK 1 DAY 2

Manipulative Chart: Gestures and Manipulative Fun

Gesturing the Song

Introduce these simple gestures to accompany the song:

Do you know	shrug shoulders with arms outstretched
What makes a seed grow	crouch down, shimmy up
A seed grow	as above
A seed grow?	as above
Do you know	shrug shoulders with arms outstretched
What makes a seed grow?	crouch down, shimmy up
It's soil, sun, and water.	point to ground, put hand above head in circle, wiggle fingers as if watering

Manipulating the Chart

- Show children how to open and close the flaps on the Manipulative Chart. The items under each flap can be substituted for the word in pink. Open the bottom flap for *root*, sing the verse, and emphasize using *root* instead of *seed* when it appears in the song. Continue opening the other flaps from bottom to top.
- Play Part 4 of the Oral Language Audio CD while you say *root* in the blank space.
- Continue introducing and identifying the rest of the plant parts in this manner.
- Invite volunteers to open the flaps as you sing the verse together or give Total Physical Response commands, such as *Point to the root in the soil.*
- Invite children to help you create new gestures for the song.
- You can revisit this activity many times during the unit.

WEEK 1 DAY 3

Chant Poster: Introduction

Setting the Scene

- Display real seeds, such as pumpkin, sunflower, grapefruit, and dried beans, such as kidney beans and lentils. Share the names of the seeds and beans. Encourage children to call out, in English or their home languages, names of the seeds and beans they recognize.
- Show Picture Card 2: seeds. Using gestures and pointing, help children understand that seeds come in many colors, patterns, textures, and sizes.

Creating Comprehensible Input

- Displaying the Chant Poster, point to and name the seeds one by one, making comparisons to the Picture Card as appropriate.
- Read the text, pausing often, as you use gestures, pointing, and other techniques to make the chant comprehensible.

Brown seeds, black seeds	point to acorns, then to kiwi seeds
Green seeds, more!	point to lima beans, then stretch arms out wide
Speckled seeds, striped seeds,	poke palm with index finger, then point to pinto beans draw lines on palm, then point to sunflower seeds
Wrinkled seeds, more!	wrinkle face, then point to orange seeds stretch arms out wide
Flying seeds, floating seeds,	point to dandelion seeds, then flap arms point to coconut, then wave arms and sway slowly
Sticking seeds, more!	point to burrs, then press hands together as if glued stretch arms out wide

Chanting the Poster

- Encourage children to chime in as you chant the rhyme together several times. Use gestures to emphasize the words *flying, floating,* and *sticking*.
- Introduce the chant on the Oral Language Audio CD as you and the children move to the rhythm of the chant. Tell them they can listen to it on their own later at the Listening Post.
- Practice saying the chant in different ways, sometimes clapping or tapping out the beat, sometimes changing the speed or volume. Emphasize the beat to *more!*
- Revisit the chant often. Invite children to gesture the actions of the chant.

Brown seeds, black seeds,
Green seeds, more!
Speckled seeds, striped seeds,
Wrinkled seeds, more!
Flying seeds, floating seeds,
Sticking seeds, more!
Chant Poster
Picture Card 2
picture
cards

Component Organizer

Other Chant Poster lessons in this unit:

- Oral Language Development, pp. U89–U90

WEEK 1 DAY 4

TPR Cards: Introduction

Introducing the Cards with Total Physical Response

- Provide one copy of page 31 of the Language Learning Masters to each child. Have children color and cut out the cards.
- Introduce a few cards at a time by holding them up one by one and saying the words clearly. Select first the words that have already been introduced in previous activities.
- Ask children to pick up the correct cards as you call out a word. Model the desired outcome. Add one new card at a time and keep reviewing in a game-like atmosphere. Children may want to say the word as they pick up the card.
- Now invite children to respond to your full-sentence commands, such as *Show me the stem. Pick up the leaf.*
- Assign partners so you can add commands like *Give the leaf to Mika.*
- As children increase their familiarity with the TPR Cards and the game, add funny commands such as *Put the stem on your nose.*
- Invite volunteers in Stages 3, 4, or 5 to give commands to their classmates.
- Extend language to discuss plant growth. ◎

Options for STAGES

❶❷ Invite these children to put the leaf TPR Card on the stem TPR Card and say *leaf* and *stem* as they are able.	❸❹❺ Have these children use the words in a sentence, such as *A leaf grows on a stem.*

- Repeat this activity several times throughout the unit.

Grammar in Context: Object Pronouns ❶❷❸❹❺

1. Have children form two lines, boys and girls.
2. Hand a TPR Card to the first boy and say *I give this flower to Eduardo. I give it to him.* Have Eduardo hand the card to the girl opposite. Model *Eduardo gives it to Lourdes. He gives it to her.*
3. Continue passing back and forth repeating *him, her,* and *it.* Add *me* by modeling *Lourdes gives it to me.*
4. Children in the lower Stages should be able to participate by at least performing the action or responding to either/or questions, such as *Did I give it to him or her?* More proficient children should be able say the entire sentence.
5. In heterogeneous pairs, have children write sentences using people's names as objects in the sentence. Then have children rewrite each sentence, replacing the object noun with a pronoun, as they are able.

You will need

- **Language Learning Master** p. 31
- Scissors

Language Learning Master

p. 34 ❶❷❸❹❺

Language Junction

Object pronouns are an area of particular difficulty for speakers of languages in which subject and object pronouns are identical, including Haitian Creole, Khmer, Cantonese, and Hmong. Speakers of these languages may at first use subject pronouns where object pronouns are needed in English: *I saw he.* Without correcting them overtly, model correct English usage: *Yes, you saw him.*

WEEK 1 DAY 5

Manipulative Chart: Focus on Oral Language Development

FUNCTION MINI-LESSON

Use Social Etiquette ❶❷❸❹❺

1. Model polite requests, such as *Juan, please put the chart on the desk* and *Thank you, Juan* using the Manipulative Chart. Explain that this is how we ask for things nicely, or politely.
2. Go around the room, asking children to either put the Manipulative Chart somewhere or to open certain flaps on it. Use *please* and *thank you.*
3. Invite children with greater language ability to make polite requests with *please* and *thank you* using the Manipulative Chart.
4. Encourage children to use polite requests and thank each other in classroom situations, such as while playing games or when asking for something.

FUNCTION MINI-LESSON

Sequence ❶❷❸❹❺

1. Display the Manipulative Chart. Say *First there is a seed.* Open the flaps one by one and say *Then the roots grow. Next the stems and leaves grow. Last a flower grows.* Emphasize the sequence words *first, then, next,* and *last* as you point to the plant parts on the chart.
2. Invite a volunteer to "finger walk" up the chart as you repeat your words.
3. Using gestures and pointing, explain that when we want to describe something in order, it helps to use sequence words.
4. Select four children and give them Picture Card 1: flower and Picture Cards 6–8: leaf, stem, root in random order. Have each child tape the card on the board in correct growth sequence from bottom to top. Have them practice using sequence words as they put the cards up. Children in Stages 3, 4, or 5 may use sentences such as *First the root grows.*

Grammar in Context: Sequence Words ❶❷❸❹❺

1. Invite children to role-play the growth of a flower as you narrate the steps using *First, next, then,* and *last.*
2. Children may then take turns opening the flaps on the Manipulative Chart, saying the steps as they are able. ◎

Options for STAGES

❶❷ These children may simply open the flaps in order, saying the sequence words and naming the plant parts as they are able.

❸❹❺ Encourage these children to use phrases or sentences, such as *First root grows.*

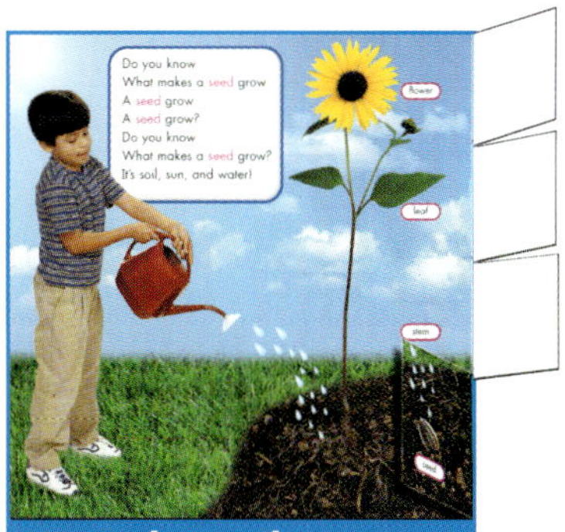

Manipulative Chart

Language Learning Strategy

Work with a friend to help you understand.

Use this strategy for children in Stages 3, 4, or 5.

- Point out that children can learn new words when they work with a friend. Tell them that when they work together, they can help each other with words they don't know. **Model** Tell children that Yuri and Ahn are working together. Yuri says *Ahn, we fold the paper in half. I know what paper is, but I don't know what "fold in half" means. Can you help me?* Explain that Ahn shows Yuri how to fold the paper into two parts that are the same size.
- Throughout the unit, encourage children to try to ask a friend for help when they come across words and phrases that they don't know.

Home-School Connection

When children have practiced manipulating the Manipulative Chart Student Version, send it home for them to practice with their family members.

Assessment

Record your observations of children during these mini-lessons on their individual assessment checklists for this unit. See page U99.

You will need

- **Language Learning Master** pp. 29–30
- Scissors
- Crayons

Assessment

Record your observations of children on their individual assessment checklists for this unit. See page U99.

Concept Poster
Picture Cards 10, 11

Guided Reading

As you work on this unit, conduct small groups of guided reading or shared-to-guided reading independent of thematic instruction. Instruction is provided in the Guided Reading section of this guide.

Component Organizer

Other Concept Poster lessons in this unit:

- Revisiting, p. U90

Manipulative Chart: Student Version

- Invite children to color and cut out the cards and the chart.
- Encourage children to place their cards correctly as you open each flap on the Manipulative Chart.
- Have children respond to your Total Physical Response commands: *Show me the roots.*
- Play Part 4 of the Oral Language Audio CD and model how children can manipulate their Student Versions as they sing along. Tell children that they will later be able to listen to the Audio CD and manipulate this mini-chart in the Listening Post.

WEEK 2 DAY 1

Concept Poster: Introduction

Setting the Scene

Prop: jar of peanut butter

- Introduce Picture Card 11: peanuts. Ask children to identify what they see and help them recognize the picture as peanuts.
- Hold up the jar of peanut butter and say *Peanut butter is made from peanuts.*

Creating Comprehensible Input

- Point out the girl eating a sandwich on the Concept Poster. Say that it is a peanut butter sandwich. Explain that you are going to find out where the peanut butter came from. Display Picture Card 10: field. Direct children's attention toward the first line of photographs on the Concept Poster. Demonstrate how to talk through the relationship between the pictures with a think-aloud. Trace with your finger as you tell how each picture follows the sequence of production.
  Model *This is a field. This arrow tells me that this picture goes with the next one on the right. These are peanut plants growing in the field. This machine in the field picks the peanuts. Then the peanuts are sent to a factory. The machines in the factory make peanut butter from the peanuts. Next boxes of peanut butter jars go to the market. Here I see the peanut butter at the store. When I follow the arrow again, I see a man buying peanut butter. Last I see a girl enjoying a peanut butter sandwich.*
- Recap this in simple language as you trace the connecting arrows: *a field; peanut plants in the field; A machine picks the peanuts; Peanut butter is made at a factory; Peanut butter goes to the store; We buy peanut butter at the store; Then we can make a sandwich with the peanut butter.*
- Invite a child in Stage 3, 4, or 5 to lead the class in talking through the pictures in the first "row." Continue with the second and third "rows." Support with appropriate academic language, such as sequence words.
- After the child has finished, recap in simple language, pointing to the pictures and the connecting arrows.

Extending Oral Language

- Engage children in reviewing these concepts by asking questions. ◎

Options for STAGES

❶❷ Ask these children specific questions that require only a *yes/no* answer or pointing, such as *Where are the peanuts?* (Child points) *Right, in the field.*	❸❹❺ Ask these children open-ended questions that require substantive answers, such as *What do you know about making peanut butter?*

- Use Total Physical Response commands to build familiarity with the concepts. For instance, say *Show me where peanuts grow. Show me what happens after the peanut butter is made.*

Language Practice Game: Version 1 ❶❷❸❹❺

Preparing the Game

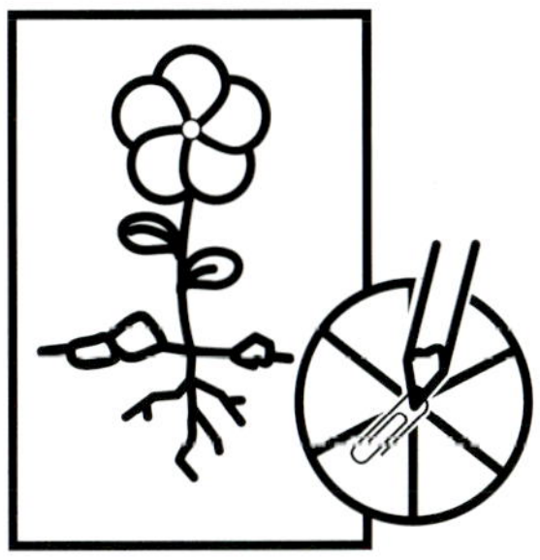

Cut out the spinners on page 33 and mount them on a file folder. Each child will have the plant game board, and each group will have a spinner with pictures. Provide a paper clip and pencil to use on the spinner.

Playing Version 1

Have children play in heterogeneous groups of mixed language abilities with four children each. Provide enough game markers for each child to be able to cover his or her board. Model the following directions.

1. Players take turns spinning the paper clip and placing a game marker on the corresponding plant part, saying, as they are able, *What makes a stem (leaf, etc.) grow? It's soil, sun, and water.* ◎

Options for STAGES

❶❷ These children can say the word as they are able or simply place their game marker on the game board.	❸ These children should be encouraged to say a few words, such as *plant grow, soil, sun.*	❹❺ Encourage these children to say the complete question and answer: *What makes a stem grow? It's soil, sun, and water.*

2. Play continues until someone fills his or her board. Remind children that they will need to spin one stem, two seeds, three leaves, and two flowers to fill the board.

You will need

- **Language Learning Master** pp. 32–33
- Scissors
- Game markers
- File folders
- Tape
- Paper clips
- Pencils

Component Organizer

Other Language Practice Game lessons in this unit:
- Version 2, p. U96

Assessment

Record your observations of children during the Language Practice Game on their individual assessment checklists for this unit. See page U99.

Newcomer Book: Small-Group Instruction

What Makes Plants Grow?

Written by Karen Clevidence

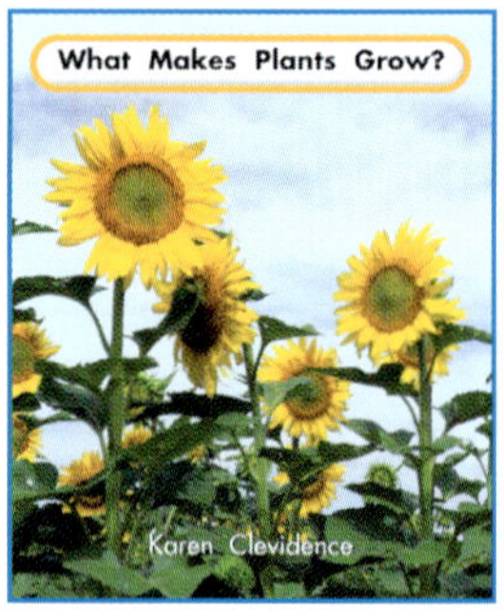

OVERVIEW *Look at all the different kinds of plants. Let's find out what makes them grow.*

The Newcomer Book is supported by the language of the Manipulative Chart and should be integrated into small-group instruction this week when children have had enough practice with vocabulary and concepts in this unit.

Language Pattern

What makes _______ grow?

Text Vocabulary

plants

Vocabulary Extenders

counting

Reading the Text

Book Talk

- Work with a small group of four children at one time who exhibit similar literacy-learning behaviors.
- Engage children in a book talk as you flip through the pages of your copy of the book. ◎

Options for STAGES

❶❷ Identify each plant for these children. Encourage them to say the names after you as they are able.

❸❹❺ Ask children to identify each plant as you encounter them.

INSTRUCTIONAL PATHS

❶❷❸❹❺ All Readers:	❶❷❸❹❺ Emergent Readers:	❶❷❸❹❺ Early Readers:
Shared-to-Guided Reading	Guided Reading	Independent Reading no lesson provided

INDIVIDUAL READING

Shared-to-Guided Reading **3–4 sessions**
❶❷❸❹❺ **All Readers**

1. Read the book to children.
   - Invite children to sit near you as you read a copy of the book. Begin with the cover and title page.
   - Turn to page 2 and begin reading the words as you point to them. Draw children's attention to the pictures.
2. Read the book with children.
   - Encourage children to follow along in their own copies of the book, turning the pages as you read together and using their own fingers to point to the words.
   - Invite children to chime in when they are comfortable.
   - Reread the book in this manner over several sessions.
3. Have children buddy-read the book.
4. Invite children to read the book independently.

Assess

- Did children look from left to right as you read together?
- Did children participate in buddy-reading?

Guided Reading **2 sessions**
❶❷❸❹❺ **Emergent Readers**

1. Provide copies of the book to children. Use one child's book and turn to page 2. Introduce the book's pattern to children by reading the sentence and pointing to each word as you read *What makes sunflowers grow?*.
2. Have each child read at his or her own pace while remaining in the group. Discourage choral reading. Observe as they read.

Assess

- Did children ask for help with English when they needed it?
- Did children check the picture clue against the first letter to read a word?

REVISITING THE NEWCOMER BOOK

For those children who are ready, you may use the book to count the number of plant parts, such as flowers, in each picture.

WEEK 2 DAY 2

Big Book: Introduction

What Fine Gardeners

Written by Brenda Parkes
Illustrated by Maya González

OVERVIEW *María and Miguel are very fine gardeners. Let's find out what they do.*

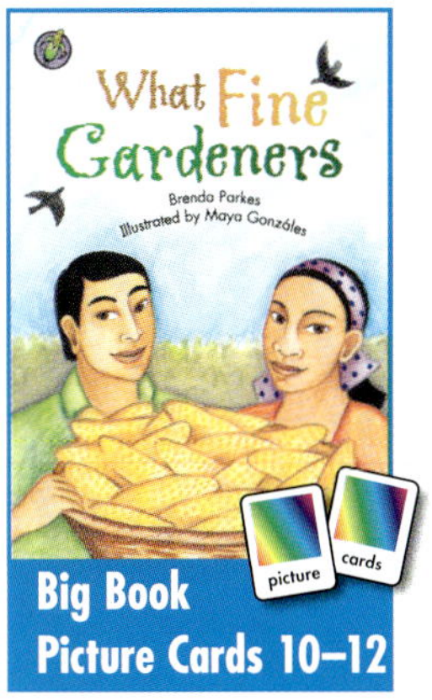

Warming Up

Begin the lesson by revisiting the Manipulative Chart, Chant Poster, or a classic such as *The Town Mouse and the Country Mouse*. You may ask a volunteer to choose one.

Setting the Scene

- Show Picture Card 11: peanuts and Picture Card 10: field. Remind children that peanuts grow in fields. Then show Picture Card 12: corn.
- Tap into children's prior knowledge. Ask *Have you seen corn? What does it look like (feel like, taste like)?* Invite children to share what they know about corn in words and gestures. Encourage children to talk about their experiences with corn in their home cultures.
- Refer to the pictures on the front cover. Identify María and Miguel, the children, the corn, the crows, and the field. Introduce the book and provide children with an overview of the story.
- Using gestures, discuss the cover of the book and help children make a prediction about the story. *What do you think María and Miguel will do in their garden?*
- Tell children that they will learn about how corn grows in the story. Point out the border feature beginning on page 4. Explain that this will help them follow the growth of the corn stalk.

Reading the Text

- Read the title page. Have children make an additional prediction based on this picture. *What will the crows do?*
- As you read through the book, use a pointer or your finger to draw children's attention to the text. Focus on the enjoyment of the book, pointing out items in the pictures to support your reading. You will return later to build children's understanding of the text. In future rereadings, children should be encouraged to chime in.
- If you have children in Stages 3, 4, or 5, pause after reading page 7 for a prediction of what will happen next. *What do you think will happen now that they have planted the corn?* Pause again after page 21 and ask *What will María and Miguel do now?*

Creating Comprehensible Input

- Open up the back flap of the book, which shows the sequencing of the main story events in four boxes. Keep this on display to help children follow the order of the steps.
- Use the comprehension supports in the following chart to help you build comprehensible input with children at all Stages of Language Acquisition.

Component Organizer

Other Big Book lessons in this unit:

- Revisiting, p. U88
- Comprehension Strategy, p. U89
- Oral Language Development, pp. U91–U92
- Literacy Skills, pp. U95–U96

PAGE	IN THE STORY	COMPREHENSION SUPPORT
2	"It's time to plant the corn, Miguel."	act out: planting
4	So they took their spades, hoes, rakes . . .	point: to each tool
6	First they dug and raked. . . . Then they hoed . . . into rows.	act out: digging, raking, and hoeing; gesture: use finger to draw rows
7	Next they planted the corn seeds . . .	act out: dropping seeds into soil
8	"What fine gardeners María and Miguel are!"	restate: people think María and Miguel are good gardeners
9	"They dig . . . their corn plants grow."	act out: digging, planting seeds, hoeing, raking, and watering
10	The rain fell and the sun shone.	gesture: wiggle fingers for rain; gesture: hands overhead for sun
10	Every day . . . would not eat the seeds.	act out: crows pecking and eating; gesture: shooing
11	. . . some tiny green shoots came out of the ground.	gesture: thumb and index finger for "tiny"
14	. . . tiny green shoots turned into stalks . . .	gesture: thumb and index finger for "tiny," expand for growing
15	. . . weeded and watered . . .	act out: pulling up weeds, watering
19	. . . cobs were as big as burritos . . .	gesture: size with hands
21	"It's time to harvest the corn," . . .	act out: excited and pleased and picking corn
23	"It's time to eat," . . .	act out: eating corn on the cob

You will need

- Magazine pictures of foods
- Scissors
- Poster board
- Spices and herbs (dill, caraway, basil, parsley, mint)
- Fresh snack foods (broccoli, spinach, peas, celery, carrots, sunflower seeds)
- Dip ingredients (cottage cheese, salsa, peanut butter)
- Napkins, paper plates

Revisiting the Big Book

- Reread the story.
- Have groups of children take on the roles of María, Miguel, neighbors, school children, and crows using props, such as toy garden tools, a watering can, backpacks, and so on.
- Invite each group to retell the story in character.

WEEK 2 DAY 3

Theme Project: Plant Parts on Our Table

1. Prepare a picture chart of food. Write the following headings across the top of the chart: *seeds, leaves, root, stem, fruit,* and *flower.* Paste food pictures from magazines under the proper headings. Write the name of the food next to each picture.
2. Every few days, present children with one or two new foods. Have children work in small groups to examine the samples and decide which heading on the chart the food goes under. Refer to the chart to determine how to categorize the foods according to their plant parts. Children may draw or paste pictures of the foods on the chart. Each food item should be labeled.
3. At the end of the project, invite children to choose or create dips and spreads. Provide assistance with mixing and stirring. Cut up or provide bite-sized foods to go with the dips and spreads.
4. Provide disposable cameras. Circulate and photograph children as they work. Allow children to photograph their finished food creations.
5. Provide copies of the photographs. Assist in writing about each photograph, including any recipes that were created.

WEEK 2 DAY 4

Big Book: Focus on Comprehension Strategy

Sequences Ideas and Story Events

1. Reread the story. Have volunteers point to and identify the corresponding border pictures at the bottom of each page.
2. Draw children's attention to the back flap of *What Fine Gardeners*. Invite a volunteer to sequentially "finger walk" from one picture to the next as you retell the story, emphasizing the sequence words *first, next, then, last*.
3. Explain that stories happen in a certain order and that the chart they see helps them keep track of that order.
4. Invite volunteers to retell the story themselves while "finger walking" on the back flap. ◎

Options for STAGES

❶❷ Invite these children to use sequence words as they are able.	❸ Encourage these children to retell with phrases and sentence approximations.	❹❺ Encourage these children to retell each part of the story using phrases or complete sentences.

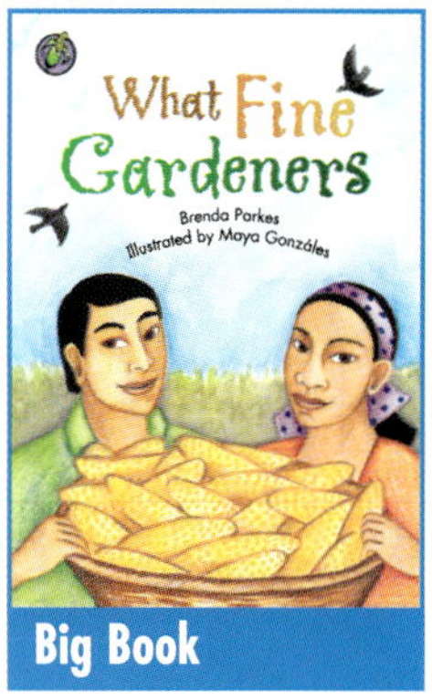
What Fine Gardeners
Brenda Parkes
Illustrated by Maya Gonzáles
Big Book

A Assessment

Use a retelling of the Big Book to assess comprehension. See page U99.

Chant Poster: Focus on Oral Language Development

FUNCTION MINI-LESSON

Use Social Etiquette ❶❷❸❹❺

- Revisit the chant, saying it several times.
- Review using polite language, which was introduced in Week 1 Day 5. Have one child ask *May I touch the brown seed?* Have a child respond *Yes, you may.* Have another pair demonstrate polite language, such as *May I please taste the lima beans? Yes, you may taste them. Thank you.* ◎

Options for STAGES

❶❷ Invite these children to ask for and grant permission as they are able, using gestures and/or words such *please* and *thank you*.	❸❹❺ Encourage these children to use full sentences such as *Yes, you may touch the brown seeds.*

Brown seeds, black seeds.
Green seeds, more!
Speckled seeds, striped seeds.
Wrinkled seeds, more!
Flying seeds, floating seeds.
Sticking seeds, more!
Chant Poster

Home-Culture Sharing

Invite children to share the names of seeds that they eat in their home cultures. They may respond with the names in their home languages as well as any names they know in English.

Assessment

Record your observations of children during these mini-lessons on their individual assessment checklists for this unit. See page U99.

Revisiting the Concept Poster

- Revisit the Concept Poster, inviting volunteers to tell what happens first, next, and last.
- Invite small groups of children to take on roles and act out the process of bringing peanuts from field to table.

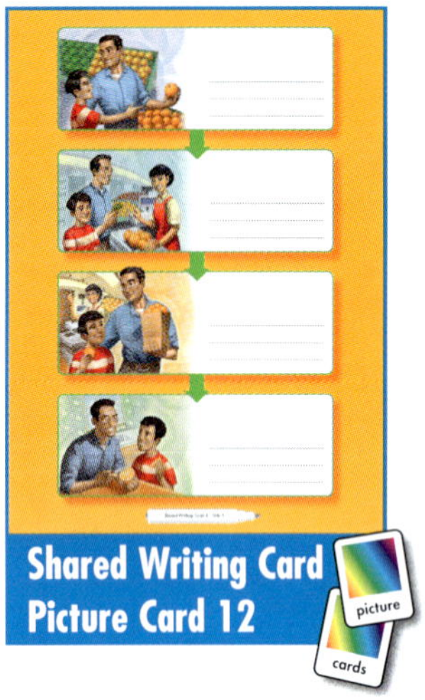

Shared Writing Card
Picture Card 12

You will need

- Shared Writing Card 4
- Wipe-off marker
- Regular marker
- Easel pad

FUNCTION MINI-LESSON

Sequence 1 2 3 4 5

- Review the sequence words introduced in Week 1 Day 5: *first, next, then* and *last.*
- Write the Chant Poster onto a piece of paper and make several photocopies of it. Cut each page into strips with one line of the chant on each strip and put the strips into envelopes.
- Divide the class into heterogeneous groups with 3 children each. Give each group the chant in strips. Model putting the chant together in order using sequence words.
- Have groups do the same. Display the Chant Poster for reference.

Grammar in Context: Adjectives with *-ing* 1 2 3 4 5

1. Review adjectives children learned in Unit 3. Help children understand that these words tell us more about the thing they describe.
2. Then point to the coconut. Say *This is floating in the water. It is a floating seed.* Emphasize and gesture *floating*. Say *The word* floating *tells us more about the coconut.* Repeat the procedure with dandelion seeds and *flying*.
3. Encourage volunteers to tell which word in the chant tells about the burrs (*sticking*).

WEEK 2 DAY 5

Shared Writing Card: Introduction of Side A

Setting the Scene

- Display the back flap of the Big Book. Follow the pictures down, and summarize the events using sequence words. Invite volunteers to chime in with sequence words they remember from earlier discussions. As you review the back flap, remind children that it is important to tell things in order.
- Show Picture Card 12: corn. Remind children that corn is a vegetable. Talk about where we buy fruits and vegetables to bring home.

Creating Comprehensible Input

- Display Shared Writing Card 4 Side A with the illustrations of buying oranges inside a flow chart graphic organizer. Begin by pointing to and naming the people and the food items.

  Model *Let's see . . . This looks like a father and his son. They are in a store. Here are some oranges. Oh, I see, they are buying oranges. Now I see that they are leaving the store. Ah, this looks like they are at home. They are eating the oranges.*
- Go back to the first illustration and use think-alouds to talk through the illustrations. Point to the illustrations one by one and track the sequential order.

  Illustration 1: *Here the father and boy are choosing some oranges.*
  Illustration 2: *Now they are paying for the oranges.*
  Illustration 3: *Here they are taking their oranges home.*
  Illustration 4: *Now Dad and his son can eat the oranges.*
- Explain that the boxes and arrows on the Shared Writing Card help us understand the order of the events. Point to each illustration in turn saying *first, next, then* and *last.*

- Invite a volunteer from Stages 3, 4, or 5 to retell the illustrations in his or her own words. Repeat with other volunteers.

Scribing with the Graphic Organizer

- After children have become comfortable with the content of the illustrations, you can use the wipe-off marker provided to scribe while you brainstorm together labels for the graphic organizer. Since you are creating a graphic organizer, not a finished product, well-crafted sentences are not necessary.
- Think aloud as you write so that children gain insight in the writing process.
- Here is an example of simple shared writing labeling for the illustrations.
  Illustration 1: *choose oranges at store*
  Illustration 2: *pay for oranges*
  Illustration 3: *take oranges home*
  Illustration 4: *eat oranges*

Writing Together from the Graphic Organizer

- You will again use the pen as you work together with children to create a shared writing piece. In this instance, you will model how to use the words and phrases from the shopping graphic organizer to create a finished paragraph on your easel pad.
- Begin with a think-aloud.
  Model *First I need to say what my paragraph is going to be about. Let me look at the pictures and words on my graphic organizer. Hmm . . . I think I'll write* The boy and his dad go to the store to buy some oranges to eat. *For the first picture we wrote "choose oranges." This should be a complete sentence. We also want to say that this is the first thing the boy and his dad do. I'll try this:* First the boy and his dad choose some oranges. *That's a complete sentence, right?*
- Write down the sentences that you and the children agree upon. You might say why the sequence word *First* is very important here.
- As you move down to the second illustration, read the label and then invite children to help create a sentence based on the picture and label. Write down what children say as you work to make sentences with them. When children offer sentences with errors in them, correct them discreetly. Encourage children to use classroom resources, such as the Word Wall.
- When you have finished your shared writing piece, read it together several times. Then hang it up on the wall where it can be displayed during the rest of the unit and reread many times. For now, do not erase your labels on Side A.

WEEK 3 DAY 1

Big Book: Focus on Oral Language Development

Reread the Big Book and return to the text to focus on oral language development.

Grammar in Context: Infinitives ❶❷❸❹❺

1. Using the back flap of the Big Book, point to each picture. Summarize the events using the sentence pattern from the book *It's time to plant (to harvest, to eat) the corn. It's time to rest.* Emphasize the word *to* and point to it in the Big Book on pages 2 and 21–24.

Phonics in Context

Shared writing provides an ideal opportunity for reviewing the phonics skills children are learning. Highlight the sounds in words like ***take***, ***pay*** and ***home*** as you reread the writing.

Sample Shared Writing

The boy and his dad go to the store to buy some oranges to eat. First the boy and his dad choose some oranges. Then they pay for the oranges. Next the boy and his dad take the bag of oranges home. Last they eat the sweet oranges.

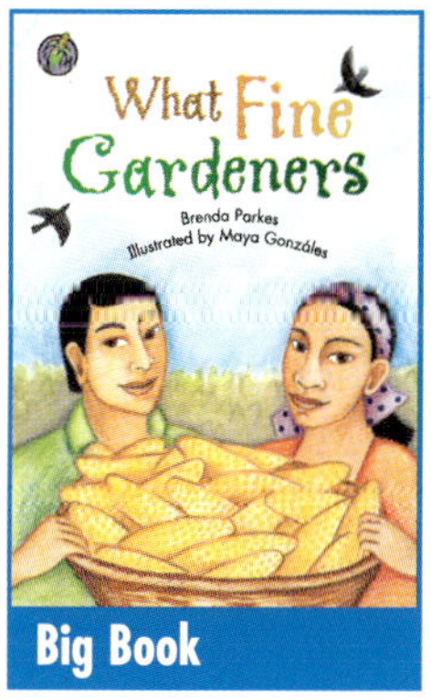

Guided Reading

As you work on this unit, conduct small groups of guided reading or shared-to-guided reading independent of thematic instruction. Instruction is provided in the Guided Reading section of this guide.

2. Invite a volunteer to act out the planting actions. Remind them of what María and Miguel in the story did to plant their corn. Encourage the class to help with role playing the different actions involved with tending a garden. Have a Stage 3, 4, or 5 child call out *It's time to . . .* as a signal for which action to do. Continue with the rest of the verbs.
3. Go through the story again, and have children look for all the infinitives after *It's time . . .* Use your finger to circle the infinitives that you find (*to plant, to water, to harvest, to eat, to rest*).
4. Work together to come up with and act out other infinitives related to the story, such as *to cook, to dig, to rake,* and so on.

Language Learning Master

p. 35 ❶❷❸❹❺

Grammar in Context: Sequence Words ❶❷❸❹❺

1. Point out the bottom border, starting with page 4. Invite Stage 1 volunteers to "finger walk" across the border. Say *The pictures are in order. They tell us that to plant corn you start with kernels. Then you plant them in rows.* Continue explaining what each border picture shows. Have children point to the pictures in order as you tell about them using sequence words.
2. Go through the text identifying sequence clue words, such as *last of all, after a week, another two weeks, soon.*
3. Ask *When did this happen? When did the green shoots come out?* Encourage children to use sequence words in their answers. Children in Stages 1 or 2 may use one-word responses, such as *first, next.*

WEEK 3 DAY 2

Shared Writing Card: Brainstorming Side B

Brainstorming a Topic

- Use Side A of the Shared Writing Card and your finished shared writing piece about buying oranges. Review how you used the graphic organizer pictures and labels as the basis of your finished piece.
- Turn the card over to Side B. Tell the children that you will now think of your own topic together to draw in the graphic organizer. Brainstorm together a topic that involves an activity or process. You can steer them either toward planting a garden or toward a more general process that they can do by themselves, such as making a peanut butter and jelly sandwich. (Your process should have four steps or fewer.)

You will need

- Shared Writing Card 4
- Wipe-off marker

Scribing with the Graphic Organizer

- Once the class has chosen a topic, you should decide together what the first step is. Model how to draw the first picture, such as putting soil in the pot. Invite volunteers to step up to the card and draw subsequent steps as the class decides on them. Continue drawing until the process is complete; some boxes may be left empty.
- Now it's time to put labels on your graphic organizer. Elicit suggestions for labels from the group in the same manner as you did for Side A and record them on the Shared Writing Card.
- You will create the shared writing paragraph in the next session.

Active Social Studies: Working Together

1. Set up four workstations and assign a heterogeneous group to each station. As children in each workstation receive the bowl, they will contribute to making the bean salad.
   - Station 1: Put canned beans and corn into the bowl.
   - Station 2: Break up celery stalks and place in bowl.
   - Station 3: Mix the ingredients.
   - Station 4: Add salad dressing and stir.
2. Circulate to provide assistance and to discuss the tasks and how they contribute to the finished product.
3. After completing the salad, form groups that include one child from each station. Have them work together to draw and label a graphic organizer about the activity.

You will need

- 1 can each kidney beans, chickpeas, corn
- 3 stalks celery
- 1 bottle salad dressing
- Large bowl and mixing spoon
- Paper
- Markers

WEEK 3 DAY 3

Shared Writing Card: Writing Together with Side B

- As with Side A, you will scribe as you work together with the children to create a finished writing piece from the graphic organizer on Side B of Shared Writing Card 4.
- Model writing from the first drawing, using think-alouds as you go. Show children how to use resources like the Word Wall. Work together to figure out difficult spellings and passages.
- When you have finished with your shared writing piece, read it together several times. Then hang it up on the wall where it can be displayed during the rest of the unit. At the end of the unit, you should erase both sides of the Shared Writing Card.

Manipulative Chart: Focus on Oral Language Development

Grammar in Context: Present Continuous Tense 1 2 3 4 5

1. Ask a volunteer to hop. Say *Ari is hopping.* Continue having children act out verbs. Emphasize the present continuous verb during each action saying, for example, *Juanita is clapping. Edgar and Jun are smiling.*
2. Point out the picture of the boy on the Manipulative Chart. Say *The boy is watering the plant.* Model holding a watering can as you move slightly to suggest a continued action.
3. Emphasize the word *grow* on the chart. As you open the flaps one by one, say *The stem is growing. The leaves are growing.* Demonstrate growing by crouching down and then shimmying up.
4. Point out that when children hear or see the word *is* or *are* and a word that ends with *-ing,* it usually names an action that is happening now.

Language Learning Master

p. 36 1 2 3 4 5

WEEK 3 DAY 4

You will need

- 4 beans, soaked overnight
- 2 paper cups
- Soil
- Easel pad
- Marker

Active Science: Soil, Sun, and Water

Sunny
Dark
September 14
2 inches tall
September 14
$1\frac{1}{2}$ inches tall
September 20
3 inches tall
September 20
2 inches tall

1. Refer children to the Manipulative Chart and review the parts of the plant and what they need to grow. Explain to children that they will investigate how their own plants grow.
2. Plant two beans each in two paper cups of soil. Place one cup in a sunny spot and water it. Place the other in a dark place and water it. Have children touch the moist soil.
3. Assign teams to check the moisture level of the soil every day. Explain that the soil should not get too dry. Remind them to touch the soil to see whether it needs more water.
4. Have children work in heterogeneous groups of two or three to monitor and chart the plants' growth from sprouting through full growth. Invite children to pantomime and describe the growth of the plant in each container.
5. Make and label a class growth chart, with one column for the plant in the sun and one column for the plant in the dark. Use drawings and labels to show the different stages of growth. Help children draw conclusions from the chart about which plants grew well and why.

WEEK 3 DAY 5

You will need

- Overhead transparency of Writing Resource Guide, p. 86
- Overhead marker

Writing Resource Guide: A Simplified Graphic Organizer

This activity is optional and necessary only if you wish to use the simplified sequence graphic organizer in cooperative-group or independent writing.

Brainstorming a Topic

- Review the drawings and labels you used on Side B of the Shared Writing Card. Trace the sequence of the pictures with your fingers.
- On the overhead projector, display a transparency of page 86 of the Writing Resource Guide, which is a flow chart graphic organizer with only three boxes.
- Brainstorm together a simple topic that involves steps in a process, such as washing your hands. Your process should have only three steps.

Scribing with the Graphic Organizer

- Once the class has chosen a topic, you should decide together what the steps might be. Model drawing each of the three steps.
- Label each of the three drawings on your graphic organizer. Elicit suggestions for labels from the group in the same manner as you did with the Shared Writing Card.

You will need

- Writing Resource Guide, pp. 85–86
- Markers

Writing Resource Guide: Cooperative-Group Writing

- Form cooperative groups of heterogeneous Stages with three to four children each to work together on a writing piece using the flow chart graphic organizer. You may hand out a copy of Writing Planner A or B to each group.

- Review the shared writing graphic organizers and finished pieces you have made together. Remind children that the drawings help them remember the order of things.
- Have the groups work together first to complete their graphic organizers and then to write their finished pieces. Circulate to provide assistance. ◎

Options for STAGES

1 2 These children should draw the pictures for the group.	**3 4 5** These children should take responsibility for the writing of the finished piece.

Writing Mini-lessons

See the Writing Resource Guide for mini-lessons to use as children write. Here are some suggestions:
- Mini-lesson 27: Writing a How-To
- Mini-lesson 42: Checking Sequence

WEEK 4 DAY 1

Big Book: Focus on Literacy Skills

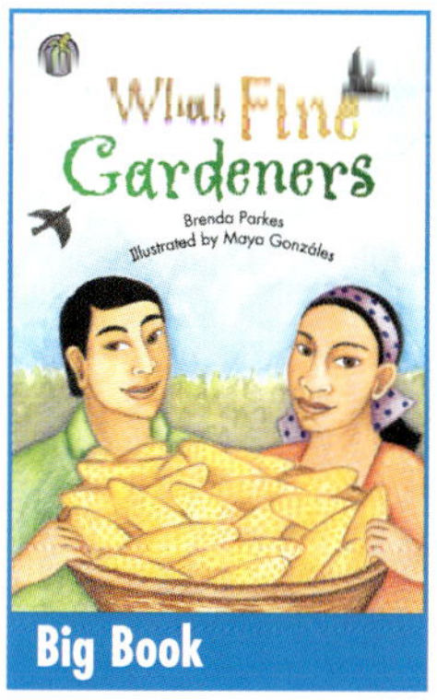

Word Level: Phonics in Context

1. You will need the Word Wall Starters with the corn symbol on them: *r__ake__*, *p__ail__*, *w__oke__*, *r__oad__*. These are pictured in the back of the Big Book.
2. Tell children that you want to choose some special words from the book for them to look at more closely.
3. Introduce the word *rake* by saying it clearly, elongating the *ake* sound, and drawing attention to the highlighting behind *ake*. Then repeat the *ake* sound several times. Say *The letter* e *at the end of* rake *makes the letter* a *have the long* a *sound. Let's say the word* rake *together:* rake. *Let's sing a song!* Review Phonics Song Chart 14 together.
4. Say *I'm going to put the word* rake *underneath the* long a. Walk over to the Word Wall and place the card *rake* under the *long a* label, taking care to group word families together. Remind children to use the symbol to help them remember where they "met" that word before.
5. Repeat a similar procedure for the other words and phonics skills.

Sentence Level: Rhythm, Rhyme, and Alliteration

1. Have children read page 9 of the Big Book as you say the words in a sing-song voice. Have everyone clap along to the beat. This is repeated on pages 13 and 17.
2. Point out the rhyming words *sow, hoe, grow*. Say *These words sound alike. They end with long* o. Invite children to add other long *o* words.
3. Read the last sentence on page 9. Emphasize /w/ at the beginning of *water* and *watch*. Say *These words begin with /w/.* Go to page 12 and read the first sentence. Emphasize /b/ at the beginning of *big, black,* and *branches*. Say *These words all begin with /b/. It's fun to read sentences that have lots of words with the same beginning sound. Let's read them together.* Read the sentences on pages 9 and 12 with alliteration.
4. You might extend this by presenting simple tongue twisters for children to enjoy, such as *Blake baked a big, brown cake.*

Guided Reading

As you work on this unit, conduct small groups of guided reading or shared-to-guided reading independent of thematic instruction. Instruction is provided in the Guided Reading section of this guide.

Home-School Connection

Send home page 47 of the Home-School Connection Masters for children to use in retelling of *What Fine Gardeners* to their families. They should retell the story in English and then talk about it in either English or their home language.

Text Level: Understanding Characters and Setting

1. Tell the children that this story has different people and animals in it. Read pages 2 and 3 and point to María and Miguel. Say *Who are they?* Reread the text pointing to María and Miguel as you say their names. Ask children to tell you something about them. For example, they might tell you that María and Miguel are hard-working.
2. Continue with the other characters such as the neighbors, children, and crows.
3. Next ask *Where do María and Miguel live?* Reread pages 2 and 3 and help children understand that the story takes place on their farm in a rural area. Continue to page through the story, identifying the different locations as the pictured settings change. Ask questions to elicit responses, such as *Where are María and Miguel? (in the field; in the house) Where are the neighbors? (on the porch).* ◎

Options for STAGES

1 2 Allow these children to point to or use one-word answers to identify characters and settings.

3 4 5 These children can reply with phrases and sentences, according to their ability.

You will need

- Previously prepared game boards
- Spinners with words only
- Game markers
- Paper clips
- Pencils

Language Practice Game: Version 2 1 2 3 4 5

Have children in Stages 3, 4, or 5 work in pairs. Provide a game board for each pair and the spinner with only words. This game should be played as in Version 1.

1. Children take turns spinning a paper clip around a pencil tip. Then the player says the word indicated on the spinner.
2. Children then place a game marker on the corresponding plant part and say *What makes a stem grow? It's soil, sun, and water.*
3. The first player to cover his or her game board is the winner.
4. Remind children that they will need to spin the same word more than once in order to cover all the parts of the board.

WEEK 4 DAY 2

You will need

- Dry beans
- One tens frame per child

Active Math: Bean Counters

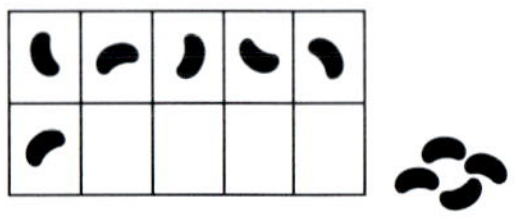

1. Have the children work in pairs. Provide a tens frame box for each pair of children.
2. Distribute 10 beans to each pair.
3. Draw a tens frame on the board and use different colors to fill in 6 boxes. Have children place 6 beans in their tens frame. Then ask *How many more beans do we need to make ten?*
4. Fill in the remaining boxes and say *6 plus 4 equals 10.* Write the equation on the board and have children place their remaining beans. After repeating the procedure with other sums, invite children to continue with their own addition sentences.

End-of-Unit Assessment

- While children are engaged in activities this week, pull them individually for the Big Book retelling, using page U99 at the end of this unit.
- Select a number of children with whom you would like to use the Open-Ended Oral Language Assessment on pages U98–U99 of this unit and pull them individually during activities this week. We recommend assessing about one-fourth of your class each unit.
- You should also have gathered the following for their assessment portfolio:
  - page 36 of the Language Learning Masters
  - page 37 of the Language Learning Masters
  - finished writing piece assessed according to the Writing Rubric on page A6.

You will need

A copy of page U99 at the end of this unit for each child

WEEK 4 DAY 3–4

Writing Resource Guide: Individual Writing

- Children have engaged in a step-by-step writing process moving toward independence. They began with teacher-led shared writing, moved to cooperative groups, and are now ready to work individually.
- Provide a copy of the four-step or three step organizer to each child. They may need individual conferencing on choosing a topic. ◎

Options for STAGES

❶❷ and Emergent Level
These children should draw the steps of their process on their graphic organizer. They should write labels on their own or dictate labels to you.

❸❹❺ Early Level and Above
These children should also use drawings and labels on the graphic organizer to record their topic. They should then use the graphic organizer to create a finished piece.

- When children have completed their finished product, whether graphic organizer or paragraph, you should assess it using the Writing Rubric on page A6 of this Teacher's Guide.

You will need

- Writing Resource Guide pp. 85–86
- Markers

Assessment

Continue pulling some children for the Big Book Retelling and Open-Ended Oral Language Assessment as others write.

WEEK 4 DAY 5

Theme Project: Sharing

- Have each group share its photos and writing pieces with the class. Ask children to describe any photographs that were taken. Encourage children to describe the work they were doing. You might ask, *Did you like the work? What was hard? What was easy? What parts did you like to do?*
- Each group should allow time for questions and feedback from the class. Model appropriate feedback for the class by making the first comment yourself—for example, *Great! You used the words* first *and* next. *Are there any other places that might need sequence words?*

Open-Ended Oral Language Assessment Reassess children's Language Acquisition Stages. Begin with an open-ended prompt like the first one below. If children are unable to respond, intervene with increasingly directed prompts, such as the second and third ones below.

What can you tell me about the picture?

What are the people in the garden doing?

I see a stem. Show me a leaf.

Assessment Directions: Copy this form for each child and place the completed form in the child's portfolio. Locate the child's Language Acquisition Stage for each of the first four activities and assess his or her performance during the unit according to expectations for that Stage. For the Big Book Retelling, pull children to retell the Big Book during end-of-unit assessment time. Use the Open-Ended Oral Language Assessment to reassess children's Language Acquisition Stages with one-fourth of your students for each unit, using the back side of the sheet to take notes. *For more guidance on assessment, see pages T33 and T34.*

Unit 4 Assessment

Name ______________________ **Date** ____________

On Our Way to English Grade 2	STAGE EXPECTATIONS ❶	❷	❸	❹	❺
Fluency Manipulative Chart Student Version, page U84 *How does the child respond when manipulating the mini-chart along with the Oral Language CD?*	Lays down the correct parts. ☐ Yes ☐ Not yet	Lays down the correct parts, naming them. ☐ Yes ☐ Not yet	Lays down the correct parts, approximating sentences and substitutions. ☐ Yes ☐ Not yet	Lays down the correct parts, singing the verse with few, if any, errors. ☐ Yes ☐ Not yet	
Content Area Knowledge Language Practice Game: Version 1, page U85 *How does the child demonstrate an understanding of plant parts and growth while playing the game?*	Puts the game marker on the appropriate plant parts saying the name of the plant parts as they are able. ☐ Yes ☐ Not yet		Puts the game markers on the appropriate plant parts and uses some appropriate vocabulary, such as *plant grow, soil, sun.* ☐ Yes ☐ Not yet	Puts the game marker on the appropriate plant parts and says complete sentences with appropriate vocabulary, such as *What makes a seed grow? It's soil, sun, and water.* ☐ Yes ☐ Not yet	
Social Language Function Social Etiquette, page U89 *How does the child respond during the Function Mini-lesson?*	Responds nonverbally or with a basic word or short phrase. ☐ Yes ☐ Not yet		Responds with a sentence approximation or a complete sentence. ☐ Yes ☐ Not yet		
Academic Language Function Sequence, page U90 *How does the child respond during the Function Mini-lesson?*	Puts the chant in order, using sequence words as they are able. ☐ Yes ☐ Not yet		Uses sequence words with short phrases ☐ Yes ☐ Not yet	Uses sequence words with sentence approximations or complete sentences. ☐ Yes ☐ Not yet	
Big Book Retelling page U89 *Have each child retell the story in character (page U88). How does the child retell the story?*	Uses props to participate without necessarily speaking. ☐ Yes ☐ Not yet	Retells using a few words. ☐ Yes ☐ Not yet	Retells using longer phrases or simple sentences. ☐ Yes ☐ Not yet	Retells using complete sentences in connected discourse with few errors. ☐ Yes ☐ Not yet	Retells using book language similar to native-speaking peers. ☐ Yes ☐ Not yet
Open-Ended Oral Language Assessment, page U98 *Use the child's responses to the illustration to reassess the child's Stage of Language Acquisition.*	☐ **STAGE ❶** Uses few or no words; gestures or points.	☐ **STAGE ❷** Uses words or short phrases.	☐ **STAGE ❸** Uses phrases and simple sentences.	☐ **STAGE ❹** Uses sentences in connected discourse.	☐ **STAGE ❺** Uses language comparable to native-speaking peers.

UNIT 5

Water Works

OVERVIEW *Children will learn about the water cycle and a variety of ways water is used. They will also explore ways in which water can be conserved.*

Determining the Purpose

Oral Language Development

Focus on Functions

Social Context:

Express Obligation ❶❷❸❹❺

Academic Context:

Solve Problems ❶❷❸❹❺

Focus on Grammar

- Sentences with *there is/are*
- Questions with *how much/many*
- Adjectives—feelings
- Prepositions—position

Comprehension Strategy

- Self-monitors by asking questions

Literacy Skills

- Word Level: Phonics in context long *i*, long *e*, ending *y*
- Sentence Level: Understands sentences and paragraphs
- Text Level: Charts

Content Area Objectives

- Distinguishes different forms and uses of water
- Understands that water is a natural resource to conserve
- Understands the concept of the water cycle

Language Learning Strategy

- It's OK to use things written in your home language to help you.

Writing Skill

- Uses a graphic organizer to support an idea

Unit Components

Manipulative Chart

There is water everywhere.
There's water in the rain.
So stomp and splash
And have a blast.
Water is everywhere!

Chant Poster

How much water do we need?
I know we use a lot!
If we each cut back a little,
We'll always have a lot!

Concept Poster

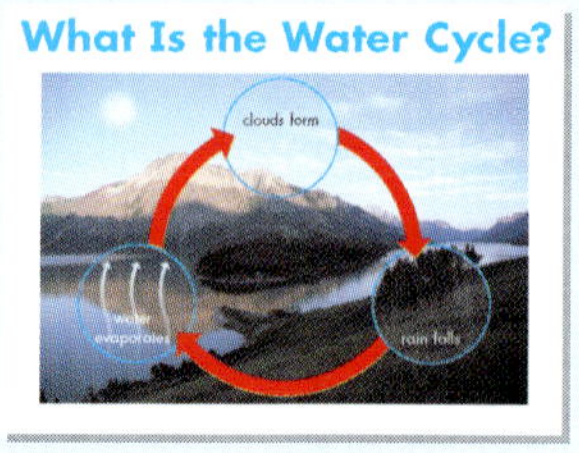
What Is the Water Cycle?
clouds form
rain falls

Water Is Everywhere

Newcomer Book

Unit at a Glance

	DURING THE WEEK	DAY 1
Week 1	**Small-Group Instruction:** • Guided Reading • Shared-to-Guided Reading **Phonics Focus:** *ike* and *ide* word families Phonics Song Chart 18, pp. P40–P41	**Manipulative Chart:** Introduction with Audio CD p. U103
Week 2	**Small-Group Instruction:** • Guided Reading • Shared-to-Guided Reading • Newcomer Book **Phonics Focus:** *ie* and *ight* word families Phonics Song Chart 19, pp. P42–P43	**Concept Poster:** Introduction p. U108 **Language Practice Game:** Version 1 p. U109
Week 3	**Small-Group Instruction:** • Guided Reading • Shared-to-Guided Reading • Newcomer Book **Phonics Focus:** *eed* and *eam* word families Phonics Song Chart 20, pp. P44–P45	**Big Book:** Oral Language Development p. U115
Week 4	**Small-Group Instruction:** • Guided Reading • Shared-to-Guided Reading • Newcomer Book **Phonics Focus:** Words ending with *y* Phonics Song Chart 21, pp. P46–P47	**Big Book:** Literacy Skills p. U119 **Language Practice Game:** Version 2 p. U120

STAGES ❶ Preproduction ❷ Early Production ❸ Speech Emergence ❹ Intermediate Fluency ❺ Advanced Fluency

Oral Language Audio CD

Big Book with Audio CD and Small Book

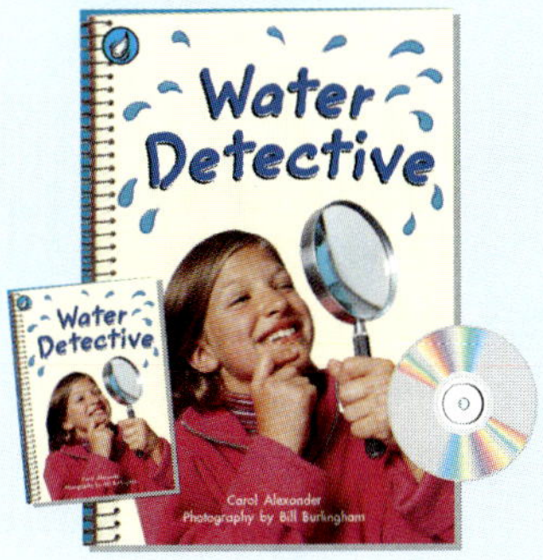

Home-School Connection Masters

Picture Cards

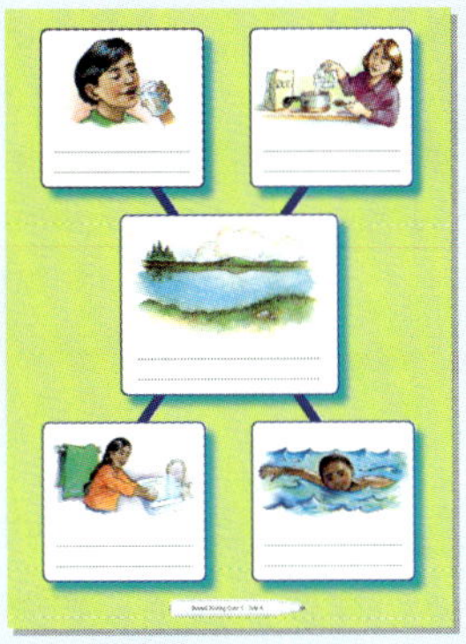

Shared Writing Card

Writing Resource Guide

Language Learning Masters

DAY 2	DAY 3	DAY 4	DAY 5
Manipulative Chart: Gestures and Manipulative Fun p. U104	**Chant Poster:** Introduction p. U105	**TPR Cards:** Introduction p. U106	**Manipulative Chart:** Oral Language Development Student Version p. U107
Big Book: Introduction p. U111	**Theme Project:** Operation Conservation p. U112 **Big Book:** Revisiting p. U112	**Big Book:** Comprehension Strategy p. U113 **Chant Poster:** Oral Language Development p. U113	**Shared Writing Card:** Introduction of Side A p. U114 **Concept Poster:** Revisiting p. U114
Shared Writing Card: Brainstorming Side B p. U116 **Active Social Studies:** Water Maps p. U116	**Shared Writing Card:** Writing Together with Side B p. U117 **Manipulative Chart:** Oral Language Development p. U117	**Active Science:** Rain Model p. U117	**Writing Resource Guide:** A Simplified Graphic Organizer Cooperative-Group Writing p. U118
Active Math: Water Evaporation p. U120 **Assessment** p. U121	**Writing Resource Guide:** Individual Writing p. U121 **Assessment** p. U121	**Writing Resource Guide:** Individual Writing p. U121 **Assessment** p. U121	**Theme Project:** Sharing p. U121

Center Activities

Number Nook

Provide measuring cups and containers of different shapes and sizes. Have children conduct measuring experiments to compare the volume of water in different containers.

Artist's Studio

Provide watercolors and drawing paper and allow children to draw their own pictures of clouds, rain, oceans, lakes, rivers, and puddles.

You will need

- Measuring cups, plastic tubs, milk cartons, and other containers
- Watercolors
- Paintbrushes
- Drawing paper
- Recycling bins
- Modeling clay
- Foil pans

Content Corner

Provide modeling clay and foil pans. Invite children to create model landscapes with areas for lakes and rivers, and then fill the waterways with the water. They can reshape these landforms as they experiment with water flow and drainage.

CENTERS

Listening Post

After introducing each element in class, children may revisit the Manipulative Chart and Chant Poster on the Oral Language Audio CD. If you include a laminated copy of the Manipulative Chart Student Version, children can manipulate it as they sing to Part 4 of the CD (with blanks). Children may also listen to *Water Detective* on the Big Book Audio CD while following along in the small copy.

Language Workshop

Any time they are not in use during the unit, place the Picture Cards for the unit in this center. Encourage children to review the water-related vocabulary with each other for additional practice. After introducing the Language Practice Game in class, add the game board, game markers and TPR Cards to the center for independent group play.

Writer's Den

Establish a journal writing center with prompts to spark children's writing. Change the prompt every two weeks:

- What do you use water for?
- What can you do to save water?

Children should be encouraged to draw pictures to support their writing. Provide blank Writing Planners in center materials for prewriting.

More Books

- *Rain* by Robert Kalan (Morrow, 1991)
- *Follow the Water from Brook to Ocean, Stage 2* by Arthur Dorros (Harper Collins, 1993)
- *Mushroom in the Rain* by Mirra Ginsburg (Simon & Schuster Children's Books, 1997)
- *Water* by Frank Asch (Harcourt, 2000)
- *Water Dance* by Thomas Locker (Harcourt, 1997)

WEEK 1 DAY 1

Manipulative Chart: Introduction with Audio CD

Sung to the tune of the last two verses of "Over the River and Through the Woods"

Setting the Scene

- Hold up a glass of water and ask children to join in as you introduce the word *water.*
- Hold up Picture Card 1: rain. Say *Rain is water. It falls from the sky.* Invite children to use words and gestures to tell what they know about rain.
- Hold up Picture Card 2: river. Explain that rivers are made up of water from rain.
- In a similar way, introduce the words *snow, puddle, lake,* and *hail* using Picture Cards 3–6, inviting children to tell what they know about each.

Options for STAGES

❶❷ These children may answer either/or questions about the cards, such as *Is this a puddle or snow?*

❸❹❺ These children should use phrases or complete sentences in their descriptions, such as *swim in lake* or *There is a big puddle outside my house.*

Creating Comprehensible Input

- Begin by opening to the inside and pointing out items in the pictures, such as the river, puddle, and so on.
- Put the top of the chart back in place and point to the cut-out shapes, saying *This is water* each time.
- Read the text, pausing often, as you use gestures, pointing, and other techniques to make the chant comprehensible. Open to the inside and point to the rain when you come to the word *rain* in red.

There is water everywhere.	point to each cut out
There's water in the rain.	open and point to the picture of rain
So stomp and splash	stomp on the ground and lift hands in splashing gesture
And have a blast.	clap happily
Water is everywhere!	motion to chart with open hand

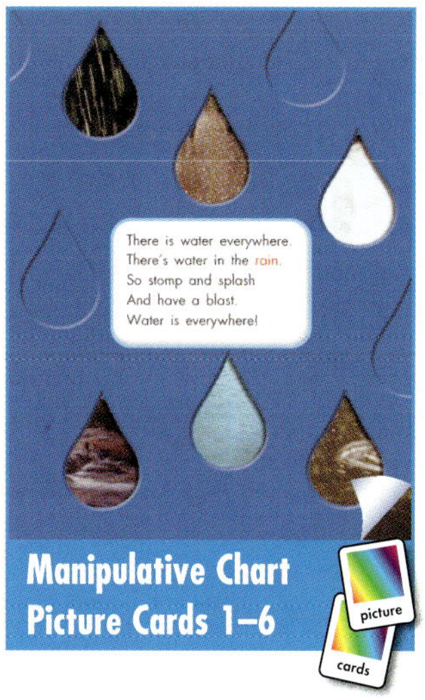

There is water everywhere.
There's water in the rain.
So stomp and splash
And have a blast
Water is everywhere!
picture
cards

Manipulative Chart
Picture Cards 1–6

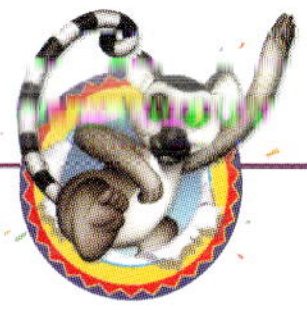

Guided Reading

As you work on this unit, conduct small groups of guided reading or shared-to-guided reading independent of thematic instruction. Instruction is provided in the Guided Reading section of this guide.

Component Organizer

Other Manipulative Chart lessons in this unit:

- Gestures and Manipulative Fun, p. U104
- Oral Language Development and Student Version, pp. U107–U108
- Oral Language Development, p. U117

Real-World Touch

Bring in water-related clothing, such as umbrellas, rain boots, raincoats, snow suits, and so on. Children may wear these items as they practice reciting the chant.

Home-School Connection

Choose one of the versions of the parent letter to send home with each child, according to the child's home language (pages 48–55 in the Home-School Connection Masters). Also send home the activity on page 56.

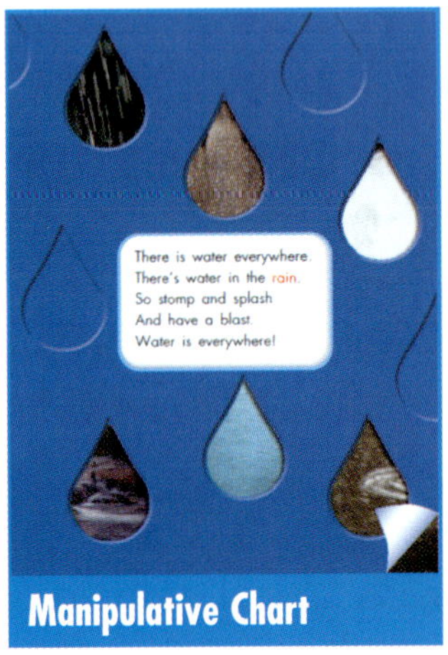
There is water everywhere.
There's water in the rain.
So stomp and splash
And have a blast.
Water is everywhere!
Manipulative Chart

Journal Writing Reminder

Children should be writing in their journals during the course of the unit. Journal writing provides an opportunity to reinforce content area vocabulary. See Writer's Den for suggested journal prompts.

Introducing the Audio CD

- Play Part 1 of the Oral Language Audio CD, the spoken song, as you say the song and track the print on the Manipulative Chart with your finger or a pointer. Replay Part 1 several times, encouraging children to chime in whenever they can.
- Introduce the song by playing the song at natural speed, Part 2 of the Audio CD, to help children get a feel for the song. Allow the Audio CD to continue playing through Part 3, the song at instructional pace. Track the print as the Audio CD plays. Repeat Part 3 again, this time singing along, making clear lip movements without exaggerating. Revisit Part 3 several times to help children learn the song.

WEEK 1 DAY 2

Manipulative Chart: Gestures and Manipulative Fun

Gesturing the Song

Introduce these simple gestures to accompany the song:

There is water everywhere.	circle with arms in encompassing gesture
There's water in the rain.	wiggle fingers to show rain
So stomp and splash	stomp as if in puddle
And have a blast.	stretch arms up over head
Water is everywhere!	circle with arms in encompassing gesture

Manipulating the Chart

- Show children how to flip back the top sheet on the Manipulative Chart to reveal the different scenes behind each cut out. The words behind each cut out can be substituted for the word in red. Close the top sheet so that only the front with raindrops is showing. Sing the first two lines, opening to the back sheet when you come to the word in red. Emphasize using *river* instead of *rain* when it appears in the song.
- Play Part 4 of the Oral Language Audio CD while you say *river* in the blank space.
- Continue introducing and naming the different forms of water behind each cut out in this manner.
- Invite volunteers to manipulate the Manipulative Chart for the class as you sing the verse together or give Total Physical Response commands, such as *Show me the people playing in the snow.*
- Invite children to help you create new gestures for the forms of water behind each cut out.
- You can revisit this activity many times during the unit.

WEEK 1 DAY 3

Chant Poster: Introduction

Setting the Scene

- Display Picture Cards 7, 8, 9, 10: sink, hose, faucet, shower. Talk with children about the ways that water is used at home.
- Using gestures, show how you used water today. Then invite children to tell how they used water today.

Options for STAGES

❶❷ Encourage these children to use gestures or one-word responses, such as *drink* or *teeth* to tell how they used water.	❸ These children can use single words or simple phrases, such as *shower, wash hands,* and so on.	❹❺ Encourage these children to use phrases or complete sentences to talk about how they used water.

- Show Picture Card 7: sink and ask children how we use the sink at home. You can use gestures to help talk about brushing teeth, washing hands, and getting a glass of water.

Creating Comprehensible Input

- Displaying the Chant Poster, explain that the boy is brushing his teeth and that he has turned off the faucet to save water.
- Read the text, pausing often, as you use gestures, pointing, and other techniques to make the chant comprehensible.

How much water do we need?	hold up hands in questioning gesture
I know we use a lot!	nod head and gesture "a lot" with arms out
If we each cut back a little,	gesture turning off faucet
We'll always have a lot!	raise hand to show rising level of water

Chanting the Poster

- Encourage children to chime in as you chant the rhyme together several times. You can form four groups, each chanting a line.
- Introduce the chant on Oral Language Audio CD as you and the children move to the rhythm of the chant. Tell them they can listen to it on their own later at the Listening Post.
- Practice saying the chant in different ways, such as varying the tempo and volume.
- Revisit the chant often with children. Invite them to act out turning on a faucet, putting toothpaste on a brush, and turning off the faucet as they chant the rhyme.

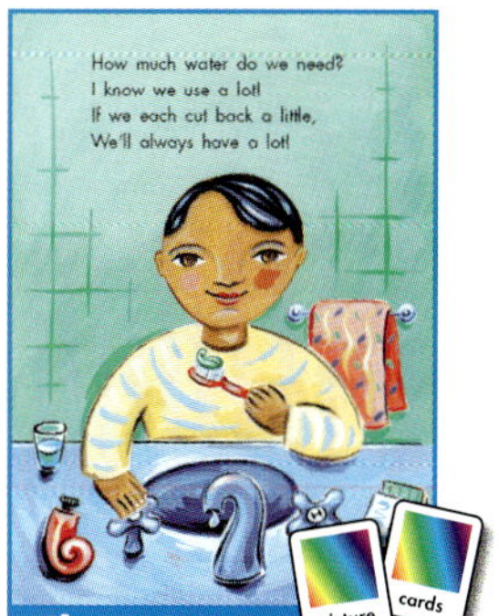

Chant Poster
Picture Cards 7–10

Component Organizer

Other Chant Poster lessons in this unit:

- Oral Language Development, pp. U113–U114

WEEK 1 DAY 4

You will need

- **Language Learning Master** p. 39
- Scissors

TPR Cards: Introduction

Introducing the Cards with Total Physical Response

- Provide one copy of page 39 of the Language Learning Masters to each child. Have children color and cut out the cards.
- Introduce a few cards at a time by holding them up one-by-one and saying the words clearly. Select first the words that have already been introduced in previous activities.
- Ask children to pick up the correct cards as you call out a word. Model the desired outcome. Add one new card at a time and keep reviewing in a game-like atmosphere. Children may want to say the word as they pick up the card.
- Now invite children to respond to your full-sentence commands, such as *Show me the faucet. Pick up the hose.*
- Assign partners so you can add commands like *Give the bucket to Eduardo.*
- As children increase their familiarity with the TPR Cards and the game, add funny commands such as *Sit on the sink.*
- Invite volunteers in Stages 3, 4, or 5 to give commands to their classmates.
- Extend language to discuss how items such as the sink and the hose are used. ◎

Options for STAGES

❶❷ Ask these children either/or questions or yes/no questions, such as *Do you wash your hands in a sink?*

❸❹❺ Ask these children to name in phrases or complete sentences as many ways to use a sink as they can.

- Repeat this activity several times throughout the unit.

Grammar in Context: Sentences with *There is/are* ❶❷❸❹❺

1. Use classroom objects and place them on a desk or around the room. For example, place three pencils on your desk and say *There are three pencils on my desk.* Take two away and say *There is one pencil on my desk.*
2. Place one TPR Card for bucket on your desk saying *There is a bucket on my desk.* Point to the bucket, hold up one finger, and say *one bucket.* Then place multiple copies of the bucket TPR card and say *There are buckets on my desk.* Explain that we use *is* to tell about one thing and *are* to tell about more than one thing.
3. Invite volunteers to make sentences with *There is* and *There are* using multiple copies of the TPR Cards river, puddle, lake, sink, and bucket. ◎

Options for STAGES

❶ Have children point as you prompt them with statements, such as *There is a river on the desk.*

❷❸ Encourage these children to approximate a sentence, such as *There is a river.*

❹❺ Encourage these children to say a complete sentence, such as *There is a river on the desk.*

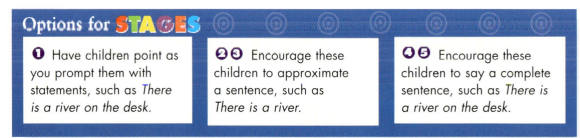

WEEK 1 DAY 5

Manipulative Chart: Focus on Oral Language Development

FUNCTION MINI-LESSON

Express Obligation 1 2 3 4 5

1. Model how to express an obligatory action. Look out the window and make a statement that corresponds to the weather, such as *It's very sunny outside. I have to wear my sunglasses.*
2. Display the Manipulative Chart and ask children questions to elicit similar statements. For example, point to the picture of snow and ask *What do you have to do on snowy days?* Reinforce children's statements or actions with other ideas, such as *On snowy days, I have to shovel the sidewalk.*
3. Continue in this way, asking questions about the pictures on the Manipulative Chart.
4. Extend the activity by asking children questions about their own activities and chores. *Do you have to do your homework after school? What do you have to do on the weekend?* and so on.
5. Begin the discussion with children in Stage 3, 4, or 5. Validate approximations such as nodding and one-word answers for children in lower Stages, and phrases and sentences for Stages 3, 4, or 5.

FUNCTION MINI-LESSON

Solve Problems 1 2 3 4 5

1. Point to the picture of rain on the Manipulative Chart and ask *What kinds of problems do people have on rainy days?* Prompt them with ideas such as *getting wet.* Write or sketch children's ideas in a column on the board.
2. Next brainstorm solutions for each problem. Write or sketch these in another column. For example, a solution for *getting wet* is *carry an umbrella.*
3. Invite volunteers to tell about problems and solutions for days with snow and hail. After each volunteer has finished, recap in simple language to model necessary vocabulary and usage.

Grammar in Context: Sentences with *There is/are* 1 2 3 4 5

1. Point to the picture of rain in the first picture on the Manipulative Chart. Say *There is water in the rain* and have children repeat the phrase.
2. Point to the river and say *There is water in the river. There are fish in the river.* Continue in this way, following the same sentence pattern. Children may chime in after each sentence.
3. Sing the song on the chart together. Point out *There is water* and *There's water* in the text.
4. Extend the activity by asking *Where else is there water?* Have children participate as they are able.

There is water everywhere.
There's water in the rain.
So stomp and splash
And have a blast.
Water is everywhere!
Manipulative Chart

Language Learning Strategy

It's OK to use things written in your home language to help you.

- Tell children that sometimes they may want to use a book or a dictionary with words in their home language and that it's OK. **Model** *If I want to know more about rivers, I might want to read about them in my language first. Or if I know how to say something in my language, but not in English, I can use a Spanish-English dictionary for help.*
- Provide resources for as many home-languages as possible. Children may want to bring some from home, too. If possible have a bilingual person demonstrate how to use a bilingual dictionary. Throughout the unit, encourage children to use these resources.

Language Learning Master

p.42 1 2 3 4 5

Home-School Connection

When children have practiced manipulating the Manipulative Chart Student Version, send it home for them to practice with their family members.

Options for STAGES

1 2 These children can point to pictures in the chart. Model a sentence, such as *There is water in the puddle* and encourage them to repeat it as they are able.

3 4 5 Encourage these children to create sentences following the pattern, such as *There is water in the ocean.*

5. You can use ideas from this activity to create new verses for the song on the chart, such as *There is water in the pool*, and so on.

You will need

- **Language Learning Master** pp. 37–38
- Scissors
- Tape

Manipulative Chart: Student Version

- Model assembling the pages according to the directions.
- Circulate to provide assistance as children assemble their charts. Encourage children to color and decorate their charts.
- Invite children to carefully open and close the top page on their charts as you do the same on the Manipulative Chart. Then encourage them to point to the appropriate pictures as you say different words in the song.
- Have children respond to your Total Physical Response Commands: *Point to the picture of snow.*
- Play Part 4 of the Oral Language Audio CD and model how children can manipulate their Student Versions as they sing along. Tell children that they will later be able to listen to the Audio CD and manipulate this mini-chart in the Listening Post.

Assessment

Record your observations of children on their individual assessment checklists for this unit. See page U123.

WEEK 2 DAY 1

Concept Poster: Introduction

Setting the Scene

1. Show children Picture Card 1: rain and Picture Card 11: clouds. Say *Rain falls from clouds.* Wiggle your fingers downward to help with comprehension.
2. Then display Picture Card 5: lake. Explain that rain falls into lakes and keeps them full of water.
3. Say *Let's see how water goes back into the clouds.*

Creating Comprehensible Input

- Direct children's attention to the diagram. Point out the lake, the sun, the clouds, and the rain. Talk through the relationship between the pictures with a think-aloud. **Model** *This label says* rain falls. *This arrow tells me what happens next. The next label says* water evaporates. *This means that the sun heats the water on the ground and makes it go up. This arrow points to the next thing that happens. After the water evaporates, clouds form. This arrow shows me that after the clouds form, rain falls.*
- Recap this in simple language, pointing to the pictures and connecting arrows: *rain falls in lake; sun heats lake; water evaporates; clouds form; rain falls from clouds.*
- Invite a child in Stages 3, 4, or 5 to lead the class in talking through the cycle. Support with appropriate academic language.

Guided Reading

As you work on this unit, conduct small groups of guided reading or shared-to-guided reading independent of thematic instruction. Instruction is provided in the Guided Reading section of this guide.

- After the child has finished, recap as you point to the rain falling, the lake, the sun, the evaporating water, the clouds, and then the rain again.
- Explain to children that this is the water cycle. Explain that cycles happen again and again and that we often show a cycle in a circular diagram like this one.

Extending Oral Language

- Engage children in reviewing these concepts by asking questions.

Options for STAGES

❶❷ Ask these children yes/no questions, such as *Do clouds form in the sky?*

❸❹❺ Ask these children open-ended questions that require substantive answers, such as *Tell me about the water cycle.*

- Use Total Physical Response commands to build familiarity with the concepts. For example, *Point to the lake. Point to rain falling.*

Component Organizer

Other Concept Poster lessons in this unit:

- Revisiting, p. U114

Language Practice Game: Version 1 ❶❷❸❹❺

Preparing the Game

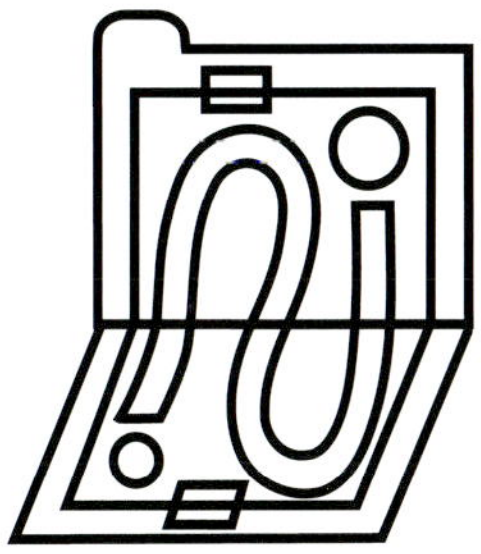

Tape the copies of pages 40 and 41 of the Language Learning Masters to two facing sides of a file folder to give each game board some durability. Assemble one file folder for each group.

Playing Version 1

Divide the class into heterogeneous groups of mixed language abilities with four children each and provide a game board to each group. Distribute a set of rain, river, snow, puddle, and lake TPR Cards to each player. Also, give each player a game marker. Then model the following directions.

1. Players shuffle and put their set of TPR cards facedown in front of them.
2. The first player draws a card and moves his or her game piece from the starting point on the board to the closest matching image. ◎

Options for STAGES

❶ These children can simply move their game marker to the appropriate space on the board, naming the water form as they are able.

❷❸ These children should be encouraged to say simple phrases about the water form shown on the space, for example, *water in river.*

❹❺ Encourage these children to say a sentence following the pattern *There is water in the lake.*

3. The player then returns the card to the bottom of the deck and the next player takes a turn. If a child lands on a square with a rope, the player "climbs" up to the connected square, naming the water forms shown on both squares. If a child lands on a square with a water slide, the player "slides" down the chute into the connected square and shouts "Splash!"
4. The first player to reach the end of the path wins, saying "I am home now. I am wet!"

You will need

- **Language Learning Master** pp. 40–41
- TPR Cards
- File folder
- Tape
- Game markers

Component Organizer

Other Language Practice Game lessons in this unit:

- Version 2, p. U120

Assessment

Record your observations of children during the Language Practice Game on their individual assessment checklists for this unit. See page U123.

Water Is Everywhere

Written by Karen Clevidence

OVERVIEW *There is water in the rain and in the snow. Water is everywhere!*

The Newcomer Book is supported by the language of the Manipulative Chart and should be integrated into small-group instruction this week when children have had enough practice with vocabulary and concepts in this unit.

Language Pattern

There is water in the ________.

Text Vocabulary

forms of water

Vocabulary Extenders

temperature: warm, cool, cold

Reading the Text

Book Talk

- Work with a small group of four children at one time who exhibit similar literacy-learning behaviors.
- Engage children in a book talk as you flip through the pages of your copy of the book.

Options for STAGES

❶❷ Identify the names of the different forms of water for these children. Encourage them to say the names as they are able.	❸❹❺ Ask children to identify each form of water as you encounter it in the text.

INSTRUCTIONAL PATHS

❶❷❸❹❺ **All Readers:** Shared-to-Guided Reading	❶❷❸❹❺ **Emergent Readers:** Guided Reading	❶❷❸❹❺ **Early Readers:** Independent Reading no lesson provided

INDIVIDUAL READING

Shared-to-Guided Reading **3–4 sessions**
❶❷❸❹❺ **All Readers**

1. Read the book to children.
   - Invite children to sit near you as you read a copy of the book. Begin with the cover and title page.
   - Turn to page 2 and begin reading the words as you point to them. Draw children's attention to the pictures.
2. Read the book with children.
   - Encourage children to follow along in their own copies of the book, turning the pages as you read together and using their own fingers to point to the words from left to right.
   - Invite children to chime in when they are comfortable.
   - Reread the book in this manner over several sessions.
3. Have children buddy read the book.
4. Invite children to read the book independently.

Assess

- Did children hold the book appropriately?
- Did children want to read the book on their own?

Guided Reading **2 sessions**
❶❷❸❹❺ **Emergent Readers**

1. Provide copies of the book to children. Use one child's book and turn to page 2. Introduce the book's pattern to children by reading the sentence and pointing to each word as you read *There is water in the rain.*
2. Have each child read at his or her own pace while remaining in the group. Discourage choral reading. Observe as they read.

Assess

- Did children use the pictures to help read the words?
- Can children identify and point to a high-frequency word?

REVISITING THE NEWCOMER BOOK

If children seem ready, you may also use the book to extend children's knowledge of temperature by pointing to the thermometer and the indicated temperature in each illustration.

WEEK 2 DAY 2

Big Book: Introduction

Water Detective

Written by Carol Alexander *Photographed by Bill Burlingham*

OVERVIEW *For her class project, Emily is a water detective. How much water can she save?*

Warming Up

Begin the lesson by revisiting the Manipulative Chart, Chant Poster, or a familiar Big Book. You may ask a volunteer to choose one.

Setting the Scene

- Review the word *sink* by displaying Picture Card 7: sink. Point out the faucet on the sink. Say *We have sinks in our kitchens and our bathrooms.* Then display Picture Card 8: hose and Picture Card 10: shower. Say the words and allow children to say them as they are able.
- Tap into children's prior knowledge. Ask *Who uses these in your house? What do you use them for?* Allow children to share their responses in words or gestures.
- Introduce the book and provide children with an overview of the story.
- Read the title of the Big Book: *Water Detective.* Point to the picture on the cover and identify Emily and the magnifying glass. Explain that a detective looks for clues and tries to solve a mystery or problem.
- Make predictions about the book: *Where do you think Emily will find water being used in her home? What "problem" is Emily trying to solve as a "detective"? As we turn the pages, see if you can find places where Emily is solving a problem.*
- Help children determine a purpose for listening. Say *As we turn the pages of the book, see if you can find two ways people can save water.*

Reading the Text

- Read the title page. Have children make additional predictions based on this picture. *What do you think will happen with this Water Detective badge?*
- As you read through the book, use a pointer or your finger to draw children's attention to the text. Point out items in the pictures to support your reading. You will return later to build children's understanding of the text. In future rereadings, children should be encouraged to chime in.
- If you have children at Stages 3, 4, or 5, pause after reading page 21 for a prediction of what will happen next. *What do you think Emily will put on her poster?*

Creating Comprehensible Input

- Open up the back flap of the book, which shows a web of ways Emily helps her family save water. Leave it open as you read to help build comprehension of the text.
- Use the comprehension supports in the following chart to help you build comprehensible input with children at all Stages of Language Acquisition.

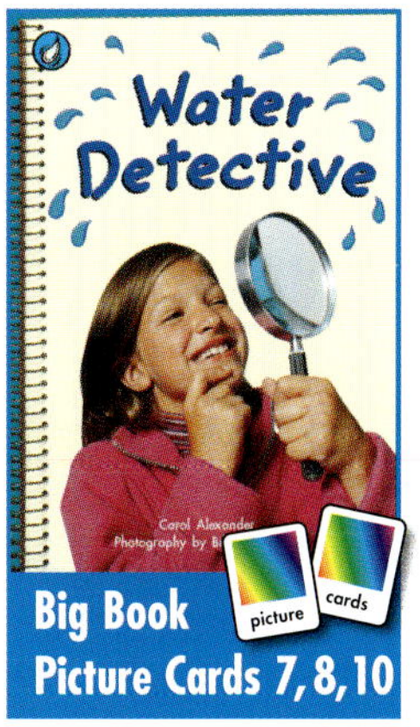

Component Organizer

Other Big Book lessons in this unit:
- Revisiting, p. U112
- Comprehension Strategy, p. U113
- Oral Language Development, pp. U115–U116
- Literacy Skills, pp. U119–U120

Idiom Note

The idioms *hand out* and *went to his head* may be unfamiliar. Demonstrate *hand out* by distributing paper and say *I am handing out paper to everyone.* Demonstrate *went to his head* by restating that it made the person feel too proud of himself.

PAGE	IN THE STORY	COMPREHENSION SUPPORT
2	. . . science fair. . . . Choose a topic.	restate: when children show something they learned about science restate: think of one thing about water, animals, or plants to show
4	She listed things to investigate . . . she wore a badge	point: to items on list; point: to badge and to your chest
5	Observe the ways my family uses water.	point: to your eyes
6	Today Mom left the water running . . .	restate: left the water on
8	So Dad filled the tub with rinse water . . .	use flap: point to Dad with dishpan
14	Today I noticed a leaky faucet.	point: to drops of water
18	. . . special showerhead . . .	use flap: point to Emily with showerhead; gesture: wiggle fingers overhead to show water
20	. . . he was impressed.	act out: smile, nod
21	He was proud of me . . .	act out: smile, hook thumbs in shirt proudly
24	Emily blushed . . .	act out: smile shyly, rub cheeks

You will need

- Chart paper
- Markers

Revisiting the Big Book

- Children can use Water Saver Awards as a retelling device. Provide construction paper, crayons, and scissors. Have children use the award shown in the Big Book as a model.
- Open the back flap of the Big Book and model how to retell the story by holding an award over each scene as you tell that part of the story. Invite children to take turns retelling the story in a similar way.

WEEK 2 DAY 3

Theme Project: Operation Conservation

1. Tell children that they will be "water detectives," just like Emily in the Big Book.
2. Form heterogeneous groups of four to five children. Have groups create questions about how water is used in their homes.
3. Over the next few days, tell groups to use the questions to look for ways that water is used in their homes.
4. As group members report their findings, help them record their observations in a log or chart using a simple spreadsheet program, if available.
5. Have groups identify examples of water waste and brainstorm ways that the waste can be minimized. They can refer to the Big Book for ideas.
6. Have groups create conservation posters showing their ideas. The posters should show ways that water is wasted, and provide suggestions for conserving it.
7. Circulate as groups plan their posters. Help children assign tasks such as drawing, writing, and assembling the poster to meet their abilities. Provide assistance as necessary.
8. Provide time to work on the conservation posters over the next two weeks. Each group will present their posters on the last day of the unit.

WEEK 2 DAY 4

Big Book: Focus on Comprehension Strategy

Self-Monitors by Asking Questions

1. Reread *Water Detective* to the children. Allow children in Stages 4 or 5 to participate by reading certain passages.
2. As you and the children read aloud, be conscious of those moments when you or a child self-monitors by asking questions to correct a miscue. For example, on page 2, you might read ". . . water, animals, and *pants*" instead of *plants*.
3. When such miscues occur, be sure to use a think-aloud to model correcting such miscues.

Model *When I read pants, that didn't sound right. The teacher is talking about studying this with water and animals. I ask myself* What sounds right with water and animals? *Let me read that again.*

Chant Poster: Focus on Oral Language Development

FUNCTION MINI-LESSON

Express Obligation ❶❷❸❹❺

1. Revisit the chant together, saying it several times.
2. Review expressing obligations, which was introduced on Week 1 Day 5.
3. Point to the poster and ask *What does the boy want us to do? Yes, he wants us to use less water.*
4. Ask children what the boy is doing to use less water.
5. Ask children what else we can do to use less water.

Options for STAGES

❶❷ Children at these Stages can gesture to show what we can do to use less water, using simple phrases, such as *Water off* as they are able.

❸❹❺ Encourage these children to use longer phrases or complete sentences, such as *We can use rinse water.*

FUNCTION MINI-LESSON

Solve Problems ❶❷❸❹❺

1. Review the chant together. Say *The chant tells us about a problem. What is the problem? How can we solve it?*
2. Invite children to respond as they are able, guiding them to state the solution that if everybody saves some water, then everybody will have the water they need.

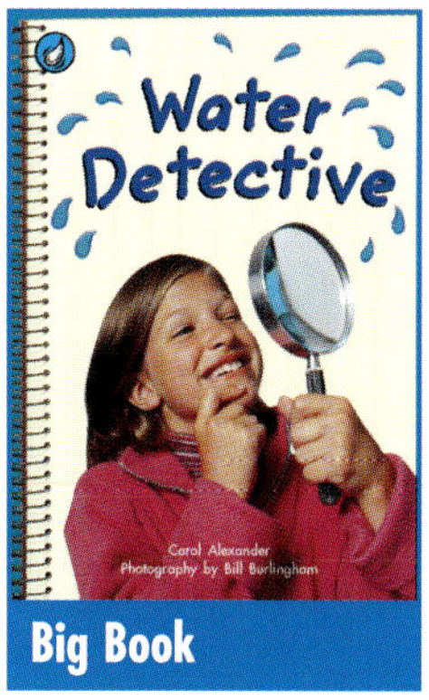

Big Book

Assessment

Use a retelling of the Big Book to assess comprehension. See page U123.

Chant Poster

Home Culture Sharing

Invite children to share cooking procedures at home that include water. For example, children may talk about the steps in preparing rice, soups, and tea.

Assessment

Record your observations of children during these mini-lessons on their individual assessment checklists for this unit. See page U123.

Grammar in Context: Questions with *How much/many* (1 2 3 4 5)

1. Use classroom items to model questions and responses with *How much?* and *How many?* For example, hold up a glass of water, saying *How much water is there? There is a little water* or *There is a lot of water.* Use other items such as pencils, paper clips, and clay.
2. Review the chant with children, emphasizing the question with *How much* at the beginning.
3. Invite partners to create their own questions and answers.

WEEK 2 DAY 5

Shared Writing Card: Introduction of Side A

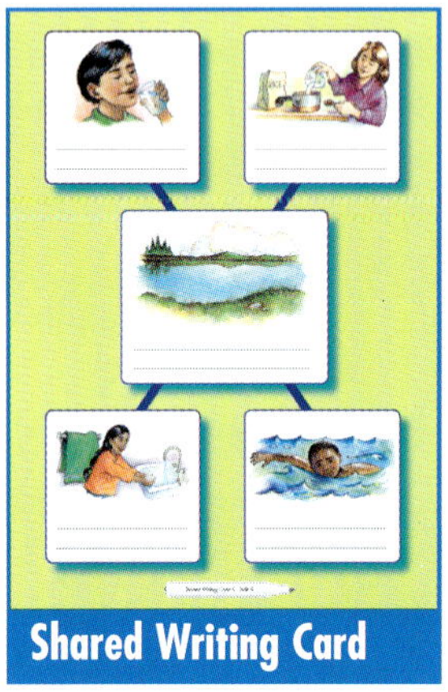

You will need

- Shared Writing Card 5
- Wipe-off marker
- Regular marker
- Easel pad

Setting the Scene

- Use the back flap of the Big Book to review the key scenes of *Water Detective*. Talk about the ways that Emily's family can reduce their water use.
- Review the things Emily's family uses water for, such as brushing teeth and washing the car. Ask children if they can think of other ways we use water. Make a list.

Creating Comprehensible Input

- Display Shared Writing Card Side A, which shows a web with different ways to use water. Begin by pointing to and describing each picture.
  Model *Look, water. Oh, a boy drinking water. Here is a woman cooking rice. Down here, a girl is washing her hands. Over here, a boy is swimming.*
- Go back to the center illustration and use think-alouds to talk through the illustrations. Point to the illustrations one by one and trace the lines with your finger.
  Center Illustration: *This is water.*
  Top left Illustration: *This boy is drinking water.*
  Top right Illustration: *This woman is using water to cook rice.*
  Bottom left Illustration: *This girl is washing her hands with water.*
  Bottom right Illustration: *This boy is swimming in water.*
- Explain that the boxes and lines on the Shared Writing Card show how the outside pictures work with the center picture. Point to the center box and say *water*. Point to the four outside boxes, saying *uses of water*.
- Invite a volunteer from Stages 3, 4, or 5 to explain the illustrations in his or her own words. Repeat with other volunteers.

Revisiting the Concept Poster

- Revisit the Concept Poster, inviting volunteers to talk you through the pictures as they are able.
- Have children draw the water cycle with other bodies of water and other forms of precipitation.

Scribing with the Graphic Organizer

- After children have become comfortable with the content of the illustrations, you can use the wipe-off marker provided to scribe while you brainstorm together labels for the graphic organizer. Since you are creating a graphic organizer, not a finished product, well-crafted sentences are not necessary.
- Think aloud as you write so that children have insight into the writing process.
- Here is an example of simple shared writing labeling for the illustrations:

Center Illustration: *water*
Top left Illustration: *we drink water*
Top right Illustration: *we cook with water*
Bottom left Illustration: *we wash with water*
Bottom right Illustration: *we swim in water*

Writing Together from the Graphic Organizer

- You will again be holding the pen while you work with children to create a shared writing piece together. This time, you will model how to use the labels from the web to create a finished paragraph on your easel pad.
- Begin with a think-aloud.
  Model *We used* water *for the first picture. We need a complete sentence that says what all the other pictures are going to be about. What would be a good way to start? Let's see, all the pictures show the different ways we use water. This might be a good sentence:* We use water in many different ways. Write down the sentence you agree upon with children.
- As you move to the next illustration, read the label and then invite children to help you create the sentence based on the picture and label. Write down what children say as you work to make sentences with them. When children offer sentences with errors in them, correct them without being overt. Encourage children to use classroom resources, such as the Word Wall.
- When you have finished your shared writing piece, read it together several times. Then hang it up on the wall where it can be displayed during the rest of the unit and reread many times. For now, do not erase your labels on Side A.

Phonics in Context

Shared writing provides an ideal opportunity for reviewing the phonics skills children are learning. Highlight the sounds in words like m***igh*t** and tr***y*** as you reread the writing.

Sample Shared Writing

We use water in many different ways. We drink water. We cook food with water. We wash our hands with water. We might swim or play with toys in the water. It's important to try to save water so we have enough to do all these things.

WEEK 3 DAY 1

Big Book: Focus on Oral Language Development

Reread the Big Book and return to the text to focus on oral language development.

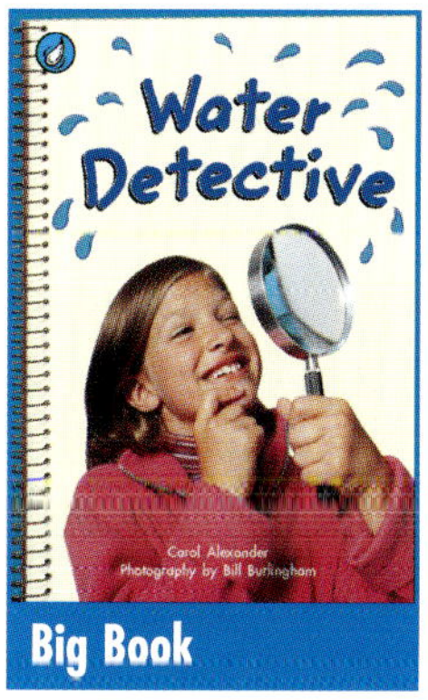

Grammar in Context: Questions with *How much/many* ❶❷❸❹❺

1. Open the Big Book to pages 2 and 3. Point to the illustration and ask *How many children do you see?* Have children count with you and repeat your answer *There are eight children.*
2. Flip through the pages of the Big Book, asking questions with *How many?* and *How much?* based on the illustrations. Emphasize that usually when we ask *How much?* we answer *There is* and when we ask *How many?* we answer *There are.* After children have had some practice hearing and answering these questions, invite volunteers to come up and take your place. ◎

Language Learning Master

p. 43 ❶❷❸❹❺

Options for STAGES

❶❷ These children can answer yes/no or either/or questions, such as *Are there three or six children?*	❸ Children at this Stage can point to the pictures and create questions using *How much?* or *How many?*	❹❺ Encourage children at these stages to create complete questions on their own with How much/many while pointing to an illustration in the Big Book.

Guided Reading

As you work on this unit, conduct small groups of guided reading or shared-to-guided reading independent of thematic instruction. Instruction is provided in the Guided Reading section of this guide.

Grammar in Context: Adjectives—Feelings ❶❷❸❹❺

1. Flip through the book with the children looking at facial expressions that show feelings. Discuss the feelings and the situations that they are related to. Write the feelings on sticky notes and put them on the pages. Explain that these words tell us more about how someone feels.
2. Extend the activity by having children tell how they feel at certain times or in certain situations. They may answer yes/no or either/or questions or use phrases or sentences as they are able.

WEEK 3 DAY 2

You will need

- Shared Writing Card 5
- Wipe-off marker

Shared Writing Card: Brainstorming Side B

Brainstorming a Topic

- Use Side A of the Shared Writing Card and your finished water shared writing piece. Review how you used the pictures on the graphic organizer to form the basis of your finished piece.
- Turn the card over to Side B. Tell children that you will now think of your own topic together to draw on the graphic organizer. Brainstorm together a topic that involves forms of water or its use and/or conservation. Your topic should be able to be supported by at least four points.

Scribing with the Graphic Organizer

- Once the class has chosen a topic, you should decide together what the center illustration will be. Model how to draw the first picture, which will represent the topic. Invite volunteers to step up to the card and draw scenes to support the central topic. Continue drawing until at least three of the outer boxes are filled.
- Now it's time to put labels on your graphic organizer. Elicit suggestions for labels from the group in the same manner as you did for Side A and record them on the Shared Writing Card.
- You will create the shared writing paragraph together in the next session.

You will need

- State map
- Drawing paper
- Markers

Active Social Studies: Water Maps

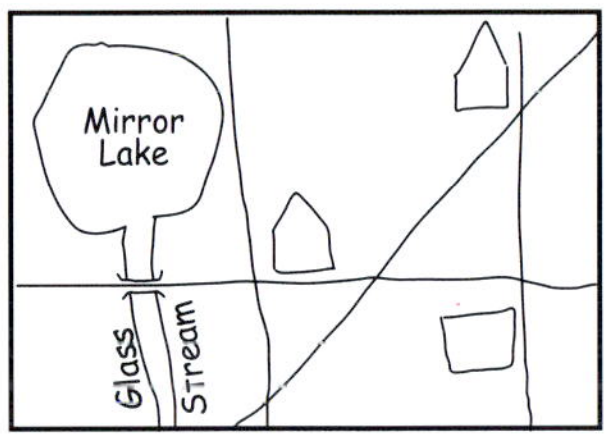

1. Display a map of your state. Point out the lakes, streams, and other forms of water on the map. Teach the names of these landmarks. Then share information about them and why they are important to the people in your state.
2. Distribute drawing paper and markers. Invite children to draw a map showing the important bodies of water in your area.
3. Circulate as children work and help them label important bodies of water on their maps.
4. Invite volunteers to present their maps to the class, pointing to and identifying the different waterways. Encourage them to share any additional information about the waterways, how they are used, and why they are important.

WEEK 3 DAY 3

Shared Writing Card: Writing Together with Side B

- As with Side A, you will scribe as you work together with children to create a finished writing piece from the graphic organizer on Side B of Shared Writing Card 5.
- Model writing from the center illustration, using think-alouds as you go. Show children how to use resources like the Word Wall. Work together on difficult spellings or tricky passages.
- When you have finished your shared writing piece, read it together several times. Then hang it up on the wall where it can be displayed during the rest of the unit. At the end of the unit, you should erase both sides of the Shared Writing Card.

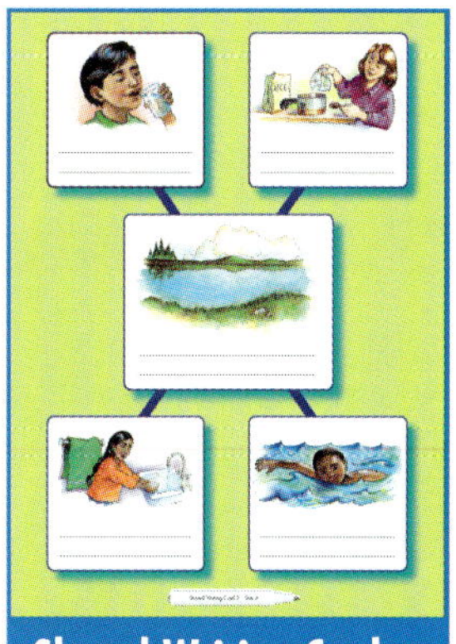

Shared Writing Card

Manipulative Chart: Focus on Oral Language Development

Grammar in Context: Prepositions—Position ❶❷❸❹❺

1. Display the Manipulative Chart and sing the song together, allowing volunteers to manipulate the top sheet as you do so.
2. Point to the first picture on the Chart and say *The boy is in the rain.* Children may want to repeat the sentence after you.
3. Model how to use prepositional phrases with the other photos in the poster. Examples: *The boy is at the river; The children are in the snow,* and so on.
4. Extend the vocabulary by modeling sentences such as *The umbrella is over the person's head. The hail is under his feet.* Use gestures to indicate *over* and *under.*
5. Ask children to use words and gestures to indicate the locations of classroom items. Encourage them to create sentences as they are able.

Language Junction

The prepositions *at, on,* and *in* are confusing for most English Language Learners. A Russian speaker might say *He study on school.* Without correcting children overtly, model correct English usage: *He studies in school.*

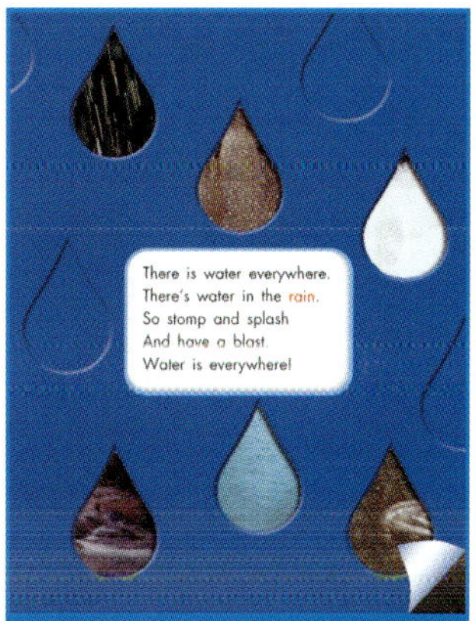

There is water everywhere.
There's water in the rain.
So stomp and splash
And have a blast.
Water is everywhere!

Manipulative Chart

Language Learning Master

p. 44 ❶❷❸❹❺

WEEK 3 DAY 4

Active Science: Rain Model

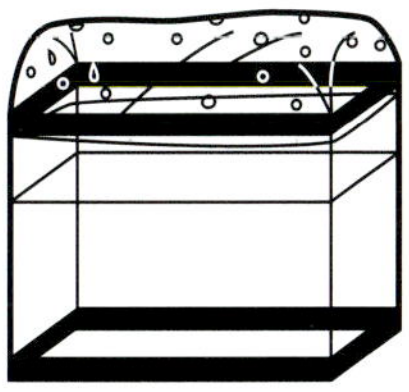

1. Obtain a small fish tank or glass case, 3 tablespoons of salt, and a clear plastic bag big enough to cover the tank.
2. Divide the class into three groups and assign them the following tasks.
   Group 1: Mix the salt into two gallons of water to create a saline solution.
   Group 2: Pour the water into the tank so that it is about $\frac{2}{3}$ full.
   Group 3: Place the bag over the tank and tape the edge of the bag to seal it.
3. Place the tank in a warm place. After a few days, observe what has happened. Point out how water droplets form and collect on the plastic and then run back into the water.
4. Engage children in a discussion to make connections between this experiment and what they have learned about the water cycle in this unit.

You will need

- 3-gallon fish tank or small glass case from a plant store
- 3 tablespoons salt
- 2 gallons water
- Mixing bowl
- Clear plastic bag
- Masking tape

WEEK 3 DAY 5

You will need

- Overhead transparency of Writing Resource Guide, p. 88
- Overhead marker

Writing Resource Guide: A Simplified Graphic Organizer

This activity is optional and necessary only if you wish to use the simplified sequence graphic organizer in cooperative-group or independent writing.

Brainstorming a Topic

- Review the drawings and labels you used on Side B of the Shared Writing Card. Trace the lines from the central picture to each outer one.
- On the overhead projector, display a transparency of Writing Planner B on page 88 of the Writing Resource Guide, which is a web with a center box and three outer boxes.
- Brainstorm together a simple topic that involves water forms, use, and/or conservation. Continue brainstorming until children have generated three ideas for the outside boxes.

Scribing with the Graphic Organizer

- Once the class has arrived at a topic, you should decide together what the center and outer boxes should show. Model drawing pictures for each box.
- Label each of the four drawings on your graphic organizer. Elicit suggestions for labels from the group in the same manner as you did with the Shared Writing Card.

You will need

- Writing Resource Guide, pp. 87–88
- Markers

Writing Mini-lessons

See the Writing Resource Guide for mini-lessons to use as children write. Here are some suggestions:

- Mini-lesson 5: Making a Class Idea List
- Mini-lesson 43: Editing Your Own Writing

Writing Resource Guide: Cooperative-Group Writing

- Form cooperative groups of heterogeneous Stages with three to four children each to work together on a writing piece using the graphic organizer. You may hand out a copy of Writing Planner A or B to each group.
- Review the shared writing graphic organizers and finished pieces you have made together. Remind children that the drawings can help them organize their ideas for writing.
- Have the groups work together first to complete their graphic organizers and then to write their finished pieces. Circulate to provide assistance.

Options for STAGES

❶❷ These children should draw the pictures for the group.	❸❹❺ These children should take responsibility for the writing of the finished piece.

WEEK 4 DAY 1

Big Book: Focus on Literacy Skills

Word Level: Phonics in Context

1. You will need the Word Wall Starters with the raindrop symbol on them: *like*, *right*, *team*, *my*. These are pictured in the back of the Big Book.
2. Tell children that you want to choose some special words from the story for them to take a closer look at.
3. Introduce the word *like* by saying it clearly, elongating the *ike* sound, and drawing attention to the highlighting behind the *ike*. Then repeat the long *i* sound several times. Say *The letter* e *at the end of* like *makes the letter* i *have the long* i *sound. Let's say the word* like *together:* like. *Can you hear the long* i *in* like? *Now let's sing a song!* Review Phonics Song Chart 18 together.
4. Say *I'm going to put the word* like *below the* ike *label.* Walk over to your Word Wall and place the *like* card under the long *i*, taking care to group word families together. Remind children that they can use the raindrop symbol to help them remember where they "met" that word before.
5. Repeat a similar procedure for the other words and phonics skills.

Sentence Level: Sentences and Paragraphs

1. Reread the first sentence on page 4 of the Big Book. With an index card, cover up all but the first sentence. Point out that a sentence is a group of words that tell a complete thought. Remind children that a sentence always begins with a capital letter and ends with a period.
2. Remove the card and show the full paragraph, indicating the indent. Say *This is a paragraph. A paragraph is a group of sentences that tells about one idea. The first word of a paragraph is often moved in a little.* Ask children to reread page 4 with you and decide what the topic is. Talk about the supporting details. Use a web graphic organizer to show how the topic and details are related.
3. Continue rereading the Big Book, pausing periodically to have children identify and read sentences and paragraphs. ◎

Options for STAGES

❶❷ Have children at these Stages identify capital letters, end punctuation, and indentations.	❸ Have these children identify sentences and paragraphs and tell how they know.	❹❺ Have these children discuss ideas and details in paragraphs.

Text Level: Charts

1. Open the Big Book to page 11. Think aloud as you identify and explain Emily's chart.
Model *Emily's chart shows how much water she uses to brush her teeth. A chart is a good way to show facts and numbers. A chart usually has a title. Then there are different columns of information. In the first column, Emily shows how much water she used before. In the second column, she shows how much she uses now. The chart helps me see the difference.*

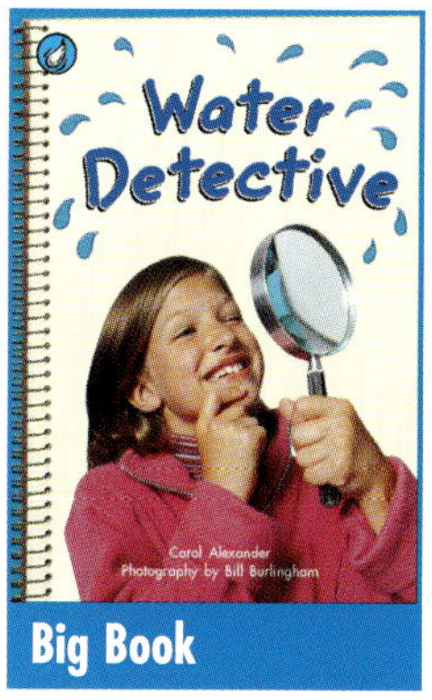

Big Book

Guided Reading

As you work on this unit, conduct small groups of guided reading or shared-to-guided reading independent of thematic instruction. Instruction is provided in the Guided Reading section of this guide.

Home-School Connection

Send home page 57 of the Home-School Connection Masters for children to use in retelling *Water Detective* to their families. They should retell the story in English and then talk about it in either English or their home language.

2. Then open the Big Book to page 19 and point out the chart. Use a think-aloud as you explain the chart.
   Model *This chart shows how much water is used. The first column shows how much water is used with the special showerhead. The second column shows how much water is used with the old showerhead. The chart helps me to compare the two showerheads.*
3. Revisit other nonfiction books. Invite children to locate charts and to explain them as they are able.

You will need

- TPR Cards

Language Practice Game: Version 2 ❶❷❸❹❺

Divide children in Stages 3, 4, and 5 into pairs. Give each pair a full set of TPR Cards. Model the following directions for this Information Gap game.

1. Have the partners sit back to back.
2. Player 1 is the clue giver and Player 2 is the clue receiver.
3. Player 2 lays out all of his or her cards faceup in rows.
4. Player 1 chooses one card to describe but does not show it.
5. Player 2 asks questions about the chosen card, such as *Does it fall from the sky?*
6. With each answer or hint, Player 2 turns over any of his or her cards that can be eliminated.
7. Play continues in this way until Player 2 can correctly guess the secret card through this process of elimination. If Player 2 cannot guess, Player 1 reveals the card.
8. Players then switch roles, shuffle the cards, and play again.

WEEK 4 DAY 2

You will need

- Plastic measuring cups
- Water
- Observation logs
- Markers

Active Math: Water Evaporation

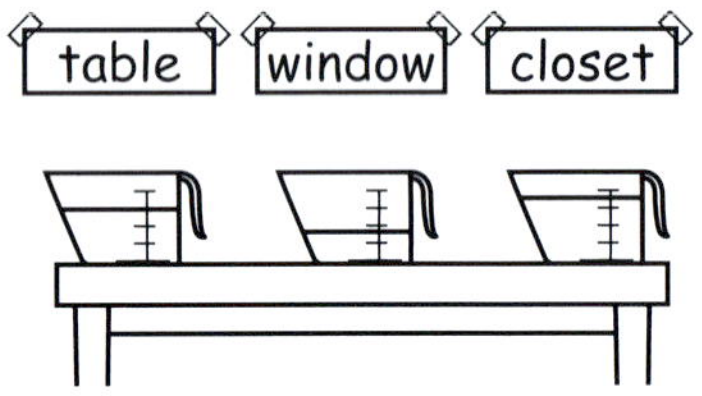

1. Form heterogeneous groups of four or five children. Provide a clear plastic measuring cup to each group.
2. Have groups fill the containers with water. Tell some groups to place their containers in an area of the classroom away from light. Have other groups place their containers on the window sill.
3. Direct groups to record the water level in their containers once each day.
4. When the water has evaporated from all the containers, ask groups to share their measurements with the class. Discuss how temperature affects varying rates of evaporation.

A End-of-Unit Assessment

- While children are engaged in activities this week, pull them individually for the Big Book retelling, using page U123 at the end of this unit.
- Select a number of children with whom you would like to use the Open-Ended Oral Assessment on pages U122–U123 of this unit and pull them individually during activities this week. We recommend assessing about one-fourth of your class each unit.
- You should also have gathered the following for their assessment portfolio:
  - page 42 of the Language Learning Masters
  - page 44 of the Language Learning Masters
  - finished writing piece assessed according to the Writing Rubric on page A6

You will need

A copy of page U123 at the end of this unit for each child

WEEK 4 DAY 3–4

Writing Resource Guide: Individual Writing

- Children have engaged in a step-by-step writing process moving toward independence. They began with teacher-led writing, moved to cooperative groups, and are now ready to work individually.
- Provide a copy of Writing Planner A or B to each child. They may need individual conferencing on choosing a topic. ◎

Options for STAGES

❶❷ and Emergent Level
These children should draw their ideas in the blank spaces on the graphic organizer. They should label pictures on their own or dictate labels to you.

❸❹❺ Early Level and Above
These children should also use drawings and labels on the graphic organizer to record their topic. They should then use the graphic organizer to create a finished piece.

- When children have completed the finished product, whether graphic organizer or paragraph, you should assess it using the Writing Rubric on page A6 of this Teacher's Guide.

You will need

- Writing Resource Guide, pp. 87–88
- Markers

A Assessment

Continue pulling some children for the Big Book Retelling and Open-Ended Oral Language Assessment as others write.

WEEK 4 DAY 5

Theme Project: Sharing

- Invite groups to share their conservation posters with the class. Some group members can display the poster while others read them aloud to the class. You may want to help children display their posters in the school cafeteria or library after the class presentations.
- Each group should allow time for questions and feedback from the class. Model appropriate feedback for the class by making the first comment yourself—*I like all the ideas on your poster. Can you think of a good title for all these ideas?*

Open-Ended Oral Language Assessment Reassess children's Language Acquisition Stages. Begin with an open-ended prompt like the first one below. If children are unable to respond, intervene with increasingly directed prompts, such as the second and third ones below.

What can you tell me about the picture?

How are people using water?

I see water in the lake. Where do you see water?

Assessment Directions: Copy this form for each child and place the completed form in the child's portfolio. Locate the child's Language Acquisition Stage for each of the first four activities and assess his or her performance during the unit according to expectations for that Stage. For the Big Book Retelling, pull children to retell the Big Book during end-of-unit assessment time. Use the Open-Ended Oral Language Assessment to reassess children's Language Acquisition Stages with one-fourth of your students for each unit, using the back side of the sheet to take notes. *For more guidance on assessment, see pages T33 and T34.*

Unit 5 Assessment

Name ______________________ **Date** ______________

On Our Way to English Grade 2	STAGE EXPECTATIONS ❶	❷	❸	❹	❺
Fluency Manipulative Chart Student Version, page U108 *How does the child respond when manipulating the mini-chart along with the Oral Language Audio CD?*	Shows the correct answers. ☐ Yes ☐ Not yet	Shows the correct answers, naming the water form. ☐ Yes ☐ Not yet	Shows the correct answers, approximating sentences and substitutions. ☐ Yes ☐ Not yet	Shows the correct answers, singing the verse with few, if any, errors. ☐ Yes ☐ Not yet	
Content Area Knowledge Language Practice Game: Version 1, page U109 *How does the child demonstrate an understanding of water forms while playing the game?*	Moves the marker to the appropriate squares. ☐ Yes ☐ Not yet	Moves the marker to the appropriate squares, naming the water form with simple phrases. ☐ Yes ☐ Not yet		Moves the marker to the appropriate square and says a sentence following the pattern *There is water in the lake.* ☐ Yes ☐ Not yet	
Social Language Function Express Obligations, page U113 *How does the child respond during the Function Mini-lesson?*	Uses gestures or simple phrases to express ways to conserve water. ☐ Yes ☐ Not yet		Uses longer phrases or complete sentences to express ways to conserve water. ☐ Yes ☐ Not yet		
Academic Language Function Solve Problems, page U113 *How does the child respond during the Function Mini-lesson?*			Offers ideas which may be expressed as incomplete sentences. ☐ Yes ☐ Not yet	Participates in the discussion by asking questions and offering solutions. ☐ Yes ☐ Not yet	
Big Book Retelling page U112 *Have each child hold their own Water Saver awards over different scenes on the back flap to retell the story. How does the child retell the story?*	Uses the manipulative to point to each scene in sequential order. ☐ Yes ☐ Not yet	Retells using a few words. ☐ Yes ☐ Not yet	Retells using longer phrases or simple sentences. ☐ Yes ☐ Not yet	Retells using complete sentences in connected discourse with few errors. ☐ Yes ☐ Not yet	Retells using story language similar to native-speaking peers. ☐ Yes ☐ Not yet
Open-Ended Oral Language Assessment, page U122 *Use the child's responses to the illustration to reassess the child's Stage of Language Acquisition.*	☐ **STAGE ❶** Uses few or no words; gestures or points.	☐ **STAGE ❷** Uses words or short phrases.	☐ **STAGE ❸** Uses phrases and simple sentences.	☐ **STAGE ❹** Uses sentences in connected discourse.	☐ **STAGE ❺** Uses language comparable to native-speaking peers.

Disaster Alert

OVERVIEW *This theme introduces concepts and vocabulary related to extreme weather conditions and natural disasters. Children then learn how people prepare for and respond to these disasters.*

Determining the Purpose

Oral Language Development

Focus on Functions

Social Context:

Warn ❶❷❸❹❺

Academic Context:

Analyze ❶❷❸❹❺

Focus on Grammar

- Preposition *in* + season
- Commands
- Conjunction *as*
- Past continuous
- Location words *here* and *there*

Comprehension Strategy

- Recognizes cause and effect

Literacy Skills

- **Word Level:** Phonics in context long *u*, *r*-controlled vowels, initial blends
- **Sentence Level:** Descriptive language and imagery
- **Text Level:** Identifying sequence of events, problem, and solution

Content Area Objectives

- Understands safety procedures for a disaster-related emergency
- Understands the type and effects of disasters

Language Learning Strategy

- Use different kinds of words in different settings

Writing Skill

- Uses a graphic organizer to organize writing about cause and effect.

Unit Components

Manipulative Chart

Chant Poster

Concept Poster

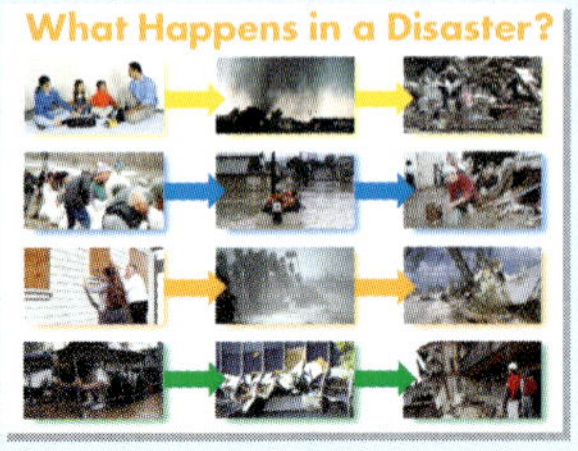

Newcomer Book

Unit at a Glance

	DURING THE WEEK	DAY 1
Week 1	**Small-Group Instruction:** • Guided Reading • Shared-to-Guided Reading **Phonics Focus:** long u: *uCe* Phonics Song Chart 22, pp. P48–P49	**Manipulative Chart:** Introduction with Audio CD p. U127
Week 2	**Small-Group Instruction:** • Guided Reading • Shared-to-Guided Reading • Newcomer Book **Phonics Focus:** *r*-controlled vowels Phonics Song Chart 23, pp. P50–P51	**Concept Poster:** Introduction p. U132 **Language Practice Game:** Version 1 p. U133
Week 3	**Small-Group Instruction:** • Guided Reading • Shared-to-Guided Reading • Newcomer Book **Phonics Focus:** *cl, pl* Phonics Song Chart 24, pp. P52–P53	**Big Book:** Oral Language Development p. U139
Week 4	**Small-Group Instruction:** • Guided Reading • Shared-to-Guided Reading • Newcomer Book **Phonics Focus:** *sl, bl* Phonics Song Chart 25, pp. P54–P55	**Big Book:** Literacy Skills p. U143 **Language Practice Game:** Version 2 p. U144

STAGES ❶ Preproduction ❷ Early Production ❸ Speech Emergence ❹ Intermediate Fluency ❺ Advanced Fluency

Oral Language Audio CD

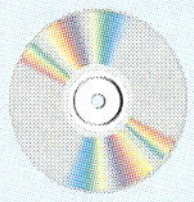

Big Book with Audio CD and Small Book

Home-School Connection Masters

Picture Cards

Shared Writing Card

Writing Resource Guide

Language Learning Masters

DAY 2	DAY 3	DAY 4	DAY 5
Manipulative Chart: Gestures and Manipulative Fun p. U128	**Chant Poster:** Introduction p. U129	**TPR Cards:** Introduction p. U130	**Manipulative Chart:** Oral Language Development Student Version p. U131
Big Book: Introduction p. U135	**Theme Project:** Disaster Theme Book p. U136 **Big Book:** Revisiting p. U136	**Big Book:** Comprehension Strategy p. U137 **Chant Poster:** Oral Language Development p. U137	**Shared Writing Card:** Introduction of Side A p. U138 **Concept Poster:** Revisiting p. U138
Shared Writing Card: Brainstorming Side B p. U140 **Active Social Studies:** Safety Posters p. U140	**Shared Writing Card:** Writing Together with Side B p. U141 **Manipulative Chart:** Oral Language Development p. U141	**Active Science:** Earthquake Model p. U141	**Writing Resource Guide:** A Simplified Graphic Organizer Cooperative-Group Writing p. U142
Active Math: Earthquake Sort p. U144 **Assessment** p. U144	**Writing Resource Guide:** Individual Writing p. U145 **Assessment** p. U144	**Writing Resource Guide:** Individual Writing p. U145 **Assessment** p. U144	**Theme Project:** Sharing p. U145

Center Activities

Number Nook

Provide empty water bottles, bean and tuna cans, and cracker boxes. Have children use these as visual aids to plan and list how much water and food they would need in a two- or three-day disaster emergency.

Artist's Studio

Provide shoe boxes, magazines, play figures, and art supplies. Guide children in making dioramas of natural disasters. They can make models of buildings in the center, and decorate the sides with magazine pictures of extreme weather conditions.

You will need

- Empty water bottles, tuna and bean cans, cracker boxes
- Construction paper
- Crayons and markers
- Scissors
- Glue
- Shoe boxes
- Newspapers and magazines
- Play figurines

Content Corner

Cut out captioned newspaper and magazine photos of extreme weather and natural disasters. Display these photos in the content corner and encourage children to discuss them.

Listening Post

After introducing each element in class, children may revisit the Manipulative Chart and Chant Poster on the Oral Language Audio CD. If you include a laminated copy of the Manipulative Chart Student Version, children can manipulate it as they sing to Part 4 of the CD (with blanks). Children may also listen to *Barge Cat* on the Big Book Audio CD while following along in the small copy.

CENTERS

Language Workshop

Any time they are not in use during the unit, place the Picture Cards for the unit in this center. Encourage children to review disaster-related vocabulary with each other for additional practice. After introducing the Language Practice Game in class, add the game board, TPR Cards and foil balls, to the center for independent group play.

Writer's Den

Establish a journal writing center with prompts to spark children's writing. Change the prompt every two weeks:

- What was the scariest storm you remember?
- What should you do during a disaster? Make a list.

Children should be encouraged to draw pictures to support their writing. Provide blank Writing Planners in center materials for prewriting.

More Books

- *Tikvah Means Hope* by Patricia Polacco (Doubleday, 1996)
- *Brave Irene* by William Steig (Farrar, Straus & Giroux, 1986)
- *Flood* by Mary Calhoun (Morrow, 1997)
- *Earthquakes* by Seymour Simon (Scholastic, 2001)
- *Hill of Fire* by Thomas P. Lewis (HarperCollins, 1985)

WEEK 1 DAY 1

Manipulative Chart: Introduction with Audio CD

Sung to the tune of "Mary Had a Little Lamb"

Setting the Scene

- Hold up a real or imaginary umbrella and pretend to walk in a rainstorm. Use gestures to describe what you are doing and why. Encourage volunteers to tell about a storm they have been in or remember. Have them use gestures and familiar language to describe it.
- Hold up Picture Card 1: earthquake. Say *This is a picture of an earthquake.* Explain that an earthquake happens when the ground moves and shakes. Use gestures and props to show how furniture shakes, people rock back and forth, and things fall.
- Use a similar procedure to introduce Picture Cards 2–5: blizzard, tornado, flood, hurricane. Use gestures, props, and sound effects to show what these disasters are like. For example, whistle and motion a spiral movement to show a tornado. ◎

Options for STAGES

❶	❷❸	❹❺
Ask these children either/or questions, such as *Is this an earthquake or tornado?*	Hold up each of the cards, and ask *What is this?* Confirm or modify answers as necessary.	Ask these children to summarize what happens during these disasters. Invite them to share anything else they may know about them.

Creating Comprehensible Input

- Prepare the chart for use by bending back the flaps and then shutting them. Doing this in advance will make the flaps more flexible.
- Point out items on the chart, such as the TV, the weather forecaster, the map of the United States, and the disaster icons. Explain that the icons point to where these disasters often happen.
- Read the text, pausing often, as you use gestures, pointing, and other techniques to make the chant comprehensible.

A tornado's coming to town,	point to Picture Card 3: tornado
Coming to town, coming to town.	point to tornado icon on Manipulative Chart
Watch the weather on the news.	point to TV and forecaster on Manipulative Chart
Stay safe and sound.	cross wrists and place hands on chest to show "safe"

Manipulative Chart Picture Cards 1–5

Guided Reading

As you work on this unit, conduct small groups of guided reading or shared-to-guided reading independent of thematic instruction. Instruction is provided in the Guided Reading section of this guide.

Component Organizer

Other Manipulative Chart lessons in this unit:

- Gestures and Manipulative Fun, p. U128
- Oral Language Development and Student Version, pp. U131–U132
- Oral Language Development, p. U141

Real-World Touch

Bring in a first-aid kit and introduce the items. Explain that these are kept handy in case of an emergency. Remove any medications, and then leave the kit in the Content Corner for individual exploration.

Home-School Connection

Choose one of the versions of the parent letter to send home with each child, according to the child's home language (pages 58–65 in the Home-School Connection Masters). Also send home the activity on page 66.

Manipulative Chart

Journal Writing Reminder

Children should be writing in their journals during the course of the unit. Journal writing provides an excellent opportunity for children to experiment with descriptive words and imagery. See Writer's Den for suggested journal prompts.

Introducing the Audio CD

- Play Part 1 of the Oral Language Audio CD, the spoken song, as you say the song and track the print on the Manipulative Chart with your finger or a pointer. Replay Part 1 several times, encouraging children to chime in whenever they can.
- Introduce the song by playing the song at natural speed, Part 2 of the Audio CD, to help children get a feel for the song. Allow the Audio CD to continue playing through Part 3, the song at instructional pace. Track the print as the Audio CD plays. Repeat Part 3 again, this time singing along, making clear lip movements without exaggerating. Revisit Part 3 several times to help children learn the song.

WEEK 1 DAY 2

Manipulative Chart: Gestures and Manipulative Fun

Gesturing the Song

Introduce these simple gestures to accompany the song:

A tornado's coming to town,	hold one hand palm up then point other index finger down at palm and make spiral motion
Coming to town, coming to town.	tap the open palm in rhythm to the beat
Watch the weather on the news.	point to your eyes then gesture TV's shape
Stay safe and sound.	hug self

Manipulating the Chart

- Show children how to open the flaps to see pictures of the disasters. The disasters in the pictures can be substituted for *tornado* in red. Point to the earthquake icon, sing the verse, and emphasize using *earthquake* instead of *tornado* each time it appears in the song.
- Play Part 4 of the Oral Language Audio CD as you say *earthquake* in the blank space.
- Continue introducing and naming the disasters behind the other flaps in this manner.
- Invite volunteers to manipulate the Manipulative Chart for the class as you sing new verses together or give Total Physical Response commands, such as *Show me the blizzard.*
- Invite children to help you create new gestures for the disasters on the chart.
- You can revisit this activity many times during the unit.

WEEK 1 DAY 3

Chant Poster: Introduction

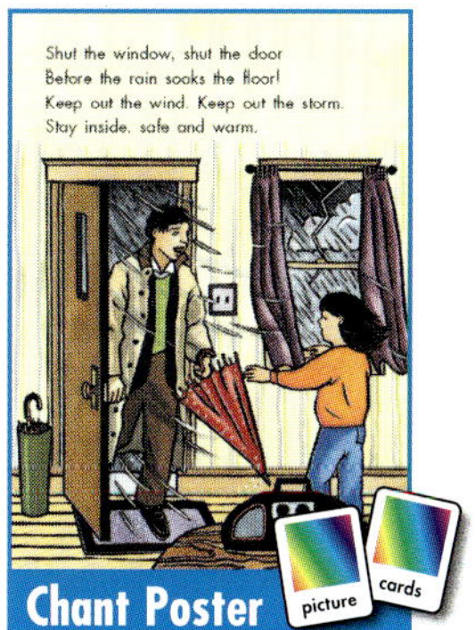
Shut the window, shut the door
Before the rain soaks the floor!
Keep out the wind. Keep out the storm.
Stay inside, safe and warm.
picture
cards

Chant Poster
Picture Cards 6–8

Setting the Scene

- Illustrate key vocabulary for the chant using gestures and items from the classroom. Close the classroom door, for example, and have children repeat as you say *Shut the door.* ◎

Options for STAGES

❶❷ These children can pantomime actions as you say them.

❸❹❺ Have these children take turns giving commands with the target vocabulary.

- Show Picture Cards 6–8: rain, wind, storm. Say each word and allow children to repeat them. Then hold Picture Cards 6 and 7 in one hand and Picture Card 8 in the other hand. Say *Rain and wind together make a rainstorm.* Put the cards down and use finger gestures and sound effects to indicate rain and wind.

Creating Comprehensible Input

- Display the Chant Poster and ask volunteers to point to the window, door, floor, and the rain. Ask *Is it raining? Is it windy?* Confirm by telling children that there is a storm outside.
- Read the text slowly as you use gestures, pointing, and other techniques to make the chant comprehensible.

Shut the window, shut the door	act out shutting a window and door
Before the rain soaks the floor!	gesture rain and point to the floor
Keep out the wind. Keep out the storm.	gesture "Stop!" with both hands out in front of you
Stay inside, safe and warm.	hug self

Chanting the Poster

- Encourage children to chime in as you chant the rhyme together several times. One group can chant the first two lines, and another group the second two lines.
- Introduce the chant on the Oral Language Audio CD as you and the children move to the rhythm of the chant. Tell them they can listen to it on their own later at the Listening Post.
- Practice saying the chant in different ways, such as very softly, very loudly, or using tone to show emotions such as urgency.
- Revisit the chant often with children. Invite them to gesture the different actions in the chant as they recite it.

Component Organizer

Other Chant Poster lessons in this unit:

- Oral Language Development, pp. U137–U138

WEEK 1 DAY 4

You will need

- **Language Learning Master** p. 47
- Scissors

TPR Cards: Introduction

Introducing the Cards with Total Physical Response

- Provide one copy of page 47 of the Language Learning Masters to each child. Have children color and cut out the cards.
- Introduce a few cards at a time by holding them up one by one and saying the words clearly. Start with words that have already been introduced in previous activities.
- Ask children to pick up the correct cards as you call out a word. Model the desired outcome. Add one new card at a time and keep reviewing in a game-like atmosphere. Children may want to say the word as they pick up the card.
- Now invite children to respond to your full-sentence commands, such as *Show me the clouds. Pick up the lightning.*
- Assign partners so you can add commands, such as *Pass the tornado to Gabriel.*
- As children increase their familiarity with the TPR cards and the game, add funny commands such as *Sit on the clouds.*
- Invite volunteers in Stages 3, 4, or 5 to give commands to their classmates.
- Repeat this activity several times throughout the unit.

Language Learning Master

p. 50 ❶❷❸❹❺

Grammar in Context: Preposition *in* + season ❶❷❸❹❺

1. Hold up TPR cards for tornado, hurricane, thunderstorm, and blizzard one at a time, encouraging children to say each word with you.
2. Using a calendar or other classroom prop, review the names of the four seasons.
3. Hold up the blizzard card and say *Blizzards happen in the winter.* Point to the winter months on the calendar. Ask *When do blizzards happen?* Elicit the previous statement as the answer.
4. Use a similar procedure for the other cards. ◎

Options for STAGES

❶❷ Have these children hold up the appropriate cards as children in the higher stages verbalize sentences with the target structure.

❸❹❺ Have these children take turns creating new sentences using the target structure. Model correct usage as necessary.

WEEK 1 DAY 5

Manipulative Chart: Focus on Oral Language Development

FUNCTION MINI-LESSON

Warn ①②③④⑤

1. Hold up Picture Card 8: storm. Act out pulling a jacket close around you and peer at the sky as you say *The sky is dark. It is starting to rain.* Point to the picture as you describe the sky. Then change your voice to one of warning and say *A storm is coming! Stay inside!*
2. Refer to the Manipulative Chart and use a similar method to give mock warnings for an impending blizzard, tornado, hurricane, and flood.
3. Invite volunteers to take turns giving warnings to the class for a storm, blizzard, tornado, hurricane, and flood. Repeat your original warning to reinforce the pattern of *A ______ is coming!* Then have volunteers take turns choosing a Picture Card and using the pattern.

   Although all children can be exposed to the function *warn,* do not expect childen in lower language Stages to produce it.

FUNCTION MINI-LESSON

Analyze ①②③④⑤

1. Invite children in Stages 3, 4, and 5 to join you while others play games with the TPR cards.
2. Point to various scenes under the flaps on the Manipulative Chart and verbally analyze the effects of each scene. As you point to the earthquake, for example, say *During an earthquake, the earth shakes. It makes the ground crack and buildings fall down.* Use actions as well as simple language to illustrate cause and effect in the picture.
3. Continue with the other pictures on the chart. Encourage children to point to or tell other effects of disasters that are part of the pictures.
4. Ask yes/no questions such as *Does the earth shake during a flood?* to help Stage 3 children identify the various effects of each disaster. Children in Stages 4 and 5 can respond to more open-ended questions like *What happens during a flood?* as they analyze each scene.

Grammar in Context: Commands ①②③④⑤

1. Review classroom rules with the children. List them on the board if they are not already posted in the classroom.
2. Look at the Manipulative Chart. Ask children to find the two rules in the chart for what to do in a disaster. (*Watch TV. Stay safe and sound.*) Start a list on the board.
3. Elicit other rules for staying safe in the particular disasters shown on the Manipulative Chart, such as *Go to the basement* when there's a tornado. Add them to the list.

Manipulative Chart Picture Card 8

Language Learning Strategy

Use different kinds of words in different settings.

Use this strategy for children in Stages 3–5.

- Tell children that we use different kinds of words at different times. Explain that some words are used to learn certain things in school, and they can be different from words we might use with friends after school. Hold up a handful of soil from a classroom plant.

  Model *I took this from our plant. When I talk in school about this, I use the word* soil. *When I'm talking about soil with my friends, I might use the word* dirt *instead.*
- Continue demonstrating the difference between academic and non-academic language with word pairs, such as *blizzard/snowstorm* and *tornado/twister.*

Home-School Connection

When children have practiced manipulating the Manipulative Chart Student Version, send it home for them to practice with their family members.

You will need

- **Language Learning Master** pp. 45–46
- Scissors

Assessment

Record your observations of children on their individual assessment checklists for this unit. See page U147.

Concept Poster
Picture Cards 1–5, 9, 10

Guided Reading

As you work on this unit, conduct small groups of guided reading or shared-to-guided reading independent of thematic instruction. Instruction is provided in the Guided Reading section of this guide.

Manipulative Chart: Student Version

- Have children color and cut out the cards on page 46 of the Language Learning Masters.
- Invite children to place their cards on their Manipulative Chart Student Version as you sing the song and open the flaps on the Manipulative Chart. Then encourage them to match the picture to what you do as you say different words in the song.
- Invite children to respond to your Total Physical Response commands: *Show me the tornado.*
- Play Part 4 of the Oral Language Audio CD and model how children can manipulate their Student Versions as they sing along. Tell children that they will later be able to listen to the Audio CD and manipulate this mini-chart in the Listening Post.

WEEK 2 DAY 1

Concept Poster: Introduction

Setting the Scene

- Display the Manipulative Chart. Remind children that this shows a TV weather report. Point to the broadcaster and the pictures. Using gestures, say *The weather report can warn us that bad weather is coming! Then we can be ready.*
- Display Picture Cards 1–5: earthquake, blizzard, tornado, flood, hurricane. Elicit from children ideas for staying safe in each of these natural disasters. Encourage children in lower Stages to use gestures to share their ideas. Explain that by preparing and practicing safety procedures for disasters, they will know what to do in an emergency.

Creating Comprehensible Input

- Direct children's attention to the first row of photographs on the Concept Poster. Demonstrate how to talk through the relationship between the pictures with a think-aloud.

  Model *This family is in the basement of their house. This arrow tells me that this picture goes with the next one on the right. A tornado is coming. They got ready by going to the basement. This tornado looks dangerous. I follow the arrow to the right and see what the tornado did. Some houses were ruined. The family went to the basement and stayed safe during the tornado.*
- Recap this in simple language as you point at the pictures and connecting arrows: *Family in basement; A tornado is coming; The family went to the basement to be safe during the tornado.*
- Introduce the word *river* using Picture Card 9: river. Then help children relate *river* to *flood* using Picture Card 4: flood. Also introduce the word *sandbag* by pointing to and explaining the first picture in the second row of the Concept Poster. Show Picture Card 10: bank. Use simple language and gestures to explain that sandbags are put along the banks of the river to help stop the water from flooding.
- Invite a child at Stages 3, 4, or 5 to lead the class in talking through the rest of the pictures in the second row. As necessary, review what children have learned about floods. Support with appropriate academic language.

- After the child has finished, recap in simple language, pointing to pictures and connecting arrows.
- Repeat the procedure for the third and fourth rows. You may want to use Picture Card 5: hurricane and Picture Card 1: earthquake to review what children have already learned about these two disasters.

Extending Oral Language

1. Engage children in reviewing these concepts by asking questions.

Options for STAGES

1 2 Ask these children questions that allow for physical, nonverbal responses, such as *What do you do during an earthquake? That's right. You get under a table and cover your head.*

3 4 5 Ask these children open-ended questions that require elaboration, such as *How can we get ready for a hurricane? What should you do during an earthquake?*

2. Use Total Physical Response commands to build familiarity with the concepts. For instance, *Point to the flood. Show me the picture of what happens after a hurricane.*

Language Practice Game: Version 1 (1 2 3 4 5)

Preparing the Game

Tape copies of pages 48 and 49 of the Language Learning Masters to two facing sides of a file folder. Squeeze aluminum foil into balls, one for each group of four children. Prepare sets of the fire, earthquake, tornado, hurricane, thunderstorm, blizzard, and volcano TPR cards, one set per child.

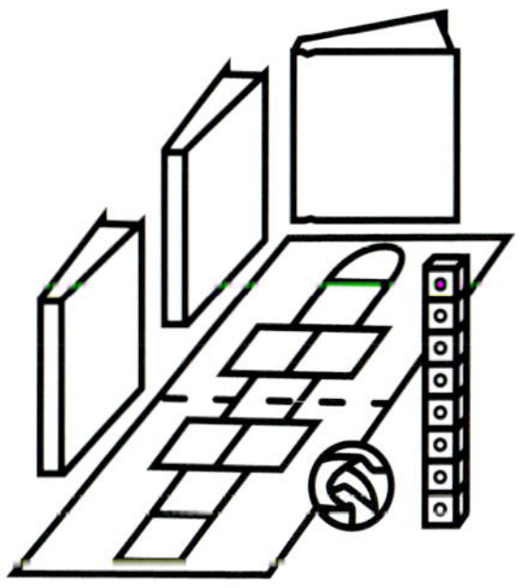

Playing Version 1

Divide the class into heterogeneous groups of mixed language abilities with four children each. Provide a game board and aluminum foil ball for each group and the set of seven TPR cards for each child. Model the following directions.

1. Children place their set of cards faceup and spread out in front of them.

2. Position books as barriers around the game. The first player rolls the foil ball onto the board and turns over the corresponding card. If the ball lands nearest the fire scene, for example, the player would turn over the fire card.

Options for STAGES

1 These children may simply turn over their card, naming it as they are able.

2 3 These children should be encouraged to say a few words, such as *tornado,* or *tornado coming.*

4 5 Encourage these children to say the complete sentence: *A tornado is coming!*

3. Children continue taking turns rolling the ball. If a player lands on a picture for which his or her corresponding card has already been turned over, the turn is lost and the next player goes.

4. The first player to turn over all of his or her cards is the winner.

Component Organizer

Other Concept Poster lessons in this unit:
- p. U138

You will need

- **Language Learning Master** pp. 48–49
- File Folder
- Tape
- TPR Cards
- Foil balls

Component Organizer

Other Language Practice Game lessons in this unit:
- Version 2, p. U144

Assessment

Record your observations of children during the Language Practice Game on their individual assessment checklists for this unit. See page U147.

Newcomer Book: Small-Group Instruction

A Disaster Is Coming!

Written by Karen Clevidence

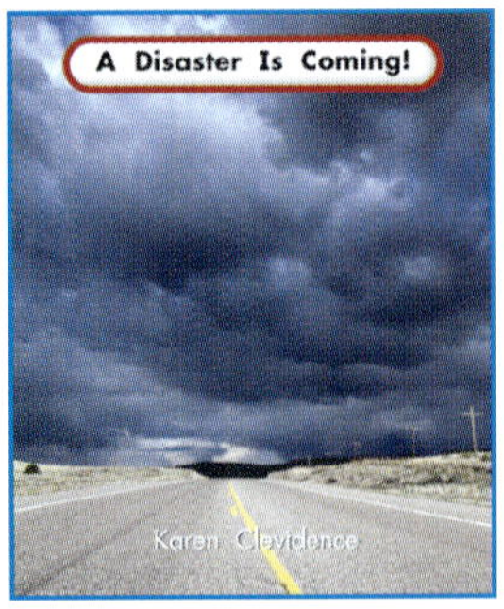

OVERVIEW *When a disaster comes, it is time to stay safe!*

The Newcomer Book is supported by the language of the Manipulative Chart and should be integrated into small-group instruction this week when children have had enough practice with vocabulary and concepts in this unit.

Language Pattern

A ______ is coming!

Text Vocabulary

names of disasters

Vocabulary Extenders

colors

Reading the Text

Book Talk

- Work with a small group of four children at one time who exhibit similar literacy-learning behaviors.
- Engage children in a book talk as you flip through the pages of your copy of the book.

Options for STAGES

1 2 Identify the names of the disasters for these children. Encourage them to repeat the names with you as they are able.

3 4 5 Ask children to identify each disaster as you encounter it.

INSTRUCTIONAL PATHS

1 2 3 4 5 All Readers:	1 2 3 4 5 Emergent Readers:	1 2 3 4 5 Early Readers:
Shared-to-Guided Reading	Guided Reading	Independent Reading — no lesson provided

INDIVIDUAL READING

Shared-to-Guided Reading — **3–4 sessions**

1 2 3 4 5 All Readers

1. Read the book to children.
   - Invite children to sit near you as you read a copy of the book. Begin with the cover and title page.
   - Turn to page 2 and begin reading the words as you point to them. Draw children's attention to the pictures.
2. Read the book with children.
   - Encourage children to follow along in their own copies of the book, turning the pages as you read together and using their own fingers to point to the words from left to right.
   - Invite children to chime in when they are comfortable.
   - Reread the book in this manner over several sessions.
3. Have children buddy read the book.
4. Invite children to read the book independently.

A Assess

- Did children look at the pictures?
- Did children finger point to each word as you read together?

Guided Reading — **2 sessions**

1 2 3 4 5 Emergent Readers

1. Provide copies of the book to children. Use one child's book and turn to page 2. Introduce the book's pattern to children by reading the sentence and pointing to each word as you read *A tornado is coming!*
2. Have each child read at his or her own pace while remaining in the group. Discourage choral reading. Observe as they read.

A Assess

- Did children look at the words from left to right?
- Did children use the first letter of words to figure them out?

REVISITING THE NEWCOMER BOOK

If children seem ready, you may also extend children's knowledge of colors by naming the border colors on each page.

WEEK 2 DAY 2

Big Book: Introduction

Barge Cat

Written by Martin Waddell *Illustrated by Troy Howell*

OVERVIEW *Barge Cat and her kittens live on a boat by a river. What will they do when a flood comes?*

Warming Up

Begin the lesson by revisiting the Manipulative Chart, Chant Poster, or a familiar classic such as *Brave Irene*. You may ask a volunteer to choose one.

Setting the Scene

- Tap into children's prior knowledge. Ask *Do all cats live with people? Where do other cats live?*
- Show Picture Card 12: barge. Say *Sometimes cats live on barges.* Show Picture Card 9: river, and explain that barges are boats that carry things up and down rivers.
- Display Picture Card 4: flood and Picture Cards 8–10: storm, river, bank. Using gestures and pointing, remind children that a flood happens when there's so much rain that the river can't hold it all. Then the water goes over the riverbank.
- Ask children what they think happens to barges when there's a flood.
- Introduce the book. Provide an overview of the story.
- Tell children that when we listen to a book, we listen for different purposes. Guide children to understand that when we listen to *Barge Cat*, our purpose will be to enjoy and appreciate it.
- Display and describe the book cover. Support your words with gesturing and pointing. *Have you ever seen cats that live outside? The mother cat must protect her kittens from many dangers like storms and floods.*
- Make predictions. *What will Barge Cat do if there's a storm and a flood?*

Reading the Text

- Read the title page. Have children make additional predictions based on this picture. *Where will Barge Cat and her kittens live after the flood?*
- As you read through the story, draw children's attention to the text. Focus on the enjoyment of the book, pointing out items in the pictures to support your reading. You will return later to build children's understanding of the text. In future rereadings, children should be encouraged to chime in.
- If you have children in Stages 3, 4, or 5, pause after reading page 10. Did their prediction come true so far? What do they think will happen next?

Creating Comprehensible Input

- Open the flap at the back of the book to show the effects of the flood. Leave it open as you read to support comprehension of the effects of the flood in the story.
- Use the comprehension supports in the following chart to help you build comprehensible input with children at all Stages of Language Acquisition.

Big Book
Picture Cards 4, 8–10, 12

Component Organizer

Other Big Book lessons in this unit:
- Revisiting, p. U136
- Comprehension Strategy, p. U137
- Oral Language Development, pp. U139–U140
- Literacy Skills, p. U143

PAGE	IN THE STORY	COMPREHENSION SUPPORT
2	Barge Cat and her kittens lived . . . barges . . . by the bank of the . . . River.	point: to cat, kittens, barge, and bank
6	Then came thunder and lightning and rain.	act out: clap hands and flash fingers to imitate thunder and lightning
7	Skid and Little and Bounce were scared.	act out: make frightened facial expression
8	The water rose and . . . rose.	gesture: move hand up in increments for rose
9	The three kittens were very frightened.	act out: make frightened facial expression
10	The old barge creaked and groaned . . .	act out: rock back and forth while making creaking noise
11	Then it stirred . . . shifted . . . started to sink.	gesture: show hand stirring, shifting, and "sinking" down
12	Barge Cat clung to a plank . . .	act out: use "claws" to cling to something
13	. . . afraid they would drown . . . terrified . . .	act out: drowning with frightened facial expression
15	Barge Cat . . . scrambled up on a branch . . .	act out: "scramble" up something
16	Little fell . . . water . . . close over his head.	act out: fall and go under water
18	Barge Cat quickly grabbed Little . . . pulled him safely . . .	act out: grab something below you, pull it up and hold it
19	. . . there was water everywhere.	gesture: water everywhere with sweeping hands
21	Then the flood waters went slowly down.	gesture: move hand down in increments
23	Barge Cat has moved . . .	point: to new barge, comparing it to first barge on pages 2–3
24	Barge Cat's kittens are grown cats now.	gesture: move hand from low to higher

You will need

- Chart paper
- Crayons and markers
- Magazine pictures of disasters
- Drawing paper
- Glue
- Hole punch
- Yarn

Revisiting the Big Book

- Cut out two rectangles of construction paper and staple them together to form an envelope. Then cut out four cat shapes, one larger than the others.
- Ask a volunteer to move the cat figures in and out of the "barge" envelope as you reread the story. The volunteer can also push the "barge" along to represent the movement of the barge.

WEEK 2 DAY 3

Theme Project: Disaster Theme Book

1. Remind children that they have learned about many different disasters and that now they can choose one to learn more about. Put children in heterogeneous groups with three to four children each. Make a list of different disasters with the children and have each group choose one to learn more about.
2. Help each group start a K-W-L Chart with three columns: *Know, Want to Learn,* and *Learned*. Help groups fill in what they already know and what they want to learn. What they want to learn should be a list of questions, including questions about where it occurs, how to prepare for it, and its aftermath.
3. After orienting children to the library using the Newcomer Language Learning Master, have groups bring their K-W-L Charts to the library. Help children find and use resources to answer their questions, filling in their *Learned* column as they find answers to their questions. Lower Stage children can participate by drawing pictures of what they learn. This may take more than one trip to the library.
4. Groups can then make booklets using information from their *Learned* column. Their booklets should include at least four pages: one about what the disaster looks like, another about where it happens, another about preparation and/or safety precautions, and the fourth showing the aftermath. Lower Stage children can participate by drawing or cutting and pasting the accompanying pictures.
5. Once children have completed their booklets, leave them in the Reading Center so children can return to them when they choose.

WEEK 2 DAY 4

Big Book: Focus on Comprehension Strategy

Recognizes Cause and Effect

1. Display the back flap of the book. Have a volunteer point to the pictures as you reread the story.
2. Establish cause and effect relationships. Start with the top picture. Say *Here the barge is sinking. Why did this happen? Oh, all the flood water made it sink.* Point back to the picture on the left of the flood. Point out the label *cause*. Say *The flood caused the barge to sink,* tracing along the arrow.
3. Point to the middle picture and have volunteers use words or gestures to tell what is happening. Then work together to determine the cause of Little's trouble. Repeat the procedure with the bottom picture.
4. Invite volunteers to explain other cause and effect relationships in the story, such as why Barge Cat moved her kittens to the top of the barge. ◎

Options for STAGES

❶❷ Invite children to trace the cause and effect arrows, naming as they are able.

❸❹❺ Ask these children to tell about the effects of the flood, such as *Little almost drowned because of the flood.*

Chant Poster: Focus on Oral Language Development

FUNCTION MINI-LESSON

Warn ❶❷❸❹❺

1. Revisit the chant together, saying it several times.
2. Review imperatives, which were introduced in Week 1 Day 5.
3. Point to the window and door in the Chant Poster saying *Shut the window! Shut the door!* Review warnings, phrased as imperatives, for other disasters, such as *Go to the basement!* Ask children to help you think of other such warnings for one disaster. Record their ideas in a word web, with the central idea being *Warnings for a Tornado,* for example.

FUNCTION MINI-LESSON

Analyze ❶❷❸❹❺

1. Ask children *What happens during a rainstorm?* If necessary, reread the chant and direct their attention to the illustration on the poster. Confirm *Yes, there can be wind and rain during a storm.*
2. Write *What Happens During a Rainstorm* in the middle of a word web. Draw spokes from the center and put the words you and children come up with, such as *wind* and *rain.*
3. Follow a similar procedure to have children analyze the elements of a *hurricane, blizzard,* and *tornado.* Create a separate web for each topic.

Big Book

Assessment

Use a retelling of the Big Book to assess comprehension. See page U147.

Shut the window, shut the door
Before the rain soaks the floor!
Keep out the wind. Keep out the storm.
Stay inside, safe and warm.

Chant Poster

Home Culture Sharing

- Some children may have moved to the United States after a devastating disaster. Invite them to share disaster-related experiences. Be sensitive to any loss they may have experienced.

Assessment

Record your observations of children during these mini-lessons on their individual assessment checklists for this unit. See page U147.

Language Learning Master

p. 51 ❶❷❸❹❺

Grammar in Context: Commands ❶❷❸❹❺

1. Review the list of ideas for staying safe from Week 1 Day 5.
2. Look for other ideas in the Chant Poster (*Shut the window, Shut the door*).
3. Give commands from the list that children can act out. Invite Stage 4 and 5 children to give their classmates commands from the list.

Options for STAGES

❶❷ These children can perform the actions as commanded.	❸❹❺ These children can give commands to lower Stage children.

WEEK 2 DAY 5

Shared Writing Card: Introduction of Side A

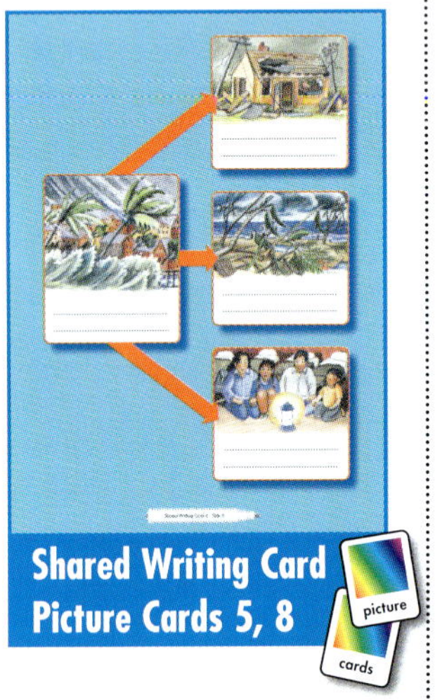

Shared Writing Card
Picture Cards 5, 8

You will need

- Shared Writing Card 6
- Wipe-off marker
- Regular marker
- Easel pad

Setting the Scene

- Use the back flap of the Big Book to review cause and effect relationships in *Barge Cat*. Ask volunteers to restate what happened because of the flood. Allow them to flip through the book to find pictures that help them make connections.
- Hold up Picture Card 8: storm. Review with words and gestures what often happens in a storm. Then show Picture Card 5: hurricane. Ask *What happens during a hurricane?* Encourage volunteers to tell about or act out experiences or information they know about hurricanes. Point out that a hurricane is a very strong and dangerous storm that usually occurs along the shores of an ocean.

Creating Comprehensible Input

- Display Writing Card 6 Side A showing the effects of a hurricane. Begin by pointing to and naming the elements in each illustration.
  Model *Look, a hurricane! See the big waves and the rain? It's very windy! See the trees? Oh, there's a hole in this roof. And look at the power lines down. Look at all these branches and boards. Here a family is in a shelter. They need a lantern for light.*
- Go back to the first illustration. Use think-alouds to talk through the illustrations on the Writing Card. Point to the illustrations one by one and trace the arrow with your finger to show the cause-effect relationship.
  Illustration 1: *The wind is blowing really hard. It is raining. There are big waves, too. It looks like a hurricane!*
  Illustration 2: *Look what happened. The hurricane broke the roof and electric lines.*
  Illustration 3: *The trees are all bent and broken. Hurricanes can do this, too.*
  Illustration 4: *What's happening here? They are using a lantern because there is no electricity. Hurricanes can cause the power to go off.*
- Explain that these pictures show the effects of a hurricane. Trace the arrows and point to each illustration saying, for example *The hurricane broke the roof.*
- Invite a volunteer from Stages 3, 4, or 5 to explain other effects of the hurricane in the illustrations.

Revisiting the Concept Poster

- Revisit the Concept Poster, inviting children to use the poster to review safety procedures for each disaster.
- Children can role-play preparing for each disaster.

Scribing with the Graphic Organizer

- After children have become comfortable with the content of the illustrations, you can use the wipe-off marker provided to scribe while you brainstorm labels together for the graphic organizer. Since you are creating a graphic organizer, not a finished product, well-crafted sentences are not necessary.
- Think aloud as you write so that children have insight into the writing process.
- Here is an example of simple shared writing labeling for the illustrations:
  Illustration 1: *wind, rain, and big waves in hurricane*
  Illustration 2: *huge hole in roof*
  Illustration 3: *trees blown over*
  Illustration 4: *no electric lights*

Writing Together from the Graphic Organizer

- Display the Shared Writing Card and refer to it as you work with children to create a shared writing piece on your easel pad. You will again be writing as you and the children develop the text of the piece.
- Begin with a think-aloud.
  Model *In the first picture, we wrote* wind, rain, and big waves in hurricane. *That's not a complete sentence. How can I make it a complete sentence? That's right,* There is rain, wind, and big waves in a hurricane. *Wait a minute. I need to say what my paragraph will be about. Let's look at the other pictures and labels. They are about the damage hurricanes cause. Maybe my first sentence should be* The rain, wind, and big waves in a hurricane cause a lot of damage.
- Write down the sentence you agree upon with children.
- As you move to the second illustration, read the label and then invite children to help you create a sentence based on the picture and label. Record what children dictate as you work together to create complete sentences for each illustration. When children offer sentences with errors in them, correct these errors without being overt. Encourage children to use classroom resources, such as the Word Wall.
- When you have finished your shared writing piece, read it together several times. Then hang it up on the wall where it can be displayed during the rest of the unit and reread many times. For now, do not erase your labels on Side A.

Phonics in Context

Shared writing provides an ideal opportunity for reviewing the phonics skills children are learning. Highlight the sounds in words like ***bl**ow* and *h**uge***.

Sample Shared Writing

The rain, wind, and big waves in a hurricane cause a lot of damage. Hurricanes can put huge holes in roofs. They also cause trees to blow over. People lose electricity because of hurricanes, too. We need to stay safe during a hurricane.

WEEK 3 DAY 1

Big Book: Focus on Oral Language Development

Reread the Big Book and return to the text to focus on oral language development.

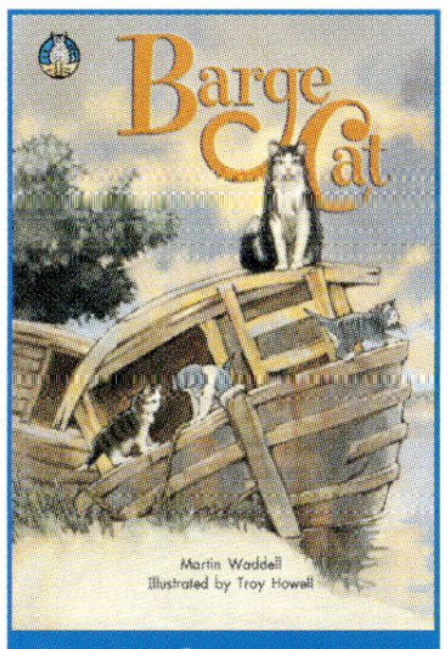

Big Book

Grammar in Context: Clauses with *as* ①②③④⑤

1. Ask two children to come to the front of the class. Ask one child to clean the board and the other to put away some books. When they are finished, say *Esai cleaned the board as Mei Ling put away the books.* Children may chime in as you repeat the sentence.
2. Open the Big Book to page 10. Read and gesture the following sentence: *The old barge creaked and groaned as the water swirled around it.* Circle *as* with your finger while children say it with you. Say *The word* as *here tells us that two things happened at the same time. Here it means that the water swirled around the boat at the same that the boat was making noises.*

Guided Reading

As you work on this unit, conduct small groups of guided reading or shared-to-guided reading independent of thematic instruction. Instruction is provided in the Guided Reading section of this guide.

Language Junction

Cantonese and Vietnamese speakers generally have trouble forming correct verb phrases. Thus, they may form verb phrases within clauses incorrectly (*She grabbed him as he going under water*). These speakers also have trouble forming verb tenses correctly because verbs in their languages do not have tense markers. As such, they may form sentences containing at least one verb with no tense such as *The kittens watched from the tree while Barge Cat rescue Little.*

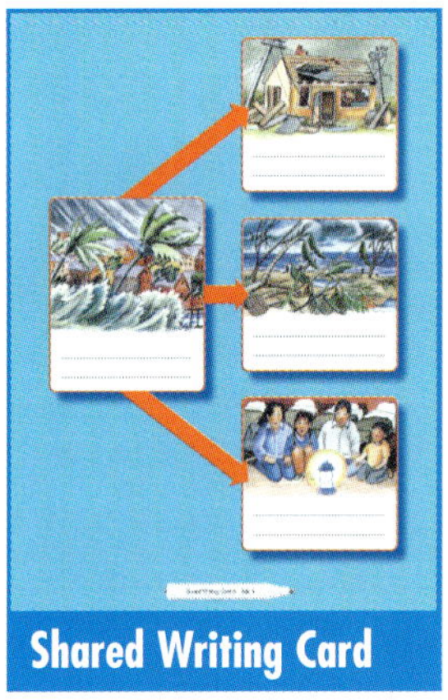

You will need

- Shared Writing Card 6
- Wipe-off marker

You will need

- Butcher paper
- Markers, pencils, and crayons

3. Turn to page 16 and read the second sentence, emphasizing *as*. Work with children to identify the two things that happened at once. Continue with pages 18 and 19. Invite volunteers to locate *as* on these pages. Then read the sentences and have children tell the two things that are happening.

Grammar in Context: Past Continuous ❶❷❸❹❺

1. Read the text on page 18 of the Big Book. Ask children to listen for the word with *-ing*. Confirm by tracking the phrase *was going*.
2. Ask a volunteer to clean the board for you. When the child is finished, ask *What was Chan doing? Yes, he was cleaning the board.* Emphasize *was cleaning* as you repeat your sentence. Explain that *was* before an action word with *-ing* tells us that it was happening before but now it's finished.
3. Ask children questions to prompt past continuous responses, such as *What was Juan doing when he raised his hand?*

WEEK 3 DAY 2

Shared Writing Card: Brainstorming Side B

Brainstorming a Topic

- Use Side A of the Shared Writing Card and your finished piece about the hurricane. Review how you used the graphic organizer's pictures and labels to form the basis of your finished piece.
- Turn the card over to Side B. Tell children that you will now think of a new topic to write about. Brainstorm a cause-effect topic related to the theme. You can use the Manipulative Chart or Concept Poster to help generate ideas. With these components and the content discussed thus far in the unit, children should be able to recall enough information to write about a tornado, earthquake, flood, or blizzard.

Scribing with the Graphic Organizer

- Once the class has chosen a topic, you should decide together what effect to include in the first box. Model how to draw the first picture, such as sandbagging. Invite volunteers to step up to the card and draw other effects as the class decides on them. Continue drawing until the process is complete.
- Now it's time to put labels on your graphic organizer. Elicit labels from the group in the same manner as you did for Side A and record them on the Shared Writing Card.
- You will create the shared writing paragraph together in the next session.

Active Social Studies: Safety Posters

1. Use gestures and simple language to review the school rules for fire drills. Ask children what kinds of rules they should have for other disasters.
2. Then form heterogeneous groups of mixed language ability with four children each. Tell each group to choose a disaster that they want to make a safety poster about.
3. Distribute butcher paper and markers. Guide children in drawing step-by-step instructions for their safety poster. Have children write or dictate a label or rule for each picture.

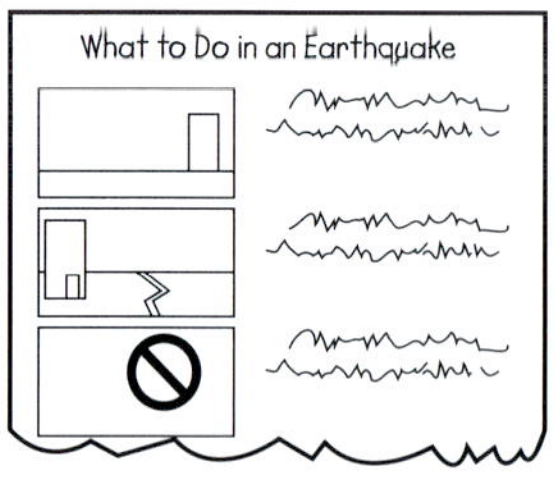

4. Display finished posters around the room and have each group present their safety tips to the class.

WEEK 3 DAY 3

Shared Writing Card: Writing Together with Side B

- As with Side A, you will scribe as you work together with children to create a finished writing piece from the graphic organizer on Side B of Shared Writing Card 6.
- Model writing from the first drawing, using think-alouds as you go. Show children how to use resources like the Word Wall. Work together to include special phrases or figure out tricky passages.
- When you have finished your shared writing piece, read it together several times. Then hang it up on the wall where it can be displayed during the rest of the unit. At the end of the unit, you should erase both sides of the Shared Writing Card.

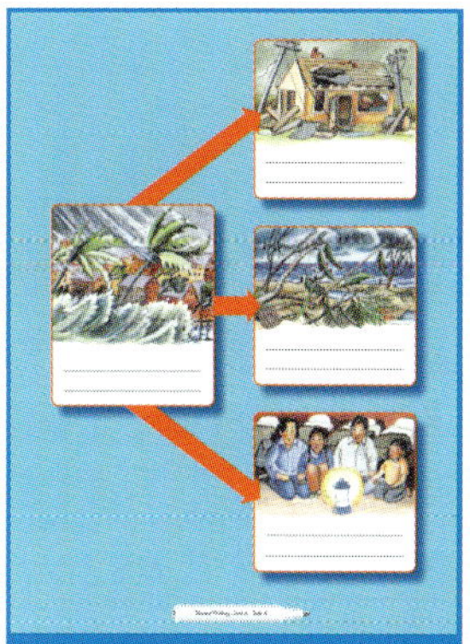

Shared Writing Card

Manipulative Chart: Focus on Oral Language Development

Manipulative Chart

Grammar in Context: Location Words (1 2 3 4 5)

1. Place a variety of familiar classroom objects in a central location of the classroom that you and the children can gather around. Place other familiar objects in a visible location away from the central location.
2. Gather around the central items with the children. Say *Here is a pencil.* Encourage children to say what else is "here."
3. Point to one of the far away objects. Say *There is a book.* Encourage children to say what else is "there."
4. Explain to children that we use *here* to talk about the location we are in and *there* to talk about locations we are not in.
5. Have children look at the Manipulative Chart. Discuss where you are on the map. Say *Here we have tornadoes,* for example. Point out another location on the chart. Say, for example, *There they have hurricanes.*

Language Learning Master

p. 54 (1 2 3 4 5)

WEEK 3 DAY 4

Active Science: Earthquake Model

You will need

- Plastic jars with lids
- Sand
- Water
- Miniature house
- Rocks and pebbles

1. Tell children that they will watch as you create an "earthquake." Have children gather around as you fill a plastic jar with sand. Saturate the sand with water. Put in a miniature house and a rock or two to represent mountains.
2. Put a lid on the jar and place it on the table. Move it back and forth for a few seconds. When you stop, ask children to notice changes. The heavier items will probably sink into the sand. Other items will be tossed about. Explain that these are some of the effects of an earthquake. Also, point out that most earthquakes only last a few seconds.

3. Allow groups to take turns creating their own "earthquakes." Invite them to explain in words or gestures what happened when they shook their jars.

WEEK 3 DAY 5

You will need

- Overhead transparency of Writing Resource Guide, p. 90
- Overhead marker

Writing Resource Guide: A Simplified Graphic Organizer

This activity is optional and only necessary if you wish to use the simplified sequence graphic organizer in cooperative-group or independent writing.

Brainstorming a Topic

- Review the drawings and labels you used on Side B of the Shared Writing Card. Trace the cause and effect arrows with your fingers.
- On the overhead projector, display a transparency of Writing Planner B on page 90 of the Writing Resource Guide, which is a cause and effect graphic organizer with only two boxes.
- With the class, brainstorm a weather-related disaster, such as a blizzard or flood. Label the first box with the name of the disaster and draw a quick sketch in the box to reinforce the concept.

Scribing with the Graphic Organizer

- Have children help you think of two effects of the disaster. Draw quick sketches in the two remaining boxes in the graphic organizer.
- Label the two drawings on your graphic organizer. Elicit suggestions for labels from the group in the same manner as you did with the Shared Writing Card.

You will need

- Writing Resource Guide, pp. 89–90
- Markers

Writing Resource Guide: Cooperative-Group Writing

- Form cooperative groups of heterogeneous Stages with three to four children each to work together on a writing piece using the graphic organizer. You may hand out a copy of Writing Planner A or B to each group.
- Review the shared writing graphic organizers and finished pieces you have made together. Remind children that the drawings help them remember how one thing makes other things happen.
- Have the groups work together first to complete their graphic organizers and then to construct finished pieces. Circulate to provide assistance. ◎

Options for STAGES

❶❷ These children should draw the pictures for the group.	❸❹❺ These children should take responsibility for the writing of the finished piece.

Writing Mini-lessons

See the Writing Resource Guide for mini-lessons to use as children write. Here are some suggestions:
- Mini-lesson 15: Exclamation Point
- Mini-lesson 21: Describing Words

Big Book

WEEK 4 DAY 1

Big Book: Focus on Literacy Skills

Word Level: Phonics in Context

1. You will need the Word Wall Starters with the cat symbol on them: *huge, barge, plank, slowly.* These words are shown in the back of the Big Book.
2. Tell children that you want to choose some special words from the story for them to take a closer look at.
3. Introduce the word *huge* by saying it clearly, elongating the long *u* sound and drawing attention to the highlighting behind the *uge*. Then repeat the long *u* sound several times. Say *The letter* e *at the end of* huge *makes the letter* u *have the long* u *sound. Let's say the word* huge *together:* huge. *Now let's sing a song together!* Review Phonics Song Chart 22 together.
4. Say *I'm going to put the word* huge *below* long u. Walk to your Word Wall and place the card *huge* under the *long u* label. Remind children that they can use the cat symbol to help them remember where they "met" that word before.
5. Repeat a similar procedure for the other words and phonics skills.

Sentence Level: Descriptive Language and Imagery

1. Reread the first sentence on page 6 of the Big Book, emphasizing *inky blue*. Talk about the special words writers use to help readers see what is happening.
   Model *It says* The sky grew inky blue. *See the sky? It means that the sky was a very, very dark blue. It looked like the ink in this pen. Writers use words like* inky *to help us see what things look like in a story.*
2. Read the text on pages 13 and 14. Ask children which words help them see what's happening in the story. Add or confirm that the phrases *soaking wet* and *huge fallen tree* are "special words" the writer uses to help us see how things look.

Text Level: Identifying Sequence of Events, Problem, and Solution

1. Reread the text, pausing at pages 9, 13, 18, 21, and 24 to summarize the story with sequence words such as *First, Next, Then,* and *Last*. As you summarize the story in sequence, invite children to point to supporting pictures or act out the story.
2. Encourage children to tell why Barge Cat and her kittens left their barge, why they were in the water, why they had to sit in a tree, and why they had to move to new barges.
3. Help the children understand that many stories contain problems. Explain that in *Barge Cat* the flood is the story problem.
4. Discuss the cats' solutions to their problem (climbing into the tree and staying there and getting a new barge). ◎

Options for STAGES

❶❷❸ Have these children point to relevant illustrations and use sequence words to indicate the correct order as they are able.	❹❺ Have these children take turns telling the story or parts of it in their own words.

Guided Reading

As you work on this unit, conduct small groups of guided reading or shared-to-guided reading independent of thematic instruction. Instruction is provided in the Guided Reading section of this guide.

Home-School Connection

Send home page 67 of the Home-School Connection Masters for children to use in retelling *Barge Cat* to their families. They should first retell the story in English and then in either English or the home language.

You will need

- Two copies of the TPR Cards

Language Practice Game: Version 2 ❶❷❸❹❺

Have children in Stages 4 and 5 play Concentration with partners. Copy two sets of the TPR Cards used in Version 1 on Week 2 Day 1. To prepare for the game, shuffle the two sets of cards together and lay them face down in rows. Model the following rules of play.

1. The first player turns up two cards. If the cards match, the player must say an appropriate warning. This provides practice with the language function *Warn.* For example, if two tornado cards are turned up, the player should say *A tornado is coming! Go to the basement.* The player then gets to keep the two cards.
2. If there is no match, the player turns the cards facedown again. It is then the partner's turn.
3. Players continue until all cards have been matched. The winner is the player with the most pairs of cards.

WEEK 4 DAY 2

You will need

- Index cards
- Markers
- Earthquake photos
- Tape

Active Math: Earthquake Sort

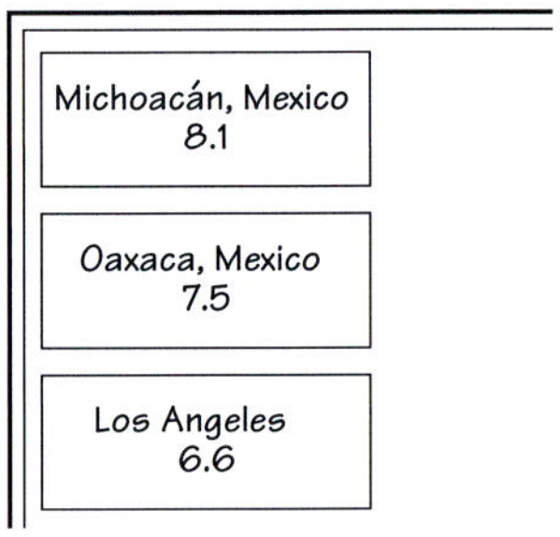

1. On each of three cards, write the names of cities that had strong earthquakes. Also include the Richter scale measurement. For example: Los Angeles, 6.6; Michoacán, Mexico, 8.1; Oaxaca, Mexico, 7.5.
2. Tell children about the city, the earthquake, and the damage done. Use photos from books such as *Earthquake!* by Seymour Simon to show some earthquakes. Say *These numbers tell how strong the earthquake was. The strongest earthquake is a "10."*
3. Ask children to help you order the cards from the strongest to the weakest earthquake. Help children focus on the first number in each measurement. Make sure the first number for each city is not the same as others to avoid confusion in differentiating decimal amounts. Extend the activity by adding new cities and measurements.

You will need

A copy of page U147 at the end of this unit for each child

End-of-Unit Assessment

- While children are engaged in activities this week, pull them individually for the Big Book retelling, using page U147 at the end of this unit.
- Select children with whom you would like to use the Open-Ended Oral Language Assessment on pages U146–U147 and pull them individually during activities this week. We recommend assessing about one-fourth of your class each unit.
- You should also have gathered the following for their assessment portfolio:
  - page 53 of the Language Learning Masters
  - page 54 of the Language Learning Masters
  - finished writing piece assessed according to the Writing Rubric on page A6.

WEEK 4 DAY 3–4

Writing Resource Guide: Individual Writing

- Children have engaged in a step-by-step writing process moving toward independence. They began with teacher-led shared writing, moved to cooperative groups, and are now ready to work individually.
- Provide a copy of Writing Planner A or B to each child. Some children may need individual conferencing to help them choose a topic. ◎

Options for STAGES

❶❷ and Emergent Level
These children should draw a cause and its effects on their graphic organizer. They can label writing on their own or dictate labels to you.

❸❹❺ Early Level and Above
These children should also use drawings and labels on the graphic organizer to record their topic. They should then use the graphic organizer to create a finished piece.

- When children have arrived at the finished product, whether graphic organizer or paragraph, you should assess it using the Writing Rubric on page A6 of this Teacher's Guide.

You will need

- Writing Resource Guide, pp. 89–90
- Markers

Assessment

Continue pulling some children for the Big Book Retelling and Open-Ended Oral Language Assessment as others write.

WEEK 4 DAY 5

Theme Project: Sharing

- Invite groups to take turns presenting their Disaster Books to the class. Stage 1 members can turn the pages of the book as other members take turns reading or summarizing the content of each page.
- Encourage class members to ask questions and give feedback after each presentation. Model appropriate feedback by making the first comment yourself—for example, *I like the section at the end on how to prepare for a tornado. I especially like the way you made a list of things to have in case of a tornado.*

Open-Ended Oral Language Assessment Reassess children's Language Acquisition Stages. Begin with an open-ended prompt like the first one below. If children are unable to respond, intervene with increasingly directed prompts, such as the second and third ones below.

What can you tell me about the picture?

What can you see outside?

I see a flood. Show me a torrado.

Assessment Directions: Copy this form for each child and place the completed form in the child's portfolio. Locate the child's Language Acquisition Stage for each of the first four activities and assess his or her performance during the unit according to expectations for that Stage. For the Big Book Retelling, pull children to retell the Big Book during end-of-unit assessment time. Use the Open-Ended Oral Language Assessment to reassess children's Language Acquisition Stages with one-fourth of your students for each unit, using the back side of the sheet to take notes. *For more guidance on assessment, see pages T33 and T34.*

Unit 6 Assessment

Name ______________________ **Date** ____________

On Our Way to English Grade 2	STAGE EXPECTATIONS ❶	❷	❸	❹	❺
Fluency Manipulative Chart Student Version, page U132 *How does the child respond when manipulating the mini-chart along with the Oral Language CD?*	Shows the correct answer. ☐ Yes ☐ Not yet	Shows the correct answer, naming the disaster. ☐ Yes ☐ Not yet	Shows the correct answer, approximating sentences and substitutions. ☐ Yes ☐ Not yet	Shows the correct answer, singing the verse with few, if any, errors. ☐ Yes ☐ Not yet	
Content Area Knowledge Language Practice Game: Version 1, page U133 *How does the child demonstrate an understanding of concepts and vocabulary?*	Turns the appropriate card face down. ☐ Yes ☐ Not yet	Turns over the appropriate card and uses some appropriate vocabulary, such as *tornado* or *tornado coming.* ☐ Yes ☐ Not yet		Turns the appropriate card face down and says a complete sentence with appropriate vocabulary, such as *A hurricane is coming.* ☐ Yes ☐ Not yet	
Social Language Function Warn, page U137 *How does the child respond during the Function Mini-lesson?*			Approximates a sentence, such as *Go basement.* ☐ Yes ☐ Not yet	Generates commands and warnings using complete sentences. ☐ Yes ☐ Not yet	
Academic Language Function Analyze, page U137 *How does the child respond during the Function Mini-lesson?*			Provides some words for the web, such as *wind, rain.* ☐ Yes ☐ Not yet	Contributes a variety of content-related vocabulary to the word web and is able to use these to formulate approximate or complete sentences, such as *There is wind and rain during a storm.* ☐ Yes ☐ Not yet	
Big Book Retelling page U136 *Have each child use the "barge" envelope to retell* Barge Cat. *How does the child retell the story?*	Uses the figures to show what happened. ☐ Yes ☐ Not yet	Retells using a few words. ☐ Yes ☐ Not yet	Retells using longer phrases or simple sentences. ☐ Yes ☐ Not yet	Retells using complete sentences in connected discourse with few errors. ☐ Yes ☐ Not yet	Retells using story language similar to native-speaking peers. ☐ Yes ☐ Not yet
Open-Ended Oral Language Assessment, page U146 *Use the child's responses to the illustration to reassess the child's Stage of Language Acquisition.*	☐ **STAGE ❶** Uses few or no words; gestures or points.	☐ **STAGE ❷** Uses words or short phrases.	☐ **STAGE ❸** Uses phrases and simple sentences.	☐ **STAGE ❹** Uses sentences in connected discourse.	☐ **STAGE ❺** Uses language comparable to native-speaking peers.

UNIT 7

How Things Work

OVERVIEW *This theme focuses on how machines and tools work and how they help us. The unit begins by introducing basic tools, machines, and magnets and then provides details about their functions.*

Determining the Purpose

Oral Language Development

Focus on Functions

Social Context:

Give instructions ❶❷❸❹❺

Academic Context:

Predict and hypothesize ❶❷❸❹❺

Focus on Grammar

- Future tense with *going to*
- Helping verbs *can/can't*
- Passive verbs
- Commands

Comprehension Strategy

- Visualizes information from text and diagrams

Literacy Skills

- **Word Level:** Phonics in context initial blends
- **Sentence Level:** End punctuation
- **Text Level:** Alphabet knowledge to locate information

Content Area Objectives

- Understands how various machines and tools work and their uses
- Identifies certain machines and their parts
- Demonstrates an understanding of magnetic force

Language Learning Strategy

- Sometimes you don't need to know the meaning of every single word to understand.

Writing Skill

- Labels a diagram as the basis for expository writing

Unit Components

Manipulative Chart

Chant Poster

Concept Poster

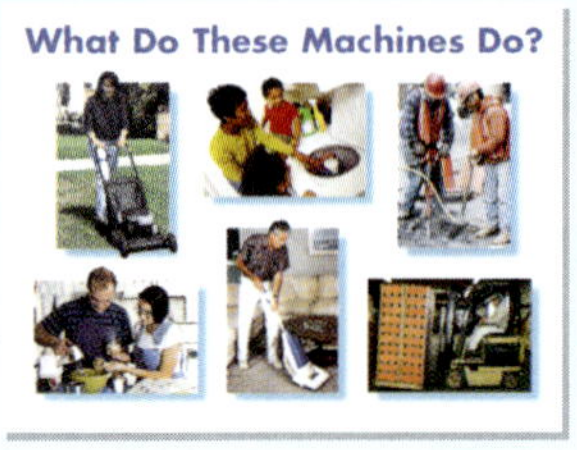

Newcomer Book

Unit at a Glance

	DURING THE WEEK	DAY 1
Week 1	**Small-Group Instruction:** • Guided Reading • Shared-to-Guided Reading **Phonics Focus:** *gr* /gr/, *tr* /tr/ Phonics Song Chart 26, pp. P56–P57	**Manipulative Chart:** Introduction with Audio CD p. U151
Week 2	**Small-Group Instruction:** • Guided Reading • Shared-to-Guided Reading • Newcomer Book **Phonics Focus:** *br* /br/, *pr* /pr/ Phonics Song Chart 27, pp. P58–P59	**Concept Poster:** Introduction p. U156 **Language Practice Game:** Version 1 p. U157
Week 3	**Small-Group Instruction:** • Guided Reading • Shared-to-Guided Reading • Newcomer Book **Phonics Focus:** *st* /st/, *sk* /sk/ Phonics Song Chart 28, pp. P60–P61	**Big Book:** Oral Language Development p. U163
Week 4	**Small-Group Instruction:** • Guided Reading • Shared-to-Guided Reading • Newcomer Book **Phonics Focus:** *sw* /sw/, *sm* /sm/ Phonics Song Chart 29, pp. P62–P63	**Big Book:** Literacy Skills p. U167 **Language Practice Game:** Version 2 p. U168

STAGES ❶ Preproduction ❷ Early Production ❸ Speech Emergence ❹ Intermediate Fluency ❺ Advanced Fluency

Oral Language Audio CD

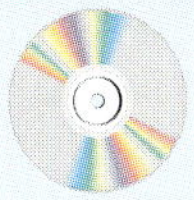

Picture Cards

Shared Writing Card

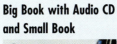

Big Book with Audio CD and Small Book

Home-School Connection Masters

Writing Resource Guide

Language Learning Masters

DAY 2	DAY 3	DAY 4	DAY 5
Manipulative Chart: Gestures and Manipulative Fun p. U152	**Chant Poster:** Introduction p. U153	**TPR Cards:** Introduction p. U154	**Manipulative Chart:** Oral Language Development Student Version p. U155
Big Book: Introduction p. U159	**Theme Project:** Dream Machines p. U160 **Big Book:** Revisiting p. U160	**Big Book:** Comprehension Strategy p. U161 **Chant Poster:** Oral Language Development p. U161	**Shared Writing Card:** Introduction of Side A p. U162 **Concept Poster:** Revisiting p. U162
Shared Writing Card: Brainstorming Side B p. U164 **Active Social Studies:** Jobs and Tools p. U164	**Shared Writing Card:** Writing Together with Side B p. U165 **Manipulative Chart:** Oral Language Development p. U165	**Active Science:** Magnet Power p. U165	**Writing Resource Guide:** A Simplified Graphic Organizer Cooperative-Group Writing p. U166
Active Math: Machine Tally p. U168 **Assessment** p. U168	**Writing Resource Guide:** Individual Writing p. U169 **Assessment** p. U168	**Writing Resource Guide:** Individual Writing p. U169 **Assessment** p. U168	**Theme Project:** Sharing p. U169

Center Activities

Number Nook

Provide measuring instruments such as rulers, tape measures, and measuring cups. Invite children to estimate and measure the length and width of materials such as bricks, blocks, and wooden boards as well as volume of containers of water and sand.

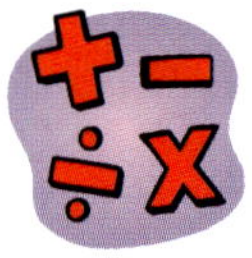

Artist's Studio

Provide drawing paper, crayons, and markers. Encourage children to use their imaginations and draw pictures of a new machine. Have them label the various parts of their inventions, and to describe what their inventions do.

You will need

- Rulers, tape measures, measuring cups
- Cardboard building bricks, wooden blocks and planks, plastic cups and bowls
- Drawing paper
- Crayons and markers
- Play tools
- Toy cars, construction vehicles, and so on

Content Corner

Provide an array of job-related tools such as play hammers, saws, and so on. Also provide models of cars and other machinery. Invite children to role-play the jobs of people who make and repair things, such as mechanics and carpenters.

CENTERS

Listening Post

After introducing each element in class, children may revisit the Manipulative Chart and Chant Poster on the Oral Language Audio CD. If you include a laminated copy of the Manipulative Chart Student Version, children can manipulate it as they sing to Part 4 of the CD (with blanks). Children may also listen to *How Bicycles Work* on the Big Book Audio CD while following along in the small copy.

Language Workshop

Any time they are not in use during the unit, place the Picture Cards for the unit in this center. Encourage children to review the names of the tools and machines with each other for additional practice. After introducing the Language Practice Game in class, add the game board, game markers, and TPR Cards to the center for independent group play.

Writer's Den

Establish a journal writing center with prompts to spark children's writing. Change the prompt every two weeks:

- What tools do people use at home?
- What tools and machines help us at school?

Children should be encouraged to draw pictures to support their writing. Provide blank Writing Planners in center materials for prewriting.

More Books

- *Charlie Needs a Cloak* by Tomie DePaola (Simon & Schuster Children's Books, 1982)
- *Tools* by Ann Morris (Morrow, 1998)
- *Home Depot Big Book of Tools* by Kimberly Weinberger (Scholastic, 2001)
- *Who Uses This?* by Margaret Miller (Morrow, 1999)
- *Construction Zone* by Tana Hoban (Greenwillow Books, 1997)

WEEK 1 DAY 1

Manipulative Chart: Introduction with Audio CD

Sung to the tune of "Alouette"

Setting the Scene

- Show Picture Card 1: tools. Use gestures and simple language to talk about common household tools. Children can either act out using tools or talk about tools they know. Record their tools in a list.
- Show Picture Card 2: birdhouse. Using gestures to facilitate comprehension, explain that a birdhouse can be made with tools.
- Return to your list and Picture Card 1: tools and ask children which tools they think are used to make a birdhouse. Validate responses.

Options for STAGES

❶❷ Invite these children to gesture how the tools are used, naming them as they are able.

❸❹❺ Ask children at these levels to tell you the name of each tool and its use.

Creating Comprehensible Input

- The Manipulative Chart has five pockets labeled *screwdriver, hammer, saw, tape measure,* and *paintbrush*. There are also five action cards to be placed in corresponding pockets. Slide the cards in and out of the pockets to make sure they will slide in easily.
- Point out items on the work bench, such as nails, screws, boards, paint, goggles, and the birdhouse. Say *This is a girl. This is her father. They are building a birdhouse. They will use all these tools.*
- Read the text, pausing often, as you use gestures, pointing, and other techniques to make the chant comprehensible.

Pound a hammer.	gesture pounding show Picture Card 3: hammer
You can pound a hammer.	as above
Pound a hammer.	as above
Build a birdhouse.	show Picture Card 2: birdhouse
Build a birdhouse with your tools.	point to birdhouse and tools on chart
Build a birdhouse with your tools,	as above
With your tools, with your tools.	point to tools on chart
Oh!	smile broadly

Manipulative Chart Picture Cards 1, 2

Guided Reading

As you work on this unit, conduct small groups of guided reading or shared-to-guided reading independent of thematic instruction. Instruction is provided in the Guided Reading section of this guide.

Component Organizer

Other Manipulative Chart lessons in this unit:

- Gestures and Manipulative Fun, p. U152
- Oral Language Development and Student Version, pp. U155–U156
- Oral Language Development, p. U165

Real-World Touch

Bring a tool box from home and introduce each of the tools. Allow children to examine the tools one at a time under close supervision.

Home-School Connection

Choose one of the versions of the parent letter to send home with each child, according to the child's home language (pages 68–75 in the Home-School Connection Masters). Also send home the activity on page 76.

Manipulative Chart

Journal Writing Reminder

Children should be writing in their journals during the course of the unit. Journal writing provides children with a stronger sense of participation in the classroom.

Introducing the Audio CD

- Play Part 1 of the Oral Language Audio CD, the spoken song, as you say the song and track the print on the Manipulative Chart with your finger or a pointer. Replay Part 1 several times, encouraging children to chime in whenever they can.
- Introduce the song by playing the song at natural speed, Part 2 of the Audio CD, to help children get a feel for the song. Allow the Audio CD to continue playing through Part 3, the song at instructional pace. Track the print as the Audio CD plays. Repeat Part 3 again, this time singing along, making clear lip movements without exaggerating. Revisit Part 3 several times to help children learn the song.

WEEK 1 DAY 2

Manipulative Chart: Gestures and Manipulative Fun

Gesturing the Song

Introduce these simple gestures to accompany the song:

Pound a hammer.	make a pounding gesture in rhythm to the song
You can pound a hammer.	nod your head in rhythm while still pounding
Pound a hammer.	pound with the opposite hand in rhythm
Build a birdhouse.	put fingertips and thumbs together to form a house
Build a birdhouse with your tools.	keep fingertips together and then point to tools
Build a birdhouse with your tools,	as above
With your tools, with your tools.	pound with one hand and then the other
Oh!	raise hands in "Oh!" gesture

Manipulating the Chart

- Show children how to slide the cards into the pockets. The items on the cards can be substituted for the words in blue. Take the cards out and show the hammer card from the chart. Read the word *pound* printed at the top of the card. Put the hammer card in the hammer pocket as you lead children in singing the song. Introduce the saw card in a similar way. Sing the verse using *push* and *saw* in place of *pound* and *hammer.*
- Play Part 4 of the Oral Language Audio CD while you say *saw* in the blank space.
- Continue introducing and naming the various actions and tools on each card in this manner.
- Invite volunteers to manipulate the Manipulative Chart for the class as you sing the verse together or give Total Physical Response commands, such as *Pull the tape measure.*
- Invite children to help you create new gestures for the actions associated with each tool.
- You can revisit this activity many times during the unit.

WEEK 1 DAY 3

Chant Poster: Introduction

Setting the Scene

- Display a magnet and tell children what it is called: *magnet*. Hold up a metal pin and show how it is pulled to the magnet. Say *A magnet can pick up a pin.*
- Hold up Picture Card 4: nails and Picture Card 5: screws. Invite children to chime in as you pronounce these words.
- Assemble various magnetic and non-magnetic items, including nails and screws, and display them on a desk. Have children gather around the desk and experiment with the magnet. Ask them to predict whether the magnet will be able to pick up each item.

Options for STAGES

1 2 Ask these children to respond to yes/no questions or to commands, such as *Pick up the paper clip with the magnet.*

3 These children can respond to either/or questions, such as *Can a magnet pick up paper or a pin?*

4 5 Have these children choose an item and use a sentence to tell whether or not a magnet can pick it up.

Creating Comprehensible Input

- Display the Chant Poster, pointing to and naming the pictured items as you describe the scene: *The boy has a magnet. Can the magnet pick up a pin?*
- Read the text with frequent pauses as you use gestures, pointing, and other techniques to make the chant comprehensible.

If we had a magnet,	gesture to all for "we"; point to magnet
Would it pick up a pin?	gesture "pick up" with thumb and index finger; point to pin
I'll get a magnet.	point to self, then magnet
Can you get a pin?	point to class, shrug; point to pin
Let's see what these things will do.	point to items on the floor in the poster
Then we'll try something new.	nod emphatically; point to other items

Chanting the Poster

- Encourage children to chime in as you chant the rhyme together several times. Form three groups of children and assign a pair of lines to each group.
- Introduce the chant on the Oral Language Audio CD. Invite children to move to the rhythm of the chant. Tell them they can listen to it later at the Listening Post.
- Practice saying the chant in different ways, such as very softly or very loudly. Children can also clap whenever they hear *magnet* and *pin*.
- Revisit the chant often with children. Invite them to point to themselves (*I'll*), to others (*you*), and to the whole class (*we, we'll*) as they sing.

Chant Poster
Picture Cards 4–5

Component Organizer

Other Chant Poster lessons in this unit:

- Oral Language Development, pp. U161–U162

WEEK 1 DAY 4

You will need

- **Language Learning Master** p. 55
- Scissors

TPR Cards: Introduction

Introducing the Cards with Total Physical Response

- Provide one copy of page 55 of the Language Learning Masters to each child. Have children color and cut out the cards.
- Introduce a few cards at a time by holding them up one by one and saying the words clearly. Select first the words that have already been introduced in previous activities.
- Ask children to pick up the correct cards as you call out a word. Model the desired outcome. Add one new card at a time and keep reviewing in a game-like atmosphere. Children may want to say the word as they pick up the card.
- Now invite children to respond to your full-sentence commands, such as *Put the vacuum cleaner on the table. Pick up the wheel.*
- Assign partners so you can add commands, such as *Give the hammer to Jin.*
- As children increase their familiarity with the TPR Cards and the game, add commands such as *Put the magnet under the saw.*
- Invite volunteers in Stages 3, 4, or 5 to give commands to their classmates.
- Extend language to discuss the actions *push* and *pull* as well as the machines and tools.

Options for STAGES

❶❷ Have these children answer either/or questions, such as *Is this a hammer or a saw?*

❸ Ask these children to identify each tool and machine.

❹❺ Ask children at these Stages to make sentences for each tool or machine, such as *A lawn mower cuts grass.*

- Repeat this activity several times throughout the unit.

Grammar in Context: Future Tense with *going to* ❶❷❸❹❺

1. Give one child a Total Physical Response command such as *Push the chair.* Before the child actually does the action, say *Sarita's going to push the chair.* Have the child walk to the chair as you repeat the sentence. Then have her push the chair as you say *Sarita is pushing the chair.* Explain that *going to* means it hasn't happened yet.
2. Display the TPR Cards. Say *I'm going to put the hammer on the table.* Repeat the sentence as you reach for the card. As you place the card, say *Now I am putting the hammer on the table.* Emphasize *am going to put* and *am putting* to distinguish between the intent and the actual action.
3. Invite volunteers to contribute phrases or sentences to be acted out.

Options for STAGES

❶❷ These children may simply respond to Total Physical Response commands as higher Stage children narrate what they are about to do.

❸❹❺ Ask these children *What are you going to do?* or *What is Saba going to do?* Invite volunteers to tell what they or their classmates are going to do before acting.

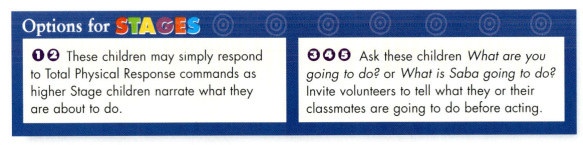

WEEK 1 DAY 5

Manipulative Chart: Focus on Oral Language Development

FUNCTION MINI-LESSON

Give Instructions 1 2 3 4 5

1. Give children instructions for making a birdhouse "card." First, distribute sheets of paper and scissors. Demonstrate as you say: *First, fold the paper in half. Hold it with the folded side to your left, like a birthday card or a book. Cut off the top two corners of the card to form a triangle at the top. Now color the front of your birdhouse. When you are finished, open the card and draw a bird inside the birdhouse.*
2. Recap the process with the class. Now have Stage 3, 4, or 5 children give you the same instructions. Ask *How did I know what to do?* Help children understand that they gave you instructions. Explain that following instructions helps us learn to do new things.
3. Repeat by having children give and follow simple instructions for other tasks, such as making a pattern with colored cubes or drawing a face.

Options for STAGES

1 2 These children can follow the instructions given by their classmates.	3 4 5 These children can give simple instructions using gestures and modeling to aid comprehension.

FUNCTION MINI-LESSON

Predict and Hypothesize 1 2 3 4 5

1. Direct children's attention to the Manipulative Chart. Review the steps that the father and child go through to make the birdhouse.
2. Point to the birdhouse and ask *Where will they put the birdhouse? What tools will they use to hang the birdhouse? What will the birds use the birdhouse for?* Invite children to use words or gestures to make their predictions.

Grammar in Context: Helping Verbs *can/can't* 1 2 3 4 5

1. Sing the song together, allowing volunteers to substitute appropriate cards in the pockets with each new verse.
2. Lead children in making sentences about what you can do with each tool. Hold up the pound/hammer TPR Card and say *You can pound a hammer.* Then hold up the pull/tape measure TPR Card and say *You can pull a tape measure.* Encourage children to chime in after you and gesture each action.
3. Ask funny questions, such as *Can you dip a hammer?* Follow up by asking *What can you do with a hammer? That's right, you can pound a hammer.*
4. Continue in this way until all the cards have been used. Encourage children to suggest verbs and tools.

Manipulative Chart

Language Learning Strategy

Sometimes you don't need to know the meaning of every single word to understand.

Use this strategy for children in Stages 3, 4 or 5.

- Tell children that sometimes they can skip over a word that they don't know and still understand what is happening. Write the sentence below as you say it. **Model** *Let's look at this sentence:* The girl and her father build a lovely birdhouse. *Even if I don't know exactly what* lovely *means, I still can understand what the girl and her father are doing.*
- Throughout the unit, remind children to use this strategy.

Language Junction

Children may have difficulty hearing *can* in a sentence because we say it quickly, reducing the /a/. Hearing the difference between *can* and *can't* is also a problem.

You will need

- **Language Learning Master** pp. 53–54
- Scissors

Assessment

Record your observations of children on their individual assessment checklists for this unit. See page U171.

Home-School Connection

When children have practiced manipulating the Student Version of the Manipulative Chart, send it home for them to practice with their family members.

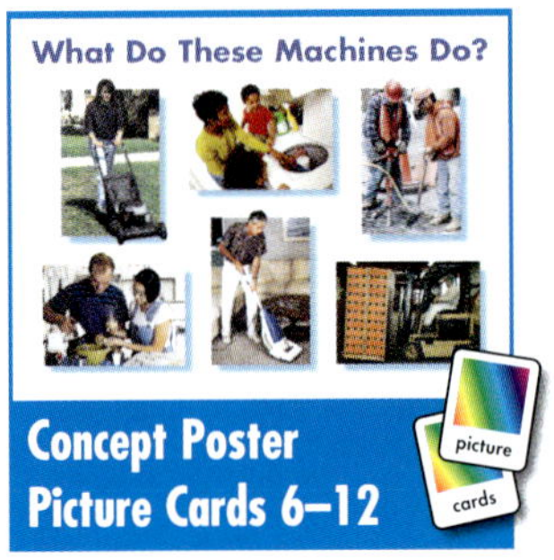

Guided Reading

As you work on this unit, conduct small groups of guided reading or shared-to-guided reading independent of thematic instruction. Instruction is provided in the Guided Reading section of this guide.

Manipulative Chart: Student Version

- Model assembling the pages according to the directions.
- Circulate to provide assistance as children color and cut out their cards. Encourage children to color their charts, too.
- Invite children to lay down the hammer card as you read the verse on the chart. Then encourage them to match their cards to what you do as you say different words in the song.
- Have children respond to your Total Physical Response commands: *Pick up the tape measure.*
- Play Part 4 of the Oral Language Audio CD and model how children can manipulate their Student Versions as they sing along. Tell children that they will later be able to listen to the Audio CD and manipulate this mini-chart in the Listening Post.

WEEK 2 DAY 1

Concept Poster: Introduction

Setting the Scene

1. Display Picture Card 12: machines and say the word. Ask *Why do people use machines?* Discuss how machines help us do many things and that some machines are used inside and others outside.
2. Invite children to share or show what they know about the machines on the card.

Creating Comprehensible Input

- Introduce Picture Card 6: lawn mower. Direct children's attention to the first picture on the Concept Poster: lawn mower. Demonstrate how to talk through each picture shown on the poster with a think-aloud.
  Model *This is a lawn mower. The woman is pushing the lawn mower. Lawn mowers are machines that cut grass.*
- Recap this in simple language as you point to the lawn mower, the woman pushing it, and the grass: *lawn mower; she's pushing the lawn mower; lawn mowers help us cut grass.*
- Display Picture Cards 7–11: vacuum cleaner, washing machine, mixer, jackhammer, and forklift. Introduce each name and allow children to repeat it as you point to the pictures. Explain that these are all different kinds of machines. Repeat the modeling procedure with the washing machine and mixer on the Concept Poster.
- Have a child in Stage 3, 4, or 5 lead the class in talking about the vacuum cleaner. Support with appropriate language. After the child is finished, recap as you point to the vacuum cleaner, the man, and the floor. Repeat the procedure for the other two machines shown on the poster. Engage children in helping to supply missing information or to modify information as appropriate.
- Summarize the poster by pointing to the pictures and using statements, such as *Machines help us in many ways. Some machines help us inside. Other machines help us outside.*

Extending Oral Language

1. Engage children in reviewing these concepts by asking questions. ◎

Options for STAGES

❶❷ Ask these children specific questions which require only a yes/no answer or gestures, such as *How do we use a lawn mower?* (Child gestures pushing.) *Right, we push it.*	❸ Ask these children to name each of the machines shown on the Poster.	❹❺ Ask these children open-ended questions that require substantive answers, such as *How does a washing machine help us?*

2. To extend the activity, role-play using the various machines.

Component Organizer

Other Concept Poster lessons in this unit:

- Revisiting, p. U162

Language Practice Game: Version 1 ❶❷❸❹❺

Preparing the Game

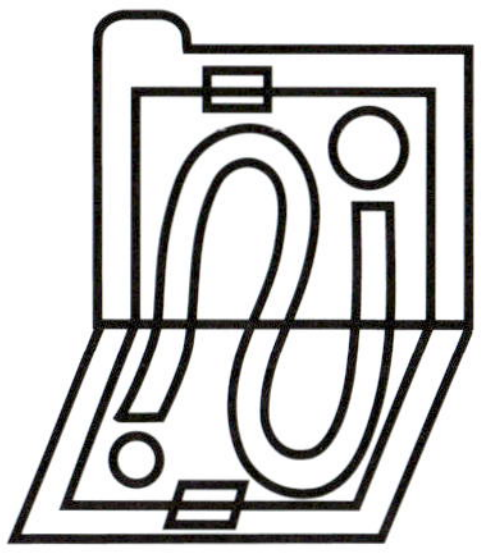

Tape copies of pages 58 and 59 of the Language Learning Masters to two facing sides of a file folder to give the game board some durability. Assemble one game board for each group. Make one set of the four TPR tool cards for each player.

You will need

- **Language Learning Master** pp. 56–57
- TPR Cards: hammer, saw, screwdriver, paintbrush
- File Folder
- Tape
- Game markers

Playing Version 1

Divide the class into heterogeneous groups of mixed language abilities with three or four children each. Shuffle the cards and place them face down in a pile where all players can reach them. Distribute one game marker to each player. Then model the following directions.

1. The first player draws the top card and moves to the appropriate square. For example, if the hammer card is drawn, the player moves his or her game marker to the first hammer square. The player should tell about the tool as the game marker is moved to the appropriate square. ◎

Options for STAGES

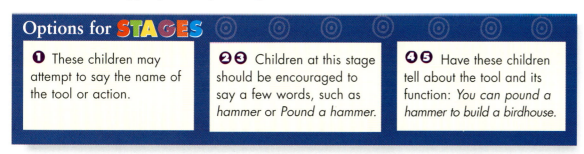

❶ These children may attempt to say the name of the tool or action.	❷❸ Children at this stage should be encouraged to say a few words, such as *hammer* or *Pound a hammer.*	❹❺ Have these children tell about the tool and its function: *You can pound a hammer to build a birdhouse.*

2. After the move is completed, the player places the card facedown at the bottom of the deck.
3. Players continue in this way, drawing cards and moving their game markers to the appropriate squares as they tell about the tool.
4. The first player to cross the finish line is the winner.

Component Organizer

Other Language Practice Game lessons in this unit:

- Version 2, p. U168

Assessment

Record your observations of children during the Language Practice Game on their individual assessment checklists for this unit. See page U171.

Newcomer Book: Small-Group Instruction

Building a House

Written by Karen Clevidence

OVERVIEW *To build a house, you need a lot of different tools.*

The Newcomer Book is supported by the language of the Manipulative Chart and should be integrated into small-group instruction this week when children have had enough practice with vocabulary and concepts in this unit.

Language Pattern

You can use _______.

Text Vocabulary

tools

Vocabulary Extenders

Directionality: left, right

Reading the Text

Book Talk

- Work with a small group of four children at one time who exhibit similar literacy-learning behaviors.
- Engage children in a book talk as you flip through the pages of your copy of the book.

Options for STAGES

1 2 Identify the names of the tools for these children. Encourage them to say the names after you as they are able.

3 4 5 Ask children to identify each tool as you encounter it in the text.

INSTRUCTIONAL PATHS

1 2 3 4 5 **All Readers:** Shared-to-Guided Reading	1 2 3 4 5 **Emergent Readers:** Guided Reading	1 2 3 4 5 **Early Readers:** Independent Reading no lesson provided

INDIVIDUAL READING

Shared-to-Guided Reading — **3–4 sessions**
1 2 3 4 5 **All Readers**

1. Read the book to children.
   - Invite children to sit near you as you read a copy of the book. Begin with the cover and title page.
   - Turn to page 2 and begin reading the words as you point to them. Draw children's attention to the pictures.
2. Read the book with children.
   - Encourage children to follow along in their own copies of the book, turning the pages as you read together and using their own fingers to point to the words from left to right.
   - Invite children to chime in when they are comfortable.
   - Reread the book in this manner over several sessions.
3. Have children buddy read the book.
4. Invite children to read the book independently.

A Assess

- Did children chime in on rereadings?
- Did children mimic your modeled intonation and phrasing?

Guided Reading — **2 sessions**
1 2 3 4 5 **Emergent Readers**

1. Provide copies of the book to children. Use one child's book and turn to page 2. Introduce the book's pattern to children by reading the sentence and pointing to each word as you read *You can use a tape measure.*
2. Have each child read at his or her own pace while remaining in the group. Discourage choral reading. Observe as they read.

A Assess

- Did children point to the words as they read?
- Did children check the picture clue against the first letter to read a word?

REVISITING THE NEWCOMER BOOK

If children seem ready, you may also use the book to extend their knowledge of directionality. On each page, tell whether the pencil is on the right or the left.

WEEK 2 DAY 2

Big Book: Introduction

How Bicycles Work

Written by Lloyd Kajikawa

OVERVIEW *Bikes are everywhere! Let's find out about their parts, history, and uses.*

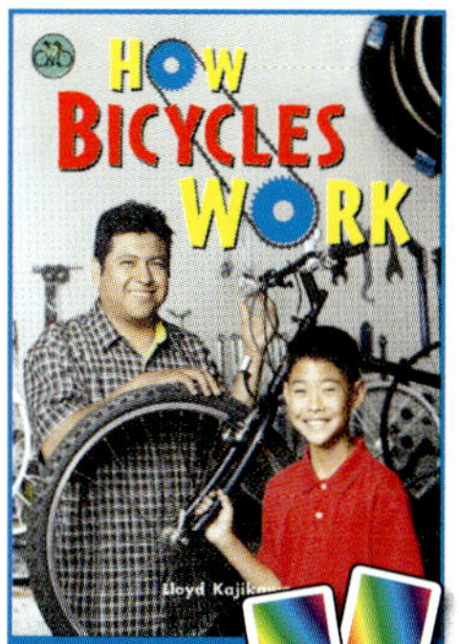

Big Book
Picture Cards 6, 8, 11, 13

Warming Up

Begin the lesson by revisiting the Manipulative Chart, Chant Poster, or a familiar Big Book. You may ask a volunteer to choose one.

Setting the Scene

- Display Picture Cards 6, 8, and 11: lawn mower, washing machine, and forklift. Say the names with children and review that these are machines that help us do things.
- Display Picture Card 13: bicycle. Say *bicycle* and act out riding a bike. Ask *What am I doing?* As children respond, support and confirm their responses. Explain that a bicycle is a kind of machine, too. Elicit from children that it is a machine that helps us go from one place to another.
- Tap into children's prior knowledge. *Have you ever ridden a bicycle before? Where?* Invite them to share their own experiences. Record responses on a K-W-L chart.
- Introduce the book and give children an overview of the information.
- Read the title of the book aloud and point to the bicycle on the cover.
- Elicit from children that the purpose for reading the book together is to get information by asking *What would you like to learn from this book?* Continue to write children's responses and some key words on the K-W-L chart.

Reading the Text

- Read the title page and show children the Contents. Explain that the Contents lets us know what the book will be about. Review the list of things children want to learn. As you read the Contents page, discuss whether children think they will find the information they want to learn in the book. Display the diagram on pages 2–3. Read the labeled parts of the bicycle and have children chime in as you repeat them.
- As you read through the book, use a pointer or your finger to draw children's attention to the text. Focus on finding answers to items in the W column of your K-W-L chart. After returning to build children's understanding of the text, complete the L column. In future rereadings, children should be encouraged to chime in.
- If you have children in Stages 3, 4, or 5, pause at page 16 and ask children what they think this section will be about.

Creating Comprehensible Input

- Open up the back flap of the book, which shows a labeled diagram of a bicycle. Leave it open and refer to it as necessary to assist comprehension.
- Use the comprehension supports in the following chart to help you build comprehensible input with children. Words in bold face are defined in a glossary in the book. You might refer to the glossary as you read to explain these terms.

Component Organizer

Other Big Book lessons in this unit:

- Revisiting, p. U160
- Comprehension Strategy, p. U161
- Oral Language Development, pp. U163–U164
- Literacy Skills, p. U167

Idiom Note

On page 14 is the idiomatic phrase "work out." Tell children that this phrase means "exercise."

PAGE	IN THE STORY	COMPREHENSION SUPPORT
4	. . . push the pedals . . . move the chain . . . moves the gear . . . turns the wheel . . . makes the bike move!	point: to each part and gesture as it is mentioned
6	going up hills . . . going fast.	gesture: hand rising then going fast
7	steer . . . handlebars. . . . brakes to stop . . .	act out: move arms to steer and hands and feet to brake
8	. . . hard to stop!	act out: not being able to stop
9	. . . easier and safer to ride.	act out: riding with ease and assurance
10	You push backward . . .	act out: pushing backward with foot
11	. . . strong frame, flat handlebars, and wide tires.	gesture: hold up arm, bent at elbow to make a "muscle"; hold hand level for *flat*, hold hands apart for *wide*
13	. . . transportation.	restate: this is how we go from one place to another
14	. . . exercise.	act out: familiar exercises
15	Bike racing . . .	gesture: racing and winning with hands and arms
16	. . . interview the owner.	restate: interview is when you ask someone questions
19	Elbow and knee pads . . . protection . . .	point: to elbow and knee pads on page 5
20	. . . tune-up . . .	restate: this is when you have your bike checked for any problems
22	. . . tires have enough air.	act out: filling tires with air
23	Use hand signals . . .	act out: a few basic hand signals

You will need

- Instruction manuals for appliances
- Various household and school scraps: toilet paper and paper towel rolls, egg and milk cartons, cereal boxes, and so on
- Pipe cleaners
- Drawing paper
- Pens, crayons, and markers
- Construction paper or poster board
- Fasteners
- Glue and tape
- Paint

Revisiting the Big Book

- Display pages 2–3 of the Big Book. Have children copy the diagram shown on these pages. Provide assistance as needed.
- As you reread the book, have children point to the part of their diagrams featured in the text.
- Invite volunteers to present their diagrams to the class. Ask these volunteers to explain the function of each part of the bicycle.

WEEK 2 DAY 3

Theme Project: Dream Machines

1. Display manuals for common appliances, such as a digital clock or VCR. Point out the diagram that shows the parts of the machine and indicate the operating instructions. Tell children that they will make manuals for machines that they create.
2. Form heterogeneous groups of mixed language abilities with four to five children each. Ask each group to create a machine from the materials listed in the margin. Distribute art supplies to groups.
3. Groups should begin by constructing the machine. They then need to decide what the machine does. They should then create a diagram and label each machine part. Circulate as children work and provide assistance as needed.
4. Ask children to create a written set of instructions for operating the machine. You can help the scribes or have them dictate these instructions to you.
5. Provide construction paper or poster board to each group. Have them brainstorm ideas for creating a cover illustration and title for their manuals. Gather each group's diagrams and instructions in booklets and fasten the pages together.
6. Leave the manuals along with their machines in the Reading Center for children to read throughout the unit.

WEEK 2 DAY 4

Big Book: Focus on Comprehension Strategy

Visualizes Information from Text and Diagrams

1. Display the back flap of *How Bicycles Work*. Say *This is a diagram. It is a picture with labels. A line goes from each word to the picture. This diagram shows the parts of a bicycle. The words tell the names of the different bicycle parts. Diagrams can help you understand when you read informational books.*
2. Open the book to page 4 and read the text. As you read, pause at the words *seat, pedals, chain, gear,* and *wheel* and point to each word. Then point to the same word in the diagram on the back flap, and trace the line from the word to the part. Say *I can use the diagram to see what the book is talking about. This helps me see what the words mean.*
3. Invite volunteers to stand with you and help the class use the diagram as you read. Volunteers can assist according to their proficiency levels. ◎

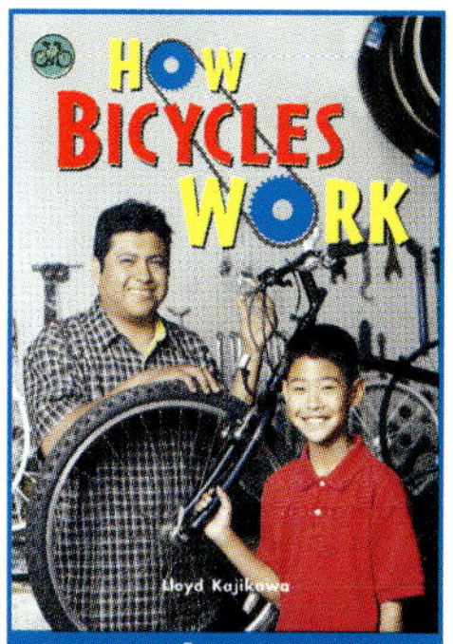

Big Book

Assessment

Use a retelling of the Big Book to assess comprehension. See page U171.

Options for STAGES

❶❷ Pause as elements in the diagram are mentioned in the text. Encourage children to say the names as they are able.

❸❹❺ Allow these children to point to the different elements in the diagram as they are mentioned in the text. Encourage them to summarize small chunks of information using the diagram as an aid.

Chant Poster: Focus on Oral Language Development

Chant Poster

FUNCTION MINI-LESSON

Give Instructions ❶❷❸❹❺

1. Revisit the chant, inviting children to say it along with you.
2. Place items from the poster on a table. Have a volunteer come up and follow instructions such as *Pick up the magnet. Then pick up the paper clip with the magnet.* Act out instructions for Stage 1 or 2 children.
3. Have Stage 3, 4, or 5 children give instructions to one another and to lower Stage children.

FUNCTION MINI-LESSON

Predict and Hypothesize ❶❷❸❹❺

1. Hold up a magnet and a classroom object. Using gestures, ask *What will happen when I put this magnet next to this pencil?* Have children gesture or call out their predictions. Then hold the magnet to the item to see what happens. Acknowledge the result.
2. Continue with other classroom objects, as children continue predicting. Encourage higher Stage children to tell what their predictions are based on.
3. Ask children what they have learned from this experiment. Guide them to form a simple hypothesis, such as *Magnets can pick up metal, but not paper or plastic.*

Assessment

Record your observations of children during these mini-lessons on their individual assessment checklists for this unit. See page U171.

Language Learning Master

p. 58 ①②③④⑤

Grammar in Context: Helping Verbs *can/can't* ①②③④⑤

1. Display a variety of metal objects, including those on the Chant Poster. Include both magnetic and nonmagnetic metal. Distribute magnets and allow groups to experiment with the objects to see which are attracted to the magnet.
2. Point out that magnets can pick up some but not all metal objects. Have children sort items into two categories: magnetic and non-magnetic. Have children contribute as you verbalize about each object: *A magnet can pick up a paper clip. A magnet can't pick up aluminum foil.*
3. Review the hypothesis you made about magnets in the Function Mini-lesson. Change it according to this new discovery: *Magnets can pick up some metal objects, but not all.*
4. Point to various items in the Chant Poster and ask *Can a magnet pick up a pin?* Allow children to nod, say yes or no, or to respond in complete sentences.

WEEK 2 DAY 5

Shared Writing Card: Introduction of Side A

Shared Writing Card
Picture Cards 6, 11, 14

Setting the Scene

- Use the back flap of the Big Book to review the concept of a diagram. Remind children that a diagram is a picture with labels. Reinforce that this diagram shows a bicycle and the labels tell the names of different parts.
- Hold up Picture Card 6: lawn mower and Picture Card 11: forklift. Review that these are machines that are used outside the home. Show Picture Card 14: bulldozer, saying its name clearly. Tell children that this is another machine used outside. Ask *Who has seen a bulldozer? What was it doing?* Invite volunteers to share what they know about bulldozers.

Creating Comprehensible Input

- Display Shared Writing Card Side A, which shows a diagram of a bulldozer with spaces for labels. Begin by pointing to and naming individual items.
  Model *This is a bulldozer. It has different parts. This is the cab. Here are the lights. This is the shovel. These are the wheels. This is the exhaust pipe.*
- Go back to the bulldozer and use think-alouds to talk through the illustration, pointing to the parts one by one.
  Bulldozer: *This is a bulldozer. It is used to move rocks and dirt. It has different parts that help it do its job.*
  Cab: *This is the cab. This is where the driver sits.*
  Lights: *These are the lights. They help the driver see better.*
  Shovel: *This is the shovel. It's what pushes the rocks and dirt.*
  Wheels: *These are the wheels. They are very big because the bulldozer is very heavy.*
  Exhaust: *This is the exhaust pipe. Smoke from the engine comes out of this pipe.*
- Remind children that labeling a picture can help us remember the names of the parts.
- Invite a volunteer from Stages 3, 4, or 5 to name and explain the function of each part in his or her own words.

You will need

- Shared Writing Card 7
- Wipe-off marker
- Regular marker
- Easel pad

Revisiting the Concept Poster

- Revisit the Concept Poster, inviting volunteers to tell about the machines as much as possible.
- Have children play charades, pantomiming the different actions associated with each machine.

Scribing with the Graphic Organizer

- After children have become familiar with the vocabulary, you can use the wipe-off marker to scribe while the class dictates labels for the diagram. Add a few words about the part to help with understanding. Draw lines from each part to its label. Since you are creating a graphic organizer, not a finished product, well-crafted sentences are not necessary.
- Think aloud as you write so that children have insight into the writing process.
- Here is an example of simple shared writing labeling for the diagram.

Cab: where driver sits
Lights: help driver see
Shovel: lifts rocks and dirt
Wheels: big for heavy bulldozer
Exhaust: smoke from engine

Writing Together from the Graphic Organizer

- You will again be holding a pen while you work with children to create a shared writing piece together. This time, you will model how to use the labels on the diagram to create a finished expository paragraph.
- Begin with a think-aloud.
Model *We are going to write about a bulldozer and its parts. We labeled some of the parts, but the labels aren't complete sentences. How can we start? Let's try this:* A bulldozer is a heavy machine with many parts. *Now let's look at the labels in the diagram. In the first space, we wrote* cab *where driver sits. I think I will change this to* The driver sits in the cab. *How does that sound? Good. That's what I will write.*
- Write down the sentence you agree upon with the children. Sound out the spelling of *bulldozer* as you write it, calling attention to the double consonant and the *z* sound.
- Move to another label on the diagram, asking children to help you make a complete sentence from the information given. Record what children say as you make sentences with them. When children offer sentences with errors correct them without being overt. Encourage children to use classroom resources, such as the Word Wall.
- When you have finished your shared writing piece, read it together several times. Then hang it up on the wall where it can be displayed during the rest of the unit and reread many times. For now, do not erase your labels on Side A.

WEEK 3 DAY 1

Big Book: Focus on Oral Language Development

Reread the Big Book and return to the text to focus on oral language development.

Grammar in Context: Passive Verbs ①②③④⑤

1. Display a book, pencil, eraser, a piece of paper, and other common items on a table. Invite two volunteers to come to the front of the class. Tell the rest of the class to close their eyes while the two volunteers manipulate the items.
2. Tell the children to open their eyes and notice the changes. Point to items as you say *The book was opened. The pencil was moved. The paper was ripped* and so on. Encourage children to chime in with similar responses. Explain *When we don't know who did something, we put* was *or* were *in front of the action word.*

Phonics in Context

Shared writing provides an ideal opportunity for reviewing the phonics skills children are learning. Highlight the sounds in words ***bri**ght* and ***sm**oke*.

Sample Shared Writing

A bulldozer is a heavy machine with many parts. The driver sits in the cab. The bright lights help the driver see. The shovel lifts rocks and dirt. The big wheels move the bulldozer. The engine sends smoke out the exhaust pipe.

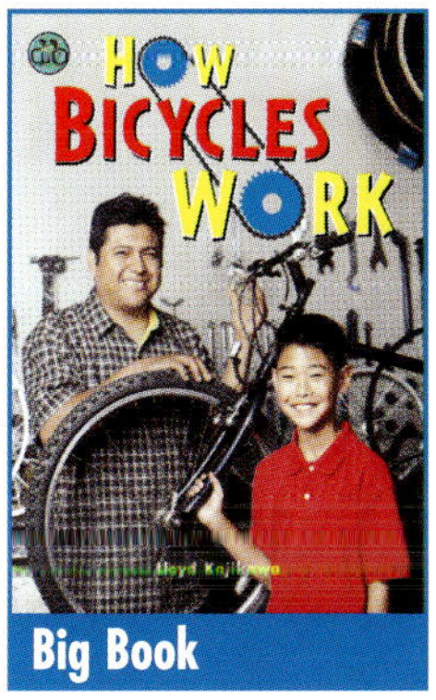

Guided Reading

As you work on this unit, conduct small groups of guided reading or shared-to-guided reading independent of thematic instruction. Instruction is provided in the Guided Reading section of this guide.

Language Learning Master

p. 59 ①②③④⑤

3. Check for comprehension by pointing to items and asking, *What happened to the book?* and so on.
4. Read the text on page 8 of the Big Book. Draw children's attention to the sentence *It was called a high-wheeler.* Ask *What was it called?* Ask children comprehension questions about other sentences with passive constructions on pages 8, 9, and 14.

Language Learning Master

p. 60 ❶❷❸❹❺

Grammar in Context: Future Tense with *going to*

❶❷❸❹❺

1. Show magazine pictures with imminent action and ask *What do you think is going to happen?* Provide a few possibilities to serve as a model. For example, show a picture of a family in a car and brainstorm where they are going.
2. Turn to page 16 of the Big Book. Ask children to find *going to* on the page. Ask *What is Jason going to do?* Remind children that *interview* means ask questions. Turn to page 23 and ask *Where do you think Jason is going to ride his bike?*
3. Invite volunteers to share what they are going to do today after school.

WEEK 3 DAY 2

Shared Writing Card: Brainstorming Side B

You will need

- Shared Writing Card 7
- Wipe-off marker

Brainstorming a Topic

- Use Side A of the Shared Writing Card and your finished piece about the bulldozer. Review how you used the picture and labels on the diagram as the basis for your finished piece.
- Turn the card over to Side B. Tell children that you will now think of your own topic together to draw in the graphic organizer. Brainstorm together a topic about another machine. Suggest other construction equipment or household appliances. The machine should have several parts that are visible and easy enough to explain.

Scribing with the Graphic Organizer

- Once the class has chosen a topic, decide together what the drawing of the machine should look like. Model how to draw the picture and label the first part.
- Continue adding labels to the diagram. Elicit suggestions for labels from the group in the same manner as you did for Side A and record them on the Shared Writing Card.
- You will create the shared writing paragraph together in the next session.

You will need

- Easel pad
- Marker

Active Social Studies: Jobs and Tools

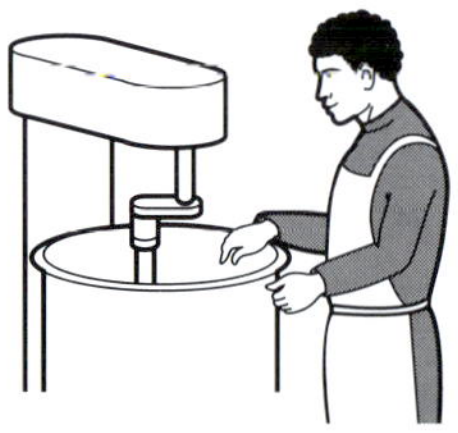

1. Take children on a field trip to visit a worker on the job. You might visit the cook in your school cafeteria, for example. Ask about the duties and tools or appliances associated with the job. If this is not possible, you can bring books and magazines to class that feature different occupations.
2. Have children dictate a language experience story to you about the job. Make sure that they tell about or show the tools and any protective clothing that is used.
3. Have children create illustrations to go with the story.

WEEK 3 DAY 3

Shared Writing Card: Writing Together with Side B

- As with Side A, you will work together with children to create a finished writing piece from the graphic organizer on Side B of Shared Writing Card 7.
- Model writing from the first label, using think-alouds as you go and creating a topic sentence. Show children how to use resources like the Word Wall. Work together on difficult spellings. Use labels to create complete sentences.
- When you have finished your shared writing piece, read it together several times. Then hang it up on the wall where it can be displayed during the rest of the unit. At the end of the unit, you should erase both sides of the Shared Writing Card.

Shared Writing Card

Manipulative Chart: Focus on Oral Language Development

Manipulative Chart

Grammar in Context: Commands ❶❷❸❹❺

1. Use realia or gestures to review the action verbs featured on the Manipulative Chart. Show how to turn a screwdriver, push a saw, pull a tape measure, and dip a paint brush. Then give Total Physical Response commands, such as *Push the saw.* Introduce negative commands, such as *Don't push the saw.* Shake your head and put your hands behind your back. Repeat the negative command until all the children understand.
2. Ask a volunteer in Stages 3, 4, or 5 to come to the front of the class. Give the volunteer commands with the five action verbs from the Chart. Have other children confirm that each of the commands is performed correctly or, in the case of negative commands, that children refrain from the action.
3. Ask another child to come to the front of the class. Have the first volunteer now give this child commands. The class should help confirm responses.
4. Pair children up and have them take turns giving each other commands. ◎

Options for STAGES

❶ These children may simply follow commands, as they are able.	❷❸ These children can use short phrases, such as *push saw* to give commands.	❹❺ Encourage these children to use complete or multi-step commands.

WEEK 3 DAY 4

Active Science: Magnet Power

1. Have children work in small groups. Provide a magnet and a paper clip to each group. Also provide a variety of flat materials: cloth, plastic sheet, foil, wooden ruler, paper, and book.
2. Have children make predictions about whether the magnet will attract the paper clip through each of the objects.

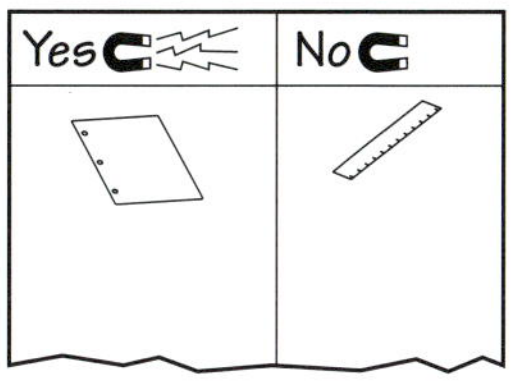

You will need

- Magnet
- Paper clip
- Cloth
- Plastic sheet
- Aluminum foil
- Wooden ruler
- Sheet of paper
- Book

3. Children can then experiment with the various objects to test their predictions, recording the results. In either a *yes* column or a *no* column.
4. Have groups share their findings with the class. Which predictions were confirmed? Which were changed?

WEEK 3 DAY 5

You will need

- Overhead transparency of Writing Resource Guide p. 92
- Overhead marker

Writing Resource Guide: A Simplified Graphic Organizer

This activity is optional and only necessary if you wish to use the simplified sequence graphic organizer in cooperative-group or independent writing.

Brainstorming a Topic

- Review the diagram you made on Side B of the Shared Writing Card. Trace the lines from the labels to the corresponding elements in the diagram.
- On the overhead projector, display a transparency of Writing Planner B on page 92 of the Writing Resource Guide, which is a blank diagram with spaces for two labels.
- Brainstorm together a simple machine featured in this unit, such as a lawn mower, mixer, or washing machine. The machine should be a simple one that has at least two logical parts to identify and label.

Scribing with the Graphic Organizer

- Once the class has arrived at a topic, you should decide together what the labels and captions for the diagram will be. Model creating a label and a brief explanatory caption.
- Elicit suggestions for labels from the group in the same manner as you did with the Shared Writing Card.

You will need

- Writing Resource Guide pp. 91–92
- Markers

Writing Mini-lessons

See the Writing Resource Guide for mini-lessons to use as children write. Here are some suggestions:
- Mini-lesson 47: Matching Words and Pictures
- Mini-lesson 51: Finishing Illustrations and Labels

Writing Resource Guide: Cooperative-Group Writing

- Form groups of heterogeneous Stages with three to four children each to work together on a writing piece using the graphic organizer. You may hand out a copy of Writing Planner A or B to each group.
- Review the shared writing graphic organizers and finished pieces you have made together. Remind children that the labels help them know the names of the parts of the machine.
- Have the groups work together first to complete their graphic organizers and then to write their finished pieces. Circulate to provide assistance. ◎

Options for STAGES

❶❷ These children should draw the pictures for the group.	❸❹❺ These children should take responsibility for the writing of the finished piece.

WEEK 4 DAY 1

Big Book: Focus on Literacy Skills

Word Level: Phonics in Context

1. You will need the Word Wall Starters with the bicycle symbol on them: *trails, brake, stop, small.* These are pictured in the back of the Big Book.
2. Tell children that you want to look at some special words from the story.
3. Introduce the word *trails* by saying it clearly, elongating the *tr* sound, and drawing attention to the highlighting behind the *tr.* Then say */tr/-/tr/-/tr/. If we put the letters* t *and* r *together, we say /tr/. Let's say the word* trails *together:* trails. *Can you hear how* trails *starts with /tr/? Let's sing a song!* Review Song Chart 26 together.
4. Say *I'm going to put the word* trails *below the* tr *label.* Walk over to your Word Wall and place the card *trails* below the *tr.* Remind children that they can use the bicycle symbol to help them remember where they "met" that word before.
5. Repeat a similar procedure for the other words and phonics skills.

Sentence Level: End Punctuation

1. Reread pages 16–18 of the Big Book. Explain the function of periods, exclamation points, and question marks.
   Model *When I come to a period, I know I'm at the end of a sentence. The period tells me to rest before reading the next sentence.*
   Continue in the same manner for exclamation points and question marks.
2. Read page 20 aloud, reviewing what periods, exclamation points, and question marks cue. Invite children to mimic your falling intonation and pauses with periods, your excited tone with exclamation points, and your rising intonation with question marks. ◎

Options for STAGES

❶❷	❸	❹❺
Ask these children to respond to prompts, such as *Point to the question mark.*	Encourage these children to approximate appropriate speech patterns with periods, exclamation points, and question marks.	Ask these children what the punctuation marks tell them about each sentence. Have them demonstrate how the sentence is supposed to be read.

Text Level: Alphabet Knowledge to Locate Information

1. Read Rudy's first sentence on page 19. Point out how *helmet* is in bold print. Explain that words in bold type can be found in the glossary at the back of the book.
2. Turn to the glossary on page 24. Point to *helmet* and read the definition. Explain that a glossary gives definitions for words in boldface in the book.
3. Show how we use alphabetic order to find words in a glossary. Show how the alphabet guide along the border can help if you don't know where the first letter of a word falls in the alphabet.
4. Have children find other words in boldface in the Big Book to look up in the glossary.

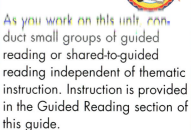

Big Book

Guided Reading

As you work on this unit, conduct small groups of guided reading or shared-to-guided reading independent of thematic instruction. Instruction is provided in the Guided Reading section of this guide.

Home Culture Sharing

The Big Book tells about the use of pedicabs in some parts of the world. Invite children to tell about forms of transportation in their home countries. Allow them to draw pictures on the board to facilitate their description.

Home-School Connection

Send home page 77 of the Home-School Connection Masters for children to use in retelling *How Bicycles Work* to their families. They should first retell the story in English and then in either English or the home language.

You will need

- TPR Cards

Language Practice Game: Version 2 ❶❷❸❹❺

Arrange children in Stages 3, 4, or 5 into groups of six. Then model the following directions for this version of Simon Says.

1. One child is selected as the leader. That child stands in front of the group and chooses a TPR Card. The leader then gives a command to do or not to do something using the tool on that card.
2. The other members must comply with the command. Players who do something when they are told not to do it, or vice versa, must sit down.
3. The leader continues giving commands until one child is left. That child then becomes the next leader and the group reassembles for play.
4. Play continues in this way until all players have had a chance to be the leader.

WEEK 4 DAY 2

You will need

- Easel pad
- Marker

Active Math: Machine Tally

1. Talk with children about machines and vehicles they know. Create a small chart that lists the kinds of machines children can see in their neighborhood.
2. Assign one or two of the machines listed to heterogeneous groups of mixed language ability with four children each.
3. Spend some time with children looking around the school neighborhood together.
4. As children dictate machines they see, make tally marks on the chart for each machine mentioned.
5. When you return to the classroom, ask children to help you tally the totals for each machine.

Machines	Tally	Total
cars	II	2
trucks	III	3
bikes	IIII	4

You will need

A copy of page U171 at the end of this unit for each child.

End-of-Unit Assessment

- While children are engaged in activities this week, pull them individually for the Big Book retelling, using page U171 at the end of this unit.
- Select a number of children with whom you would like to use the Open-Ended Oral Language Assessment on pages U170–U171 of this unit and pull them individually during activities this week. We recommend assessing about one-fourth of your class each unit.
- You should also have gathered the following for their assessment portfolio:
  - page 58 of the Language Learning Masters
  - page 60 of the Language Learning Masters
  - finished writing piece assessed according to the Writing Rubric on page A6.

WEEK 4 DAY 3-4

Writing Resource Guide: Individual Writing

- Children have engaged in a step-by-step writing process moving toward independence. They began with teacher-led shared writing, moved to cooperative groups, and are now ready to work individually.
- Provide a copy of Writing Planner A or B to each child. Children may need individual conferencing on choosing a topic. ◎

Options for STAGES

❶❷ and Emergent Level
These children can draw the machine of their choice in the center of the diagram. They should label parts on their own or dictate labels to you.

❸❹❺ Early Level and Above
These children should also begin by drawing a machine at the center of the diagram. They should label parts to prepare to write about their topic. They should then use the graphic organizer to create a finished piece.

- When children have completed the finished product, whether graphic organizer or paragraph, you should assess it using the Writing Rubric on page A6 of this Teacher's Guide.

You will need

- Writing Resource Guide pp. 91–92
- Markers

Assessment

Continue pulling some children for the Big Book Retelling and Open-Ended Oral Language Assessment as others write.

WEEK 4 DAY 5

Theme Project: Sharing

- Invite groups to present their dream machines and manuals to the class. One Stage 2 or 3 member can tell what the machine is and point out the various features of the machine. Another Stage 4 or 5 member can read the instructions aloud.
- Each group should allow time for questions and responses from the class. Model appropriate feedback for the class by making the first comment yourself, such as *I understand what your machine does, but where do you use it?*

Open-Ended Oral Language Assessment Reassess children's Language Acquisition Stages. Begin with an open-ended prompt like the first one below. If children are unable to respond, intervene with increasingly directed prompts, such as the second and third ones below.

What can you tell me about the picture?

What machines do you see?

I see a person using a hammer. Do you see another tool?

Assessment Directions: Copy this form for each child and place the completed form in the child's portfolio. Locate the child's Language Acquisition Stage for each of the first four activities and assess his or her performance during the unit according to expectations for that Stage. For the Big Book Retelling, pull children to retell the Big Book during end-of-unit assessment time. Use the Open-Ended Oral Language Assessment to reassess children's Language Acquisition Stages with one-fourth of your students for each unit, using the back side of the sheet to take notes. *For more guidance on assessment, see pages T33 and T34.*

Unit 7 Assessment

Name ______________________ **Date** ____________

On Our Way to English Grade 2	STAGE EXPECTATIONS ❶	❷	❸	❹	❺
Fluency Manipulative Chart Student Version, page U156 *How does the child respond when manipulating the mini-chart along with the Oral Language Audio CD?*	Shows the correct answers. ☐ Yes ☐ Not yet	Shows the correct answers, naming the tool or the action associated with it. ☐ Yes ☐ Not yet	Shows the correct answers, approximating sentences and substitutions. ☐ Yes ☐ Not yet	Shows the correct answers, singing the verse with few, if any, errors. ☐ Yes ☐ Not yet	
Content Area Knowledge Language Practice Game: Version 1, page U157 *How does the child show an understanding of tools and their related actions while playing the game?*	Places the game marker on the appropriate square. ☐ Yes ☐ Not yet	Places the game marker on the appropriate square and uses some appropriate vocabulary, such as *hammer* or *Pound a hammer.* ☐ Yes ☐ Not yet		Places the game marker on the appropriate square and says a complete sentence with appropriate vocabulary, such as *You can pound a hammer to build a birdhouse.* ☐ Yes ☐ Not yet	
Social Language Function Give Instructions, page U161 *How does the child respond during the Function Mini-lesson?*	Responds nonverbally or with a basic word or phrase, such as *pick clip.* ☐ Yes ☐ Not yet		Delivers simple instructions to others, such as *Pick up clip.* ☐ Yes ☐ Not yet	Delivers more complex instructions, such as *Pick up the clip with the magnet.* ☐ Yes ☐ Not yet	
Academic Language Function Predict and Hypothesize, page U161 *How does the child respond during the Function Mini-lesson?*			Responds using a short phrase, such as *pick up pin.* ☐ Yes ☐ Not yet	Responds with a complete sentence, such as *It will pick up the pin.* ☐ Yes ☐ Not yet	
Big Book Retelling, page U161 *Have children copy the diagram on pages 2–3 of the Big Book (page U160) and use that to retell the book. How does the child process the text?*	Points to elements in the diagram in response to questions. ☐ Yes ☐ Not yet		Points to elements in the diagram and identifies the names of key parts ☐ Yes ☐ Not yet	Identifies key elements in the diagram and supplies some commentary, although it may be fragmented in nature. ☐ Yes ☐ Not yet	Identifies key elements in the diagram and supplies commentary with near native-like fluency. ☐ Yes ☐ Not yet
Open-Ended Oral Language Assessment, page U170 *Use the child's responses to the illustration to reassess the child's Stage of Language Acquisition.*	☐ **STAGE ❶** Uses few or no words; gestures or points.	☐ **STAGE ❷** Uses words or short phrases.	☐ **STAGE ❸** Uses phrases and simple sentences.	☐ **STAGE ❹** Uses sentences in connected discourse.	☐ **STAGE ❺** Uses language comparable to native-speaking peers.

UNIT 8

Choices We Make

OVERVIEW *Children will explore choices and consequences in everyday life, including how they might spend or earn money. In addition, they will learn vocabulary related to jobs and professions.*

Determining the Purpose

Oral Language Development

Focus on Functions

Social Context:

Agree and disagree ❶❷❸❹❺

Academic Context:

Justify and persuade ❶❷❸❹❺

Focus on Grammar

- Questions with *what* and *which*
- Ordinal numbers
- Appositives
- Adjectives with *-ing*

Comprehension Strategy

- Draws conclusions

Literacy Skills

- **Word Level:** Phonics in context final blends, initial and final digraphs
- **Sentence Level:** Dialogue in text
- **Text Level:** Distinguishing fantasy from reality

Content Area Objectives

- Identifies professions
- Understands responsibilities of community members
- Chooses food to create a balanced meal
- Counts and sorts coins and bills

Language Learning Strategy

- Talk around the problem word.

Writing Skill

- Uses a graphic organizer as an outline for writing

Unit Components

Manipulative Chart

Chant Poster

Concept Poster

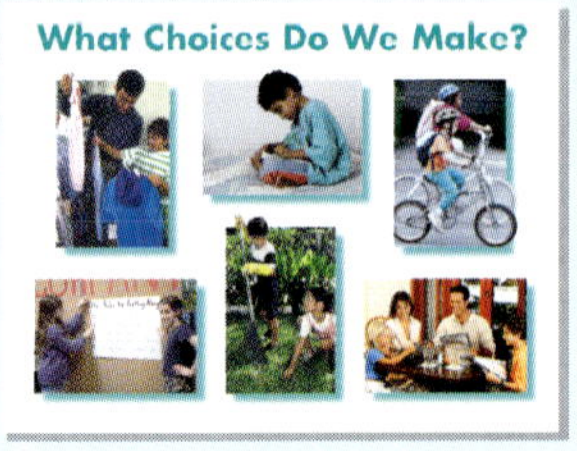

Newcomer Book

Unit at a Glance

	DURING THE WEEK	DAY 1
Week 1	**Small-Group Instruction:** • Guided Reading • Shared-to-Guided Reading **Phonics Focus:** *-nd, -nt* Phonics Song Chart 30, pp. P64–P65	**Manipulative Chart:** Introduction with Audio CD p. U175
Week 2	**Small-Group Instruction:** • Guided Reading • Shared-to-Guided Reading • Newcomer Book **Phonics Focus:** *-st, -mp* Phonics Song Chart 31, pp. P66–P67	**Concept Poster:** Introduction p. U180 **Language Practice Game:** Version 1 p. U181
Week 3	**Small-Group Instruction:** • Guided Reading • Shared-to-Guided Reading • Newcomer Book **Phonics Focus:** *ch, sh* Phonics Song Chart 32, pp. P68–P69	**Big Book:** Oral Language Development p. U187
Week 4	**Small-Group Instruction:** • Guided Reading • Shared-to-Guided Reading • Newcomer Book **Phonics Focus:** *th, wh* Phonics Song Chart 33, pp. P70–P71	**Big Book:** Literacy Skills p. U191 **Language Practice Game:** Version 2 p. U192

STAGES ❶ Preproduction ❷ Early Production ❸ Speech Emergence ❹ Intermediate Fluency ❺ Advanced Fluency

Oral Language Audio CD

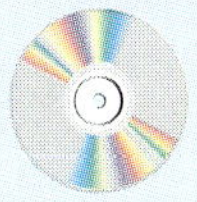

Picture Cards

Shared Writing Card

Big Book with Audio CD and Small Book

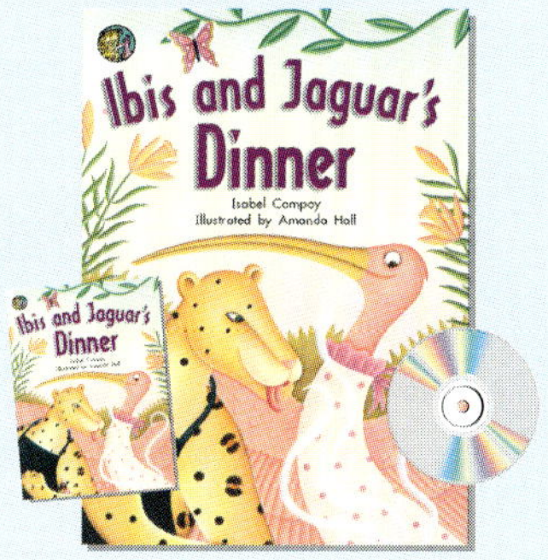

Home-School Connection Masters

Writing Resource Guide

Language Learning Masters

DAY 2	DAY 3	DAY 4	DAY 5
Manipulative Chart: Gestures and Manipulative Fun p. U176	**Chant Poster:** Introduction p. U177	**TPR Cards:** Introduction p. U178	**Manipulative Chart:** Oral Language Development Student Version p. U179
Big Book: Introduction p. U183	**Theme Project:** Restaurant Role-Play p. U184 **Big Book:** Revisiting p. U184	**Big Book:** Comprehension Strategy p. U185 **Chant Poster:** Oral Language Development p. U185	**Shared Writing Card:** Introduction of Side A p. U186 **Concept Poster:** Revisiting p. U186
Shared Writing Card: Brainstorming Side B p. U188 **Active Social Studies:** A Good Citizen p. U189	**Shared Writing Card:** Writing Together with Side B p. U189 **Manipulative Chart:** Oral Language Development p. U189	**Active Science:** A Balanced Diet p. U190	**Writing Resource Guide:** A Simplified Graphic Organizer Cooperative-Group Writing p. U190
Active Math: Money Math p. U192 **Assessment** p. U193	**Writing Resource Guide:** Individual Writing p. U193 **Assessment** p. U193	**Writing Resource Guide:** Individual Writing p. U193 **Assessment** p. U193	**Theme Project:** Sharing p. U193

Center Activities

Number Nook

Display play money for children. Have children arrange the bills and coins by value, and then create a variety of equivalent combinations.

Artist's Studio

Provide magazines, scissors, construction paper, and glue. Children can create collages about their future career goals.

You will need

- Classroom objects
- Cards or tags
- Markers
- Construction paper
- Magazines
- Scissors
- Glue
- Play paper and coin money

CENTERS

Content Corner

Set up a store of classroom objects with price tags and stacks of play money. Have children take independent "shopping sprees" to practice addition and subtraction as they choose purchases and count money.

Listening Post

After introducing each element in class, children may revisit the Manipulative Chart and Chant Poster on the Oral Language Audio CD. If you include a laminated copy of the Manipulative Chart Student Version, children can manipulate it as they sing to Part 4 of the CD (with blanks). Children may also listen to *Ibis and Jaguar's Dinner* on the Big Book Audio CD while following along in the small copy.

Language Workshop

Any time they are not in use during the unit, place the Picture Cards and TPR cards for the unit in this center. Encourage children to review the names of the items on the cards with each other for additional practice. After introducing the Language Practice Game in class, add the game board and spinner to the center for independent group play.

Writer's Den

Establish a journal writing center with prompts to spark children's writing. Change the prompt every two weeks:

- What choices did you make yesterday?
- What do you want to be when you grow up?

Children should be encouraged to draw pictures to support their writing. Provide blank Writing Planners in center materials for prewriting.

More Books

- *Benny's Pennies* by Pat Brisson (Doubleday, 1993)
- *My Rows and Piles of Coins* by Tololwa M. Mollel (Clarion, 1999)
- *General Store* by Rachel Field (Little, Brown, 1988)
- *I Want to Be an Astronaut* by Byron Barton (HarperCollins, 1997)
- *Pickles to Pittsburgh* by Judi Barrett (Simon & Schuster Children's Books, 1997)

WEEK 1 DAY 1

Manipulative Chart: Introduction with Audio CD

Sung to the tune of "Oh My Darling, Clementine"

Setting the Scene

- Share some of your favorite things. You might tell about your favorite CD or your favorite food. Display as many of these items as possible. Say *These are my favorite things.*
- Ask children about their favorite things. Encourage them to name as many items as they can. Stages 1 and 2 children may be able to point to items you displayed. Record these items on the board using simple sketches and labels.
- Display Picture Cards 1 and 2: bills and coins. Explain that these are kinds of money, which we use to buy things. Say *When you only have a little money to spend, can you buy everything you like? No, you have to choose.* Ask *What would you choose?*

Options for STAGES

❶❷❸ Have these children point to and name as they are able what they would buy.

❹❺ Have these children tell what they would buy and why.

Creating Comprehensible Input

- Display the chart. Point out the spinner and the bills and coins on the spinner. Tell children that this is money to buy items for sale in the "store."
- Point out items for sale on the left side of the chart. Teach the names of the stuffed animal, zoo ticket, popcorn, and so on by gesturing and pointing to these items and asking children to chime in.
- Read the text, pausing often as you use gestures, pointing, and other techniques to make the chant comprehensible.

How much money	shrug and point to money on the spinner
How much money	repeat
How much money can I spend?	pretend to count out money from your hand
If I only have two dollars,	hold up two fingers
What choices will I make?	shrug and point to items for sale

Manipulative Chart
Picture Cards 1, 2

Guided Reading

As you work on this unit, conduct small groups of guided reading or shared-to-guided reading independent of thematic instruction. Instruction is provided in the Guided Reading section of this guide.

Component Organizer

Other Manipulative Chart lessons in this unit:

- Gestures and Manipulative Fun, p. U176
- Oral Language Development and Student Version, pp. U179–U180
- Oral Language Development, p. U189

Real-World Touch

Bring in some of the items shown on the Manipulative Chart and play money to reinforce this vocabulary.

Home-School Connection

Choose one of the versions of the parent letter to send home with each child, according to the child's home language (pages 78–85 in the Home-School Connection Masters). Also send home the activity on page 86.

Introducing the Audio CD

- Play Part 1 of the Oral Language Audio CD, the spoken song, as you say the song and track the print on the Manipulative Chart with your finger or a pointer. Replay Part 1 several times, encouraging children to chime in whenever they can.
- Introduce the song by playing the song at natural speed, Part 2 of the Audio CD, to help children get a feel for the song. Allow the Audio CD to continue playing through Part 3, the song at instructional pace. Track the print as the Audio CD plays. Repeat Part 3 again, this time singing along, making clear lip movements without exaggerating. Revisit Part 3 several times to help children learn the song.

Manipulative Chart

WEEK 1 DAY 2

Manipulative Chart: Gestures and Manipulative Fun

Gesturing the Song

Introduce these simple gestures to accompany the song:

How much money	pretend to count on your fingers
How much money	repeat
How much money can I spend?	shrug shoulders in questioning gesture
If I only have two dollars,	hold up two fingers
What choices will I make?	hold chin in pensive gesture

Manipulating the Chart

- Demonstrate how to spin the spinner and point to the money indicated by the arrow. Count the amount of money aloud, encouraging children to count along. The money amounts on the spinner can be substituted for the words in green. Spin to *five dollars*, sing the verse, and emphasize using *five dollars* instead of *two dollars*.
- Play Part 4 of the Oral Language Audio CD while you say *five dollars* in the blank space.
- Continue introducing and saying money amounts on the spinner in this manner.
- Invite volunteers to manipulate the Manipulative Chart for the class as you sing the verse together or give Total Physical Response commands, such as *Show me the soccer ball.*
- Invite children to create new gestures for the new money amounts in each verse.
- You can revisit this activity many times during the unit.

Journal Writing Reminder

Children should be writing in their journals throughout the unit. Journal writing provides an opportunity to express personal needs and wants freely. See Writer's Den for suggested journal prompts.

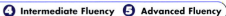

WEEK 1 DAY 3

Chant Poster: Introduction

Chant Poster
Picture Cards 3–5

Setting the Scene

- Introduce Picture Cards 3–5: doctors, writers, sailors. Say each word allowing children to repeat. Use simple language and appropriate gestures to describe what each one does. Say, for example, *Sailors work on a ship* and move your hand to indicate water as you point to the ship on the Picture Card.
- Invite children to act out or tell what they know about these or other jobs. ◎

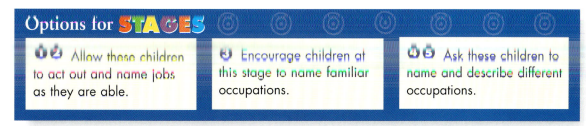

Options for STAGES

- Allow these children to act out and name jobs as they are able.
- Encourage children at this stage to name familiar occupations.
- Ask these children to name and describe different occupations.

- Ask children what job they want to do when they are older.

Creating Comprehensible Input

- Displaying the Chant Poster, point to the girl, the doctor, the writer, and the sailor, making comparisons to the Picture Cards. Explain that the girl is thinking about what she will be when she is older.
- Read the text, pausing often as you use gestures, pointing, and other techniques to make the chant comprehensible.

When I grow up,	raise hand from knee level to head
What will I be?	shrug
A doctor, a writer,	point to doctor and writer
A sailor at sea?	point to the sailor, then make a wave movement with hand
I'll have to make choices	point to doctor, writer, sailor
And see what fits me.	tap chest
What will I be?	shrug
I'll just wait and see!	put hands on hips and tap foot

Chanting the Poster

- Encourage children to chime in as you chant the rhyme several times. You can form two groups and have them alternate every two lines.
- Introduce the chant on the Oral Language Audio CD as you and the children move to the rhythm of the chant. Tell them that they can listen to it on their own later at the Listening Post.
- Practice saying the chant in different ways. Snap or clap to accentuate the beat.
- Revisit the chant often with children. Invite children to substitute *a doctor, a writer* with the names of other jobs they might like to have when they grow up.

Component Organizer

Other Chant Poster lessons in this unit:

- Oral Language Development, p. U185

WEEK 1 DAY 4

You will need

- **Language Learning Master** p. 65
- Scissors

TPR Cards: Introduction

Introducing the Cards with Total Physical Response

- Provide one copy of page 65 of the Language Learning Masters to each child. Have children color and cut out the cards.
- Introduce a few cards at a time by holding them up one by one and saying the words clearly. Select first the words that have already been introduced in previous activities.
- Ask children to pick up the correct cards as you call out a word. Model the desired outcome. Add one new card at a time and keep reviewing in a game-like atmosphere. Children may want to say the word as they pick up the card.
- Now invite children to respond to your full-sentence commands, such as *Hold up a penny in one hand. Hold up a nickel in the other hand.*
- Assign partners so you can add commands like *Trade quarters with Yosef.*
- As children increase their familiarity with the TPR Cards and the game, add funny commands such as *Sit on the menu.*
- Invite volunteers in Stages 3, 4, or 5 to give commands to their classmates.
- Extend language by discussing choices made in the activities shown: doing homework, buying something, riding a bike. ◎

Options for STAGES

❶❷	❸	❹❺
These children may act out the activities being discussed, perhaps using single words as they demonstrate.	These children may say a few words, such as *choose food.*	Ask these children to describe choices made, using phrases or complete sentences.

- Repeat this activity several times throughout the unit.

Grammar in Context: Questions ❶❷❸❹❺

1. Display the penny card and ask *What is this?* Confirm their responses *Yes, it is a penny.*
2. Continue asking *what* questions for each of the TPR Cards. For the cards that show actions instead of nouns, ask *What did the boy choose to do?* You can then model the answer *His homework.*
3. Invite volunteers to take turns asking the class *what* questions with the cards in the same way you have demonstrated.
4. Arrange the cards in a grid on a desktop and have children gather around. Ask *Which card shows a dime?* Wait for children to point and then select the correct card, saying, *Yes, this card shows a dime.* Remove the card from the group.
5. Model how to ask *which* questions in this way, selecting and removing cards until they are all gone.
6. Replace the cards, and ask volunteers to take turns asking *which* questions. Each volunteer should wait for the correct response and then remove the appropriate card. Volunteers continue taking turns until all the cards are gone.

Language Junction

In Spanish, question word order is flexible, and, unlike English, helping verbs play no part in question formation. As a result, Spanish-speaking learners of English might produce questions such as *What John want?* When learners start to use helping verbs, expect them to have difficulty with forms: *What did they wanted?* Without correcting them overtly, you might model correct forms: *What did they want?*

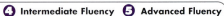

WEEK 1 DAY 5

Manipulative Chart: Focus on Oral Language Development

FUNCTION MINI-LESSON

Agree and Disagree ❶❷❸❹❺

1. Turn the wheel on the Manipulative Chart to $2.00. Say *The best way to spend $2.00 is to buy two boxes of popcorn.* Ask *Who likes my choice?* while nodding and smiling. Count how many children agree. Write *Agree* on the board and the number who agree. Say *Ten people agree with my choice.*
2. Ask *Who doesn't like my choice? Who wants to buy something different with two dollars?* Count how many disagree. Write *Disagree* on the board and the number who disagree. Say *Six people don't agree with my choice.* Explain that when we have the same idea as someone, it's called agreeing, and when we have a different idea, it's called disagreeing.
3. Have children make choices with $2.00 on the Manipulative Chart and add these to your list, noting how many children agree and disagree with each choice. ◎

Options for STAGES

❶❷ Encourage these children to respond to yes/no questions, such as *Do you like my choice?*

❸❹❺ These children can agree or disagree in complete phrases or sentences.

FUNCTION MINI-LESSON

Justify and Persuade ❶❷❸❹❺

1. Invite children in Stages 3, 4, and 5 to join you while others play games with the TPR Cards.
2. Ask children to take turns spinning the spinner on the Manipulative Chart. Ask each child how she or he would spend the money indicated.
3. Ask children to justify their choices. Encourage them to share why the chosen items were more appealing or necessary to them than the other items.

Grammar in Context: Ordinal Numbers ❶❷❸❹❺

1. Display the Manipulative Chart and review the names of the items.
2. Tell children they can buy whatever they want. Ask them to look at the chart and think about their preferences.
3. Invite volunteers to take turns pointing to items on the chart and sharing their choices using ordinal numbers. Model by saying *My first choice is the teddy bear. My second choice is the soccer ball,* and so on. Have children use pointing, phrases, or complete sentences as they are able.

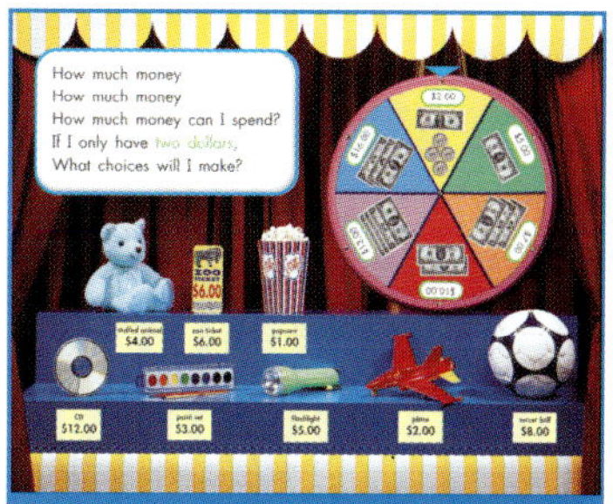

Manipulative Chart

Language Learning Strategy

Talk around the unknown word.

Use this strategy for children in Stages 3, 4, and 5

- Tell children when they don't know the word for something they want to say, they can use other words and gestures to describe it. They can talk around the problem word.
  Model *I want to buy this item, but I don't know the word for it, so I'll talk around the word. You hold it in your hand. It gives light. You use it in the dark. Do you know what I want to buy?* Wait for children to supply the answer and say *See, I didn't have to say the word for you to know what I was talking about.*
- Throughout the unit, encourage children to keep trying to communicate when they get stuck by talking around the unknown words.

Home-School Connection

When children have practiced manipulating the Manipulative Chart Student Version, send it home for them to practice with their family members.

You will need

- **Language Learning Master** pp. 61–64
- Scissors
- Pencils
- Paper clips

Assessment

Record your observations of children on their individual assessment checklists for this unit. See page U195.

Manipulative Chart: Student Version

- Model assembling the pages according to the directions.
- Circulate to provide assistance as children cut out the spinner and money. Encourage children to color and decorate their charts.
- Have children spin their spinners as you do the same on the Manipulative Chart. Then encourage them to match the monetary value to what you do as you say different amounts of money in the song. Model making a statement about how you will spend the money shown.
- Have children respond to your Total Physical Response commands: *Show me five dollars.*
- Play Part 4 of the Oral Language Audio CD and model how children can manipulate their Student Versions as they sing along. Tell children that they will later be able to listen to the Audio CD and manipulate this mini-chart in the Listening Post.

WEEK 2 DAY 1

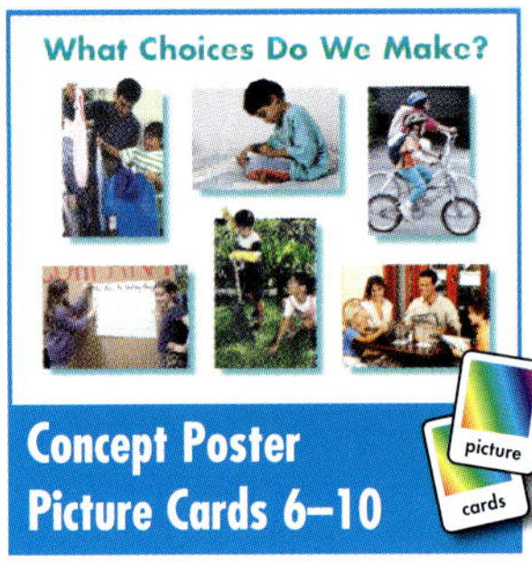

Concept Poster
Picture Cards 6–10

Concept Poster: Introduction

Setting the Scene

- Show children Picture Card 6: menu and Picture Card 7: food, saying each word.
- Use the cards to talk through a decision-making process. Say *Let's see, what do I want to order for dinner?*
- Display Picture Cards 8–10: bicycle, bicycle helmet, dress. Encourage children to talk about other decisions they make. You may prompt them with questions such as *Is wearing a bicycle helmet a good choice?*

Creating Comprehensible Input

- Display the Concept Poster. Read the poster title aloud. Introduce the vocabulary items in the upper left picture. Demonstrate how to talk through the decision-making process and consequences behind the picture with a think-aloud.
  Model *Look at this picture of the children working in their yard. They chose to work in the yard to help their family, and they chose to work together. The two children will feel good about helping, and the job will get done faster because they're working together.*
- Recap this in simple language as you point at the pictures and connecting arrows: *children helping and working together; children feel good; job gets done faster; good choice.*
- Use similar language to talk about the decisions and consequences involved in the next photo on the poster.
- Invite a child in Stages 4 or 5 to talk through the other pictures shown on the poster. Supply necessary vocabulary to facilitate the process.
- After the child has finished, recap in simple language, pointing to the pictures as you go.
- Repeat the procedure for the remaining pictures. You may use appropriate Picture Cards as needed.

Guided Reading

As you work on this unit, conduct small groups of guided reading or shared-to-guided reading independent of thematic instruction. Instruction is provided in the Guided Reading section of this guide.

Extending Oral Language

- Engage children in reviewing these concepts by asking questions. ◎

Options for STAGES

❶❷ Ask these children specific questions which require only a yes/no answer or pointing, such as *What is the girl choosing?*	❸ Ask children at this stage either/or questions, such as *Did the boy choose to do his homework or play outside?*	❹❺ Ask these children open-ended questions that require substantive answers, such as, *Tell me about the choice.*

Language Practice Game: Version 1 ❶❷❸❹❺

Preparing the Game

Tape copies of page 66 of the Language Learning Masters to poster board for durability. Make enough copies for each child. Provide pencils and paper clips to use with the spinners.

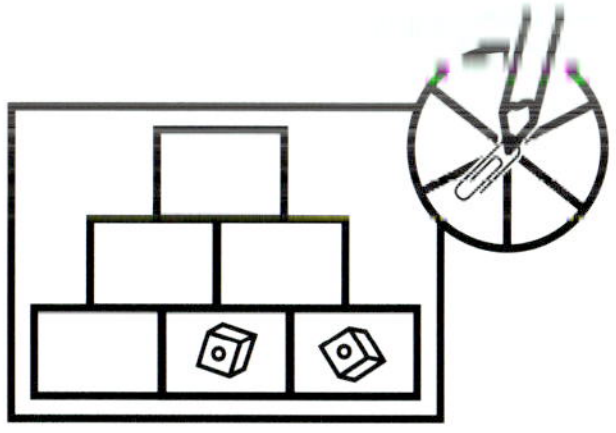

Playing Version 1

Form heterogeneous groups of mixed language ability with four children each. Provide each group with a copy of page 68. Give each child a copy of the spinner with pictures and words. Provide each child with six game markers. Model the following directions.

1. The first player spins the spinner. That player must say the amount indicated and which item or items on the pyramid he or she will buy with that amount, such as *I have two dollars. I will buy a baseball cap.* ◎

Options for STAGES

❶ These children can point to or name the item he or she wishes to buy.	❷❸ These children should be encouraged to simply say the amount of money and the item they wish to buy without having to form complete sentences.	❹❺ Encourage these children to form complete sentences as modeled above.

2. Players should verify that their partners have chosen items that they can afford to buy with the amount of money indicated on the spinner.
3. Then the player places a game marker on the desired items.
4. Players take turns spinning and placing markers on the pyramid. The first player to fill all the spaces on his or her pyramid is the winner.

Component Organizer

Other Concept Poster lessons in this unit:
- Revisiting, p. U186

You will need

- **Language Learning Master** pp. 66–67
- Poster board
- Tape
- Pencils
- Paper clips
- Game markers

Component Organizer

Other Language Practice Game lessons in this unit:
- Version 2, p. U192

Assessment

Record your observations of children during the Language Practice Game on their individual assessment checklists for this unit. See page U195.

Newcomer Book: Small-Group Instruction

I Have Some Money

Written by Karen Clevidence

OVERVIEW *It's exciting to have some money!*

The Newcomer Book is supported by the language of the Manipulative Chart and should be integrated into small-group instruction this week when children have had enough practice with vocabulary and concepts in this unit.

Language Pattern

I have _______ dollars.

Text Vocabulary

cardinal numbers; money

Vocabulary Extenders

more/less

Reading the Text

Book Talk

- Work with a small group of four children at one time who exhibit similar literacy-learning behaviors.
- Engage children in a book talk as you flip through the pages of your copy of the book. ◎

Options for STAGES

1 2 Identify the amounts of money shown for these children. Encourage them to say these dollar amounts after you as they are able.

3 4 5 Ask children to identify the amounts of money shown as you encounter these in the text.

INSTRUCTIONAL PATHS

1 2 3 4 5 **All Readers:**	1 2 3 4 5 **Emergent Readers:**	1 2 3 4 5 **Early Readers:**
Shared-to-Guided Reading	Guided Reading	Independent Reading no lesson provided

INDIVIDUAL READING

Shared-to-Guided Reading **3–4 sessions**

1 2 3 4 5 **All Readers**

1. Read the book to children.
   - Invite children to sit near you as you read a copy of the book. Begin with the cover and title page.
   - Turn to page 2 and begin reading the words as you point to them. Draw children's attention to the pictures.
2. Read the book with children.
   - Encourage children to follow along in their own copies of the book, turning the pages as you read together and using their own fingers to point to the words from left to right.
   - Invite children to chime in when they are comfortable.
   - Reread the book in this manner over several sessions.
3. Have children buddy read the book.
4. Invite children to read the book independently.

A Assess

- Did children anticipate the words as you read them?
- Did children participate in buddy reading?

Guided Reading **2 sessions**

1 2 3 4 5 **Emergent Readers**

1. Provide copies of the book to children. Use one child's book and turn to page 2. Introduce the book's pattern to children by reading the sentence and pointing to each word as you read *I have one dollar.*
2. Have each child read at his or her own pace while remaining in the group. Discourage choral reading. Observe as they read.

A Assess

- Did children ask for help with English when they needed it?
- Can children identify and point to a high-frequency word?

REVISITING THE NEWCOMER BOOK

If children seem ready, you may also use the book to extend children's knowledge of *more* and *less* by comparing amounts on facing pages.

WEEK 2 DAY 2

Big Book: Introduction

Ibis and Jaguar's Dinner

Written by Isabel Campoy *Illustrated by Amanda Hall*

OVERVIEW *Ibis and Jaguar played together when they were young. But when they grow up, they play tricks on each other. What other stories do you know with characters that play tricks, like Anansi the spider?*

Warming Up

Begin the lesson by revisiting the Manipulative Chart, Chant Poster, or a familiar Big Book. You may ask a volunteer to choose one.

Setting the Scene

- Introduce Picture Card 11: ibis. Tell children that an ibis is a bird that lives near the water. Point out its long beak. Invite children to imagine how the ibis might drink through its beak. Bend over and pretend to sip through a straw. This will be an important concept to understanding the story.
- Introduce Picture Card 12: jaguar. Tell children that the jaguar is in the cat family. It lives in the jungle. Again, invite children to imagine how the jaguar might drink. Pretend to lap at water with your tongue.
- Tap into children's prior knowledge. *Have you ever seen animals like these? Where?* Allow children to share their responses in words or gestures.
- Introduce the book and provide children with an overview of the story.
- Show the cover and point as you say: *Ibis and Jaguar are friends.*
- Make predictions about the story. *What will Ibis and Jaguar do together as friends? How will they change as they grow up? What will Jaguar do to make Ibis angry?*

Reading the Text

- Read the title page. Have children make predictions based on the picture. *Which dish do you think Ibis can eat from easily? Which can Jaguar eat from easily? Why?*
- As you read through the story, use a pointer or your finger to draw children's attention to the text. In future rereadings, children should be encouraged to chime in. Point out items in the pictures to support your reading. You will return later to build children's understanding of the text.
- If you have children in Stages 3, 4, or 5, pause after reading page 18 for a prediction of what will happen next. *What do you think will happen at Ibis's home?*

Creating Comprehensible Input

- Open up the back flap of the book, which shows the two major cause-effect events in the story. Leave it open as you read to help build comprehension of cause-effect events in the story.
- Use the comprehension supports in the following chart to help you build comprehensible input with children at all Stages of Language Acquisition.

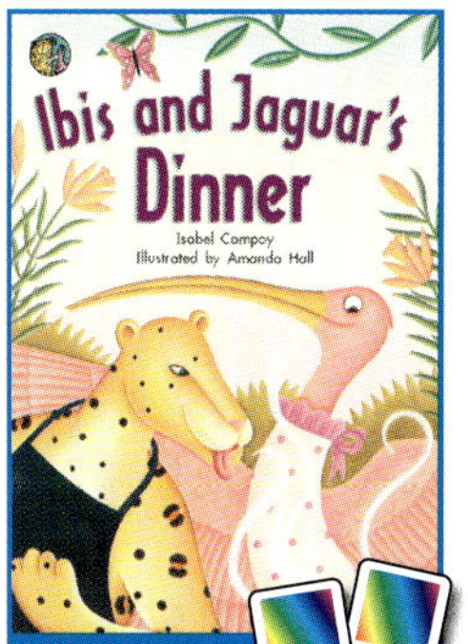

Big Book
Picture Cards 11, 12

Component Organizer

Other Big Book lessons in this unit:

- Revisiting, p. U184
- Comprehension Strategy, p. U185
- Oral Language Development, pp. U187–U188
- Literacy Skills, pp. U191–U192

PAGE	IN THE STORY	COMPREHENSION SUPPORT
2	. . . it was spring . . .	explain: spring is the season after winter and before summer
2	. . . long skinny beak . . . spotted	point: to long skinny beak, tracing and emphasizing length
7	. . . grew up . . .	gesture: put hand level with knee and move up to your height
7	What a surprise!	act out: look surprised, with hand to mouth and eyes big
10	. . . plenty of good food . . .	gesture: a lot of something with arms
14	. . . steamy oatmeal on a large flat shell.	explain: oatmeal is a soupy food we eat hot
14	Ibis looked puzzled.	act out: look confused with head tilted
14	. . . poked and pecked . . .	gesture: poke and peck with your nose
21	. . . dish with a long skinny neck . . . gourd . . .	point: to gourd in story, tracing and accentuating neck explain: a gourd is a hollowed-out dried vegetable
21	. . . delicious . . .	gesture: rub tummy and smack lips

You will need

- Sample menus
- Light-colored construction paper or manila folders
- Markers and crayons
- Magazine pictures of food

Revisiting the Big Book

- Copy Picture Card 11: ibis and Picture Card 12: jaguar for each child. Guide children in coloring their copies and taping them to craft sticks.
- Invite children to manipulate their puppets as you reread the story together.
- Use a pointer to draw children's attention to the text. Pause to provide time for your actors to manipulate their puppets.

WEEK 2 DAY 3

Theme Project: Restaurant Role-Play

1. Display several restaurant menus. Discuss any restaurant experiences children have had, and talk about different types of restaurants and the foods they serve. Using gestures to support comprehension, point out and explain the different categories on the menus (appetizers, main courses, beverages, and desserts). Also point out the prices. Work together to compare some prices. For example, ask *Which costs more, the soup or the chicken?*
2. Form heterogeneous groups of mixed language abilities with four to five children each. Tell groups that they will create their own menus and then use these menus to pretend they are ordering food.
3. Groups should brainstorm items they want to include on the menu. Have children organize the items into categories and begin to plan their menu. Ask them to try to include appetizers, main courses, beverages, and desserts. Provide groups with pictures of food for reference.
4. Distribute folded sheets of light-colored construction paper or manila folders to each group. Group members can dictate the content of their menus to a scribe within their group or to you. They should remember to include the prices. The prices should reflect the relative value of the different items. They may also want to include illustrations for many of the items.
5. When they are finished, have groups decorate the front of their menus and name their restaurants.
6. Gather the menus and keep them until the end of the unit, when children will conduct a restaurant role-play.

WEEK 2 DAY 4

Big Book: Focus on Comprehension Strategy

Draws Conclusions

1. Explain how readers draw conclusions. Say *You can use clues from your reading and information that you already know to answer questions. This is called drawing conclusions.*
2. Open the book to pages 4 and 5 and ask children, *Did Ibis and Jaguar like to be together? How do we know?* Validate responses, such as *They played together* and *They looked for rainbows together.* Say *These are good conclusions.*
3. Open the book to page 10, and have children tell why Ibis says "That sounds very good!" Validate responses, such as *He was hungry, He hasn't seen his friend in many years,* and *He doesn't want to look for food.* Point out to children that they are using information from the text to draw conclusions.
4. Continue asking questions and encouraging children to support conclusions with examples drawn from the text.

Big Book

Assessment

Use a retelling of the Big Book to assess comprehension. See page U195.

Chant Poster: Focus on Oral Language Development

FUNCTION MINI-LESSON

Agree and Disagree ❶❷❸❹❺

1. Revisit the chant together, saying it several times.
2. Review agreeing or disagreeing with a statement, which was introduced on Week 1 Day 5.
3. Ask a child in Stage 4 or 5 to choose one profession for the girl. Write the choice on the board. Ask *Who agrees with this choice?* Write how many children agree. Then ask *Who does not agree with this choice?* Write that number on the board.

Options for STAGES

❶❷	❸❹❺
Encourage these children to nod/shake their heads and/or say yes or no.	Encourage these children to approximate a full answer.

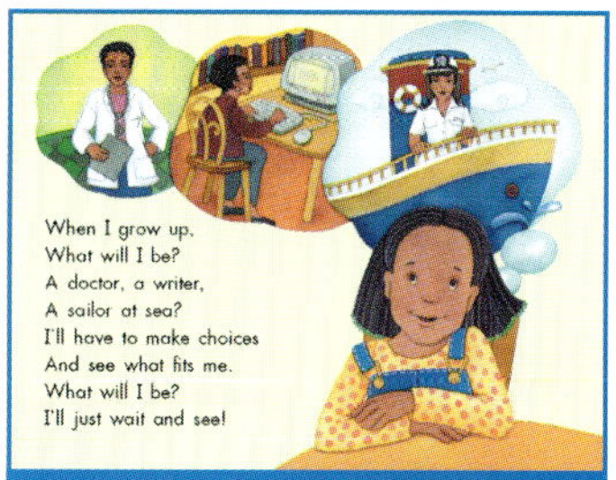

Chant Poster

Home-Culture Sharing

- Have children interview a family member about what job they want the child to have when grown up and why.
- Accept all answers children may bring back to the class without judgment. What is appropriate for one culture may not be for another.

FUNCTION MINI-LESSON

Justify and Persuade ❶❷❸❹❺

1. Read the chant again, encouraging children to chime in. Have them supply the names of other occupations for the third line.
2. Invite children to tell about what they want to be when they grow up.
3. Ask children to tell why that particular occupation might be a good choice for them. Engage children in a discussion about the pros and cons of each occupation. Help them use this information to persuade others that it might be a good job for them, too.

Assessment

Record your observations of children during these mini-lessons on their individual assessment checklists for this unit. See page U195.

Language Learning Master

p. 68 ①②③④⑤

Shared Writing Card

You will need

- Shared Writing Card 8
- Wipe-off marker
- Regular marker
- Easel pad

Revisiting the Concept Poster

- Revisit the Concept Poster, engaging children in a discussion about the choices being made in the pictures and their potential consequences.
- Have children talk about choices they make in similar situations. Ask *Do you choose to follow class rules? What happens when you do? What about when you don't?*

Grammar in Context: Ordinal Numbers ①②③④⑤

1. Review with children the ordinal numbers that they learned in Week 1, Day 5: *first, second, third,* and so on.
2. Model ranking the jobs in order of preference: *My first choice is a doctor. My second choice is a writer. My third choice is a sailor.*
3. Invite children to share their preferences. Children in Stages 4 or 5 can justify their choices by giving reasons, such as *My first choice is a doctor because I like to help people.*

WEEK 2 DAY 5

Shared Writing Card: Introduction of Side A

Setting the Scene

- Display various warm- and cold-weather clothing and review the names. You may use pictures, simple sketches, or real clothing to introduce these items.
- Tell children to pretend it is a warm, sunny day. Ask children what they would choose to wear. Ask them what would happen if they chose heavy clothing. Then ask them to pretend it is a cold and rainy day and to choose the appropriate clothes. Ask them what would happen if they chose light clothing.

Creating Comprehensible Input

- Display Shared Writing Card 8 showing a boy choosing clothing and doing homework. Begin by pointing to and naming individual items in the first cause-effect boxes: choose clothing–being outside.
  Model *Here is a boy. It's morning—See the time, and he is wearing pajamas. Here are clothes on the bed. Oh, I see—he's choosing what to wear today. Here he is outside. He seems cold. The other children are wearing warm clothes. He chose the wrong clothes and now he's cold.*
- Go back to the top illustration and use a think-aloud to talk through the illustrations. Point to the illustrations and trace the arrow with your finger.
  Top Illustration: *The boy is choosing what to wear.*
  Bottom Illustration: *The boy chose clothing for warm weather, but it's cold outside. He did not choose the right clothing for a cold day, and now he's cold.*
- Explain that the boxes and arrow on the Shared Writing Card help us understand choices and consequences just like on the back flap of the Big Book.
- Invite a volunteer from Stages 4 or 5 to summarize the choice and consequence represented in the two boxes on the left.
- Repeat the procedure for the two boxes on the right, emphasizing the positive consequences of his choosing to do his homework.

Scribing with the Graphic Organizer

- After children have become comfortable with the content of the illustrations, you can use the wipe-off marker provided to scribe while you brainstorm together captions for the graphic organizer. Since you are creating a graphic organizer, not a finished product, well-crafted sentences are not necessary.

- Think aloud as you write so that children have insight into the writing process.
- Here is an example of a simple shared writing labeling for the illustrations.
  Top-left Illustration: *boy chooses clothing*
  Bottom-left Illustration: *boy is cold in his clothing*
  Top-right Illustration: *boy chooses to do his homework*
  Bottom-right Illustration: *boy and teacher happy*

Writing Together from the Graphic Organizer

- You will again be holding the pen while you work with children to create a shared writing piece together. This time, you will model how to use the labels on the graphic organizer to create a finished paragraph on your easel pad.
- Begin with a think-aloud.
  Model *First let's give the boy a name. How about* Ivan? *Now we need to say what our writing is about. How does* Ivan makes choices every day *sound?*
- Write down the sentence you agree upon with the children.
- As you move from box to box, read the labels and then invite children to help you create sentences based on the pictures and labels. Write down what children say as you work to make sentences with them. When children offer sentences with errors in them, correct them without being overt. Encourage children to use classroom resources, such as the Word Wall. Be sure to write a concluding sentence about both good and bad choices.
- When you have finished your shared writing piece, read it together several times. Then hang it up on the wall where it can be displayed during the rest of the unit and reread many times. For now, do not erase your labels on Side A.

Phonics in Context

Shared writing provides an ideal opportunity for reviewing the phonics skills children are learning. Highlight the sounds in words like ***ch**oose* and ***wh**en* as you reread the writing.

Sample Shared Writing

Ivan makes choices every day. Sometimes Ivan does not choose the right clothes for the weather. He does not choose to wear a jacket when it is cold outside. He makes a bad choice and then he is uncomfortable. When Ivan chooses to do his homework, he feels good. His teacher is happy. He's glad he made a good choice. Sometimes Ivan makes bad choices. Other times he makes good ones.

WEEK 3 DAY 1

Big Book: Focus on Oral Language Development

Reread the Big Book and return to the text to focus on oral language development.

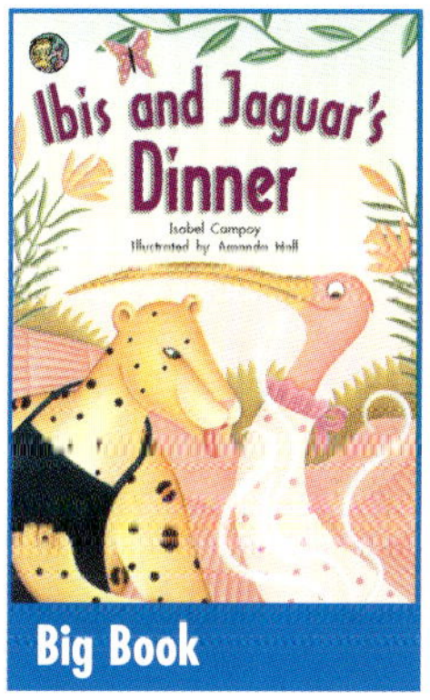

Grammar in Context: Appositives ❶❷❸❹❺

1. Model how to use appositives by describing a child sitting near the front of the class. Say, for example, *Ashok, a boy with black hair, is sitting in front of the class.* Point out that *a boy with black hair* tells us a little more about Ashok.
2. Continue in this way, making straightforward statements about various children in the class. Include an identifying piece of information about each child in the form of an appositive.
3. Encourage children to use appositives themselves by prompting them *Tell me something about Marta.* If they do not include an appositive, repeat their sentence, along with another one and then combine the two. For example, *Marta is my best friend. She is very nice. Marta, my best friend, is very nice.*
4. Reread page 2 of the Big Book. With your finger, underline the sentence "Who are you, my spotted friend?" Tell children *my spotted friend* tells a little more about *you.*
5. Go around the class, saying for example, *Who are you, young man?* and so on. Invite volunteers to take turns asking each other similar kinds of questions.

Guided Reading

As you work on this unit, conduct small groups of guided reading or shared-to-guided reading independent of thematic instruction. Instruction is provided in the Guided Reading section of this guide.

Language Learning Master

p. 69 ❶❷❸❹❺

You will need

- Shared Writing Card 8
- Wipe-off marker

Grammar in Context: Adjectives with *-ing* ❶❷❸❹❺

1. Open the Big Book to pages 18 and 19. Use adjectives with *-ing* endings to describe the animals shown. Invite children to point to the animal you're describing. *I see a monkey hanging from a tree. I see a fish jumping out of the water.* Encourage children to repeat this by asking them *What do you see?* Help children understand that the words *hanging* and *jumping* tell us more about who or what we're talking about. Continue describing the other animals in a game-like fashion. ◎

Options for STAGES

❸ These children may be able to respond with just the noun and the participle: *monkey hanging*

❹❺ These children should respond in phrases or sentences, such as *a monkey hanging from a tree.*

2. Turn to page 7. Ask children to find the *-ing* word that tells us more about Ibis.

WEEK 3 DAY 2

Shared Writing Card: Brainstorming Side B

Brainstorming a Topic

- Use Side A of the Shared Writing Card and your finished shared writing piece about the boy. Review how you used the graphic organizer's pictures and labels to form the basis of your finished piece.
- Turn the card over to Side B. Tell children that you will now think of your own topics together to draw in the graphic organizer. Brainstorm together a topic that involves making choices. For example, you can suggest writing a piece about what to do on a Saturday afternoon, what to eat for a snack, or how to spend an allowance.

Scribing with the Graphic Organizer

- Once the class has chosen a topic, you should decide on two options. If the topic is spending an allowance, for example, the class should think of at least two ways that it can be spent. Invite the class to tell you how the choices and the final decision can best be illustrated. Draw simple scenes in the blank boxes based on the children's suggestions.
- Now it's time to put labels on your graphic organizer. Elicit suggestions for labels from the group in the same manner as you did for Side A and record them on the Shared Writing Card.
- You will create the shared writing paragraph together in your next session.

Active Social Studies: A Good Citizen

1. Using gestures and examples to support comprehension, talk with children about what it means to be a good citizen, emphasizing the responsibility for common good and working together with others to improve the community.
2. Form heterogeneous groups of four or five children. Give each group an easel pad and a marker to record their ideas.
3. Tell children to list activities they could do to improve their school or community. One example might be to pick up litter around the school.
4. Invite groups to share their lists with the class.
5. Choose and implement a class community service project. Be sure to lead into the project and wrap up with a discussion of their chosen project.

You will need

- Easel pad
- Markers

WEEK 3 DAY 3

Shared Writing Card: Writing Together with Side B

- As with Side A, you will work together with children to create a finished writing piece from the graphic organizer on Side B of Shared Writing Card 8.
- Model how to start a paragraph for both sets of boxes, using think-alouds as you go. Show children how to use resources like the Word Wall. Work through wording for difficult concepts together.
- When you have finished your shared writing piece, read it together several times. Then hang it up on the wall where it can be displayed during the rest of the unit. At the end of the unit, you should erase both sides of the Shared Writing Card.

Manipulative Chart: Focus on Oral Language Development

Grammar in Context: Questions ❶❷❸❹❺

1. Sing the song together several times. Keep the spinner on $2.00 as you sing.
2. Draw children's attention to the spinner. Point to a section and say *This picture shows two dollars.* Introduce each of the successive sections, telling the money amount of each.
3. Ask *Which picture shows ten dollars?* Have volunteers respond with pointing or words, such as *the red one.* Confirm their responses *That's right. This picture shows ten dollars.*
4. Continue in this way, asking *which* questions about the sections in the spinner.
5. Display the Manipulative Chart and review the items. Ask *What do you want to buy? How much money will you need?* Invite volunteers to respond by pointing or with words.
6. Allow children to take turns posing questions and responding as they are able, such as *Which thing will you buy? Buy book.*

Language Learning Master

p. 70 ❶❷❸❹❺

WEEK 3 DAY 4

You will need

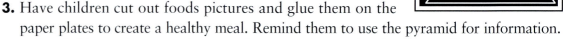

- Food or cooking magazines, supermarket flyers
- Scissors
- Paper plates
- Glue

Active Science: A Balanced Diet

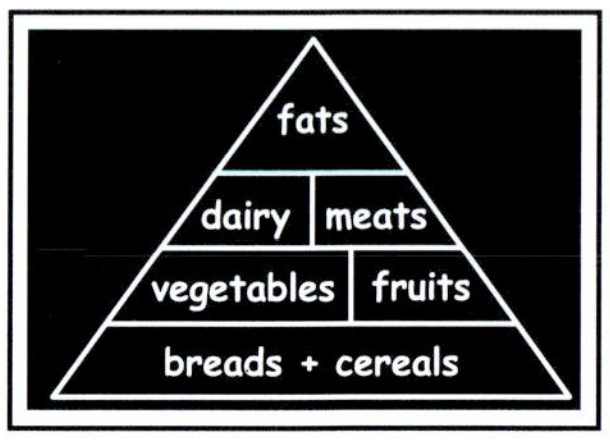

1. Draw a food pyramid on the board. Identify the foods within each group. Explain that we should eat more of the foods at the bottom and less of the foods toward the top.
2. Tell children that they will plan a healthy meal. Distribute food or cooking magazines, paper plates, scissors, and glue.
3. Have children cut out foods pictures and glue them on the paper plates to create a healthy meal. Remind them to use the pyramid for information.
4. Have children take turns showing their "meals" to the class and telling or showing why they chose each of the food items.

WEEK 3 DAY 5

You will need

- Overhead transparency of Writing Resource Guide, p. 94
- Overhead marker

Writing Resource Guide: A Simplified Graphic Organizer

This activity is optional and necessary only if you wish to use the simplified sequence graphic organizer in cooperative-group or independent writing.

Brainstorming a Topic

- Review the drawings and labels you used on Side B of the Shared Writing Card. Trace the arrow from the top boxes to the bottom boxes, telling about the choices and consequences shown.
- On the overhead projector, display a transparency of Writing Planner B on page 94 of the Writing Resource Guide, which is a choice-consequence graphic organizer with two boxes.
- Brainstorm together a simple topic that involves a choice and its consequence.

You will need

- Writing Resource Guide, pp. 93–94
- Markers

Scribing with the Graphic Organizer

- Once the class has arrived at a topic, you should decide together on the choices and the outcome. Model drawing scenes in each of the two boxes.
- Write labels for each of the boxes. Elicit suggestions for labels from the group in the same manner as you did with the Shared Writing Card.

Writing Resource Guide: Cooperative-Group Writing

- Form cooperative groups of heterogeneous Stages with three to four children each to work together on a writing piece using the graphic organizer. You may hand out a copy of Writing Planner A or B to each group.
- Review the shared writing graphic organizers and finished pieces you have made together. Remind children that the drawings can help them to organize their writing.
- Have the groups work together first to complete their graphic organizers and then to write their finished pieces. Circulate to provide assistance. ◎

Writing Mini-lessons

See the Writing Resource Guide for mini-lessons to use as children write. Here are some suggestions:

- Mini-lesson 34: Focusing on Meaning
- Mini-lesson 39: Adding Details

Options for STAGES

❶❷ These children should draw the pictures for the group.

❸❹❺ These children should take responsibility for the writing of the finished piece.

WEEK 4 DAY 1

Big Book: Focus on Literacy Skills

Word Level: Phonics in Context

1. You will need the Word Wall Starters with the Ibis and Jaguar symbol on them: *friend*, *must*, *show*, *when*. These are pictured in the back of the Big Book.
2. Tell children that you want to choose some special words from the story for them to take a closer look at.
3. Introduce the word *friend* by saying it clearly, elongating the *nd* sound, and drawing attention to the highlighting behind the *nd*. Then repeat /end/ several times. *The letters* end *make the /end/ sound. Let's say the word* friend *together*: friend. *Can you hear how* friend *ends with* end? *Let's sing a song.* Review Phonics Song Chart 30 together.
4. Say *I'm going to put the word* friend *below the* nd *label.* Walk over to your Word Wall and place the card *friend* under the *nd* label. Remind children that they can use the Ibis and Jaguar symbol to help them remember where they "met" that word before.
5. Repeat a similar procedure for the other words and phonics skills.

Sentence Level: Dialogue in Text

1. Reread page 2 of the Big Book. When you come to the first quotation marks, point them out to children. Think aloud about how quotation marks cue dialogue.
   Model *When I come to a quotation mark, I know that someone is about to talk. I read the words after the mark to see what the character is saying. When I see the quotation mark again, I know that the speaker is finished talking. Here, I know Jaguar is speaking because it says "asked Jaguar."*
2. Ask children what Ibis says in response to Jaguar's question. Help children recognize the quotation marks and "said the bird" as signals that help us know who is talking and what they are saying.
3. Turn to pages 8 and 9 and ask children to identify who is speaking and what they are saying. Encourage children to articulate how they know.
4. Continue in this manner through the rest of the story.

Text Level: Distinguishing Fantasy from Reality

1. Display the cover of the Big Book. Compare it to Picture Card 11: ibis and Picture Card 12: jaguar. Discuss what is real about the cover and what is fantasy. For example, they look like the real animals, but animals don't wear aprons.
2. Flip through pages 2 through 11, which depict the animals' friendship. Ask *Do you really think an ibis and jaguar would be friends?* Explain that this is fantasy, like their wearing aprons.

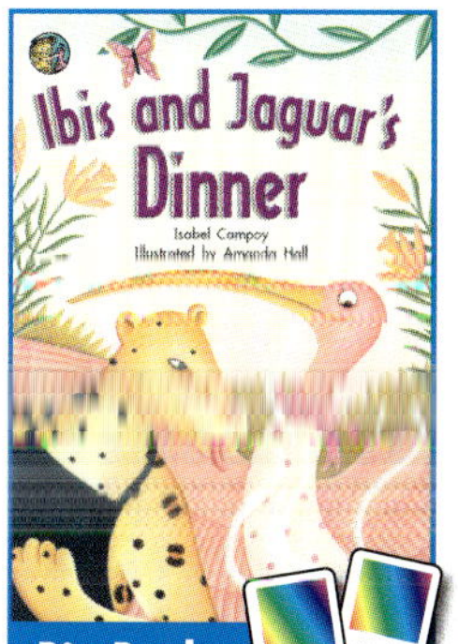

Big Book
Picture Cards 11, 12

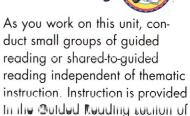

Guided Reading

As you work on this unit, conduct small groups of guided reading or shared-to-guided reading independent of thematic instruction. Instruction is provided in the Guided Reading section of this guide.

Home-School Connection

Send home page 87 of the Home-School Connection Masters for children to use in retelling *Ibis and Jaguar's Dinner* to their families. They should retell the story in English, and then talk about it in either English or their home language.

3. Continue looking through the story. Invite children to point out other elements of fantasy, such as their eating at a table, using dishes, and so on.
4. Extend the discussion by asking children to point out elements of reality in the story, such as their living in the jungle.

Options for STAGES

❶❷ Ask these children yes/no questions: *Do jaguars really use dishes?* Use pantomime and gestures to support comprehension of questions.

❸❹❺ These children can discuss elements of fantasy and reality in the story using phrases or sentences.

You will need

- Previously prepared game boards, spinners, and markers

Language Practice Game: Version 2 ❶❷❸❹❺

Have children at Stages 3, 4, and 5 form partners. Provide a copy of the spinners with words only to each pair and a game sheet with the pyramid to each child. Give each child six game markers, one for each square in the pyramid. Model the following directions for this innovation on the game.

1. Player 1 spins and sees the amount of money indicated by the spinner. The player must state what he or she wants to buy on the pyramid with that amount and why: *I have two dollars. I will buy the puzzle. It will be fun to do on a rainy day.* This provides practice with the language function *Justify*.
2. Player 2 should confirm that Player 1 can indeed afford to buy what he or she has chosen with the money available. Player 1 then places a marker on his or her choice or choices.
3. Players continue to take turns. The first player to cover all six squares on his or her pyramid is the winner.

WEEK 4 DAY 2

You will need

- Play coins and bills

Active Math: Money Math

1. Form heterogeneous groups of mixed language abilities with two or three children each. Distribute one of each play coin and bill shown to each group.
2. Have children arrange their money from lowest value to highest. Invite groups to name the coins and bills.
3. Next, distribute multiple play coins and bills to each group. Write a dollar value on the board, such as $3.75. Have groups count out that amount of money. Encourage children to tell or show which coins and bills they used. Continue the activity with other money amounts.

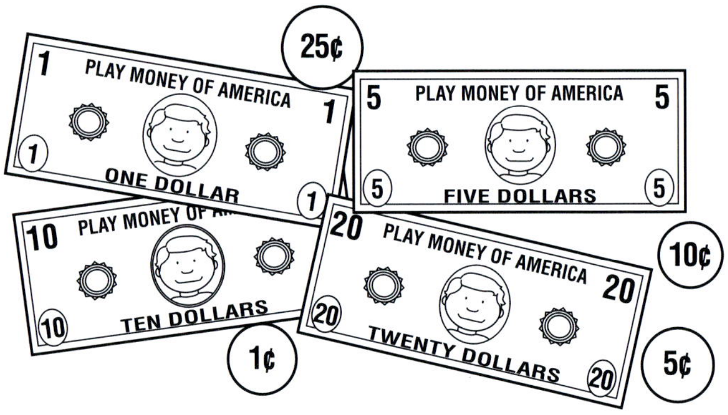

End-of-Unit Assessment

- While children are engaged in activities this week, pull them individually for the Big Book retelling, using page U195 at the end of this unit.
- Select children with whom you would like to use the Open-Ended Oral Assessment on pages U194 and U195 of this unit and pull them individually during activities this week. We recommend assessing about one-fourth of your class each unit.
- You should also have gathered the following for their assessment portfolio:
  - page 68 of the Language Learning Masters
  - page 69 of the Language Learning Masters
  - finished writing piece assessed according to the Writing Rubric on page A6.

You will need

A copy of page U195 at the end of this unit for each child

WEEK 4 DAY 3–4

Writing Resource Guide: Individual Writing

- Children have engaged in a step-by-step writing process moving toward independence. They began with teacher-led writing, moved to cooperative groups, and are now ready to work individually.
- Provide a copy of Writing Planner A or B to each child. They may need individual conferencing on choosing a topic. ◎

You will need

- Writing Resource Guide pp. 93–94
- Markers

Options for STAGES

❶❷ and Emergent Level
These children should draw a choice and a consequence on their graphic organizer. They should label their drawings on their own or dictate labels to you.

❸❹❺ Early Level and Above
These children can work more independently to draw pictures and write labels on their graphic organizers to record their topic. They should then use the graphic organizer to create a finished piece.

- When children have completed the finished product, whether graphic organizer or paragraph, you should assess it using the Writing Rubric on page A6 of this Teacher's Guide.

Assessment

Continue pulling some children for the Big Book Retelling and Open-Ended Oral Language Assessment as others write.

WEEK 4 DAY 5

Theme Project: Sharing

- Have groups present their menus to the class. Have one member point out items as another member reads the names and prices of some of the items.
- Tell groups that they will pretend they are going to a restaurant. Have groups exchange menus and role-play looking over the menus and ordering food.
- After sharing time is over, allow time for questions and feedback. Model appropriate feedback by making the first comment yourself—for example, *I like the choices on this menu. Can you add dollar signs to the prices so they are easier to read?*

Open-Ended Oral Language Assessment

Reassess children's Language Acquisition Stages. Begin with an open-ended prompt like the first one below. If children are unable to respond, intervene with increasingly directed prompts, such as the second and third ones below.

What can you tell me about the picture?

What prices do you see?

Do you see a price tag?

Assessment Directions: Copy this form for each child and place the completed form in the child's portfolio. Locate the child's Language Acquisition Stage for each of the first four activities and assess his or her performance during the unit according to expectations for that Stage. For the Big Book Retelling, pull children to retell the Big Book during end-of-unit assessment time. Use the Open-Ended Oral Language Assessment to reassess children's Language Acquisition Stages with one-fourth of your students for each unit, using the back side of the sheet to take notes. *For more guidance on assessment, see pages T33 and T34.*

Unit 8 Assessment

Name ______________________ **Date** ____________

On Our Way to English Grade 2	STAGE EXPECTATIONS ❶	❷	❸	❹	❺
Fluency Manipulative Chart Student Version, page U180 *How does the child respond when manipulating the mini-chart along with the Oral Language CD?*	Chooses an appropriate item for the monetary value. ☐ Yes ☐ Not yet	Chooses an appropriate item, naming it correctly. ☐ Yes ☐ Not yet	Chooses an appropriate item, approximating sentences and substitutions. ☐ Yes ☐ Not yet	Chooses an appropriate item, singing the verse with few, if any, errors. ☐ Yes ☐ Not yet	
Content Area Knowledge Language Practice Game: Version 1, page U181 *How does the child demonstrate an understanding of correspondence between available money and prize?*	Places markers on items that are within the amount indicated on the spinner. ☐ Yes ☐ Not yet	Places markers on items within the amount indicated, naming the monetary value or the items. ☐ Yes ☐ Not yet	Places markers on items within the amount indicated on the spinner while telling what he or she will buy, with short phrases, such as *five dollars choose flashlight.* ☐ Yes ☐ Not yet		Places markers on items within the amount indicated on the spinner, telling in complete sentences what he or she will buy. ☐ Yes ☐ Not yet
Social Language Function Agree/Disagree, page U185 *How does the child respond during the Function Mini-lesson?*	Responds nonverbally or with a basic word or phrase such as *agree.* ☐ Yes ☐ Not yet		Approximates a sentence such as *I agree.* ☐ Yes ☐ Not yet	Responds with complete, full sentence. ☐ Yes ☐ Not yet	
Academic Language Function Justify and Persuade, page U185 *How does the child respond during the Function Mini-lesson?*			Gives reason for choice in a short phrase, such as *because I like.* ☐ Yes ☐ Not yet	Is able to give reasons for choosing a particular occupation, using phrases or sentences. ☐ Yes ☐ Not yet	
Big Book Retelling page U185 *Have each child use stick puppets (page U184) to retell by dramatizing key scenes from the story. How does the child retell the story?*	Manipulates the puppets in a meaningful way while listening to the teacher or others retell the story. ☐ Yes ☐ Not yet	Retells using a few words while manipulating the puppets. ☐ Yes ☐ Not yet	Retells using longer phrases or simple sentence. ☐ Yes ☐ Not yet	Retells using complete sentences in connected discourse with few errors. ☐ Yes ☐ Not yet	Retells using story language approximating or similar to native-speaking peers. ☐ Yes ☐ Not yet
Open-Ended Oral Language Assessment, page U194 *Use the child's responses to the illustration to reassess the child's Stage of Language Acquisition.*	☐ **STAGE ❶** Uses few or no words; gestures or points.	☐ **STAGE ❷** Uses words or short phrases.	☐ **STAGE ❸** Uses phrases and simple sentences.	☐ **STAGE ❹** Uses sentences in connected discourse.	☐ **STAGE ❺** Uses language comparable to native-speaking peers.

Appendix

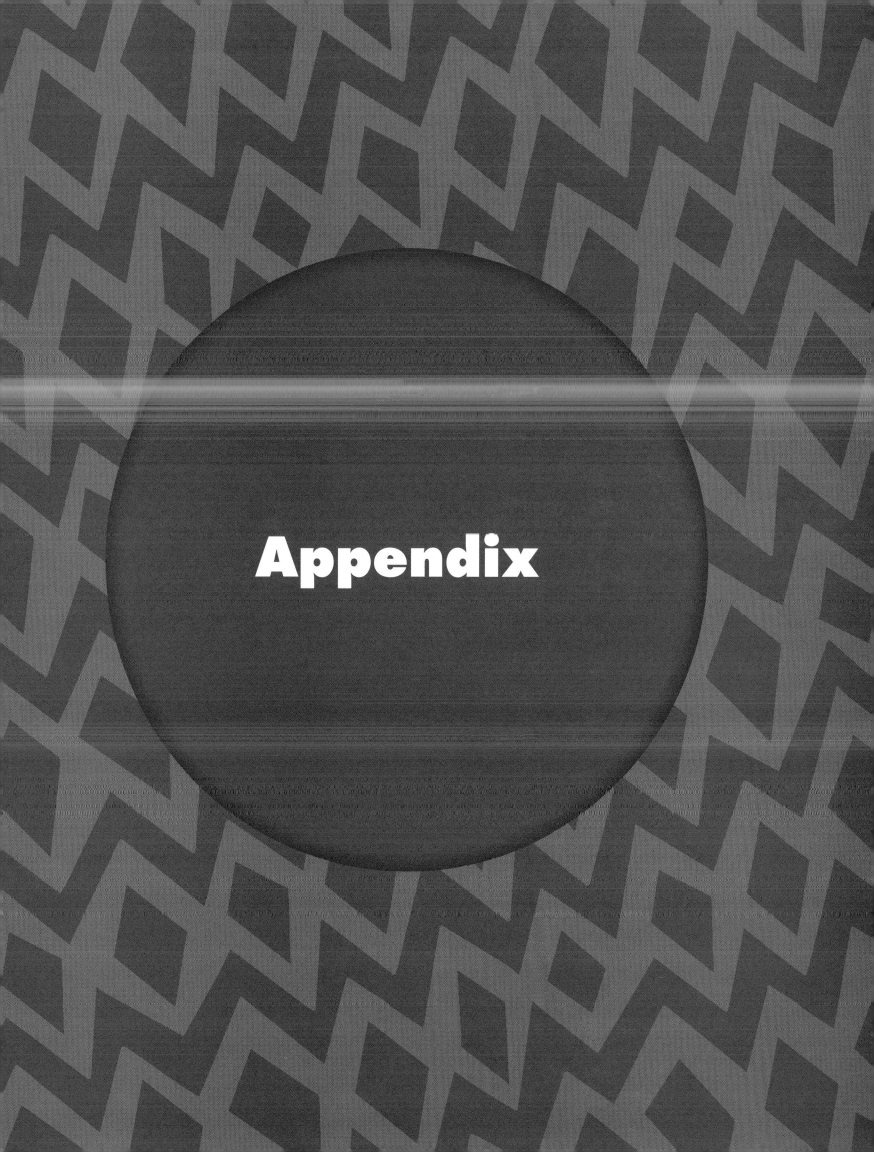

Appendix

Ongoing Records Schedule A2

Pre- and Post-Retelling A3

Oral Language Rubric A5

Writing Rubric for English Language Writers A6

Snapshots of Young English Language Writers A8

Thematic Unit Assessment Summary Sheet A10

K–5 Scope and Sequence A11

Language Functions Scope A18

Language Learning Strategies Scope A20

Bibliography A22

Ongoing Records Schedule

Assessment	When to Record	Information Provided	Page Reference
Retelling Pre- and Post-Test (used with Oral Language Rubric)	Month 1 Month 8	• Stage of Language Acquisition for program entry/exit	A3
Oral Language Rubric	Used with Retelling Pre- and Post-Test and Open-Ended Oral Language Assessment	• Stage of Language Acquisition	A5
Writing Rubric	Used with Writing Sample and Unit Writing Sample	• Writing Level	A6
Writing Sample (used with Writing Rubric)	Month 1	• Writing Level	None
Writing Self-Assessment	Month 1 Month 4 Month 8	• writing attitudes and perceptions	Writing Resource Guide pp. 95 and 96
Unit Assessment	Monthly during each unit	• fluency • content-area knowledge • language function facility • shared reading retelling	U24, U49, U73, U97, U121, U125, U168, U193
Open-Ended Oral Language Assessment	Monthly following each unit	• oral language development	U26, U50, U74, U98, U122, U146, U170, U194
Unit Writing Sample (Writing Planners)	Monthly during each unit	• Writing Level	Writing Resource Guide pp. 79–94
Language Learning Masters	Monthly following each unit	• grammar development	See Thematic Unit lessons

Pre- and Post-Retelling

The *On Our Way to English* Pre- and Post-Retelling is an oral language assessment intended as an initial screening tool for Stage placement within the program. Using the five Stages of Language Acquisition, this assessment tool helps you to determine a child's level of language proficiency from Stage 1 Preproduction to Stage 5 Advanced Fluency. This tool is also intended to measure progress—you can reuse it at the program level to assess students' language proficiency over the course of the year.

To use the assessment, copy the stories and retelling prompts on page A3. Administer the test to one child at a time. Allow about ten minutes per child. Invite the child to look at the pictures on page A4. Read the story aloud, pointing to the pictures as you read to provide comprehensible input. When you have finished reading, start the cassette recorder and tell the child, "Please use the pictures to retell the story." If the child is having difficulty, use the retelling prompts provided below the story one at a time as needed. Later, listen to the recorded retelling and refer to the criteria in the Oral Language Rubric provided on page A5 to determine the child's appropriate Stage of Language Acquisition.

Grade 2

The Bike Ride

[1] One day in early spring, Carlos and his brother Felipe decided to ride their bikes to the park. Felipe was older and stronger, so it was easy for him to ride more quickly than Carlos. [2] When Carlos pedaled hard to catch up, they heard a big BANG! Carlos had a flat tire. "Oh no!" said Carlos. "What can I do?" Carlos was very disappointed.

[3] "I'll help you," answered Felipe. Together they walked the bikes home, where Felipe could fix the tire. He took the tire off and began to work on it. After he had finished, Felipe put the tire back on the bike and pumped air into it. He said, "Here you go, Carlos!"

[4] Soon the two set out again and rode all the way to the park without stopping. They had a wonderful time there, and Carlos realized that it's good to have a big brother.

Retelling Prompts

1. Tell me about Carlos and Felipe.
2. What made Carlos and Felipe stop riding?
3. Why was Carlos disappointed?
4. Why do Carlos and Felipe go home?
5. What happens at the end of the story?

Pre- and Post-Retelling Point to each illustration as you read the story to the child. Then start the cassette recorder and say *Please use the pictures to retell the story.* Use the retelling prompts provided on A3 as needed.

Oral Language Rubric for *On Our Way to English*

STAGE 1: Preproduction	**Comprehension** Understands little of everyday English. **Message** Communicates primarily through gestures or single-word utterances. Able to communicate only the most rudimentary needs. **Fluency and Sentence Structure** Produces little, if any, spoken English.
STAGE 2: Early Production	**Comprehension** Understands some social conversation but limited academic conversation. **Message** Uses routine expressions to convey basic needs and ideas. To some extent, continues to rely on gestures to communicate. **Fluency and Sentence Structure** Uses some basic words and simple phrases. **Word Choice and Academic Language** Relies on routine language expressions. May use some academic words in isolation.
STAGE 3: Speech Emergence	**Comprehension** Understands most of what is said in social and academic conversation but exhibits occasional lack of understanding. **Message** Participates in everyday conversations about familiar topics. Although speech contains errors that sometimes hinder communication, child can often convey his or her basic message. **Fluency and Sentence Structure** Produces longer, complete phrases and some sentences. **Word Choice and Academic Language** Relies on high-frequency words and sometimes cannot fully communicate ideas due to a lack of sufficient vocabulary. Uses some academic language although not always successfully.
STAGE 4: Intermediate Fluency	**Comprehension** Rarely experiences a lack of understanding in social and academic situations. **Message** Engages in ordinary conversation. Although errors may be present, they generally do not hinder communication. Successfully communicates most ideas to others. **Fluency and Sentence Structure** Engages in ordinary conversation with some complex sentences. Errors no longer hinder communication. **Word Choice and Academic Language** Range of vocabulary and academic language allows child to communicate well on everyday topics. Begins to use idioms. Occasionally uses inappropriate terms and/or must rephrase to work around unknown vocabulary.
STAGE 5: Advanced Fluency	**Comprehension** Understands social and academic conversation without difficulty. **Message** Uses English successfully to convey his or her ideas to others. **Fluency and Sentence Structure** Speech appears to be fluent and effortless, approximating that of native-speaking peers. **Word Choice and Academic Language** Use of vocabulary, academic language, and idioms approximates that of native-speaking peers.

Writing Rubric for English Language Writers

Use the following writing rubric in evaluating the writing of your English language learners. The rubric was designed specifically with English language learners in mind and focuses on providing criteria for evaluating informational writing, the focus of the *On Our Way to English* program.

Writing Level 1	**Message and Content** Unable to respond or draws a picture or dictates a message (in English or primary language). **Conventions of English** May know the direction that print goes and use some conventional symbols in a random fashion.
Writing Level 2	**Message and Content** Copies environmental print or labels drawings or writes a simple message. **Conventions of English** Begins to use spacing between words and sound-symbol relationships to produce temporary spelling. **Word Choice and Academic Language** May use isolated academic terms in labeling or dictation.
Writing Level 3	**Message and Content** With the support of a graphic organizer and a topic about which he or she can produce connected oral discourse, the child produces phrases or sentences that convey a message on one topic. **Conventions of English** Uses sound-symbol relationships to spell and groups words in phrases or sentences. Begins to use uppercase and lowercase conventionally. May make spelling errors that reflect his or her nonnative English pronunciation or native-language spelling patterns. **Word Choice and Academic Language** If academic language is included, it is often used inappropriately or imprecisely. **Fluency and Sentence Structure** Phrases or sentences can generally be understood by adults but may be repetitive and simple. Word order may reflect native-language word order.

There are four areas of evaluation within the levels: Message and Content, Conventions of English, Word Choice and Academic Language, and Fluency and Sentence Structure. The first two writing levels use only some of these areas since all are not appropriate.

Writing Level 4	**Message and Content** With the support of a graphic organizer, the child produces a piece of writing that has a beginning, middle, and end, as well as sentences on a single topic. **Conventions of English** Spells words in common word families and uses most punctuation conventionally. **Word Choice and Academic Language** Shows a range of vocabulary and varied word choice with some academic language used appropriately. **Fluency and Sentence Structure** Word order generally reflects English word order. Sentences may be simple but complete and perhaps loosely connected to one another or run-ons.
Writing Level 5	**Message and Content** With the support of a graphic organizer, the child writes several paragraphs with cohesive structure and connected sentences. **Conventions of English** Uses spelling and punctuation accurately. Uses verb tenses and first/third person appropriately. May experiment with more complex verb forms. **Word Choice and Academic Language** Selects vocabulary, including academic language, appropriately and according to audience and purpose. **Fluency and Sentence Structure** Uses some compound sentences with conjunctions. Begins to use connecting words, although perhaps, inconsistently or inappropriately.
Writing Level 6	**Message and Content** Writes several pages with paragraphs in logical sequence and descriptions that are coherently developed. **Conventions of English** Has control of conventions appropriate to grade level. Uses complex verb forms skillfully. **Word Choice and Academic Language** Uses a wide range of vocabulary appropriate to audience, purpose, and style. Uses grade-level academic language effectively. **Fluency and Sentence Structure** Uses a range of sentence structures, including complex sentences. Uses connecting words effectively.

Snapshots of Young English Language Writers

While the English language learners in your classroom are engaged in authentic writing experiences within the Writing Resource Guide, your task is to observe their use of writing strategies, skills, and behaviors. Writing samples from young writers are powerful indicators of children's knowledge of written language. An analysis of writing samples gives you a "snapshot" of the child as a writer. Knowing what to look for in a writing sample is key to its value for assessment. This is a skill that improves with practice and with increased knowledge about literacy development. The following are samples of writing from English language learners that represent each of the six levels of the Writing Rubric.

Appropriate Mini-Lessons from the Writing Resource Guide to use with this child are:

- What Is Writing? on page 24.
- Drawing/Talking About the Pictures on page 32.
- Directionality on pages 37–39.

Sample for Level 1

Appropriate Mini-Lessons from the Writing Resource Guide to use with this child are:

- Copying Environmental Print on page 36.
- Using a Variety of Sentence Patterns on page 64.
- Using Writing Resources on page 70.

Appropriate Mini-Lessons from the Writing Resource Guide to use with this child are:

- One-to-One Correspondence on page 42.
- Describing Words on page 55.
- Reading Your Work to Yourself on page 57.

Sample for Level 2

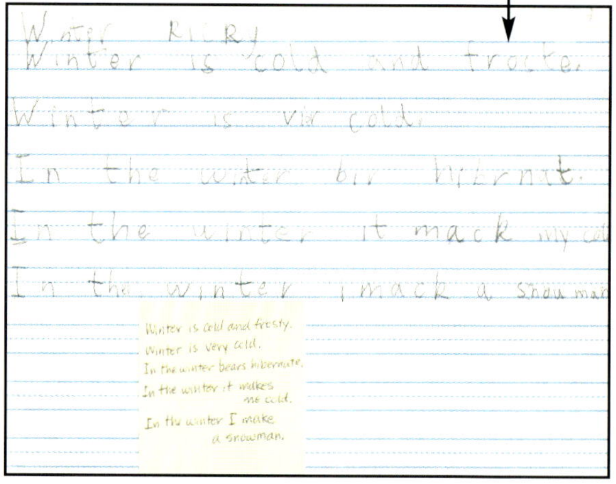

Sample for Level 3

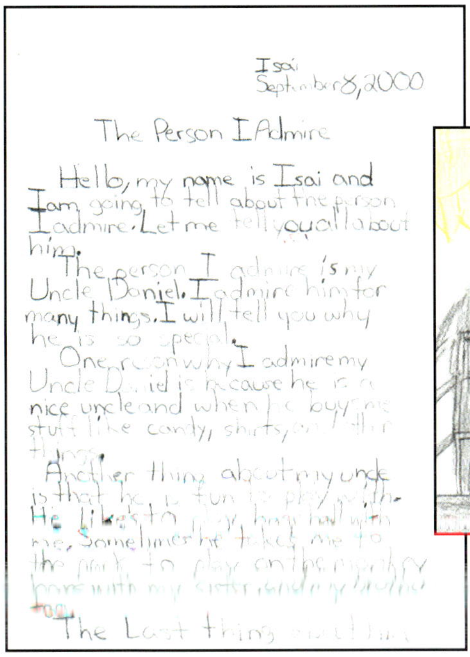

Isai
September 8, 2000

The Person I Admire

Hello, my name is Isai and I am going to tell about the person I admire. Let me tell you all about him.

The person I admire is my Uncle Daniel. I admire him for many things. I will tell you why he is so special.

One reason why I admire my Uncle Daniel is because he is a nice uncle and when he buys me stuff like candy, shirts, and other things.

Another thing about my uncle is that he is fun to play with. He likes to play baseball with me. Sometimes he takes me to the park to play on the monkey bars with my sister and my brother too.

The Last thing about him

Sample for Level 4

Appropriate Mini-Lessons from the Writing Resource Guide to use with this child are:

- Copying Environmental Print on page 36.
- Describing Words on page 55.
- Reading Your Work to Yourself on page 57.

Appropriate Mini-Lessons from the Writing Resource Guide to use with this child are:

- Describing Words on page 55.
- Reading Your Work to Yourself on page 57.
- Asking for Comments on page 59.

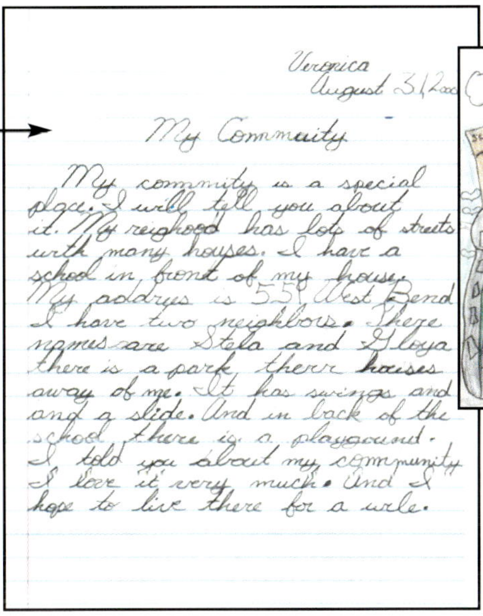

Veronica
August 31, 2000

My Commuity

My commity is a special plac. I will tell you about it. My neighood has lots of streets with many houses. I have a school in front of my house. My addrys is 551 West Bend. I have two neighbors. There names are Stela and Gloya. There is a park there houses away of me. It has swings and and a slide. And in back of the school there is a playground. I told you about my community. I love it very much. And I hope to live there for a wile.

Sample for Level 5

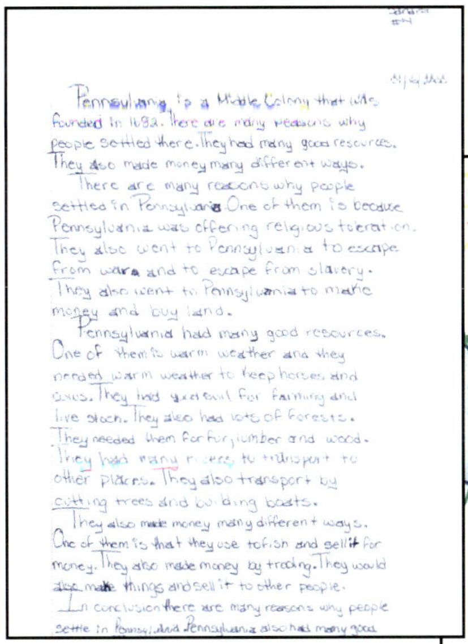

Pennsylvania is a Middle Colony that was founded in 1682. There are many reasons why people settled there. They had many good resources. They also made money many different ways.

There are many reasons why people settled in Pennsylvania. One of them is because Pennsylvania was offering religious toleration. They also went to Pennsylvania to escape from wars and to escape from slavery. They also went to Pennsylvania to make money and buy land.

Pennsylvania had many good resources. One of them is warm weather and they needed warm weather to keep horses and cows. They had good soil for farming and live stock. They also had lots of forests. They needed them for fur, lumber and wood. They had many rivers to transport to other places. They also transport by cutting trees and building boats.

They also made money many different ways. One of them is that they use to fish and sell it for money. They also made money by trading. They would also make things and sell it to other people.

In conclusion there are many reasons why people settle in Pennsylvania. Pennsylvania also had many good

Sample for Level 6

Appropriate Mini-Lessons from the Writing Resource Guide to use with this child are:

- Adding Interesting Words on page 63.
- Using a Variety of Sentence Patterns on page 64.
- Choosing a Title on page 76.

Thematic Unit Assessment Summary Sheet

Name: ______________________ **Grade:** ______

	Unit 1	Unit 2	Unit 3	Unit 4	Unit 5	Unit 6	Unit 7	Unit 8
Fluency	Does the child meet the expectations for Stage ___ ? ☐ Yes ☐ No	Does the child meet the expectations for Stage ___ ? ☐ Yes ☐ No	Does the child meet the expectations for Stage ___ ? ☐ Yes ☐ No	Does the child meet the expectations for Stage ___ ? ☐ Yes ☐ No	Does the child meet the expectations for Stage ___ ? ☐ Yes ☐ No	Does the child meet the expectations for Stage ___ ? ☐ Yes ☐ No	Does the child meet the expectations for Stage ___ ? ☐ Yes ☐ No	Does the child meet the expectations for Stage ___ ? ☐ Yes ☐ No
Content Area Knowledge	Does the child meet the expectations for Stage ___ ? ☐ Yes ☐ No	Does the child meet the expectations for Stage ___ ? ☐ Yes ☐ No	Does the child meet the expectations for Stage ___ ? ☐ Yes ☐ No	Does the child meet the expectations for Stage ___ ? ☐ Yes ☐ No	Does the child meet the expectations for Stage ___ ? ☐ Yes ☐ No	Does the child meet the expectations for Stage ___ ? ☐ Yes ☐ No	Does the child meet the expectations for Stage ___ ? ☐ Yes ☐ No	Does the child meet the expectations for Stage ___ ? ☐ Yes ☐ No
Social Language Function	Does the child meet the expectations for Stage ___ ? ☐ Yes ☐ No	Does the child meet the expectations for Stage ___ ? ☐ Yes ☐ No	Does the child meet the expectations for Stage ___ ? ☐ Yes ☐ No	Does the child meet the expectations for Stage ___ ? ☐ Yes ☐ No	Does the child meet the expectations for Stage ___ ? ☐ Yes ☐ No	Does the child meet the expectations for Stage ___ ? ☐ Yes ☐ No	Does the child meet the expectations for Stage ___ ? ☐ Yes ☐ No	Does the child meet the expectations for Stage ___ ? ☐ Yes ☐ No
Academic Language Function	Does the child meet the expectations for Stage ___ ? ☐ Yes ☐ No	Does the child meet the expectations for Stage ___ ? ☐ Yes ☐ No	Does the child meet the expectations for Stage ___ ? ☐ Yes ☐ No	Does the child meet the expectations for Stage ___ ? ☐ Yes ☐ No	Does the child meet the expectations for Stage ___ ? ☐ Yes ☐ No	Does the child meet the expectations for Stage ___ ? ☐ Yes ☐ No	Does the child meet the expectations for Stage ___ ? ☐ Yes ☐ No	Does the child meet the expectations for Stage ___ ? ☐ Yes ☐ No
Big Book Retelling	Does the child meet the expectations for Stage ___ ? ☐ Yes ☐ No	Does the child meet the expectations for Stage ___ ? ☐ Yes ☐ No	Does the child meet the expectations for Stage ___ ? ☐ Yes ☐ No	Does the child meet the expectations for Stage ___ ? ☐ Yes ☐ No	Does the child meet the expectations for Stage ___ ? ☐ Yes ☐ No	Does the child meet the expectations for Stage ___ ? ☐ Yes ☐ No	Does the child meet the expectations for Stage ___ ? ☐ Yes ☐ No	Does the child meet the expectations for Stage ___ ? ☐ Yes ☐ No
Open-Ended Oral Language Assessment	Stage Assessment ☐ Stage 1 ☐ Stage 2 ☐ Stage 3 ☐ Stage 4 ☐ Stage 5	Stage Assessment ☐ Stage 1 ☐ Stage 2 ☐ Stage 3 ☐ Stage 4 ☐ Stage 5	Stage Assessment ☐ Stage 1 ☐ Stage 2 ☐ Stage 3 ☐ Stage 4 ☐ Stage 5	Stage Assessment ☐ Stage 1 ☐ Stage 2 ☐ Stage 3 ☐ Stage 4 ☐ Stage 5	Stage Assessment ☐ Stage 1 ☐ Stage 2 ☐ Stage 3 ☐ Stage 4 ☐ Stage 5	Stage Assessment ☐ Stage 1 ☐ Stage 2 ☐ Stage 3 ☐ Stage 4 ☐ Stage 5	Stage Assessment ☐ Stage 1 ☐ Stage 2 ☐ Stage 3 ☐ Stage 4 ☐ Stage 5	Stage Assessment ☐ Stage 1 ☐ Stage 2 ☐ Stage 3 ☐ Stage 4 ☐ Stage 5

K–5 Scope and Sequence

	K	1	2	3	4	5
Comprehension						
Uses prior knowledge and experiences						
Activates existing background knowledge	●	●	●	●		
Makes connections with text based on personal experiences and knowledge					●	●
Makes connections with text based on educational experience and knowledge					●	●
Builds background knowledge	●	●	●	●		
Uses illustrations and text features to help store important new information					●	●
Determines what is important in text						
Recognizes how readers use capitalization and punctuation to comprehend	●					
Identifies main ideas or theme	●	●	●	●		
Identifies main ideas and supporting details					●	●
Utilizes text features and text structures to determine importance			●	●		
Uses personal beliefs, experiences, and prior learning to determine importance					●	●
Recognizes cause and effect			●	●	●	●
Compares and contrasts information	●	●	●	●		
Classifies and ranks important vs. unimportant information					●	●
Considers purpose for reading	●	●	●	●	●	●
Recognizes theme and relevance to reader						●
Draws inferences						
Makes and confirms predictions	●	●	●	●		
Makes, changes, and checks predictions					●	●
Draws conclusions with support drawn from text		●	●	●	●	●
Makes generalizations			●	●	●	●
Forms and supports opinions			●	●		
Creates personal interpretation			●	●		
Forms personal interpretations					●	●
Makes critical judgments					●	●
Asks questions						
Asks questions to clarify meaning	●	●	●	●		
Asks in order to clarify and extend comprehension					●	●
Asks questions to understand author		●	●	●		
Asks questions to understand key themes		●	●	●		
Asks in order to preview, plan reading, and predict					●	●
Asks in order to understand how genre influences comprehension					●	●
Asks to recognize and interpret story elements and text features				●	●	●

	K	1	2	3	4	5
Synthesizes Information						
Connects ideas from several different sources Text-to-text Text-to-self Text-to-world		●	●	●	●	●
Sequences ideas and story events	●	●	●	●	●	●
Summarizes information		●	●	●	●	●
Classifies and categorizes information	●	●	●	●		
Retells story events or key facts	●	●	●	●		
Retells in order to clarify					●	●
Considers author's viewpoint, purpose, and style			●	●	●	●
Focuses on text elements to understand overall meaning and theme					●	●
Shares, recommends, and criticizes what is read				●	●	●
Reacts to and interprets what is read				●	●	●
Uses sensory images						
Creates or uses images from all senses	●	●	●	●		
Makes connections with all 5 senses and with emotions					●	●
Visualizes information from text, illustrations, diagrams, etc.	●	●	●	●	●	●
Uses fix-up strategies to monitor comprehension						
Rereads text	●	●	●	●		
Rereads and reviews text					●	●
Reads on		●	●	●	●	●
Adjusts pace			●	●	●	●
Uses decoding skills	●	●	●	●		
Uses decoding, word analysis, syntactic and context clues for word recognition or pronunciation					●	●
Self-monitors by asking questions		●	●	●		
Changes your mind while reading						●
Identifies synonyms, antonyms, homonyms, homophones				●	●	●

Literacy Skills

	K	1	2	3	4	5
Phonological Awareness						
Identifies words within sentences *(see also Concepts of Print)*	●	●				
Identifies syllables within spoken words	●	●				
Recognizes and produces rhyming words	●	●	●	●		
Identifies and isolates initial and final sounds in spoken words	●	●	●			
Identifies and matches initial and final sounds in spoken words	●	●	●			
Blends phonemes to make words	●	●	●			
Segments one-syllable words into initial, medial, and final sounds	●	●	●			
Deletes phonemes to change words		●	●			
Adds phonemes to change words		●	●			

	K	1	2	3	4	5
Phonics and decoding						
Names and identifies letters of the alphabet	●	●				
Knows order of the alphabet	●	●				
Uses knowledge of letter-sound relationships to decode	●	●	●	●	●	●
Develops and applies knowledge of consonant sounds		●	●	●	●	●
Develops and applies knowledge of consonant blends		●	●	●	●	●
Develops and applies knowledge of consonant digraphs		●	●	●	●	●
Develops and applies knowledge consonant patterns, such as *kn, wr, dge, tch*				●	●	●
Develops and applies knowledge of short vowels	●	●	●	●	●	●
Develops and applies knowledge of long vowels		●	●	●	●	●
Develops and applies knowledge of complex vowel patterns: *oo, au, aw, al, all*			●	●	●	●
Uses knowledge of vowel diphthongs		●	●	●	●	●
Uses knowledge of vowel digraphs		●	●	●	●	●
Uses knowledge of vowel variants, i.e. one vowel sound can have more than one spelling (e.g., *clue, new, to*) or one spelling can have more than one sound		●	●	●	●	●
Demonstrates understanding of r-controlled vowels		●	●	●	●	●
Uses knowledge of word families to decode		●	●	●	●	●
Reads more complex and irregularly spelled words		●	●	●	●	●
Uses knowledge of spelling patterns to decode (CVC, CVCe, CV)		●	●	●	●	●
Uses knowledge of syllables to decode multi-syllable words		●	●	●	●	●

	K	1	2	3	4	5
Concepts of Print and Structural Analysis						
Develops an understanding of letters and words	●	●				
Develops an understanding of sentences and paragraphs		●	●	●		
Understands that a sentence begins with a capital letter	●	●	●			
Uses knowledge of word order and context to support word identification and confirm word meaning [e.g., Child uses decoding skills and predicts meaning, then sees if predicted meaning makes sense given the position of the word in the sentence (subject, verb, object) and given the context.]		●	●	●	●	●
Demonstrates book-handling skills	●	●	●	●	●	●
Demonstrates directionality	●	●	●	●	●	●
Identifies uppercase and lowercase letters	●	●	●		●	
Understands words are separated by spaces	●	●	●	●	●	●
Matches spoken words to print	●	●	●	●	●	●
Recognizes parts of a book (cover, title, title page)	●	●	●	●	●	●
Recognizes name and common environmental print	●	●	●	●	●	●
Locates name of author and illustrator	●	●	●	●	●	●
Identifies end punctuation	●	●	●	●	●	●
Reads one-syllable and high-frequency words	●	●	●	●	●	●

Concepts of Print and Structural Analysis *(continued)*

	K	1	2	3	4	5
Demonstrates understanding of how type treatment can convey meaning (e.g., boldface, italics, falling or slanted letters, reverse out of color)		●	●	●		
Uses picture cues to comprehend text	●	●	●	●	●	●
Demonstrates understanding of inflected endings *(-ed, -ing, -s)*	●	●	●	●	●	●
Demonstrates an understanding of noun plurals	●	●	●	●	●	●
Identifies and reads compound words		●	●	●	●	●
Identifies and reads contractions		●	●	●	●	●
Demonstrates understanding of possessives	●	●	●	●	●	●
Uses knowledge of prefixes and suffixes			●	●	●	●
Identifies root words		●		●	●	●

Literary Response/Analysis

	K	1	2	3	4	5
Distinguishes genres (e.g., play, fiction, nonfiction, poetry, fable or fairy tale, traditional tale, drama, letter, e-mail)		●	●	●	●	●
Distinguishes fantasy from reality	●	●	●	●	●	●
Distinguishes fact from opinion			●	●	●	●
Understands role of author and illustrator		●	●	●	●	●
Understands characters & setting	●	●	●	●		●
Identifies sequence of events, problem, and solution		●	●		●	
Identifies plot (story problem), conflict, and sequence of events				●		●
Identifies beginning, middle, end	●	●	●	●	●	
Recognizes table of contents and chapter titles				●	●	●
Recognizes point of view				●	●	●
Identifies mood				●	●	●
Compares and contrasts plots (story problem), settings, and characters		●	●	●	●	●
Compares and contrasts different forms of the same story			●	●	●	●
Identifies author's style of writing					●	●
Understands use of dialogue in text	●	●	●	●	●	●
Understands use of dialogue in play		●	●	●	●	●
Recognizes descriptive language and imagery			●	●	●	●
Identifies rhythm, rhyme, and alliteration	●	●	●	●	●	●
Identifies onomatopoeia		●	●	●	●	●
Identifies and understands use of figurative language			●	●	●	●
Identifies and understands use of personification			●	●	●	●
Identifies and understands use of metaphor				●	●	●
Identifies and understands use of simile				●	●	●
Recognizes humor in text	●	●	●	●	●	●
Recognizes use of exaggeration in text				●	●	●
Identifies use of flashbacks				●	●	●
Identifies use of foreshadowing				●		●

Literary Response/Analysis *(continued)*

	K	1	2	3	4	5
Recognizes idioms	●	●	●	●	●	●
Recognizes use of suspense					●	●
Discusses a range of books and stories	●	●	●	●	●	●
Takes notes on nonfiction reading				●	●	●
Uses graphic organizers to organize information				●	●	●

Nonfiction

	K	1	2	3	4	5
Text features						
Recognizes and uses contents page	●	●	●	●	●	●
Recognizes and uses picture index	●	●				
Recognizes and uses index			●	●	●	●
Uses alphabet knowledge to locate information		●	●	●	●	●
Uses glossary		●	●	●	●	●
Recognizes headings and subheadings		●	●	●	●	●
Uses photos and illustrations	●	●	●	●	●	●
Reads labels	●	●	●	●	●	●
Reads captions			●	●	●	●
Uses recipe			●	●	●	●
Uses lists and bullet points		●	●	●	●	●
Uses inserted information		●	●	●	●	●
Uses sidebars and boxes				●	●	●
Uses guide words	●	●	●	●	●	●
Graphic elements						
Uses maps			●	●	●	●
Uses charts, diagrams	●	●	●	●	●	●
Uses cross sections & cutaways				●	●	●
Uses bird's eye view			●	●	●	●
Uses graphs				●	●	●
Uses time lines			●	●	●	●
Uses scale drawings				●	●	●
Uses floor plans				●	●	●
Uses flow charts					●	●
Uses satellite or radar images				●	●	●
Uses microscopic images						●
Types of nonfiction						
Understands and uses question & answer format		●	●	●	●	●
Understands reference			●	●	●	●
Understands how-to instructions		●	●	●	●	●
Recognizes journals/observation logs			●	●	●	●

	K	1	2	3	4	5
Types of nonfiction *(continued)*						
Understands explanation		●	●	●	●	●
Understands narrative account	●	●	●	●	●	●
Recognizes description			●	●	●	●
Understands photo essay				●	●	●
Recognizes persuasive language			●	●	●	●
Recognizes compare/ contrast				●	●	●
Understands interview			●	●	●	●
Understands biography			●	●	●	●

Grammar

	K	1	2	3	4	5
Adjectives	●	●	●	●	●	●
Adverbs	●	●	●	●	●	●
Conjunctions	●	●	●	●	●	●
Interjections					●	●
Prepositions	●	●	●	●	●	●
Pronouns	●	●	●	●	●	●
Nouns	●	●	●	●	●	●
Verbs						
Future Tense	●	●	●	●	●	●
Past Tense		●	●	●	●	●
Present Tense	●	●	●	●	●	●
Continuous	●	●	●	●	●	●
Perfect			●	●	●	●
Passive			●	●	●	●
Helping Verbs			●	●	●	●
Linking Verbs	●	●	●	●	●	●
Gerunds				●	●	●
Infinitives	●	●	●	●	●	●
Commands	●	●	●	●	●	●
Exclamations	●	●	●	●	●	●
Statements	●	●	●	●	●	●
Questions	●	●	●	●	●	●
Negative Sentences	●	●	●	●	●	●
Complex Sentences		●	●	●	●	●
Compound Sentences		●	●	●	●	●
Compound-Complex Sentences				●	●	●
Comparative and Superlative	●	●	●	●	●	●
Contractions		●	●	●	●	●
Possessives	●	●	●	●	●	●

	K	1	2	3	4	5
Writing						
Strategies						
Participates in collaborative writing, shared writing, and writing to prompts	●	●	●	●	●	●
Uses a variety of prewriting strategies [drawing, graphic organizers, brainstorming, notes]	●	●	●	●	●	●
Writing process: prewriting, writing drafts, revising, proofreading, publishing		●	●	●	●	●
Evaluates own writing and peers' writing						
Applications						
Writes sentences	●	●	●	●	●	●
Writes labels, captions, lists, logs	●	●	●	●	●	●
Writes to retell personal experiences [dictation, language experience]	●	●	●			
Writes narrative text based on personal experience			●	●	●	●
Writes narrative text [humorous, realistic, fantasy]				●	●	●
Writes to entertain [stories, poems]				●	●	●
Writes letters [informal, formal]				●	●	●
Writes expository text [reports, instructions, steps in a process, research results, comparison-contrast, cause-effect]		●	●	●	●	●
Writes persuasive text [review, letter, request]				●	●	●
Writes using point of view					●	●
Organization and Focus						
Uses models and traditional structures for writing		●	●	●	●	●
Writes to communicate ideas and reflections		●	●	●	●	●
Maintains a central idea or single focus		●	●	●	●	●
Presents information in a logical sequence			●	●	●	●
Addresses purposes and audience		●	●	●	●	●
Addresses length and format					●	●
Uses descriptive words		●	●	●	●	●
Uses dialogue					●	●
Uses topic sentences with supporting sentences in writing		●	●	●	●	●
Writes with a distinct beginning, middle, and end				●	●	●
Uses paragraphs effectively in writing				●	●	●

	K	1	2	3	4	5
Evaluation and Revision						
Revises to improve progression and clarity of ideas				●	●	●
Revises to include more descriptive and sensory detail			●	●	●	●
Adds titles and headings			●	●	●	●
Revises to vary sentence structure			●	●	●	●
Combines sentences		●	●	●	●	●
Revises to improve word choice		●	●	●	●	●
Proofreads to correct spelling				●	●	●
Uses a variety of reference materials to revise [dictionary, thesaurus, Internet, proofreading checklist]				●	●	●
Comments constructively on peers' writing and revises based on peer comments		●	●	●	●	●
Uses proofreading symbols to revise		●	●	●	●	●
Sentence Structure and Grammar						
Uses complete sentences and recognizes correct word order			●	●	●	●
Uses simple and complex sentences		●	●	●	●	●
Demonstrates an understanding of subject-verb agreement		●	●	●	●	●
Uses appropriate parts of speech			●	●	●	●
Uses basic capitalization and punctuation rules		●	●	●	●	●
Penmanship						
Writes uppercase and lowercase letters of the alphabet	●	●	●	●	●	●
Writes clearly and legibly		●	●	●	●	●
Allows adequate spacing between letters, words, and sentences	●	●	●	●	●	●
Punctuation						
Uses end punctuation	●	●	●	●	●	●
Uses commas			●	●	●	●
Uses quotation marks				●	●	●
Uses apostrophes in possessive nouns and in contractions			●	●	●	●

Language Functions Scope

Social Function	Definition	Stages of Oral Language Development 1	2	3	4	5	K	1	2	3	4	5
Agree and disagree	express opinion regarding ideas, actions, etc.	●	●	●	●	●	●	●	●	●		
Apologize	express remorse for an action or something said	●	●	●	●	●	●			●		
Ask for assistance or permission	use question words to make requests or ask for clarification; request permission; make requests	●	●	●	●	●	●	●			●	●
Express feelings and needs	use words to express emotions, ideas and feelings, refuse	●	●	●	●	●	●	●		●	●	●
Express likes and dislikes	use words to express likes/dislikes and preferences; express opinions about film, print, and technological presentations with supporting examples	●	●	●	●	●	●	●	●		●	●
Express obligation	indicate that something should be done to benefit oneself or others, for example, *We should take care of our planet*			●	●	●		●	●		●	●
Give instructions	inform or direct a person by telling, explaining, or describing		●	●	●	●			●	●	●	●
Greet	use appropriate phrases for welcoming someone, greeting, making introductions, making small talk such as *How are you? What's new?*, saying and responding to farewell	●	●	●	●	●	●	●	●	●		
Negotiate	propose ways of proceeding in group work that recognize the need for compromise and diplomacy			●	●	●				●	●	●
Use appropriate register	vary degree of formality in speech (word choice, diction, and usage) according to setting, occasion, purpose, and audience			●	●	●				●	●	●
Use social etiquette	respond appropriately and courteously to directions and questions; express gratitude; appropriately use polite phrases such as *please, thank you, excuse me*	●	●	●	●	●	●	●	●	●		
Warn	inform of danger; command that someone should or should not do something for safety	●	●	●	●	●	●		●			●
Wish and hope	use words to express a desire such as *I hope I can go to the game; I wish it would snow*			●	●	●		●	●		●	
Academic Function	**Definition**	**Stages of Oral Language Development**										
Analyze	separate whole into parts; identify relationships and patterns; identify cause and effect; interpret important events and ideas			●	●	●		●	●	●	●	●
Classify	group objects or ideas according to their characteristics	●	●	●	●	●	●			●		
Compare (and contrast)	describe similarity and/or differences in objects or ideas or between print, visual, and electronic media		●	●	●	●	●	●	●		●	●
Describe	name; describe immediate surroundings; give and account of an event/action, object, person, and/or characteristics in words		●	●	●	●	●	●			●	●
Evaluate	assess and verify the worth of an object, idea or decision			●	●	●			●	●		
Explain	express an understanding of a process, an event, or idea (gleaned from video segments, graphic art, or technology presentations); give the "why" when providing information; ask questions to obtain information or directions			●	●	●		●		●	●	●
Express position	tell where something is (*here, there, right/left, up/down*); use prepositional phrases of location		●	●	●	●	●	●				
Inquire	ask questions to obtain information or directions		●	●	●	●	●	●	●			
Justify and persuade	give reasons for an action, decision, point of view; convince others by clarifying and supporting with evidence, elaborations, and examples			●	●	●			●		●	●
Predict and hypothesize	suggest cause or outcomes	●	●	●	●	●	●		●	●	●	●
Report	share or recount personal or other factual information		●	●	●	●		●		●		
Sequence	put objects, ideas, numbers, or events into a particular order through retelling, role-playing, and/or visually illustrating	●	●	●	●	●	●		●		●	
Solve problems	define and represent a problem and determine a solution			●	●	●			●	●		●
Synthesize	combine or integrate spoken ideas to form a new whole; summarize orally; draw conclusions from information gathered from multiple sources			●	●	●				●	●	●
Tell time	use words and expressions to express hours and time; talk about calendar	●	●	●	●	●	●	●			●	

Language Learning Strategies Scope

Student Language	Teacher Language	Definitions and/or Examples	STAGES OF ORAL LANGUAGE DEVELOPMENT										
			1	2	3	4	5	K	1	2	3	4	5
• Ask for help in your home language.	• Use native language for clarification.	• Student talks to someone in his or her home language to find out the meaning of an unknown word or phrase.	●	●	●	●	●	●	●				
• Show me what you mean.	• Manipulate and act out language.	• Student uses real objects and role-playing to communicate.	●	●	●	●	●	●					
• Ask or show me when you need help.	• Ask for adult assistance.	• Student requests help from an adult (verbally and nonverbally).	●	●	●	●	●	●					
• Look at what I do when I talk.	• Compare verbal and nonverbal cues.	• Ex: Teacher said "Smile." Student is confused until seeing the teacher point to his/her mouth, then student performs the action.	●	●	●	●	●	●					
• When you talk to an adult, call them *Mr., Ms.,* or *Mrs.* with their last name. • Use different kinds of words in different settings.	• Rehearse variations of language in different social and academic settings.	• Ex: Student calls friends by their first names, but knows to address a teachers with a title such as *Mr.* and *Mrs.* • Ex: Student learns the difference between using the term *soil* in the classroom and *dirt* when playing.		●	●	●	●	●		●			
• Practice what you learn.	• Test new expressions through use.	• Student learns new word or phrase and practices using it.		●	●	●	●	●	●				
• Say what another child says.	• Imitate others' language use.	• Ex: Student hears a classmate use the word *please* or *it's your turn* and imitates.	●	●	●	●	●	●					
• Put new words in sentences you know. • Use language you know.	• Learn to use language patterns.	• Student identifies and correctly uses a phrase or sentence pattern. Ex: *We have* _____. • Student identifies and correctly uses a phrase or sentence pattern. Ex: *I got five* when sharing answers to a math problem		●	●	●	●	●			●	●	●
• Ask or show me when you don't understand. • Ask me "What do you mean?" when you don't understand.	• Seek clarification.	• Student uses gesture, word, or phrase to ask for clarification. Ex: *What do you mean? What is* _____*?*	●	●	●	●	●		●	●			
• Try saying that again another way.	• Clarify and restate information.	• Students restate what they have said when communication breaks down.			●	●	●		●				
• Tell a friend how to say that. • Teach a friend.	• Teach a peer.	• Student practices recently learned vocabulary, phrases, and expressions by teaching a peer.		●	●	●	●		●			●	
• Talk around the problem word.	• Paraphrase.	• Student "talks around" an unknown word, hoping to get the meaning across. Ex: *The things that you use to put flowers in.* (vase)			●	●	●		●	●	●	●	●
• Ask "Do you understand?" • Ask "Did I say that right?"	• Seek feedback. • Get feedback.	• Ex: Students seek feedback on language use.			●	●	●		●		●	●	●
• Try a word and see if it works.	• Coin a word.	• Student makes up a word to describe something, hoping that someone will supply the target word. Ex: *bee house* (bee hive)			●	●	●		●				●

Student Language	Teacher Language	Definitions and/or Examples	STAGES OF ORAL LANGUAGE DEVELOPMENT 1	2	3	4	5	K	1	2	3	4	5
• Use your home language to help you understand a word. • How can your home language help you?	• Use a cognate.	• Student uses a home language word, hoping that it is similar to a word in the target language. Ex: *I went to the parque.* (park) • Student uses the meaning of a similar word in the home language to understand English.	●	●	●	●	●			●	●		●
• Listen for parts you know. • Listen for important parts.	• Attend selectively to input.	• Student focuses on breaking down a sentence into understandable language patterns or "chunks." Ex: Teacher says "We're going to do some writing. Take out your paper and pencil." Student focuses on materials needed, i.e., words *paper* and *pencil*. • Student learns to listen for key ideas and details.		●	●	●	●			●		●	
• Work with a friend to help you understand. • Ask a friend for help.	• Consult a peer.	• Student talks to a classmate to develop understanding. • Student asks peers, both English language learners and native English speakers, for help.	●	●	●	●	●			●	●		
• It's OK to use things written in your home language to help you. • Look in a book in your home language for help.	• Consult home language resources.	• Student uses written home language resources, such as books, picture cards, or dictionary.	●	●	●	●	●			●	●		
• Sometimes you don't need to know the meaning of every single word to understand. • Keep listening when you don't understand a word.	• Skip an unknown word as necessary.	• Student skims over unknown words in order to focus on the full meaning of a phrase, sentence, or paragraph. Ex: *The spotted dog played in the street* can be mostly understood without the word *spotted*. • If students keep listening, they may find that they didn't need to understand a particular word or that context may help them understand it.			●	●	●			●	●		
• Keep using words you've learned in our theme.	• Use academic language across content areas.	• Use academic language learned, such as *equal, compare,* and *soil.*	●	●	●	●	●				●	●	●
• Write down what you learn to help you remember.	• Take notes to help you remember.	• Student learns to write down key ideas and details in note form.		●	●	●	●					●	●

Bibliography

Adams, Marilyn J. *Beginning to Read: Thinking and Learning About Print*. Cambridge: MIT Press, 1990.

Adams, M., Foorman, B., I. Lundberg, and T. Beeler. *Does phoneme awareness in young children*. Baltimore: Paul Brookes, 1998.

Allen, V. *Selecting Materials for the Reading Instructions of ESL Children, Kids Come in All Languages: Reading Instructions for ESL Students*, edited by K. Spandenburg-Urbschat and R. Pritchard. Newark: International Reading Association, 1994.

Amador-Watson, C. *Introduction to Guided Reading for Emergent and Early Readers Seminar*. Crystal Lake, IL: Rigby, 1999.

Amador-Watson, Clara and Charlotte Knox. *Responsive Instruction for Success in English*. Crystal Lake, IL: Rigby, 2000.

Anderson, Neil. *Exploring Second Language Reading: Issues and Strategies*. Boston: Heinle & Heinle, 1999.

Au, Kathryn H. *Literacy Instruction in Multicultural Settings*. New York: Harcourt Brace, 1993.

August, D., and K. Hakuta, eds. *Improving Schooling for Language Minority Children: A Research Agenda*. National Research Council. Washington, DC: National Academy Press, 1997.

Baker, Colin. *Foundations of Bilingual Education and Bilingualism*. 2d. ed. Bristol, PA: Multilingual Matters, 1996.

Bear, Donald R., et al. *Words Their Way: Word Study for Phonics, Vocabulary, and Spelling Instruction*. Upper Saddle River, NJ: Merrill, 1999.

Bisplinghoff, B. and J. Allen. *Engaging Teachers: Creative Teaching and Researching Relationships*. York, ME: Stenhouse, 1998.

Boyle, O. and S. Peregoy. "Literacy Scaffolds: Strategies for First- and Second-Language Readers and Writers." *The Reading Teacher*, 1990.

Bransford, J. and D. L. Swartz. "Rethinking Transfer: A Simple Proposal with Multiple Implications." In *Review of Educational Research: Volume 24*, edited by A. Iran-Nejad and P. D. Pearson. Washington, DC: American Educational Research Association, 1999.

Brantley, Jane H. *Basically Phonics Facilitator's Manual*. Crystal Lake, IL: Rigby, 1998.

Brisk, María Estela, and Margaret M. Harrington. *Literacy and Bilingualism: A Handbook for All Teachers*. Mahwah, NJ: Lawrence Erlbaum Associates, 2000.

Brown, H. Douglas. *Teaching by Principles: An Interactive Approach to Language Pedagogy*. Englewood Cliffs, NJ: Prentice Hall Regents, 1994.

Brown, James Dean. *The Elements of Language Curriculum: A Systematic Approach to Program Development*. Boston: Heinle & Heinle, 1995.

Cambourne, B., and J. Turbill. *Responsive Evaluation: Making Valid Judgements About Student Literacy*. Portsmouth, NH: Heinemann, 1994.

Campbell, Cherry. *Teaching Second-Language Writing: Interacting with Text*. Boston: Heinle & Heinle, 1998.

Cary, Stephen. *Second Language Learners*. York, ME: Stenhouse Publishers, 1997.

Celce-Murcia, Marianne, ed. *Teaching English as a Second or Foreign Language*. 2d ed. Boston: Heinle & Heinle, 1991.

Chamot, Anna Uhl, et al. *The CALLA Handbook: Implementing the Cognitive Academic Language Learning Approach*. Reading, MA: Addison-Wesley, 1994.

Chamot, Anna Uhl, Sarah Barnhardt, Pamela Bread El-Dinary, and Jill Robins. *The Learning Strategies Handbook*. White Plains, NY: Longman, 1999.

Chard, David J., and Shirley V. Dickson. "Phonological Awareness: Instructional and Assessment Guidelines." *Intervention in School and Clinic*: Vol. 34, No. 5, 1999.

Clark, Raymond C., Patrick R. Moran, and Arthur A. Burrows. *The ESL Miscellany*. Brattleboro, VT: Pro Lingua Associates, 1991.

Clay, Marie M. *Becoming Literate: The Construction of Inner Control*. Portsmouth, NH: Heinemann, 1991.

———. *Reading Recovery: A Guidebook for Teachers in Training*. Portsmouth, NH: Heinemann, 1993.

———. *An Observation Survey of Early Literacy Achievement*. Portsmouth, NH: Heinemann, 1993.

———. *Becoming Literate: The Construction of Inner Control*. Portsmouth, NH: Heinemann, 1997.

———. *By Different Paths to Common Outcomes*. York, Maine: Stenhouse, 1998.

Cloud, Nancy, Fred Genesee, and Else Hamayan. *Dual Language Instruction: A Handbook for Enriched Education*. Boston: Heinle & Heinle, 2000.

Coles, Gerald. *Misreading Reading: The Bad Science That Hurts Children*. Portsmouth, NH: Heinemann, 2000.

Collier, V. "How Long? A Synthesis of Research on Academic Achievement in a Second Language." *TESOL Quarterly* 23(3), 509–532, 1989.

Collier, V. P. *Promoting Academic Success for ESL Students*. Jersey City: New Jersey Teachers of English to Speakers of Other Languages–Bilingual Educators, 1995.

Collins, A., J. Brown, and S. Newman. "Cognitive Apprenticeship: Teaching the Crafts of Reading, Writing, and Mathematics." In *Knowing, Learning, and Instructions: Essays in Honor of Robert Glaser*, edited by L Resnick. Hillsdale, NJ: Lawrence Erlbaum Associates, 1989.

Crystal, D. *A Dictionary of Linguistics and Phonetics*. Cambridge: Basil Blackwell, 1980.

Cummins, J. *Negotiating Identities: Education for Empowerment in a Diverse Society*. Ontario, CA: California Association for Bilingual Education, 1996.

Cummins, J. *Language, Power and Pedagogy: Bilingual Children in the Crossfire*. Tonawnada, NY: Multilingual Matters, 2000.

———. *Negotiating Identities: Education for Empowerment in a Diverse Society*. Ontario, CA: California Association for Bilingual Education, 1996.

———. "The Acquisition of English as a Second Language." In *Kids Come in All Languages: Reading for Instruction for ESL Students*. Newark, DE: International Reading Association, 1994.

———. *Empowering Minority Students*. Sacramento: CABE, 1989.

———. "Age on Arrival and Immigrant Second Language Learning in Canada: A Reassessment." *Applied Linguistics* 2, 132–149, 1981.

———. "The Role of Primary Language Development in Promoting Educational Success for Language Minority Students." In *Schooling and Language Minority Students: A Theoretical Framework*. Sacramento: California State Department of Education, Division of Instructional Support and Bilingual Education, Office of Bilingual Bicultural Education, 1981.

Cunningham, Patricia M. *Phonics They Use: Words for Reading and Writing*. New York: Longman, 2000.

Daniels, H. and M. Bizar. *Methods That Matter: Six Structures for Best Practice Classrooms*. York, ME: Stenhouse, 1998.

Day, Frances Ann. *Multicultural Voices in Contemporary Literature: A Resource for Teachers*. Portsmouth, NH: Heinemann, 1994.

DeFord, Diane E., Carol A. Lyons, and Gay Su Pinnell. *Bridges to Literacy: Learning from Reading Recovery*. Portsmouth, NH: Heinemann, 1991.

Dentler, Robert A., and Anne L. Hafner. *Hosting Newcomers: Structuring Educational Opportunities for Immigrant Children*. New York: Teachers College Press, 1997.

Dorn, L., C. French, and T. Jones. *Apprenticeship in Literacy Transitions Across Reading and Writing*. York, ME: Stenhouse, 1998.

Dulay, Heidi, Marina Burt, and Stephen Krashen. *Language Two*. Oxford: Oxford University Press, 1982.

Duthie, C. *True Stories: Nonfiction Literacy in the Primary Classroom*. York, ME: Stenhouse, 1996.

Durgunoglu, A. Y., W. E. Nagy, and B. J. Hancin-Bhatt. "Cross-language of phonological awareness." *Journal of Educational Psychology*, Vol. 85, 453–465, 1993.

Edelsky, C. "Who's Got the Floor?" *Language and Society* 10, 383–421, 1981.

Ellis, R. *Understanding Second Language Acquisition.* Oxford: Oxford University Press, 1985.

Enright, D. S. and M. L. McCloskey. *Integrating English: Developing English Language and Literacy in the Multilingual Classroom.* Reading, MA: Addison-Wesley, 1988.

Escamilla, Kathy. "Teaching Literacy in Spanish." In *The Power of Two Languages 2000: Effective Dual-Language Use Across the Curriculum* edited by J.V. Tinajero and Robert DeVillar. New York: McGraw-Hill, 2000.

Faltis, Christian Jan. *Joinfostering: Adapting Teaching Strategies to the Multilingual Classroom.* New York: Prentice Hall, 1993.

Faltis, Christian, and Sarah Hudelson. "Learning English as an Additional Language in K–12 Schools." *TESOL Quarterly,* vol. 28:3, 1994.

Ferreiro, E. and A. Teberosky. *Literacy before Schooling.* Portsmouth, NH: Heinemann, 1982.

Fountas, Irene C., and Gay Su Pinnell. *Guided Reading: Good First Teaching for ALL Children.* Portsmouth, NH: Heinemann, 1996.

Fountas, Irene C., and Gay Su Pinnell. *Matching Books to Readers: Using Leveled Books in Guided Reading, K–3.* Portsmouth, NH: Heinemann, 1999.

Fox, Barbara J. *Strategies for Word Identification.* Columbus: Prentice Hall, Inc, 1996.

Franklin, E. "Encouraging and Understanding the Visual and Written Works of Second-Language Children." In *When They Don't All Speak English: Integrating the ESL Student into the Regular Classroom* edited by P. Rigg and V. Allen. Urbana, IL: National Council of Teachers of English, 1989.

Freeman, David E., and Yvonne S. Freeman. *Teaching Reading in Multilingual Classrooms.* Portsmouth, NH: Heinemann, 2000.

———. *Between Worlds: Access to Second Language Acquisition.* Portsmouth, NH: Heinemann, 1994.

———. *ESL/EFL Teaching: Principles for Success.* Portsmouth, NH: Heinemann, 1998.

Freeman, Yvonne S., and David E. Freeman. *Closing the Achievement Gap: How to Reach Limited Formal Schooling and Long-Term English Learners.* Portsmouth, NH: Heinemann, 2002.

———. *Teaching Reading and Writing in Spanish in the Bilingual Classroom.* Portsmouth, NH: Heinemann, 1997.

Fry, Edward. *Phonics Patterns.* Laguna Beach: Laguna Beach Educational Books, 1996.

Genesee, Fred, ed. *Educating Second Language Children: The Whole Child, the Whole Curriculum, the Whole Community.* Cambridge: Cambridge University Press, 1994.

Gentile, L. "Oral Language: Assessment and Development in Reading Recovery in the United States." In *Research in Reading Recovery* edited by S. Schwartz and A. Klein. Portsmouth, NH: Heinemann, 1997.

Gibbons, Pauline. *Learning to Learn in a Second Language.* Portsmouth, NH: Heinemann, 1993.

Glatthorn, Allan A., et al. *Performance Assessment and Standards-Based Curricula: The Achievement Cycle.* Larchmont, NY: Eye on Education, 1998.

Gottlieb, M. "Promising Assessment Practices for Language Minority Students: National, State, and School Perspectives." *Excellence and Equity for Language Minority Students: Critical Issues and Promising Practices.* Chevy Chase, MD: The Mid-Atlantic Equity Consortium, 2000.

———. *The Language Proficiency Handbook: A Practitioner's Guide to Instructional Assessment.* Springfield: Illinois State Board of Education, 1999.

Griffith, Priscilla L. and Mary W. Olson. "Phonemic Awareness Helps Beginning Readers Break the Code." *The Reading Teacher* 45, No. 7, 1992.

Hadaway, Nancy L., Sylvia M. Vardell, and Terrell A. Young. *Literature-Based Instruction with English Language Learners, K–12.* Boston: Allyn & Bacon, 2002.

Hasbrouck, Jan E. and Carolyn A Denton. *Phonological Awareness in Spanish: A Summary of Research and Implications for Practice.* In *The Power of Two Languages 2000: Effective Dual-Language Across the Curriculum* edited by J. V. Tinajero and Robert DeVillar. New York: McGraw-Hill, 2000.

Hill, B., L. Norwick, and C. Ruptik. *Classroom Based Assessment.* Norwood, MA: Christopher-Gordon, 1998.

Holdaway, D. *The Foundations of Literacy.* Australia: Ashton Scholastic, 1979.

Holiman, L. *The Complete Guide to Classroom Centers.* Cypress, CA: Creative Teaching Press, 1996.

Holt, D. *Cooperative Learning: A Response to Linguistic and Cultural Diversity.* McHenry, IL: Center for Applied Linguistic/Delta Systems, 1993.

Hudelson, S. *Write On: Children Writing in ESL.* Englewood Cliffs, NJ: Prentice Hall, 1989.

———. "Children's Writing in ESL: What We've Learned, What We're Learning." In *Children and ESL: Integrating Perspectives* edited by P. Rigg and D. S. Enright. Washington, DC: TESOL, 1986.

———. "Kan yo ret an rayt in Ingles: Children Become Literature in English as a Second Language." *TESOL Quarterly* 18, 221–237 (1984).

Johnston, P. *Knowing Literacy: Constructive Literacy Assessment.* York, ME: Stenhouse, 1997.

Kang, Hee-Won. "Helping Second Language Readers Learn from Content Area Text Through Collaboration and Support." *Journal of Reading,* vol. 37:8, 1994.

Keene, Ellin Oliver, and Susan Zimmerman. *Mosaic of Thought: Teaching Comprehension in a Reader's Workshop.* Portsmouth, NH: Heinemann, 1997.

Krashen, S. *Principles and Practice in Second Language Acquisition.* New York: Pergamon Press, 1982.

Krashen, S. and T. Terrell. *The Natural Approach: Language Acquisition in the Classroom.* Hayward, CA: Alemany Press, 1983.

Krashen, S. D. *Fundamentals of Language Education.* Torrence, CA: Laredo, 1992.

Krashen, Stephen. *The Power of Reading: Insights from the Research.* Englewood, CO: Libraries Unlimited, 1993.

———. *Under Attack: The Case Against Bilingual Education.* Culver City, CA: Language Education Associates, 1996.

Kucer, Stephen B., Cecilia Silva, and Esther L. Delgado-Larocco. *Curricular Conversations: Themes in Multilingual and Monolingual Classrooms.* York, ME: Stenhouse, 1995.

Law Barbara, and Mary Eckes. *Assessment and ESL: A Handbook for K-12 Teachers.* Winnipeg: Peguis, 1995.

Manning, M., G. Manning, and R. Long. *Theme Immersion: Inquiry-Based Curriculum in Elementary and Middle Schools.* Portsmouth, NH: Heinemann, 1994.

McCloskey, Mary Lou. "Literature for Language Learning." <http://www.eslmag.com> *ESL Magazine Online,* November/December 1998.

Miramontes, O. B., A. Nadeau, N. Commins. *Restructuring Schools for Linguistic Diversity: Linking Decision Making to Effective Programs.* New York. Teachers College Press, 1997.

Moline, S. *I See What You Mean: Children at Work with Visual Information.* York, ME: Stenhouse, 1996.

Mooney, Margaret E. *Reading To, With, and By Children.* Katonah, NY: Richard C. Owen Publishers, 1990.

Moustafa, Margaret. *Beyond Traditional Phonics: Research Discoveries and Reading Instructions.* Portsmouth, NH: Heinemann, 1997.

Moustafa, M., and E. Maldonado-Colon: "Whole-to-Parts Phonics Instruction: Building on What Children Know to Help Them Know More." *The Reading Teacher* 52: 448–456, 1999 .

National Research Council Institute of Medicine. *Improving Schooling for Language-Minority Children.* Washington, DC: National Academy Press, 1997.

Newkirk, T., ed. *The Teacher as Researcher.* Portsmouth, NH: Heinemann, 1992.

Odlin, Terence. *Language Transfer: Cross-linguistic Influence in Language Learning.* Cambridge: Cambridge University Press, 1989.

Ogbu, J. "Immigrant and Involuntary Minorities in Comparative Perspective." In *Minority Status and Schooling: A Comparative Study of Immigrant and Involuntary Minorities* edited by M. Gibson and J. Ogbu. Garland Publishing: New York, 1991.

Oller, Jr., John W., ed. *Methods That Work: Ideas for Literacy and Language* Teachers. 2d ed. Boston: Heinle & Heinle, 1993.

O'Malley, J., and L. Valdez Pierce. *Authentic Assessment for English Language Learners: Practical Approaches for Teachers.* New York: Addison-Wesley, 1996

Opitz, Michael F. *Flexible Grouping in Reading: Practical Ways to Help All Students Become Better Readers.* New York: Scholastic Professional Books, 1998.

Opitz, Michael F., ed. *Literary Instruction for Culturally and Linguistically Diverse Students: A Collection of Articles and Commentaries.* Newark: International Reading Association, 1998.

Ovando, C. J., and V. Collier. *Bilingual and ESL Classrooms: Teaching in Multicultural Contexts.* 2d. ed. New York: McGraw-Hill, 1998.

Palincsar, A. S. "The Role of Dialogue in Providing Scaffolded Instruction," *Educational Psychologist 21* (1 &2), 73–98, 1986.

Parkes, B. *Something Old, Something New: An Integrated Approach to Traditional Tales.* Crystal Lake, IL: Rigby.

Parkes, B. *Guided Reading with Emergent Readers.* Train the Trainer Seminars, Crystal Lake, IL: Rigby, 1997.

Payne, C. and M. Schulman. *Getting the Most Out of Morning Message and Other Shared Writing Lessons.* New York: Scholastic, 1998.

Pearson, P.D. "Focus on Research: Teaching and Learning Reading, A Research Perspective." *Language Arts* (October), 505, 1993.

Peregoy, Suzanne F., and Owen F. Boyle. *Reading, Writing, and Learning in ESL: A Resource Book for K–12 Teachers.* 2d ed. White Plains, NY: Longman, 1997.

Peyton, Joy Kreeft, and Leslee Reed. *Dialogue Journal Writing with Nonnative English Speakers: A Handbook for Teachers.* Alexandria, VA: TESOL Publications, 1990.

Pinnell, Gay Su, et al. *Word Matters: Teaching Phonics and Spelling in the Reading/Writing Classroom.* Portsmouth, NH: Heinemann, 1998.

Power, B. *Taking Note: Improving Your Observational Notetaking.* York, ME: Stenhouse, 1997.

Power, B. and R. Hubbard, eds. *Oops: What We Learn When Our Teaching Fails.* York, ME: Stenhouse, 1996.

Reeves, D. B. *Making Standards Work*, 2d ed. Denver, CO: Advanced Learning Centers, 1998.

Rigg, Pat, and D. Scott Enright, eds. *Children and ESL: Integrating Perspectives.* Alexandria, VA: TESOL Publications, 1986.

Rogoff, B. *Apprenticeship in Thinking: Cognitive Development in Social Contexts.* New York: Oxford University Press, 1990.

Royce, Terry. "Multimodality in the TESOL Classroom: Exploring Visual-Verbal Synergy." *TESOL Quarterly* 36, no. 2, 191–205, 2002.

Samway, Katharine Davies, and Denise McKeon, eds. *Common Threads of Practice: Teaching English to Children Around the World.* Alexandria, VA: TESOL Publications, 1993.

Samway, Katharine Davies, and Denise McKeon. *Myths and Realities: Best Practices for Language Minority Students.* Portsmouth, NH: Heinemann, 1999.

Schiffini, A. "Language, Literacy, and Content Instruction: Strategies for Teachers." In *Kids Come in All Languages: Reading Instruction for ESL Students* edited by K. Spandenburg-Urbschat, and R. Pritchard. Newark: International Reading Association, 1994.

Schinke-Llano, Linda, and Rebecca Rauff, eds. *New Ways in Teaching Young Children.* Alexandria, VA: TESOL Publications, 1996.

Short, D.J., et al. *Training Others to Use the ESL Standards: A Professional Development Manual.* Alexandra, VA: TESOL, 2000.

Short, K. G., J. C. Harste, and C. Burke. *Creating Classrooms for Authors and Inquirers.* 2d ed. Portsmouth, NH: Heinemann, 1996.

Smallwood, Betty Ansin, ed. *Integrating the ESL Standards Into Classroom Practice: Grades Pre-K–2.* Alexandria, VA: TESOL, 2000.

Spangenberg-Urbschat, Karen, and Robert Pritchard. *Kids Come in All Languages: Reading Instruction for ESL Students.* Newark: International Reading Association, 1994.

Sparks, D. and Hirsch, S. *A New Vision for Staff Development.* Alexandria, VA: Association for Supervision and Curriculum Development, 1997.

Stahl, S. and B. Murray. "Defining Phonological Awareness and Its Relationship to Early Reading." *Journal of Educational Psychology* 86, Vol. 2, 221–234, 1994.

Stahl, Steven. "Saying the 'P' Word: Nine Guidelines for Exemplary Phonics Instruction." *The Reading Teacher* 45, no. 8, 618–625, 1992.

Stanovich, Keith E. "Romance and Reality." *The Reading Teacher* 47, no. 4, 280–291, 1992.

Stefanakis, E. *Whose Judgement Counts? Assessing Bilingual Children K–3.* Portsmouth, NH: Heinemann, 1998.

Swan, Michael, and Bernard Smith. *Learner English: A Teacher's Guide to Interference and Other Problems.* Cambridge: Cambridge University Press, 1987.

Teachers of English to Speakers of Other Languages. *ESL Standards for Pre-K–12 Scenarios for ESL Standards-Based Assessment.* Alexandria, VA: TESOL Publications, 2001.

———. *ESL Standards for Pre-K–12 Students.* Alexandria, VA: TESOL Publications, 1997.

Tharp, R. and R. Gallimore. *Rousing Minds to Life: Teaching, Learning, and Schooling in Social Context.* Cambridge: Cambridge University Press.

Thomas, Wayne, and Virginia Collier. *School Effectiveness for Language Minority Students.* Washington, DC: National Clearinghouse for Bilingual Education, 1997.

Tierney, Robert J., John E. Readence, and Ernest K. Dishner. *Reading Strategies and Practices: A Compendium.* 4th ed. Boston: Allyn & Bacon, 1995.

Tinajero, J., S. R. Hurley, and E. V. Lozano. *Developing Language and Literacy in Bilingual Classrooms.* In *Educating Latino Students: A Guide to Successful Practice* edited by M. L. Gonzales et al. Lancaster, PA: Technomics. 143–160, 1998.

Tomlinson, Carol Ann. "Grading for Success." *Educational Leadership* 58, no. 6, 2000.

Traill, Leana. *Highlight My Strengths.* Crystal Lake, IL: Rigby, 1995.

Trelease, Jim. *The Read-Aloud Handbook.* New York: Penguin Books, 1985.

Valdés, Guadalupe. *Con Respeto: Bridging the Distances Between Culturally Diverse Families and Schools.* New York: Teachers College Press, 1996.

Vale, David, with Anne Feunteun. *Teaching Children English: A Training Course for Teachers of English to Children.* Cambridge: Cambridge University Press, 1995.

Vygotsky, L. S. *Thought and Language.* Cambridge, MA: MIT Press, 1962.

———. *Mind in Society.* Cambridge, MA: Harvard University Press, 1978.

Wagstaff, Janiel. *Phonics That Work: New Strategies for the Reading/Writing Classroom.* New York: Scholastic, 1996.

Waterland, L. *Read With Me: An Apprenticeship Approach to Reading.* Stroud, UK: Thimble Press, 1985.

White, Lydia. *Universal Grammar and Second Language Acquisition.* Philadelphia: John Benjamin Publishing, 1989.

Wiggins, G. *Educative Assessment.* San Francisco, CA: Jossey-Bass, 1998.

Wilde, Sandra. *What's a Schwa Sound Anyway?* Portsmouth, NH: Heinemann, 1997.

Wink, Joan. *Critical Pedagogy: Notes from the Real World.* 2d ed. White Plains, NY: Longman, 1999.

Wong-Fillmore, L., and C. Valadez. *Teaching bilingual learners.* In *Handbook of Research on Teaching* edited by M. Wittrock. Washingon, DC: American Educational Research Association, 648–685, 1985.

Yopp, Hallie K. "A Test for Assessing Phonemic Awareness in Young Children." *The Reading Teacher* 49, no. 1, 20–29, 1995.

———. "Developing phonemic awareness in young children." *The Reading Teacher* 45, no. 9, pp. 696–707, 1992.